# SCHOOL CHOICE 2003

## How States are Providing Greater Opportunity in Education

Krista Kafer

Krista Kafer is Senior Policy Analyst for Education at The Heritage Foundation.

Published by
The Heritage Foundation
214 Massachusetts Avenue, NE
Washington, DC 20002-4999
800-544-4843
heritage.org

Front cover design by Suzanne Kesler
Photo copyright © photo.com and gettyone.com

# TABLE OF CONTENTS

# EDITOR'S NOTE

Education options have always been available to those who can afford them. Parents with financial means have "residential choice." They can buy a house in a neighborhood with a desirable school. They can also choose a private school. Many families sacrifice to provide the best education possible for their children. Others simply cannot afford to choose.

In the past, a few states initiated policies or programs to expand access to education options to all families. Maine and Vermont's small towns have paid to send students to private schools and public schools in other communities for more than a century. Minnesota's education tax deduction dates back to 1955. For more than two decades, controlled choice programs and magnet schools—instituted primarily to create racial balance—have provided some families with access to better schools.

However, the real drive to give parents greater voice in their children's education did not begin until the mid-1980s. In 1985, Minnesota became the first state to enact legislation permitting junior and senior high school students to take college courses at public expense. Three years later, the state enacted the first interdistrict public school choice law, enabling students to attend schools in other districts. In 1987, the Iowa legislature enacted a law establishing the first tax credit for education expenses.

In 1990, Wisconsin adopted a voucher program for low-income students in Milwaukee. A year later, Minnesota broke new ground again, enacting the nation's first charter school law, making possible the creation of innovative public schools of choice. Students in Cleveland, Ohio, were the next to be given the opportunity to choose among public and private schools, with the help of vouchers. Arizona instituted the first tax credit for contributions to tuition scholarship organizations in 1997.

As of May 2003, 40 states and the District of Columbia have charter school laws on the books, and Washington State could become the 41st under pending legislation. A number of states have initiated tax credits, public and private school choice programs, dual enrollment, and on-line schools. Home schooling is legal in every state and is growing in popularity.

Researchers have confirmed what parents have always known: School choice works. Choice engages parents and creates market competition that results in improvements in public schools. The dream of educating all children to be literate, knowledgeable, and free is fully compatible with choice and market diversity; in fact, this goal is attainable *only* when all parents are empowered with the opportunity to guide their children's education.

While the past 15 years have brought America closer to this ideal, much remains to be done. I look forward to the day when this book gathers dust because the opportunity to choose from a spectrum of education options is no longer an exception worth noting, but the rule.

*School Choice 2003* provides information on each state and the District of Columbia, including:

- Statistics on traditional public schools, public charter schools, and private schools regarding enrollment, teacher–pupil ratio, number of schools, and other data;

- The most recent results of the National Assessment of Educational Progress tests in math, science, and reading;

- Academic achievement rankings by the American Legislative Exchange Council and state rankings on the Education Freedom Index by the Manhattan Institute for Policy Research;

- A snapshot of the history of school choice in each state, updated through May 2003; and

- Education reform organizations in each state.

This book is intended to present a snapshot, rather than a comprehensive history, of each state's progress on choice. The chapters, with few exceptions, are updated through May 2003. While the cut-off date was necessary for the book to be published, it does not allow continuing updates in a rapidly progressing arena. History waits for no book. Therefore, a companion Web site has been developed for *School Choice 2003*, available through *Heritage.org*, which will provide up-to-date information on legislation, studies, commentary, and other important information on parental choice. Anyone wishing to offer new information on school choice, as well as thoughts on how the Web site and book can be improved, is urged to e-mail The Heritage Foundation at *schoolchoice@heritage.org*.

*School Choice 2003* incorporates information from a number of organizations that have done exceptional work on the issue, including (among others) the American Education Reform Council, the American Legislative Exchange Council, the Center for Education Reform, Children First America, the Children's Scholarship Fund, the Education Commission of the States, the Institute for Justice, the Manhattan Institute for Policy Research, and the U.S. Department of Education's National Center for Education Statistics.

The writing of *School Choice 2003* would not have been possible without the assistance and talents of other Heritage staff: Domestic Policy research assistants Jonathan Butcher (to whom I am especially grateful) and Derek Hunter; Research Department editors Collette Caprara, William Poole, and Richard Odermatt; Michelle Smith, Therese Pennefather, Camille Culbertson, Suzanne Kesler, and Jonathan Larsen of Publishing Services; and Research Department interns Al Canata and Matthew Carr. Special thanks also go to Pam Benigno of the Independence Institute, for her timely, play-by-play descriptions regarding the passage of Colorado's new parental choice program, and to Robert Moffit and William Poole for their encouragement.

Krista Kafer

# FOREWORD

Rod Paige,
U.S. Secretary of Education

This year marks the 20th anniversary of the groundbreaking report *A Nation at Risk*, which warned that too many children were falling through the cracks in our education system. Fifteen years after the report was issued, experts estimated that, of the approximately 45 million high school seniors in the nation during that period:

- 10 million could not read at even a basic level;

- More than 25 million did not know even the basics of U.S. history; and

- Of students in all high school levels, more than 20 million could not do even basic math.

This failure was not due to a lack of resources or effort. Between 1970 and 1995, per-pupil spending increased by 75 percent, the number of students per teacher fell by 25 percent, and the number of teachers with advanced degrees more than doubled. Yet student achievement in the United States remained flat.

With each budget cycle since he took office, President George W. Bush has worked to protect our investment in our children, with historic levels of funding targeted to areas of greatest need. But the question is, How do we turn those resources into results? How do we ensure that in another 20 years we will not still be "a nation at risk?"

We can do this with a new law that says no child will be left behind, with a new attitude that says every child can learn, and with a new era of accountability that says results matter. All of these are strengthening public education in America. Through the No Child Left Behind Act, we are working to fix the problem on the front end of each child's education, where it will do the most good.

But improving America's schools will take something else as well—new freedom for parents to choose what is best for their children academically. We must strengthen public education by empowering parents with choice.

Only in education could we consider choice an innovation. We are three years into the 21st century; we left the Industrial Age behind long ago. The great companies and organizations that have survived and prospered have done so only to the extent that they provide greater choice to their customers. Yet here we are today, preventing our schools from operating by this same formula for success.

Ours is a highly mobile, confident nation that offers the greatest range of personal choices in the history of mankind: We have instant messaging, 24-hour news, personal Web sites, global markets, overnight express mail, and e-commerce. The world is moving toward more choice, not less. Our education system must change to reflect these times—for all parents and all children, from all income levels.

I believe that one of our most grievous sins has been to tie a child to a school that is failing him—and insist that he stay at that school and continue to be crippled. Under the current monopolistic system, public schools have no incentive to embark on substantial reforms or make major improvements because, no matter how badly they perform:

- Their budgets will not be cut;

- Their enrollment will not decline; and

- The school will not close down.

But when parents are allowed to remove their children—and the money that comes with them—from failing schools, public schools are forced to respond.

The American people are demanding change:

- More than half a million children are enrolled in roughly 2,700 charter schools nationwide;

- Approximately 2 million children are home-schooled; and

- The number of students learning through virtual charter schools is growing.

Under the No Child Left Behind Act, if children are not learning and schools do not improve, their moms and dads can choose supplemental services such as one-on-one tutoring or after-school help. Or they can enroll their children in a better public school.

Choice works, and I can speak from experience. I ran the nation's seventh largest public school system, and I embraced choice. I knew that competition would make our system stronger. And it did. We strengthened our system in Houston and won a national award for closing the achievement gap. There is also evidence that choice programs that allow children to attend private schools can improve student achievement. The findings are strongest for African–American students.

As we work to implement our new education reforms, I am mindful that change can be diffi-cult. But I am also reminded of the words of Martin Luther King who said:

> Every society has its protectors of the status quo and its fraternities of the indifferent who are notorious for sleeping through revolutions. But today our very survival depends on our ability to stay awake, to adjust to new ideas, to remain vigilant and to face the challenge of change.

*—Rod Paige is the seventh U.S. Secretary of Education. The son of public school educators, he has been a teacher, a coach, a school board member, a dean of a college of education, and the superintendent of the Houston public school district. Throughout his career, Dr. Paige has been a passionate and constant advocate for children and better schools.*

# INTRODUCTION

Progress on school choice in the statehouse and courtroom during 2002 set the stage for an ambitious 2003 legislative agenda in many states and the U.S. Congress. Most significantly, the Supreme Court of the United States ruled in *Zelman* v. *Simmons-Harris* that voucher programs do not violate the U.S. Constitution, even when participating schools are overwhelmingly religious.[1] Before the one-year anniversary of the Court's decision, Colorado Governor Bill Owens signed into law the Colorado Opportunity Contract Pilot Program, which will provide vouchers to low-income students in low-performing school districts. The Maryland legislature enacted a charter school law.

Meanwhile, the body of research supporting choice has grown considerably. This research, the Supreme Court's landmark legal opinion, and increased legislative activity on choice provide a foundation for new programs that will empower parents to choose the schools that best meet their children's needs.

Nationwide, the school choice movement has made significant gains. As of May 26, 2003:

- In six states—Colorado, Florida, Maine, Ohio, Vermont, and Wisconsin—students may use state or district-funded scholarships to attend a private school of choice.[2]

- Six states offer tax credits or deductions for education expenses or contributions to scholarship programs.

- Forty states and the District of Columbia have enacted charter school laws.[3]

- Fifteen states guarantee public school choice within or between districts. (Other states have choice programs that are optional for districts, target only specific populations, and/or require that parents pay tuition.).[4]

- Thirty-nine states and the District of Columbia have privately funded scholarship organizations that provide tuition assistance to more than 60,000 students.[5]

- In all 50 states, home schooling is legal. As many as 2 million students are home-schooled nationwide.

- Twenty-one states have comprehensive dual enrollment programs that enable high school students to attend college classes for high school and postsecondary credit at minimal or no expense to the student.[6]

---

1. *Zelman* v. *Simmons-Harris*, 536 U.S. 639 (2002).

2. In 2002, 10,789 students participated in the Milwaukee Parental Choice Program; 4,523 participated in the Cleveland Scholarship and Tutoring Program; 14,185 participated in Maine's tuitioning program (8,252 went to public schools, and 5,933 went to private schools); 7,147 participated in Vermont's tuitioning program (school breakdown not available); 1,611 received Florida's Opportunity Scholarships, 702 of which were used at private schools; and 8,200 participated in the Florida McKay Scholarship Program. The Colorado Opportunity Contract Pilot Program, which will start in the 2004-–2005 school year, could aid as many as 20,000 students when fully implemented. See Marya DeGrow, "Educational Vouchers and Tax Credits: A State-by-State Summary of Current Programs," Independence Institute, December 18, 2002; "Colorado Governor Signs School Voucher Law," *The Washington Times*, April 16, 2003; and Manhattan Institute for Policy Research, Education Research Office, "Florida Facts," at *www.miedresearchoffice.org/index.html*.

3. Washington State could become the 41st state to have a charter law. At the time of publication, legislators were in special session to consider legislation that includes the charter school bill S.B. 5012.

4. In these states, laws require districts to allow students to enroll in other schools within (intradistrict choice) or outside of (interdistrict choice) their home district. Capacity, racial balance policies, and other rules may limit transfers. In other states, state law allows public school choice, but districts are not required to participate. See Education Commission of the States, "School Choice: State Laws," December 2002, at *www.ecs.org/clearinghouse/13/75/1375.doc*.

5. See Children First America, "Backgrounder/Overview," at *www.childrenfirstamerica.org/about/backgrounder.htm*.

6. The definition of a "comprehensive policy" is taken from Education Commission of the States, Center for Community College Policy, "Postsecondary Options: Dual/Concurrent Enrollment," July 2001, at *www.communitycollegepolicy.org/pdf/ECSDualEnrollStateNote.pdf*. In other states, either dual enrollment is available on an institutional basis in the absence of a statewide policy, or the statewide policy has limitations.

---

## Progress at the Federal Level

Since President George W. Bush announced a voucher plan for the District of Columbia and other communities in his fiscal year (FY) 2004 budget, several prominent D.C. leaders have voiced their support for vouchers, including D.C. Mayor Anthony A. Williams (D) and D.C. School Board President Peggy Cooper Cafritz. In an interview with *The Washington Post*, Mayor Williams explained, "We've got a model we've been using for 140 years. I think it's time to try something else." Kevin P. Chavous (D), member of the D.C. Council and chairman of its Committee on Education, Libraries, and Recreation, backs vouchers as part of a proposal to increase support for charter schools and traditional schools. According to Chavous, "No school bureaucracy will reform itself internally. It only comes through pressure. And the most effective form of pressure is choice."[7]

In January 2002, President Bush signed the No Child Left Behind Act, which requires states to compile a list of all schools that have failed to make adequate yearly progress toward meeting state standards for two consecutive years. In 2002, children attending 8,652 schools nationwide that were deemed "failing" under the provisions of this legislation were eligible to transfer to better-performing schools. Students enrolled in schools that had failed for three years were eligible to obtain supplemental services such as tutoring.

Some states and districts, however, are not providing public school choice or supplemental services for all eligible students as mandated by the Act. They cite insufficient capacity within their public school systems as the obstacle to compliance. In New York City and Albany, New York, parents of students in failing schools filed a lawsuit when the school districts did not make the educational opportunities required by the Act available to their children.[8]

In July 2002, a presidential commission recommended expanding educational options for students served under the Individuals with Disabilities Education Act (IDEA), stating that "The Commission views parental empowerment as essential to excellence in special education. Increasing parental empowerment, coupled with public accountability for results, will create better results for children and schools."[9] The commission reasoned that "Parental and student choice is an important accountability mechanism and IDEA should include options for parents to choose their child's educational setting."[10]

Although thousands of children with disabilities throughout the country are being educated in private schools at public expense under the IDEA, many children do not have this option. For a student to be placed in a private school, the members of his or her Individualized Education Plan (IEP) team—which includes the child's teachers, administrators, specialists, and parents—must agree that the child would be served more appropriately in a private program. The options are limited by the team's decisions, which may seem arbitrary to frustrated parents.[11]

On April 30, 2003, U.S. Representative Jim DeMint (R–SC) introduced an amendment to the IDEA reauthorization legislation (H.R. 1350) to give states the flexibility to establish innovative parental choice programs for students with disabilities. While the amendment failed to pass, there are still opportunities for similar legislation in the Senate.

---

7.  Craig Timberg, "Williams Sheds Light on Vouchers Stance," *The Washington Post*, May 3, 2003. p. B1.

8.  Mark Walsh and Joetta L. Sack, "Suits Contend Officials Fail to Obey ESEA," *Education Week*, February 5, 2003.

9.  U.S. Department of Education, "A New Era: Revitalizing Special Education for Children and Families," Presidential Commission on Excellence in Special Education, July 2002.

10. *Ibid.*

11. Press release "Paige Principles for Reauthorizing Individuals with Disabilities Education Act (IDEA)," February 25, 2003, at *www.ed.gov/PressReleases/02-2003/02252003.html*.

## Existing School Choice Programs

### Arizona
An Arizona law enacted in 1997 allows individuals to receive a tax credit of up to $500 and married couples to receive a credit of up to $625 for donations to a private tuition scholarship program. Individuals may also receive a credit of up to $200 for donations to public school extracurricular activities.[12]

On January 26, 1999, the Arizona Supreme Court upheld the tax credit plan, finding the program to be neutral with regard to religion and beneficial to low-income families who have been "coerced into accepting public education."[13]

From 1998 to 2002, the tax credit program generated $56 million that financed nearly 36,000 scholarships.[14] More than 80 percent of the scholarship recipients were from lower-income families. A Cato Institute report found the credit to be revenue-neutral. Because the scholarships cost less than the per-pupil expenditure at the public schools, the system saves money when students who had been educated at public expense transfer to less costly private schools, offsetting the revenue loss of the tax credit.[15]

### Colorado
Starting in 2004, the Colorado Opportunity Contract Pilot Program will provide vouchers to low-income students in districts that are designated by the state as "poor-performing." The vouchers will be worth 37.5 percent of the district's per-pupil costs for kindergarteners, 75 percent for elementary and junior high school students, and 85 percent for high school students. Only students who participate in the federal free and reduced-price lunch program and who were enrolled in a Colorado public school the previous year will be eligible to participate.

Additionally, in grades 4–12, only students who failed the state assessment or college entrance exam will be eligible. Participation is capped at 1 percent of a district's enrollment in 2004–2005, and the cap will rise yearly to a maximum of 6 percent in 2007–2008 and thereafter.[16]

### Florida
Florida has three school choice programs: Opportunity Scholarships, McKay Scholarships for students with disabilities, and a tax credit for donations to scholarship funds for poor students.

The A+ Plan provides Opportunity Scholarships to students in schools that have failed to achieve state assessment benchmarks twice within a four-year period. The plan allows these students to carry their state per-pupil dollars to another public school or a private school. Of the 1,611 students using the Opportunity Scholarships during the 2002–2003 school year, 702 used their vouchers to attend a private school, and the rest are attending other public schools.[17]

During the 2002–2003 school year, approximately 8,200 disabled students used McKay Scholarships to attend another public or private school.[18] The McKay Scholarship program, enacted as a pilot program by the Florida legislature in 1999 and expanded statewide in 2001, provides vouchers to special-needs students if their parents are dissatisfied with their academic progress.[19]

In addition, 15,000 students statewide are using scholarships under Florida's corporate income tax credit program during the 2002–2003 school year. Under this program, which was approved by the state legislature in 2001, corporations can receive tax credits for scholarship-fund donations of up to 75 percent of the amount of their corporate income tax bill. The

12. DeGrow, "Educational Vouchers and Tax Credits."
13. *Kotterman v. Killian*, 972 P, 2nd 606 at 615 (1999).
14. Dan Lips, "The Arizona Scholarship Tax Credit: A Model for Federal Reform," Goldwater Institute, August 1, 2002.
15. Carrie Lips and Jennifer Jacoby, "The Arizona Scholarship Tax Credit: Giving Parents Choices, Saving Taxpayers Money," Cato Institute, September 17, 2001, at *www.cato.org/pubs/pas/pa414.pdf*.
16. See Colorado General Assembly Web site at *www.state.co.us/gov_dir/stateleg.html*.
17. Manhattan Institute for Policy Research, Education Research Office, "A+ Accountability Program Opportunity Scholarships," at *www.miedresearchoffice.org/accountability.htm*, and DeGrow, "Educational Vouchers and Tax Credits."
18. DeGrow, "Educational Vouchers and Tax Credits."
19. Lisa Fine, "Florida's 'Other' Voucher Program Taking Off," *Education Week*, August 8, 2001.

tuition scholarship organizations give low-income students scholarships worth $3,500 or the full cost of tuition, whichever is less, to attend a private school or a $500 voucher to attend a public school in another school district. Income thresholds apply.[20]

## Illinois

In 1999, the Illinois legislature approved a tax credit plan for education expenditures (S.B. 1075). The law provides an annual tax credit of up to 25 percent of education-related expenses—including tuition, book fees, and lab fees—that exceed $250, up to a maximum of $500 per family.[21]

After the law's enactment, opponents brought two lawsuits against the credit. The plaintiffs lost in both circuit and appeals courts, however, and in 2001, the Illinois Supreme Court refused to reconsider the two district appeals court rulings that upheld the tax credit.[22]

## Iowa

In 1987, the Iowa legislature enacted a law providing tax credits and deductions for education expenses. Under the original law, families earning less than $45,000 could deduct up to $1,000 per child from their state income tax liability for education expenses. Taxpayers using the standard deduction could take a tax credit of up to $50 for education expenses for each child.[23] The law was amended in 1996 and again in 1998, and all families may now take a tax credit of 25 percent of the first $1,000 spent on their children's education.[24]

## Maine

Maine has been paying for students to attend private schools since colonial times. A century ago, the state enacted the town "tuitioning" law that serves students today. Under the law, school districts without public schools allow students to attend public schools in other districts or nonsectarian private schools.[25] In 1981, the legislature enacted a law preventing students from selecting religious schools.[26]

## Minnesota

Since 1955, Minnesota families have been able to deduct education expenses from their state taxes.[27] In 1997, the legislature enacted legislation giving Minnesota families who earn $33,500 or less a refundable tax credit of up to $1,000 per student (up to $2,000 per family) for education expenses, excluding tuition. The law increased the maximum deduction to $1,625 for expenses associated with elementary school education, including tuition, and up to $2,500 for junior high school and senior high school expenses.[28]

## Ohio

Enacted in 1995, the Cleveland Scholarship and Tutoring Program provides elementary school students with vouchers worth up to $2,250 for tuition at a private school of choice.[29] Although the number of vouchers was increased from 4,523 in the 2001–2002 school year to 5,523 for the 2002–2003 school year, officials say they had to turn away more than 1,100 Cleveland parents who applied for vouchers because there were not enough to meet the demand.[30]

20. Manhattan Institute for Policy Research, Education Research Office, "Corporate Tax Credit Scholarships," at *www.miedresearchoffice.org/corporatetaxscholarships.htm*.

21. State of Illinois, 91st General Assembly, Public Acts, at *www.legis.state.il.us/legislation/publicacts/pubact91/acts/91-0009.html*.

22. *Griffith v. Bower,* 319 Ill. App. 3d 993 (5th Dist.), *app. denied,* 195 Ill. 2d 577 (2001); *Toney v. Bower,* 318 Ill. App. 3d 1194 (4th Dist.), *app. denied,* 195 Ill. 2d 573 (2001).

23. Tom Mirga, "Tuition Tax Credits Are Challenged in Iowa," *Education Week,* October 28, 1987.

24. "Legislative Update," *Education Week,* June 5, 1996, and Robert C. Johnston, "Despite Talk, Lawmakers Slow to Copy Tax Credits," *Education Week,* June 3, 1998.

25. Institute for Justice, "The Case for School Choice: Raymond, Maine," *Litigation Backgrounder,* 1997, at *www.ij.org/cases/index.html*.

26. John Gehring, "Legal Battle Over School Vouchers Returns to Maine," *Education Week,* September 25, 2002.

27. See Minnesota House of Representatives, Research Department, "Minnesota's Public School Fee Law and Education Tax Credit and Deduction," *Information Brief,* January 2003, at *www.house.leg.state.mn.us/hrd/pubs/feelaw.pdf*.

28. *Ibid.*

29. "State Voucher Programs," *Education Week,* October 3, 2001.

## Pennsylvania

In 2001, the Pennsylvania legislature approved an education tax credit program that permits corporations to receive credits of up to $100,000 for contributions to organizations that provide scholarships to private schools or grants to public schools for innovative programs. The state may award a maximum of $30 million in tax credits per year. Scholarship recipients must meet income eligibility guidelines.[31]

## Vermont

Since 1869, Vermont has operated a tuitioning program for students in school districts without a public school.[32] Students may attend a public school in another district or an approved non-sectarian private school. As was the case in Maine, students in Vermont could attend religious schools during the first 100 years that the program was in existence. An estimated 7,147 students participated in the program during the 2001–2002 school year.[33]

## Wisconsin

More than 10,000 students participate in the Milwaukee Parental Choice Program. Established in 1990 and expanded in 1995, the program provides vouchers to Milwaukee families with incomes that are at or below 175 percent of the poverty level to enable their children to attend private or religious schools of choice. The Wisconsin Supreme Court upheld the program in 1998 and the U.S. Supreme Court declined to review the decision.[34]

## Privately Funded School Choice

Thanks to such private foundations as Children First America (CFA) and the Children's Scholarship Fund (CSF), the number of privately funded scholarships enabling low-income public school students to attend a private school of choice continues to grow.

These scholarship organizations have been active for over 10 years and have served more than 100,000 children. During that period, approximately 100 privately funded organizations have invested $500 million in the future of America's children, providing vouchers that range from $1,500 to $5,000 per year. Because vouchers typically do not cover the entire tuition, some financial commitment from the parents is usually required.[35]

Children First America has played a central role in developing many of the scholarship programs and continues to provide support for new and existing scholarship organizations. CFA also provides information on parental choice to parents; local, state, and federal elected leaders; and the general public.[36]

The Children's Scholarship Fund, founded in 1998, is a multimillion-dollar foundation that matches funds raised in communities throughout the country. The CSF provides scholarships to nearly 34,000 students at 7,000 schools. In 2001, *Worth* magazine named it one of "America's 100 Best Charities."[37]

## Charter School Developments

Maryland recently joined 39 other states and the District of Columbia in enacting a law to establish charter schools. The first charter school opened its doors in 1992 in St. Paul, Minnesota. In 2002, Wyoming and Indiana opened their first charter schools, and the number of charter schools increased by 14 percent, bringing the total to approximately 2,700 schools. The states with the most charter schools in 2002 included Arizona, with 465; California, with 427; Florida, with 227; Texas, with 221; and Michigan, with 196.[38]

---

30. Caroline Hendrie, "Applications for Cleveland Vouchers Soar After High Court Ruling," *Education Week*, September 4, 2002.

31. DeGrow, "Educational Vouchers and Tax Credits."

32. Libby Sternberg, "Lessons from Vermont: 132-Year-Old Voucher Program Rebuts Critics," Cato Institute *Briefing Paper* No. 67, September 10, 2001.

33. DeGrow, "Educational Vouchers and Tax Credits."

34. *Jackson v. Benson*, 578 NW.2d 602 (Wis. S. Ct. 1998), cert. denied, 525 U.S. 997 (1998). See also Institute for Justice, "Milwaukee School Choice Case," at *www.ij.org*, and DeGrow, "Educational Vouchers and Tax Credits."

35. See Children First America Web site at *www.childrenfirstamerica.org*.

36. *Ibid.*

37. See Children's Scholarship Fund Web site at *www.scholarshipfund.org*.

The number of "virtual charter schools" that implement educational programs via the Internet is also on the rise. There are approximately 50 virtual charter schools throughout the nation.[39]

A U.S. Department of Education report released in June 2001 confirmed existing research indicating that public schools and school districts respond positively to the formation of charter schools. *Challenge and Opportunity: The Impact of Charter Schools on Districts* reported that districts improved their services and operations in response to competition from charter schools.[40] Heralding this new report, U.S. Secretary of Education Rod Paige stated:

> Charter schools offer meaningful options for parents and their children—particularly for those children who would otherwise be left behind in low-performing schools. The good news is that charter schools do not just help the students they serve directly, they also prod the entire system to improve.[41]

Research over the past two years has found that charter schools are typically smaller than traditional schools, serve predominantly at-risk populations, and show achievement gains after two years. Specifically:

- The 2000–2001 evaluations of the Public Charter Schools Program, commissioned by the U.S. Department of Education, found that charter schools are smaller than traditional public schools, enjoy strong parental involvement, and serve diverse populations of students.[42]

- Results from the Center for Education Reform's 2002 Survey of American Charter Schools show that charter schools, in addition to educating children who are poorly served by traditional public schools, are both cost-effective and innovative.[43]

- In a recent study, Harvard professor Caroline Hoxby found that increased school choice raises school productivity and student achievement within the public school system. Hoxby's report found that competition from charter schools in Michigan and Arizona, and from Milwaukee's voucher program, has compelled public schools to raise their productivity, as measured by students' achievement gains.[44]

- According to a 2002 California State University study, *California Charter Schools Serving Low SES Students: An Analysis of the Academic Performance Index*, the state's charter schools were more effective than traditional public schools in improving the academic achievement of low-income and at-risk students. Charter schools in which at least half of the students participated in the federal free and reduced-price lunch program improved at a rate of 22 percent, while academic achievement in traditional public schools improved at a rate of 19 percent. Moreover, charter schools in which 75 percent of the students participated in the lunch programs improved at a rate of 28 percent, compared with 24 percent in the other public schools.[45]

- A report released by the Georgia Department of Education in 2002 shows that the state's charter schools are outpacing their traditional counterparts. Compared with their counterparts in traditional public

38. Press release, "Growth in Charter Schools Reflects Increasing Demands for Choices," Center for Education Reform, December 20, 2002, at *www.edreform.com/press/2002/charternumbers.htm*, and e-mail correspondence with Anna Varghese, Center for Education Reform, February 24, 2003.

39. Mary Lord, "O E-pioneers!" *U.S. News & World Report*, December 9, 2002.

40. U.S. Department of Education, *Challenge and Opportunity: The Impact of Charter Schools on Districts*, June 2001, at *www.ed.gov/pubs/chartimpact*.

41. News release, "Charter Schools Prompting Improvement in School Districts, According to Two U.S. Department of Education Reports," U.S. Department of Education, June 14, 2001.

42. Lee Anderson, Nancy Adelman, Kara Finnigan, Lynyonne Cotton, Mary Beth Donnelly, and Tiffany Price, *A Decade of Public Charter Schools, Evaluation of the Public Charter Schools Program: 2000–2001 Evaluation Report*, SRI International, November 2002, at *www.sri.com/policy/cep/choice/yr2.pdf*.

43. Center for Education Reform, "Charter Schools 2002: Results from CER's Annual Survey of America's Charter Schools," October 2002, at *www.edreform.com/charter_schools/survey2002.pdf*.

44. Caroline Hoxby, "School Choice and School Productivity (Or, Could School Choice Be a Tide That Lifts All Boats?)," National Bureau of Economic Research *Working Paper* No. 8873, April 2002, at *www.nber.org/digest/aug02/w8873.html*.

schools, more charter school students passed the state's proficiency tests in all five subjects. Furthermore, fewer charter school students repeat grades or drop out of school.[46]

## Home Schooling

The home-school movement has grown steadily over the past two decades.[47] As many as 2 million children in grades K–12 were home-schooled during the 2001–2002 school year. The home-school population is growing at a rate of 7 percent to 15 percent a year.[48] From 1999 to 2002, the number of African–American home-schooling families increased nearly ten-fold. African–American families now comprise nearly 5 percent of the total number of home-schooling families.[49]

On average, home-school students have higher academic achievement than students in public or private schools. Home-schooled elementary school students tend to perform one grade level higher than their peers in traditional schools. By high school, they are achieving four grade levels above the national average.[50] Nearly all home-schooled students participate in at least two extracurricular activities such as dance, sports, music, and volunteerism. In fact, the average home-school student participates in five such activities.[51]

Barred from the National Honor Society, home schoolers have started their own honor society, Eta Sigma Alpha. Founded in 1999 by Joanne Juren, a former public school teacher and administrator, the society has 20 chapters nationwide.[52]

## Winning in the Courts

In June 2002, the Supreme Court of the United States upheld the Cleveland Scholarship and Tutoring Program, ruling that the use of public money to underwrite tuition at private and religious schools does not violate the Establishment Clause of the U.S. Constitution as long as parents make the decision regarding where the voucher is used.[53] The Cleveland program provides vouchers for tuition or tutoring fees at public, private, secular, and religious schools.

Given the range of options and the freedom parents have to choose among them, the Court concluded that the Cleveland program is neutral with regard to religion, even though most parents used vouchers to send their children to religious schools. Writing for the Court, Chief Justice William Rehnquist stated, "We believe that the program challenged here is a program of true private choice, consistent with *Mueller*, *Witters*, and *Zobrest*, and thus constitutional. As was true in those cases, the Ohio program is neutral in all respects toward religion."[54]

This momentous decision removes the constitutional cloud from policy consideration, enabling state legislators and Congress to consider, on their merits, new programs to give parents greater choice in the schooling of their children.

Other important state-level constitutional battles remain in play as the courts interpret state constitutional provisions, including discriminatory "Blaine amendments" that prohibit tax money from flowing to religious institutions. Vestiges of a 19th century anti-Catholic movement, state-level Blaine amendments have been used by some courts to strike down voucher

45. Press alert, "Achievement Gains Found at California Charter Schools: Disadvantaged Children Benefit More from Charter Schools," Center for Education Reform, March 11, 2002. For the complete study, see *www.cal-statela.edu/academic/ccoe/c_perc/rpt1.pdf*.

46. Center for Education Reform, *Education Reform Newswire*, November 19, 2002, at *www.edreform.com*. For the full report, see *www.doe.k12.ga.us/charterschools/about.html*.

47. George A. Clowes, "Homeschooling Update," *School Reform News*, January 2003, p. 13.

48. See Home School Legal Defense Association, "Homeschooling Research: Frequently Asked Questions," at *www.hslda.org/research/faq.asp#1*.

49. Clowes, "Homeschooling Update."

50. Lawrence M. Rudner, Ph.D., "The Scholastic Achievement and Demographic Characteristics of Home School Students in 1998," University of Maryland, College of Library and Information Services, ERIC Clearinghouse on Assessment and Evaluation, at *www.hslda.org/docs/study/rudner1999/Rudner2.asp*.

51. Dr. Brian D. Ray , Strengths of Their Own: Home Schoolers Across America, National Home Education Research Institute, 1997, at *www.hslda.org/docs/study/ray1997/17.asp*.

52. Ellen Sorokin, "Home-Schoolers Start a New Honor Society," *The Washington Times*, January 4, 2003, p. 1.

53. *Zelman v. Simmons-Harris*, 536 U.S. 639 (2002).

54. *Ibid.* at 652.

programs, while other courts have upheld choice programs despite the clause. Thirty-seven states have Blaine-type language, and 29 have prohibitive "compelled support" provisions. This type of constitutional language dates back to colonial times and was intended to prevent governments from compelling individuals to contribute to or attend a state-designated church.[55]

The following are among the significant developments in the courts during 2002.

- Undeterred by the U.S. Supreme Court's ruling on the Cleveland voucher program, a Florida circuit court struck down the state's voucher program in August 2002.[56] Supporters of vouchers, including Governor Jeb Bush, have challenged the decision. The state has appealed the circuit court's decision, and the judge has allowed the program to continue while the case makes its way through the courts.[57]

- On July 18, 2002, the Ninth U.S. Circuit Court of Appeals declared unconstitutional a Washington State policy that prohibits students who use state higher education scholarships to earn a degree in theology. The court declared in *Davey* v. *Locke* that "a state law may not offer a benefit to all…but exclude some on the basis of religion."[58] The case has been appealed to the U.S. Supreme Court.[59]

- In June 2002, the Washington Supreme Court overturned a previous trial court decision and ruled that the state's Educational Opportunity Grant (EOG) Program does not violate the state constitution when college students use grants for tuition at religiously affiliated colleges. Washington's Blaine amendment prohibits public-sector funding of sectarian institutions. The state

interpreted this provision to prohibit students from using state aid to attend religious K–12 schools or colleges. The court ruled that the Blaine amendment did not apply to higher education. However, it did not consider whether the Blaine amendment itself violates the U.S. Constitution, which requires that government programs must be non-discriminatory toward religion.[60]

- The Institute for Justice is representing six families in Maine who have filed suit against a 1981 statute that removed religious schools from the state's century-old voucher program. Under Maine's tuitioning law, students who live in rural towns without a public school may attend a public school in another town or a private school. Until 1981, students had been allowed to attend sectarian schools under the program.[61] Maine's constitution does not have a Blaine amendment.

- On March 2003, a number of Vermont residents filed suit against the state regarding its tuitioning policy, which enables students in rural towns without public schools to attend private schools. Since 1961, Vermont law has prohibited parents from using the tuitioning policy to send their children to religious schools. Plaintiff Dr. Blane Nasveschuk had to pay tuition for his sons to attend Mount St. Joseph's Academy, although students in nonsectarian schools could take advantage of the tuitioning policy. Dr. Nasveschuk was joined in this suit by two other families who also live in tuitioning towns but must pay for their children's education in schools with a religious affiliation. The Institute for Justice is representing these families.[62]

---

55. Richard Komer, "School Choice: The State Constitutional Challenge," *Liberty & Law*, Vol. 10, No. 5 (September 2001).

56. Michael A. Fletcher, "Florida's Voucher Law Is Struck Down," *The Washington Post*, August 6, 2002, p. A7.

57. Alan Richard, "Florida Sees Surge in Use of Vouchers," *Education Week*, September 4, 2002.

58. *Davey* v. *Locke*, 299 F.3d 748 at 754 (9th Cir. 2002).

59. Office of the Attorney General, Petition for a Writ of Certiorari, at *www.wa.gov/ago/davey/Petition.doc.*

60. News release, "Washington Supreme Court Sidesteps Key Issue in School Aid Case," Becket Fund for Religious Liberty, June 13, 2002.

61. See *Anderson* v. *Town of Durham* at *www.ij.org.*

62. Institute for Justice, "Fighting for Parental Liberty by Stopping Religious Discrimination," *Litigation Backgrounder*, March 20, 2003, at *www.ij.org/media/school_choice/vermont/3_20_03pr.shtml.*

## Research Revealing the Benefits of Choice

Lawmakers can now make decisions informed by a growing body of evidence that choice often improves the academic performance of at-risk students, promotes parental involvement and satisfaction, and fosters accountability within public school systems. Significant research over the past two years confirms earlier findings that choice improves the educational experience of students.

- A May 2003 survey by the U.S. Department of Education shows that more families, particularly those with lower incomes, are participating in "public-school choice," sending their children to schools other than their assigned schools. The number of students attending a public school of choice rose from 11 percent in 1993 to 14 percent in 1996 and 1999. Further, the National Center for Education Statistics found that parents of students in private schools or public schools of choice were "more likely to say they were 'very satisfied' with their children's schools, teachers, academic standards, and order and discipline" than were parents of students attending a public school to which they had been assigned.[63]

- According to research conducted by Harvard University professor Paul Peterson, the academic achievement of low-income African–American students who received scholarships offered by the School Choice Scholarships Foundation (SCSF) rose significantly.[64] African–American students who participated in the program for three years had scores on the Iowa Test of Basic Skills that were 9.2 percentile points higher than the scores of students who remained in the public schools. Students who participated in the program for fewer than three years also experienced gains.[65]

- In September 2002, the U.S. General Accounting Office released a report that examined research findings regarding 78 privately funded voucher programs. Several studies showed that families using vouchers were more satisfied with their children's new schools with regard to such factors as academics and safety. Parents using privately funded vouchers reported that their children's schools communicated with them more frequently and had a more positive environment than did the public schools. Other studies documented the academic gains of African–American students who had received vouchers.[66]

- In 2001, Harvard and Georgetown University researchers released a study comparing the academic experience of students using privately funded vouchers through the Washington Scholarship Fund with that of similar students in a control group who remained in public schools. Their findings on academic and social indicators were significant: Parental satisfaction was higher for parents of scholarship students. The report also found that students in private schools did more homework, were safer, and had greater respect for teachers. Significantly, African–American students using the vouchers scored 9 percentile points higher on national math and reading achievement tests than their peers in public schools.[67]

- A 2001 RAND Corporation review of existing literature on voucher and charter programs found that the voucher programs produced positive or neutral achievement benefits, resulted in higher parental satisfaction, and hold the potential for increases in school integration. Because choice programs have been small and limited, RAND researchers caution against using them to make predictions about the impact of large

63. National Center for Education Statistics, "Trends in the Use of School Choice 1993–1999," National Household Education Surveys Program, May 2003, at *http://nces.ed.gov/pubs2003/2003031.pdf*.

64. Daniel Mayer, Paul Peterson, Christina Clark Tuttle, and William Howell, "School Choice in New York After Three Years: An Evaluation of the School Choice Scholarship Program Final Report," Harvard University, Mathematica Policy Research, Inc., and University of Wisconsin, February 2002.

65. *Ibid.*

66. U.S. General Accounting Office, *School Vouchers: Characteristics of Privately Funded Programs*, GAO–02–752, September 2002, at *www.gao.gov/new.items/d02752.pdf*.

67. Patrick J. Wolf, Paul E. Peterson, and Martin R. West, "Results of a School Voucher Experiment: The Case of Washington, D.C., After Two Years," prepared for annual meeting of the American Political Science Association, San Francisco, California, August 30–September 2, 2001.

programs. Rather, they suggest, "A program of vigorous research and experimentation is called for, but not one confined to choice programs. Better information on the performance of conventional public schools and alternative reform models is needed as well."[68]

- In October 2002, Manhattan Institute scholars Jay P. Greene, Ph.D., and Greg Forster, Ph.D., released a new study that focuses on the impact of school choice on the academic achievement of public school students in Milwaukee and San Antonio. After controlling for demographic characteristics such as race and income level and differences in expenditures, the authors found increased academic achievement in public schools that had been exposed to competition from private school scholarship programs and charter schools.[69]

- A 2002 analysis of the voucher programs in Maine and Vermont (the oldest in the nation) found that choice increases productivity. In these states, students in towns without public schools may attend private schools at public expense. Schools located in areas where there was high competition in attracting students (and their per-pupil funding) had a strong incentive to improve performance. Such schools exhibited higher levels of achievement than did those in areas with less competition.[70]

- Research conducted in 2002 by Duke University professor Thomas Nechyba suggests that a citywide voucher program could alleviate neighborhood income segregation by attracting higher-income families to poorer areas. Their relocation to low-income neighborhoods would increase property values and improve the tax base, thereby generat-

ing greater revenues for the public schools. Thus, benefits flow not only to students using vouchers, but also to students who remain in the public school system. In this way, vouchers can contribute to neighborhood revitalization and public school improvement while increasing the freedom of parents to choose the school that best meets their children's needs.[71]

- A 2001 analysis of the Florida A+ program, conducted by Jay P. Greene of the Manhattan Institute, found that vouchers provided a strong incentive for schools to improve. In Florida, schools receive grades ranging from "A" to "F," based on the proportion of students who pass the state's proficiency tests. Students who attend schools that receive a failing grade twice within a four-year period can receive a voucher to attend another public or private school of choice. Greene found that schools receiving an "F" improved when they were faced with the prospect of vouchers.[72]

## Winning in the Court of Public Opinion

A poll conducted in July 2002 by Zogby International Polling on behalf of the Center for Education Reform found that 76 percent of respondents "strongly" or "somewhat" supported "providing parents with the option of sending their children to the school of their choice—either public, private or parochial—rather than only to the school to which they are assigned." When asked specifically whether they were "in favor of or against allowing poor parents to be given the tax dollars allotted for their child's education and permitting them to use those dollars in the form of a scholarship to attend a private, public, or parochial school of their choosing," 63 percent of respondents

68. Brian P. Gill, P. Michael Timpane, Karen E. Ross, and Dominic J. Brewer, "Rhetoric Versus Reality: What We Know and What We Need to Know About Vouchers and Charter Schools," RAND Corporation, RB–8018–EDU, 2001.

69. Jay P. Greene and Greg Forster, "Rising to the Challenge: The Effect of School Choice on Public Schools in Milwaukee and San Antonio," Manhattan Institute *Civic Bulletin* No. 27, October 2002.

70. Christopher Hammons, Ph.D., "The Effects of Town Tuitioning in Vermont and Maine," Milton & Rose D. Friedman Foundation, 2002.

71. Thomas Nechyba, "The Unintended Benefits of Private School Choice," Milton & Rose D. Friedman Foundation, June 2002; see also Thomas Nechyba, "School Finance, Spatial Income Segregation, and the Nature of Communities," Duke University and National Bureau of Economic Research, at *www.econ.duke.edu/~nechyba/segregation.pdf*.

72. Jay P. Greene, Ph.D., "An Evaluation of the Florida A-Plus Accountability and School Choice Program," Manhattan Institute for Policy Research, February 2001.

favored the proposal. Rates of approval were higher among minority respondents.[73]

Even a 2001 survey conducted for the National Education Association (NEA), a union that has actively opposed vouchers, found that 63 percent of those surveyed supported President Bush's plan to give parents of children in failing schools a voucher to send their children to another public, charter, or private school. According to Representative John Boehner (R–OH), chairman of the U.S. House Committee on Education and the Workforce:

> Americans support giving parents the power to do what they think is best for their children's education. The President's plan gives this power as a last resort to the parents of children trapped in chronically failing schools after those schools have been given every opportunity to change. A solid majority of Americans support this approach.[74]

Support for choice also is strong among Members of Congress—at least as far as their own children are concerned. According to a Heritage Foundation survey, among members of the 107th Congress, 47 percent of Representatives and 50 percent of Senators who have school-age children were sending their children to private schools. The percentage of Members practicing private school choice in 2001 was higher than in Heritage's previous surveys, particularly in the House of Representatives. It was also much higher than the percentage of the general population (approximately 10 percent) that sends their children to private schools.[75]

Despite the rising popularity of private schools among Members of Congress, however, many of the same policymakers who exercise choice in their own children's education voted to block legislation that would have given lower-income families the range of options that they enjoy. Had these Members voted on choice legislation in a way that was consistent with their own practices, such legislation would have passed.[76]

## Minority Support for School Choice

Potentially powerful and growing support for school choice is found among minority parents. A 2002 National Opinion Poll conducted by the Joint Center for Political and Economic Studies found that 57.4 percent of African–American respondents favored a voucher system when asked, "Would you support a voucher system where parents would get money from the government to send their children to the public, private, or parochial school of their choice?"[77] An earlier poll by the Joint Center found that, while 69 percent of black elected officials oppose vouchers, 60 percent of the black populace supports them and that 70 percent of blacks under the age of 50 support vouchers.[78]

A July 2001 poll by the Latino Coalition and Hispanic Business Roundtable found that 73 percent of Hispanic adults surveyed supported the following statement: "The government should provide taxpayer-funded vouchers to help low-income families send their children to a better public, private, or church-run school." An even larger percentage of respondents supported giving all parents a $1,000 tax credit for educational expenses, including tuition.[79]

A June 2002 poll conducted by Black America's Political Action Committee (BAMPAC) found that 63 percent of African–American parents would like to transfer their children from their current public schools to a public charter school or private school. More than half of the respondents gave their children's public school a grade

---

73. Press release, "Poll Finds 63 Percent of Americans Favor School Choice," Center for Education Reform, August 20, 2002.

74. Press release, "New Poll for NEA Shows Majority of Americans Back President Bush's Approach to School Choice," Committee on Education and the Workforce, U.S. House of Representatives, 107th Cong., 1st Sess., March 5, 2001.

75. Jennifer Garrett, "Another Look at How Members of Congress Exercise School Choice," Heritage Foundation *Backgrounder* No. 1553, May 22, 2002.

76. *Ibid.*

77. David A. Bositis, "2002 National Opinion Poll: Politics," Joint Center for Political and Economic Studies, 2002, at *130.94.20.119/whatsnew/2002_NOP_text&tables.pdf.*

78. Center for Education Reform, *Education Reform Newswire*, July 10, 2001, at *www.edreform.com.* For the full report, see *www.jointcenter.org.*

79. Latino Coalition and Hispanic Business Roundtable, "National Survey of Hispanic Adults," July 24, 2001, at *http://hbrt.org/surveys/010724.htm.*

of "C" or lower. BAMPAC President Alvin Williams declared that "African–Americans are becoming increasingly frustrated with the public school system and its failure, in many cases, to provide a quality education for their children. This just shows us that the idea of choice is widely supported by the African–American community."[80]

In September 2000, the Black Alliance for Educational Options (BAEO) began a public information campaign to highlight the importance of choice for children in inner-city communities. The campaign featured a compelling slogan: "School choice is widespread unless you're poor."[81] BAEO Chairman Howard Fuller supports the view that giving minority parents vouchers to take their children out of failing schools is the best way to close the racial achievement gap.[82]

In 2001, the Hispanic Council for Reform and Educational Options (CREO) was formed to address the education crisis among Hispanic youth. Faced with high dropout rates, illiteracy, and teen pregnancy among Hispanic youth, CREO advocates increased education options to improve the academic achievement of all Hispanic children.[83]

## Parental Support for School Choice

The following parental testimonies are reprinted with permission from the American Education Reform Council.[84] The testimonies are abridged for reasons of space.

> In third grade, my son Jonathan was making A's and B's on his report card, yet when he was tested, he could not read. My son was on the honor roll, and he could not read. My husband and I wanted to enroll Jonathan in another school, but we had no real options. Our income is limited…. But, beginning in the fourth grade, Florida's new A+ Opportunity Scholarship Program let us enroll Jonathan at Sacred Heart Catholic School in Pensacola. Everybody at Sacred Heart knows Jonathan. He feels

like he's somebody…. Since he started attending Sacred Heart, Jonathan gets up in the morning ready to go to school. Most importantly, Jonathan can now read.

> —By Cassandra, whose son Jonathan uses a publicly funded Opportunity Scholarship to attend a school of choice.

> The Milwaukee program has let me choose schools that I think are best for my girls…. My daughters are excelling. I believe both of them will have a choice to go on to college because of the voucher program. Before, I thought that wouldn't happen. I have seen how options like choice, charter schools, and privately funded scholarships through Milwaukee's PAVE organization have made a difference for many other low-income families like ours. People who once felt they had little or no voice in their children's education now have a voice. Because of these opportunities, I see young African Americans doing better.

> —By Tony, whose daughters Chronda and Tanya attend schools of choice through the Milwaukee voucher program.

> When Dylan was at the public school, the teacher was writing full-page letters every day telling me what Dylan could not do. He would come home with a full day's schoolwork, plus homework because he couldn't read the instructions. Homework became a four-hour ordeal of fighting and tears…. After he failed so many times, and he has no self-esteem and no desire to try, then he's labeled as something else and no one wants to deal with him. [At his new school] he does very well. He has learned a lot of coping mechanisms that he wasn't taught at the public school…. After just eight weeks in the private school he earned his very first, ever, perfect score on a spelling test. The

---

80. Ellen Sorokin, "Poll Finds Most Blacks Favor Charter, Private Schools," *The Washington Times*, July 19, 2002, p. A13.

81. See Black Alliance for Educational Options Web site at *www.baeo.org/*.

82. Scott Greenberger, "Many Blacks Seek Choice of Schools," *The Boston Globe*, February 26, 2001, p. B5.

83. See Hispanic CREO Web site at *www.hcreo.org/*.

84. Testimonies may also be viewed at *www.schoolchoiceinfo.org*.

skills and abilities he has attained just amaze me. I always knew he could do it, he just needed the right way to unlock that busy brain of his.

—By Susan, whose son Dylan attends a school specializing in dyslexia, using a McKay Scholarship.

Kenya is a very happy child. She likes to smile. But, she is very demanding. She's mentally and physically profoundly handicapped and she can't walk, she can't talk. The public school system has been some help, but not enough. I felt Kenya was not making enough progress in public schools…. When I learned about the McKay Scholarships, I chose one of the schools that fit her needs. The McKay Scholarship gives parents a choice—a choice in their child's future. You have an opportunity to make some decisions about the services your child will receive…. She will receive much more in the private school system: psychological services, speech therapy, and more aggressive physical and occupational therapy.

—By Selma, whose daughter Kenya has used a McKay Scholarship to attend a school that specializes in serving children with disabilities.

I care about my child's education. I would do anything, whatever it takes, to get her the best education possible. Ebony is a very bright child. I'm not saying that just because she's my child. I know she will grow up to be somebody very special. So when I found out she wasn't doing well in her social studies and math, I knew I had to do something. I was going to find a school that would help her do her best. I wanted to send her to a private school but I could never afford it. If you try to send your children to private school, you will have

to work two or three jobs to do it, and then you won't have any time for your kids. That's why the Cleveland Scholarship Program is very important to me. When I got the letter saying she got a voucher, I was so happy I didn't know what to do. It was like someone was coming to my rescue.

—By Eulanda, whose daughter Ebony receives a voucher through the Cleveland Scholarship and Tutoring Program.

## Legislative Outlook in Congress

Some of the lowest levels of achievement among public school students exist in the nation's capital. Despite per-pupil expenditures of more than $11,000, 94 percent of 4th grade students in Washington, D.C., are not proficient in math and 90 percent lack proficiency in reading, according to the National Assessment of Educational Progress (NAEP).[85] The results are similar for 8th graders. Three-quarters of D.C. 4th graders lack even basic reading and math skills. Many will never catch up. As few as 59 percent of students graduate from high school.[86]

Research strongly suggests that vouchers would improve the academic achievement of D.C. students. Researchers at Harvard and Georgetown University found improved academic achievement and higher parental satisfaction for African–American students who used privately funded scholarships through the Washington Scholarship Fund.[87] According to the NAEP test results, parochial school students consistently achieve at a higher rate than their peers in public schools.[88] Research by Heritage Foundation Analyst Kirk Johnson, Ph.D., using NAEP data confirms this trend for African–American students in the District and shows that, on average, a black 8th grader in a Catholic school outperforms 72 percent of his or her public school peers.[89]

Given the failure of other reforms to improve achievement and the growing recognition that additional funding alone will not improve the

---

85. See National Center for Education Statistics, "The Nation's Report Card State Profiles: District of Columbia," at *www.nces.ed.gov/nationsreportcard/states/*.

86. Jay P. Greene, Ph.D., "High School Graduation Rates in the United States," Manhattan Institute for Policy Research, April 2002.

87. Wolf, Peterson, and West, "Results of a School Voucher Experiment: The Case of Washington, D.C., After Two Years."

88. See U.S. Department of Education, National Center for Education Statistics, at *www.nces.ed.gov/nationsreportcard/sitemap.asp*.

system, a far better approach would be to grant families in the District of Columbia publicly funded scholarships to send their children to a public or private school of choice. In 1997, such legislation was passed by both houses of Congress but was vetoed by then-President Bill Clinton.

Representative Jeff Flake (R–AZ) introduced similar legislation, the District of Columbia Student Opportunity Scholarship Act (H.R. 684), on February 11, 2003. This bill would provide low-income students with scholarships to attend another public or private school within the D.C. metro area. The voucher would be worth the cost of tuition or $5,000 (under half the per-pupil expenditure of D.C. public schools), whichever is less, for students from families whose income is equal to or below the poverty line, and 75 percent of the cost of tuition or $3,750 for students from families earning up to 185 percent of the poverty level.

President Bush's FY 2004 budget also includes a D.C. voucher proposal as part of a $75 million Choice Incentive Fund. The fund would provide competitive grants to states, school districts, and community-based nonprofit organizations to give scholarships to students to attend a school of choice. The District of Columbia would receive a choice grant.[90]

In all, the budget provides for several school choice initiatives, including a refundable tax credit for parents who transfer their child out of a "failing" school as defined under the No Child Left Behind Act. The credit would be worth 50 percent of the first $5,000 in tuition, fees, and transportation costs. The No Child Left Behind Act currently allows students in failing schools the option of transferring to another public school within the District, but many students have been denied this opportunity because of insufficient capacity within the public school system.

Funding for a public school choice program, charter schools, and magnet schools is also included in the FY 2004 budget, along with billions of dollars of new funding for other education programs, bringing the total to the largest amount ever spent at the federal level for education. Although only a very small percentage of this funding is designated to help families find better schools for their children, such programs are an important step in the right direction. They rest squarely on the foundation of previous legislative activity, current law, legal opinion, and research.

## Remaining Challenges

Despite the growth of choice programs over the past few years, the vast majority of poor children remain trapped in low-performing schools. The nation spends more than $422 billion each year on elementary and secondary education,[91] yet the results of the most recent NAEP tests in math, science, reading, history, and geography are deeply disappointing. Nearly 60 percent of high school seniors lack even a basic knowledge of American history, and more than half of the nation's low-income 4th graders cannot read at a basic level.[92]

Moreover, America's children have fallen behind many of their international peers on tests of core academic knowledge, particularly in math and science. Despite higher than average per-pupil expenditures, American 8th graders ranked 19th among counterparts in 38 countries in math and 18th in science in the most recent international comparison of proficiency, the Third International Mathematics and Science Study–Repeat (TIMSS–R) of 1999.[93]

89. Kirk A. Johnson, Ph.D., "Comparing Math Scores of Black Students in D.C.'s Public and Catholic Schools," Heritage Foundation *Center for Data Analysis Report* No. 99–08, October 7, 1999, at *www.heritage.org/ Research/Education/CDA99-08.cfm*.

90. Press release, "President Bush's 2004 Budget Will Include an Estimated $756 Million to Expand Options for Parents, Paige Says," U.S. Department of Education, January 31, 2003.

91. This is the latest figure available from the U.S. Department of Education for 2000 and includes private, local, state, and federal spending. See U.S. Department of Education, National Center for Education Statistics, *Digest of Education Statistics 2001*, at *http://nces.ed.gov/pubs2002/digest2001/ch1.asp*.

92. NAEP assessment results provide information about what students know and can do, as well as what they should know and be able to do, on a variety of subjects. The three achievement levels for each grade (4, 8, and 12) are Basic, Proficient, and Advanced. See National Center for Education Statistics, "The Nation's Report Card," at *http://nces.ed.gov/nationsreportcard*.

93. TIMSS–R 1999, "Benchmarking Highlights," Boston College, Lynch School of Education, International Study Center, April 2001, p. 3, at *www.timss.org/timss1999b/pdf/t99b_highlights.pdf*.

While parental choice has made significant headway in the past few years, opponents have done their best to limit its success. As the eminent scholars of the Koret Task Force on K–12 Education recently stated,

> *Choice-based reforms have not had a fair test.* Most evidence to date suggests that they can boost student learning and parental satisfaction, but constraints have kept them from being tried in full. Opponents have hamstrung school-choice programs at every turn: fighting voucher programs in legislative chambers and courtrooms; limiting per-pupil funding so tightly that it's impractical for new schools to come into being; capping the number of charter schools; and regulating and harassing them into near conformity with conventional schools.

> These barriers have kept choice-based reforms from receiving the proper trials they deserve, which is significant on two counts: first, by ensuring that only half-baked versions have been adopted, opponents have made it easier to claim that the reforms were tried but they failed; second, profound changes in a system—the kind of changes that choice would bring to bear—cannot arise overnight.[94]

## Conclusion

2002 was a momentous year for the school choice movement. The Supreme Court of the United States upheld the Cleveland Scholarship and Tutoring Program, opening the door for new voucher programs. Progress was made in the state courts against Blaine amendments that have prohibited students from using publicly funded vouchers in schools with a religious affiliation.

New studies have added to the growing body of evidence showing that when parents are empowered to choose their children's schools—whether they choose public, public charter, private, or home schools—all students can benefit. This research has added to the growing recognition that competition produced by school choice improves the public school system.

Eleven states currently have publicly funded voucher or tax credit programs, and 40 states and the District of Columbia have charter school laws. This year, Colorado and Maryland adopted voucher or charter school laws. Other states and Congress may yet adopt parental choice legislation before the end of the year.

There will be numerous opportunities in the coming years to enact authentic education reform that empowers parents to provide their children with the best education that is available. The principles of parental empowerment and educational opportunity are shaping the education policy debate as more policymakers realize the benefits that choice holds for the nation's children.

---

94. Paul E. Peterson, ed., *Our Schools and Our Future...Are We Still at Risk? Findings and Recommendations of the Koret Task Force on K–12 Education* (Stanford, Cal.: Hoover Institution Press, 2003), p. 14 (emphasis in original). For the full text of the book, see *www-hoover.stanford.edu/publications/books/osof.html.*

# SNAPSHOTS OF CHOICE IN THE STATES

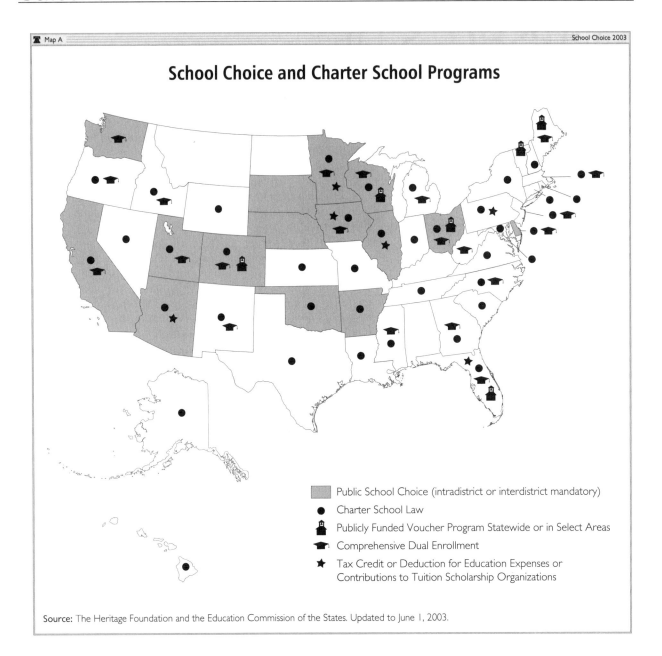

## School Choice and Charter School Programs

Public School Choice (intradistrict or interdistrict mandatory)

● Charter School Law

Publicly Funded Voucher Program Statewide or in Select Areas

Comprehensive Dual Enrollment

★ Tax Credit or Deduction for Education Expenses or Contributions to Tuition Scholarship Organizations

**Source:** The Heritage Foundation and the Education Commission of the States. Updated to June 1, 2003.

Table 1    School Choice 2003

# School Choice Programs in the States

| State | Public School Choice Within Districts (Intradistrict) | Public School Choice Between Districts (Interdistrict) | Charter School Law | Comprehensive Dual Enrollment | Scholarship/ Tax Credit | Home School Law |
|---|---|---|---|---|---|---|
| Alabama | | | | | | X |
| Alaska | | | X | | | X |
| Arizona | X | X | X | | X | X |
| Arkansas | | X | X | | | X |
| California | X | | X | X | | X |
| Colorado | X | X | X | X | X | X |
| Connecticut | | | X | | | X |
| Delaware | X | X | X | X | | X |
| Florida | | | X | X | X | X |
| Georgia | | | X | X | | X |
| Hawaii | | | X | | | X |
| Idaho | | | X | X | | X |
| Illinois | X | | X | | X | X |
| Indiana | | | X | | | X |
| Iowa | | X | X | X | X | X |
| Kansas | | | X | | | X |
| Kentucky | | | | | | X |
| Louisiana | | | X | | | X |
| Maine | | | | X | X | X |
| Maryland | | | X | | | X |
| Massachusetts | | | X | X | | X |
| Michigan | | | X | | | X |
| Minnesota | | X | X | X | X | X |
| Mississippi | | | X | X | | X |
| Missouri | | | X | | | X |
| Montana | | | | | | X |
| Nebraska | | X | | | | X |
| Nevada | | | X | | | X |
| New Hampshire | | | X | | | X |
| New Jersey | | | X | X | | X |
| New Mexico | | | X | X | | X |
| New York | | | X | | | X |
| North Carolina | | | X | X | | X |
| North Dakota | | | | | | X |
| Ohio | X | | X | X | X | X |
| Oklahoma | | X | X | | | X |
| Oregon | | | X | X | | X |
| Pennsylvania | | | X | | X | X |
| Rhode Island | | | X | | | X |
| South Carolina | | | X | | | X |
| South Dakota | X | X | | | | X |
| Tennessee | | | X | | | X |
| Texas | | | X | | | X |
| Utah | X | X | X | X | | X |
| Vermont | | | | | X | X |
| Virginia | | | X | | | X |
| Washington | X | X | | X | | X |
| West Virginia | | | | X | | X |
| Wisconsin | | X | X | X | X | X |
| Wyoming | | | X | | | X |
| District of Columbia | | | X | | | X |

**Sources:** Public School Choice: Education Commission of the States, "School Choice: State Laws," December 2002, at *www.ecs.org/clearinghouse/13/75/1375.htm*; Charter School Law: Center for Education Reform at *www.edreform.com/charter_schools/map.htm* and Heritage research; Dual Enrollment: Education Commission of the States, "School Choice: State Laws," December 2002, at *www.ecs.org/clearinghouse/13/75/1375.htm*. Scholarship/Tax Credit: Heritage research; Home-school Law: Home School Legal Defense Association at *www.hslda.org*.

Table 2      School Choice 2003

# Scholarship and Tax Credit Programs

| State | Privately Funded Voucher | Scholarships for Students in Low-Performing Schools or Districts | Rural Vouchers | Select City Vouchers | Special Education Scholarships | Tax Credit for Donations to Scholarship Organizations | Tax Credits/ Deductions for Educational Expenses |
|---|---|---|---|---|---|---|---|
| Alabama | X | | | | | | |
| Alaska | | | | | | | |
| Arizona | X | | | | | X | |
| Arkansas | X | | | | | | |
| California | X | | | | | | |
| Colorado | X | X | | | | | |
| Connecticut | X | | | | | | |
| Delaware | | | | | | | |
| Florida | X | X | | | X | X | |
| Georgia | X | | | | | | |
| Hawaii | | | | | | | |
| Idaho | | | | | | | |
| Illinois | X | | | | | | X |
| Indiana | X | | | | | | |
| Iowa | X | | | | | | X |
| Kansas | X | | | | | | |
| Kentucky | X | | | | | | |
| Louisiana | X | | | | | | |
| Maine | X | | X | | | | |
| Maryland | X | | | | | | |
| Massachusetts | X | | | | | | |
| Michigan | X | | | | | | |
| Minnesota | X | | | | | | X |
| Mississippi | X | | | | | | |
| Missouri | X | | | | | | |
| Montana | | | | | | | |
| Nebraska | X | | | | | | |
| Nevada | | | | | | | |
| New Hampshire | X | | | | | | |
| New Jersey | X | | | | | | |
| New Mexico | X | | | | | | |
| New York | X | | | | | | |
| North Carolina | X | | | | | | |
| North Dakota | | | | | | | |
| Ohio | X | | | X | | | |
| Oklahoma | X | | | | | | |
| Oregon | X | | | | | | |
| Pennsylvania | X | | | | | X | |
| Rhode Island | | | | | | | |
| South Carolina | X | | | | | | |
| South Dakota | | | | | | | |
| Tennessee | X | | | | | | |
| Texas | X | | | | | | |
| Utah | X | | | | | | |
| Vermont | X | | X | | | | |
| Virginia | X | | | | | | |
| Washington | X | | | | | | |
| West Virginia | | | | | | | |
| Wisconsin | X | | | X | | | |
| Wyoming | | | | | | | |
| District of Columbia | X | | | | | | |

**Sources:** Privately Funded Voucher: Children's Scholarship Fund at *www.scholarshipfund.org*, Children First America at *www.childrenfirstamerica.org*, and Heritage research; Vouchers for Students in Low Performing Schools or Districts: Heritage research; Rural Vouchers: Heritage research; Select City Vouchers: Heritage research; Special Education Vouchers: Heritage research; Tax Credit for Donations to Scholarship Organizations: Heritage research; Tax Credit for Educational Expenses: Heritage research.

# ABOUT THE STATE PROFILES

The *State Profiles* in this book provide snapshots of school choice options and an overview of the public and private education system in each state. This guide explains terms and sources of information used in the *State Profiles* section of each chapter.

## School Choice Status

The extent of school choice available in each state is described with respect to the following elements.

- **Public school choice and enrollment options.** Specific types of public school choice and enrollment options include the following:

  **Interdistrict choice programs** allow parents to send their child to a school in another district;

  **Intradistrict choice programs** allow parents to choose among public schools within the district;

  **Mandatory open enrollment** requires districts to permit students to transfer; and

  **Voluntary open enrollment** permits, but does not require, districts to allow students school choice. In states with voluntary open enrollment, parents may have to obtain permission from the sending and receiving districts and/or pay tuition. In most states, intradistrict policies are determined by the local board.

  *Sources:* Education Commission of the States, "School Choice: State Laws," December 2002, at *www.ecs.org/clearinghouse/13/75/1375.htm*, and The Heritage Foundation.

- **Restrictions regarding funding for religious schools.** Two types of restrictive language prohibiting the use of public money to fund religious institutions can be found in state constitutions: Blaine amendments and compelled-support language.

  **Blaine amendments** to state constitutions are adaptations (or, in some cases, precursors) of a narrowly defeated amendment to the U.S. Constitution proposed in 1875 by then-Speaker of the U.S. House of Repre-

sentatives James G. Blaine. Blaine's amendment, targeting parochial schools that were viewed by some as a threat to a then-emerging public school system, prohibited the use of public funds for sectarian schools. Blaine amendments were once a prerequisite for consideration for statehood. They were incorporated in the constitutions of 37 states.

  **Compelled-support language** dates back to colonial times and was intended to prevent governments from compelling individuals to contribute to or attend a state-designated church. Twenty-nine states have such language in their constitutions.

  Only three states—Louisiana, Maine, and North Carolina—have neither a Blaine amendment nor compelled-support language.

  *Source:* Richard D. Komer, "School Choice: Answers to Frequently Asked Questions About State Constitutions' Religious Clauses," Institute for Justice, September 6, 2002, at *www.ij.org/cases/school*.

- **Charter school laws.** Descriptions of the strength of states' charter school laws are based on rankings by the Center for Education Reform (CER), a free-market public policy organization that tracks and ranks school choice developments in the states. Considerations used in CER rankings include (1) the number of charter schools permitted; (2) the number of chartering authorities; (3) types of eligible charter applicants; (4) whether or not "new starts" are allowed; (5) whether evidence of local support is a prerequisite for creating a charter school; (6) whether charters are given automatic waivers from state and district laws and regulations governing public schools; (7) the amount of legal and operational authority charters are given; (8) guaranteed full per-pupil funding; (9) whether charters have fiscal autonomy; and (10) the exemption of charter schools from collective bargaining agreements and district work rules.

# School Choice 2003

*Source:* Center for Education Reform, "Charter Schools in the United States," at *www.edreform.com/charter_schools/map.htm.*

- **Publicly funded private school choice.** This category notes whether or not a state has publicly funded programs that enhance education options—including financial assistance to attend private or religious schools—through vouchers or scholarships, tax credits for education expenditures, and/or tax credits for individual or corporate donations to tuition scholarship organizations.

  *Source:* Heritage Foundation analysis based on state contact information, news reports, and legislative developments.

- **Privately funded school choice.** This section notes whether states have privately funded vouchers or tuition scholarship programs that provide parents with additional options for their children's education, including enrollment in private and religious schools.

  *Source:* Heritage Foundation analysis based on state contact information, news reports, and legislative developments.

- **Home-school law.** This section describes the restrictions and requirements a state places on home schoolers regarding such issues as the notification of government officials, requirements to take standardized state achievement tests or undergo professional evaluation, curriculum approval, parents' teaching qualifications, and mandated home visits by state officials. Notification requirements of states are ranked as no notice required, low, moderate, or high as follows:

  **No notice required:** Parents are not required to notify the state of their intention to homeschool.

  **Low regulation:** Parents need only notify the state or district of their intention to homeschool.

  **Moderate regulation:** Parents must give notification and report test scores, and/or be subject to professional evaluation of student achievement.

  **High regulation:** Parents must give notification and report achievement test scores, and/or submit to professional evaluations

and approval or home visits by state officials.

*Source:* Home School Legal Defense Association, at *www.hslda.org/laws.*

- **Ranking on the Education Freedom Index.** This section presents a state's ranking in terms of available options for education, based on an evaluation by the Manhattan Institute for Policy Research. The District of Columbia was not included in this evaluation. Considerations include (1) the availability of government assistance for private school options, such as vouchers or tax credits; (2) home-schooling options and regulations; (3) options within the public school system; and (4) availability of charter school options and the strength of the charter law.

  *Source:* Jay P. Greene, *The Education Freedom Index*, Manhattan Institute, Center for Civic Innovation, January 2002, at *www.manhattan-institute.org/html/cr_24_table_1.htm.*

## Sources of School Information
- **Public school enrollment**

  *Source:* U.S. Department of Education, Office of Educational Research and Improvement, National Center for Education Statistics, "Early Estimates of Public Elementary and Secondary Education Statistics: School Year 2001–02," April 2002, p. 9, at *http://nces.ed.gov/pubs2002/2002311.pdf.*

- **Students enrolled per teacher**

  *Source:* U.S. Department of Education, Office of Educational Research and Improvement, National Center for Education Statistics, "Early Estimates of Public Elementary and Secondary Education Statistics: School Year 2001–02," April 2002, p. 9, at *http://nces.ed.gov/pubs2002/2002311.pdf.*

- **Number of schools**

  *Source:* U.S. Department of Education, Office of Educational Research and Improvement, National Center for Education Statistics, "Overview of Public Elementary and Secondary Schools and Districts: School Year 2000-01," May 2002, Table 1, at *http://nces.ed.gov/pubs2002/2002356.pdf.*

- **Number of districts**

  *Source:* National Education Association, "Rankings and Estimates: Rankings of States 2001 and Estimates of School Statistics 2002," released May 2002, p. 86, at *www.nea.org/edstats/images/02rankings.pdf.*

- **Current expenditures**

  *Source:* U.S. Department of Education, Office of Educational Research and Improvement, National Center for Education Statistics, "Early Estimates of Public Elementary and Secondary Education Statistics: School Year 2001–02," April 2002, p. 9, at *http://nces.ed.gov/pubs2002/2002311.pdf.*

- **Current per-pupil expenditure**

  *Source:* U.S. Department of Education, Office of Educational Research and Improvement, National Center for Education Statistics, "Early Estimates of Public Elementary and Secondary Education Statistics: School Year 2001–02," April 2002, p. 9, at *http://nces.ed.gov/pubs2002/2002311.pdf.*

- **Amount of revenue from the federal government for 2001–2002**

  *Source:* National Education Association, "Rankings and Estimates: Rankings of States 2001 and Estimates of School Statistics 2002," released May 2002, p. 94, at *www.nea.org/edstats/images/02rankings.pdf.*

- **Number of teachers**

  *Source:* U.S. Department of Education, Office of Educational Research and Improvement, National Center for Education Statistics, "Early Estimates of Public Elementary and Secondary Education Statistics: School Year 2001–02," April 2002, p. 9, at *http://nces.ed.gov/pubs2002/2002311.pdf.*

- **Teachers' average salary**

  *Source:* National Education Association, "Rankings and Estimates: Rankings of States 2001 and Estimates of School Statistics 2002," released May 2002, p. 92, at *www.nea.org/edstats/images/02rankings.pdf.*

- **Private school enrollment, number of schools, and number of teachers**

  *Source:* U.S. Department of Education, Office of Educational Research and Improvement, National Center for Education Statistics, "Private School Universe Survey, 1999–2000," August 2001, at *http://nces.ed.gov/pubs2001/2001330.pdf.*

## Measures of Academic Performance

- **NAEP test results** show how 4th and 8th grade students in public schools performed on the National Assessment of Educational Progress (NAEP) exams in math, reading, and science, with national percentages provided in parentheses. Students achieve at four levels: Below Basic, Basic, Advanced, or Proficient. Not all states participated in each test. No state results for the state 2000 reading assessments are available.

  *Source:* National Assessment of Educational Progress Report Cards at *http://nces.ed.gov/nationsreportcard.*

- **SAT and ACT weighted ranks (2001)** indicate a state's ranking based on the average scores of students on the predominant test (either the SAT or ACT) administered in the state.

  *Source:* American Legislative Exchange Council, *Report Card on American Education: A State-by-State Analysis, 1976–2001,* October 2002, at *www.alec.org/meSWFiles/pdf/Education_Report_Card.pdf.*

- **Academic Achievement Ranking** is based on students' 2000 Grade 8 NAEP scores, 2001 ACT scores, and 2001 SAT scores.

  *Source:* American Legislative Exchange Council, *Report Card on American Education: A State-by-State Analysis, 1976-2001,* October 2002, at *www.alec.org/meSWFiles/pdf/Education_Report_Card.pdf.*

# ALABAMA

## State Profile (Updated May 2003)

### School Choice Status
- Public school choice: No
- State constitution: Blaine amendment and compelled-support language
- Charter school law: No
- Publicly funded private school choice: No
- Privately funded school choice: Yes
- Home-school law: Low regulation
- Ranking on the Education Freedom Index (2001): 41st out of 50 states

### K–12 Public Schools and Students (2001–2002)
- Public school enrollment: 726,367
- Students enrolled per teacher: 15.4
- Number of schools (2000–2001): 1,380
- Number of districts: 128
- Current expenditures: $4,312,295,000
- Current per-pupil expenditure: $5,937
- Amount of revenue from the federal government: 10.4%

### K–12 Public School Teachers (2001–2002)
- Number of teachers: 47,201
- Average salary: $39,268

### K–12 Private Schools (1999–2000)
- Private school enrollment: 73,352
- Number of schools: 374
- Number of teachers: 5,934

### K–12 Public and Private School Student Academic Performance
- NAEP test results:

| NAEP Tests Alabama Student Performance | State (National) 2000 Math Scale = 0–500 | | State (National) 2000 Science Scale = 0–300 | | State (National) 2000 Reading Scale = 0–500 | |
|---|---|---|---|---|---|---|
| | 4th Grade | 8th Grade | 4th Grade | 8th Grade | 4th Grade | 8th Grade |
| Average Scale Score | 218 (226) | 262 (274) | 143 (148) | 141 (149) | 211 (215) | 255 (261) |
| Advanced | 1% (3%) | 2% (5%) | 2% (3%) | 2% (4%) | 5% (6%) | 1% (2%) |
| Proficient | 13% (23%) | 14% (21%) | 20% (25%) | 20% (26%) | 19% (23%) | 20% (29%) |
| Basic | 43% (43%) | 36% (39%) | 37% (36%) | 29% (29%) | 32% (32%) | 45% (41%) |
| Below Basic | 43% (31%) | 48% (35%) | 41% (36%) | 49% (41%) | 44% (39%) | 34% (28%) |

For updates go to: *heritage.org*

1

- SAT weighted rank (2001): N/A
- ACT weighed rank (2001): 20th out of 26 states
- ALEC Academic Achievement Ranking: 43rd out of 50 states and the District of Columbia

## Summary

Private scholarship programs are available to enable low-income students to attend a school of choice. High school students may take college courses at two-year institutions for high school and postsecondary credit.[1]

## Background

In 1998, Birmingham became a Children's Scholarship Fund (CSF) "partner city." The CSF provided approximately 375 low-income students with scholarships to attend schools of choice with funds matched by Birmingham residents. In the program's initial year, more than 9,000 students applied for these scholarships.[2]

In 2000, then-State Senator Bill Armistead (R–14) introduced Senate Bill 549, which would have allowed students in low-achieving schools to receive publicly funded scholarships to attend K–12 private schools.[3] The bill did not move forward. In 2001, he introduced S.B. 108, which would have provided Student Opportunity Scholarships for children in failing public schools to attend another public or private school of choice. The bill died in committee.[4]

## Developments in 2002 and 2003

From 1990 to 2000, the percentage of Alabama schoolchildren attending private schools increased from 8 percent to 10 percent. U.S. census data show that an increasing number of black children in urban centers are attending private schools. The dean of the College of Education at the University of Alabama suggests that the rise in private school enrollment may indicate dissatisfaction with public schools among both black and white middle-income parents.[5]

## Position of the Governor / Composition of the State Legislature

Governor Bob Riley, a Republican, supports school choice. Democrats control both houses of the legislature.

## State Contacts

**Alabama Department of Education**
Dr. Ed Richardson, Superintendent
50 North Ripley Street
P.O. Box 302101
Montgomery, AL 36130-2101
Phone: (334) 242-9700
Web site: www.alsde.edu
E-mail: edrich@alsde.edu

**Alabama Policy Institute**
Gary Palmer, President
402 Office Park Drive, Suite 300
Birmingham, AL 35223
Phone: (205) 870-9900
Fax: (205) 870-4407
Web site: www.alabamapolicyinstitute.org
E-mail: kristind@alabamapolicy.org

**Children's Scholarship Fund Alabama**
Lesley Searcy, Director
P.O. Box 590073
Birmingham, AL 35259
Phone: (205) 428-3742
Fax: (205) 877-3387
E-mail: lesleysearcy@aol.com

**Eagle Forum of Alabama**
Eunice Smith, President
4200 Stone River Circle
Birmingham, AL 35213
Phone: (205) 879-7096
Fax: (205) 871-2859
Web site: www.alabamaeagle.org
E-mail: alaeagle@charter.net

## State School Report Card

**Alabama Department of Education**
Web site: www.alsde.edu/html/reports.asp?menu=reports&footer=general&sort=all

**Greatschools.net**
Web site: www.greatschools.net/modperl/go/AL

1. Education Commission of the States, "Postsecondary Options: Dual/Concurrent Enrollment," July 2001.
2. Toby Roth, "Choice for All," Citizens for a Sound Economy, January 2, 2000.
3. Toby Roth, "School Choice Legislation Introduced," Citizens for a Sound Economy, April 12, 2000.
4. See National School Boards Association Web site at *www.nsba.org/novouchers*.
5. Laura J. Swartley and George A. Clowes, "School Choice Roundup," *School Reform News*, October 2002.

# ALASKA

## State Profile (Updated May 2003)

### School Choice Status
- Public school choice: No
- State constitution: Blaine amendment
  Charter school law: Enacted 1995
  - Strength of law: Weak
  - Number of charter schools in operation (fall 2002): 15
  - Students enrolled in charter schools (fall 2002): 2,682
- Publicly funded private school choice: No
- Privately funded school choice: No
- Home-school law: No notice required
- Ranking on the Education Freedom Index (2001): 38th out of 50 states

### K-12 Public Schools and Students (2001–2002)
- Public school enrollment: 134,023
- Students enrolled per teacher: 16.7
- Number of schools (2000–2001): 502
- Number of districts: 53
- Current expenditures: $1,263,775,000
- Current per-pupil expenditure: $9,430
- Amount of revenue from the federal government: 12.5%

### K-12 Public School Teachers (2001–2002)
- Number of teachers: 8,025
- Average salary: $49,418

### K-12 Private Schools (1999–2000)
- Private school enrollment: 6,172
- Number of schools: 69
- Number of teachers: 572

### K-12 Public and Private School Student Academic Performance
- NAEP test results:

| NAEP Tests Alaska Student Performance | State (National) 2000 Math Scale = 0–500 | | State (National) 2000 Science Scale = 0–300 | | State (National) 2000 Reading Scale = 0–500 | |
|---|---|---|---|---|---|---|
| | 4th Grade | 8th Grade | 4th Grade | 8th Grade | 4th Grade | 8th Grade |
| Average Scale Score | N/A (226) | N/A (274) | N/A (148) | N/A (149) | N/A (215) | N/A (261) |
| Advanced | N/A (3%) | N/A (5%) | N/A (3%) | N/A (4%) | N/A (6%) | N/A (2%) |
| Proficient | N/A (23%) | N/A (21%) | N/A (25%) | N/A (26%) | N/A (23%) | N/A (29%) |
| Basic | N/A (43%) | N/A (39%) | N/A (36%) | N/A (29%) | N/A (32%) | N/A (41%) |
| Below Basic | N/A (31%) | N/A (35%) | N/A (36%) | N/A (41%) | N/A (39%) | N/A (28%) |

- SAT weighted rank (2001): 6th out of 24 states and the District of Columbia
- ACT weighted rank (2001): N/A
- ALEC Academic Achievement Ranking: 11th out of 50 states and the District of Columbia

## Summary

Alaska offers neither public school choice nor privately funded scholarships. The state has a weak charter school law. Correspondence courses are offered through school districts and through the Alaska Department of Education's Alyeska Central School (ACS).

## Background

Since 1939, the Alaska Department of Education and Early Development has operated the Alyeska Central School, a publicly funded correspondence school. The ACS offers over 250 courses and maintains close contact with enrolled students.[6]

In 1995, then-Governor Tony Knowles, a Democrat, signed the state's Charter School Act to establish a pilot charter school program. Under this legislation, charter schools are subject to the jurisdiction of, and must be approved by, the local school board. Teachers in charter schools must be certified and are covered by collective bargaining rules unless the charter school can negotiate an exemption. Charter schools receive the full state and district per-pupil funding for each student, less a portion that is retained by the public school system to cover administrative costs.[7]

State Representatives Vic Kohring and John Coghill, Jr., introduced voucher legislation in 1999. House Bill 5 would have established a statewide, publicly funded choice scholarship system, but the bill died in the House Judiciary Committee.[8]

In 2001, the governor signed H.B. 101, which strengthened the charter school law. H.B. 101 eliminated the sunset clause, doubled the cap on charter schools to 60, and extended the contract length from five to 10 years. It also clarified that charter schools were not exempt from competency testing, provided a one-time start-up grant of $500 per student, and altered the funding formula to increase charter school funding. Under this law, charter schools remain under the jurisdiction of the local school board, and there is no formal process by which applicants may appeal a rejection of a charter proposal.[9]

## Developments in 2002 and 2003

In 2002, the Alaska Department of Education and Early Development proposed regulations governing district-run correspondence schools that enroll home-school students. These innovative correspondence programs are offered by approximately 20 percent of Alaska's school districts and serve nearly 10,000 home-school students, often with the use of telecommunications technology.[10] These correspondence schools receive state funding, and their students must take statewide assessment tests that are monitored and graded by a certified teacher. State funds may not be used to purchase religious curricula for home schools that participate in these distance-learning programs.[11]

In August 2002, Senate Bill 345 was signed into law, allowing home-school correspondence students to use curricula material and textbooks not provided by the school district if these materials were purchased with private funds.[12] On November 22, 2002, the Alaska State Board of Education approved the regulations proposed earlier in the year.[13]

State Senator Fred Dyson (District I–Eagle River) introduced Senate Concurrent Resolution 10 as charter school legislation in April 2003.

6. See Alyeska Central School Web site at *www.eed.state.ak.us/Alaskan_Schools/ACS/*.
7. Center for Education Reform, "Charter School Legislation: Profile of Alaska's Charter School Law," 2001, at *http://edreform.com/charter_schools/laws/Alaska.htm*.
8. Alaska Legislature, 1999–2000 Session, H.B. 5.
9. E-mail correspondence from Wes Keller, Staff Aide, Committee on Health, Education, and Social Services, Alaska State Legislature, August 5, 2002.
10. *Ibid.*
11. Home School Legal Defense Association, "Alaska Charter School 'Benefits' May Have Strings Attached," January 24, 2002, at *www.hslda.org/docs/news/hslda/200201240.asp*.
12. See *www.legis.state.ak.us/basis/get_bill_text.asp?hsid=SB0345C&session=22* and *www.legis.state.ak.us/basis/get_bill.asp?session=22&bill=SB+345&submit=Display+Bill+Root*.

S.C.R. 10 would create a Joint Legislative Charter School Task Force charged with studying charter schools and proposing improvements in the state law. The bill was approved by the Education Committee, but no further action was taken.[14]

## Position of the Governor / Composition of the State Legislature

Governor Frank Murkowski, a Republican, supports charter schools, but his position on school choice is unclear. Republicans control both houses of the legislature.

## State Contacts

**Alaska Charter School Association**
Chinook Montessori Charter School
Terri Austin, President
3002 International Street
Fairbanks, AK 99701
Phone: (907) 452-5020
Fax: (907) 452-5048
E-mail: tla@ptialaska.net

**Alaska Department of Education and Early Development**
Shirley J. Holloway, Commissioner
801 West 10th Street
Juneau, AK 99801
Phone: (907) 465-2800
Web site: www.eed.state.ak.us

**Charter Schools**
Louie Yannotti

Phone: (907) 465-8720
Fax: (907) 465-1686
Web site: www.educ.state.ak.us/
E-mail: louie_yannotti@eed.state.ak.us

**Alaska Private and Home Educators Association**
P.O. Box 141764
Anchorage, AK 99514
Web site: www.aphea.org
E-mail: board@aphea.org

**Wes Keller**
Staff Aide
Committee on Health, Education, and Social Services
Alaska Legislature
10928 Eagle River Road, Suite 140
Eagle River, AK 99577-8052
Phone: (907) 465-2199 (January–May)
Phone: (907) 694-6683 (June–December)
E-mail: Wes_Keller@Legis.state.ak.us

## State School Report Card

**Alaska Department of Education**
Web site: www.eed.state.ak.us/DOE_Rolodex/
schools/ReportCard/ReportCardSearch1.cfm

**Greatschools.net**
Web site: www.greatschools.net/modperl/go/AK

---

13. State of Alaska Online, Online Public Notice, "Notice of Filing—4 AAC 33 Statewide Correspondence," November 27, 2002.

14. Personal communication with Wes Keller, Staff Aide, Committee on Health, Education, and Social Services, Alaska State Legislature, May 2, 2003. See also Alaska Legislature, 2003–2004 Session, S.CR. 10.

---

# ARIZONA

## State Profile (Updated May 2003)

### School Choice Status
- Public school choice: Intradistrict and interdistrict/mandatory
- State constitution: Blaine amendment
  Charter school law: Enacted 1994
  - Strength of law: Strong
  - Number of charter schools in operation (fall 2002): 464
  - Number of students enrolled in charter schools (fall 2002): 73,542
- Publicly funded private school choice: Yes
- Privately funded school choice: Yes
- Home-school law: Low regulation
- Ranking on the Education Freedom Index (2001): 1st out of 50 states

### K–12 Public Schools and Students (2001–2002)
- Public school enrollment: 903,518
- Students enrolled per teacher: 19.7
- Number of schools (2000–2001): 1,633
- Number of districts: 224
- Current expenditures: $4,919,844,000
- Current per-pupil expenditure: $5,445
- Amount of revenue from the federal government: 6.1%

### K–12 Public School Teachers (2001–2002)
- Number of teachers: 45,959
- Average salary: $36,966

### K–12 Private Schools (1999–2000)
- Private school enrollment: 44,060
- Number of schools: 276
- Number of teachers: 3,319

### K–12 Public and Private School Student Academic Performance
- NAEP test results:

| NAEP Tests Arizona Student Performance | State (National) 2000 Math Scale = 0–500 | | State (National) 2000 Science Scale = 0–300 | | State (National) 2000 Reading Scale = 0–500 | |
|---|---|---|---|---|---|---|
| | 4th Grade | 8th Grade | 4th Grade | 8th Grade | 4th Grade | 8th Grade |
| Average Scale Score | 219 (226) | 271 (274) | 141 (148) | 146 (149) | 207 (215) | 261 (261) |
| Advanced | 2% (3%) | 3% (5%) | 2% (3%) | 2% (4%) | 5% (6%) | 2% (2%) |
| Proficient | 15% (23%) | 18% (21%) | 20% (25%) | 22% (26%) | 17% (23%) | 26% (29%) |
| Basic | 41% (43%) | 41% (39%) | 35% (36%) | 33% (29%) | 31% (32%) | 45% (41%) |
| Below Basic | 42% (31%) | 38% (35%) | 43% (36%) | 43% (41%) | 47% (39%) | 27% (28%) |

- SAT weighted rank (2001): 3rd out of 24 states and the District of Columbia
- ACT weighted rank (2001): N/A
- ALEC Academic Achievement Ranking: 23rd out of 50 states and the District of Columbia

## Summary

Arizona has a strong charter school law and more charter schools than any other state in the nation. The state has public school open enrollment, and eligible high school students may enroll in higher education courses for high school and postsecondary credit. Low-income students may apply for privately funded scholarships supported by the state's education tax credit.

## Background

Under a 1984 law, qualified high school students may enroll in higher education courses for both secondary and college credit.[15]

In 1993, in a 5 to 4 decision, the Supreme Court of the United States supported public aid to a disabled student attending a religious school in the case of *Zobrest* v. *Catalina Foothills School District*. The case involved a deaf child whose parents sought a sign-language interpreter under provisions of the Individuals with Disabilities Education Act (IDEA). Several lower courts ruled with the school district that the parents' request would violate the Establishment Clause of the U.S. Constitution. However, the Supreme Court ruled that the aid to the student (the interpreter) did not violate the Constitution. Chief Justice Rehnquist, writing for the majority, found that

> IDEA creates a neutral government program dispensing aid not to schools but to individual handicapped children. If a handicapped child chooses to enroll in a sectarian school, we hold that the Establishment Clause does not prevent the school district from furnishing him with a sign-language interpreter there in order to facilitate his education.[16]

Arizona's School Improvement Act of 1994 remains the nation's strongest charter school law, according to the Center for Education Reform. Any citizen, group, or organization may apply for a 15-year charter from the Arizona State Board of Education, the Arizona State Board for Charter Schools, or the local school board. The state's charter schools have broad fiscal and legal autonomy. Like the state's other public schools, charter schools submit annual report cards to parents and the Arizona Department of Education. In addition, charter schools are audited annually.[17]

On April 7, 1997, then-Governor Fife Symington, a Republican, signed House Bill 2074, allowing residents to receive a tax credit for donations to charitable organizations that give scholarships to children to attend private or religious schools. Currently, an individual can receive a tax credit of up to $500, and a married couple can receive a credit of $625, for donations to a private tuition scholarship program. Individuals donating to public school extracurricular activities can receive a tax credit of up to $200.[18]

The Arizona Education Association (AEA), the state affiliate of the National Education Association, made several attempts to overturn the law. Partnering with the PTA, the League of Women Voters, People for the American Way, the Arizona School Boards Association, and the Arizona Democratic Women's Association, the AEA attempted to collect signatures from registered voters to place a referendum on the tax credit on the November 1998 general election ballot. Had they succeeded in getting the requisite number of signatures, these groups could have kept the tax credit law from going into effect at least until after the election.[19] In July 1998, however, opponents of the tax credit stopped their petition drive and focused instead on a lawsuit they

---

15. Education Commission of the States, "Postsecondary Options: Dual/Concurrent Enrollment," July 2001.

16. *Zobrest* v. *Catalina Foothills School District*, 509 U.S. 1 (1993); *Zobrest* v. *Catalina Foothills School District*, 113 S. Ct. 2462 (1993). See also Melanie L. Looney, "School Choice in the Courts," National Center for Policy Analysis, *Policy Backgrounder* No. 153, August 7, 2000.

17. See Center for Education Reform, "Charter School Legislation: Profile of Arizona's Charter School Law," 2001, at *http://edreform.com/charter_schools/laws/Arizona.htm*.

18. Hal Mattern, "Private-School Tax Credit Signed: Opponents Say Law Is Voucher System," *The Arizona Republic*, April 8, 1997, p. B1.

had filed, contending that the law violated the state constitution.[20]

On January 26, 1999, the Arizona Supreme Court upheld the tax credit plan in a 3–2 ruling. The majority found the program neutral with regard to religion and beneficial to poor families who have been "coerced into accepting public education." Chief Justice Thomas Zlaket, writing for the majority, declared that the poor

> have had few choices and little control over the nature and quality of their children's schooling because they have been unable to afford a private education that may be more compatible with their own values and beliefs.... Arizona's tax credit achieves a higher degree of parity by making private schools more accessible and providing alternatives to public education.[21]

The Arizona Education Association appealed the case to the Supreme Court of the United States, which in October 1999 refused to consider it.[22]

From 1998 to 2002, the tax credit program generated $56 million and financed nearly 36,000 scholarships.[23] More than 80 percent of scholarship recipients were from lower-income families.[24] A Cato Institute report found the credit to be revenue-neutral; the public school system saves money when students who had been educated at public expense leave the system to attend private schools, and these savings offset the revenue loss from the tax credit.[25]

In March 1999, the Arizona House of Representatives passed H.B. 2279, which would have enabled parents of students who qualify for free or reduced-price school lunches to send their children to a public, private, or religious school of choice. Based on a plan submitted to the legislature in January by then-State Superintendent of Public Instruction Lisa Graham Keegan, the bill would have given poor students scholarships of about $5,000 or the cost of tuition, whichever was less, to attend a school of choice. The bill did not make it through the Senate.[26]

Another school choice bill introduced during the 1999 session, Senate Bill 1371, would have provided state-funded vouchers to students in public schools that were filled beyond capacity. The bill died in Senate committee.[27]

In March 2001, the Goldwater Institute reported that spending two to three consecutive years in an Arizona charter school had a greater positive impact on students' math and reading test scores than did spending comparable time in a traditional school. This finding is based on the Stanford 9 achievement test scores of students in charter and public schools from 1997–1999. Moreover, there was no evidence that charter schools accepted only the best students or encouraged the worst-performing students to leave.[28]

In 2001, H.B. 2252, which would have authorized "opportunity scholarships" to enable students in low-performing public schools to attend a private school or another public school of choice, died in a House committee. A Senate committee rejected S.B. 1560, which would have given vouchers to students whose parents determined that a school was unsafe for their child because of gang activity, a history of violence, or students' drug use.[29]

19. Hal Mattern, "Petition Drive Under Way to Put School Tax-Credit Plan on Ballot," *The Arizona Republic*, May 2, 1997, p. A17, and Kay Lybeck, "Bill Is Divisive, Bad Policy," *The Arizona Republic*, June 29, 1997, p. EV9.
20. "Teachers End Petition Drive, to Sue in 'Pre-voucher Scheme'," *The Arizona Republic*, July 9, 1997, p. B1.
21. *Kotterman v. Killian*, 972 P.2d 606 at 615 (1999). See also "Opportunity for Poor Kids: High Court's Ruling on Tax Credits Keeps Choice in Education," *The Arizona Republic*, February 1, 1999, p. B4.
22. Robert Robb, "U.S. Inaction Helps State Tax Credit," *The Arizona Republic*, October 8, 1999, p. B9.
23. Dan Lips, "The Arizona Scholarship Tax Credit: A Model for Federal Reform," Goldwater Institute, August 1, 2002.
24. Carrie Lips and Jennifer Jacoby, "The Arizona Scholarship Tax Credit: Giving Parents Choices, Saving Taxpayers Money," Cato Institute, September 17, 2001, at *www.cato.org/pubs/pas/pa414.pdf*.
25. *Ibid.*
26. Chris Moeser, "Voucher Bill Gains Steam, Passes Education Committee," *The Arizona Republic*, February 18, 1999, p. B1.
27. See National School Boards Association Web site at *www.nsba.org/novouchers*.
28. Lewis C. Solmon, Kern Paark, and David Garcia, "Does Charter School Attendance Improve Test Scores? The Arizona Results," Goldwater Institute, March 16, 2001.
29. See National School Boards Association Web site at *www.nsba.org/novouchers*.

## Developments in 2002 and 2003

During the 2002 legislative session, S.B. 1560, a bill from the previous session that would have allowed students to transfer from unsafe schools, was reintroduced as S.B. 1127. It was rejected in committee.[30]

A pair of bills introduced during the 2002 legislative session, H.B. 2368 and H.B. 2394, would have weakened the state's tuition tax credit program. H.B. 2368 would have prevented taxpayers from claiming a tax credit if their contributions to a school tuition organization (STO) were designated for any specific student, including their own child. It also would have required school tuition organizations to report the amount of donations received, how the money was spent, and the number of students served. H.B. 2394 would have placed reporting requirements similar to those of H.B. 2368 on STOs and public schools that received contributions for extracurricular activities. Both bills died in House committees.[31]

A study released in April 2002 found that competition engendered by increased school choice raises school productivity as well as student achievement. The report's author, Harvard economist Caroline M. Hoxby, Ph.D., found that the introduction of even a small amount of competition—such as the possibility that a school could lose 6 percent of its students to a neighboring charter school—sparked a statistically significant improvement in school productivity.[32]

S.B. 1263, introduced in 2003, would have created a tax credit for corporations that donate to tuition scholarship organizations that aid low-income students. The bill was passed by the Senate but lost in the House by a vote of 27 to 31.[33] Also introduced this session was S.B. 1240, which would have forced contributors to scholarship organizations to claim either the public or private school tax credit—not both.

The bill was defeated by a vote in the Senate Education Committee in early February.[34]

H.B. 2260, which would have provided a tax credit worth $1,500 to home-schooling families, also died in committee.

Voucher legislation was introduced in 2003. Under S.B. 1141, a new A Plus Literacy Voucher Program would award publicly funded scholarships to students who perform poorly on state tests or who have a disability, and parents would submit voucher applications to the Arizona Department of Education. The bill died in committee.[35]

## Position of the Governor / Composition of the State Legislature

Governor Jane Napolitano, a Democrat, does not support school choice. Republicans control both houses of the legislature.

## State Contacts

**Arizona Charter Schools Association**
Margaret Roush-Meier, Executive Director
721 North San Francisco
Flagstaff, AZ 86001
Phone: (928) 779-2761
Fax: (928) 779-2761
Web site: http://www.azcharters.org
E-mail: mroushmeier@azcharters.org

**Arizona Department of Education**
Tom Horne, Superintendent
1535 West Jefferson Street
Phoenix, AZ 85007
Phone: (602) 542-4361
Fax: (602) 542-5440
Web site: www.ade.az.gov

**Charter School Division**
Bonnie Barclay
1535 West Jefferson Street
Phoenix, AZ 85007
Phone: (602) 542-5968
Fax: (602) 542-3590

30. *Ibid.*

31. *Ibid.*

32. Caroline Hoxby, "School Choice and School Productivity (Or Could Choice Be a Tide that Lifts All Boats?)," National Bureau of Economic Research, *Working Paper* No. 8873, April 2002, at *www.nber.org/digest/aug02/w8873.html.*

33. Arizona 46th Legislature, S.B. 1263, and Center for Arizona Policy, "Education Legislation," at *www.azpolicy.org/html/education.html.*

34. Arizona 46th Legislature, S.B. 1240 and Center for Arizona Policy, "Education Legislation," at *www.azpolicy.org/html/education.html.*

35. Arizona 46th Legislature, S.B. 1141.

Web site: www.ade.az.gov
E-mail: bbarcla@mail1.ade.state.az.us

**Arizona Dream Foundation**
Dan Lips, President
P.O. Box 2628
Phoenix, AZ 85002
Phone: (602) 712-1277
Web site: www.arizonadream.org
E-mail: lips@arizonadream.org

**Arizona Families for Home Education**
P.O. Box 2035
Chandler, AZ 85244-2035
Phone: (800) 929-3927
Web site: www.afhe.org
E-mail: Homeschool@afhe.org

**Arizona Regional Resource Center**
Rick Brown, Project Director
PPEP TEC High School
1840 East Benson Highway
Tucson, AZ 85714
Phone: (520) 294-6997
Fax: (520) 294-7738
Web site: www.resourcecenter.org
E-mail: rbrown@resourcecenter.org

**Arizona Scholarship Fund**
ChamBria Henderson, Executive Director
P.O. Box 2576
Mesa, AZ 85214-2576
Phone: (480) 497-4564
Fax: (480) 497-4737
Web site: www.Azscholarships.org
E-mail: choice@Azscholarships.org

**Arizona School Choice Trust**
Thomas Rouse, Chairman
Nelson Llumiquinga, Executive Director
3737 East Broadway Road
Phoenix, AZ 85040-2966
Phone: (602) 454-1360
Fax: (602) 454-1362
Web site: www.asct.org
E-mail: info@asct.org

**Arizona State Board for Charter Schools**
Kristen Jordison, Director
4105 North 20th Street, Suite 280
Phoenix, AZ 85016
Phone: (602) 468-6369
Fax: (602) 468-1682
Web site: www.asbcs.state.az.us
E-mail: charter_school_board@pop.state.az.us

**Goldwater Institute**
Darcy Olsen, President and CEO
500 East Coronado Road
Phoenix, AZ 85004
Phone: (602) 462-5000
Fax: (602) 256-7045
Web site: www.goldwaterinstitute.org
E-mail: info@goldwaterinstitute.org

## State School Report Card

**Arizona Department of Education**
Web site: www.ade.az.gov/srcs/main.asp

**Greatschools.net**
Web site: www.greatschools.net/modperl/go/AZ

# ARKANSAS

## State Profile (Updated May 2003)

### School Choice Status
- Public school choice: Interdistrict/mandatory
- State constitution: Compelled-support language
  Charter school law: Established 1995
    Strength of law: Weak
    Number of charter schools in operation (fall 2002): 8
    Number of students enrolled (fall 2002): 1,486
- Publicly funded private school choice: No
- Privately funded school choice: Yes
- Home-school law: Moderate regulation
- Ranking on the Education Freedom Index (2001): 32nd out of 50 states

### K–12 Public Schools and Students (2001–2002)
- Public school enrollment: 448,246
- Students enrolled per teacher: 14.4
- Number of schools (2000–2001): 1,130
- Number of districts: 310
- Current expenditures: $2,583,877,000
- Current per-pupil expenditure: $5,764
- Amount of revenue from the federal government: 8.1%

### K–12 Public School Teachers (2001–2002)
- Number of teachers: 31,097
- Average salary: $35,389

### K–12 Private Schools (1999–2000)
- Private school enrollment: 26,424
- Number of schools: 192
- Number of teachers: 2,075

### K–12 Public and Private School Student Academic Performance
- NAEP test results:

| NAEP Tests Arkansas- Student Performance | State (National) 2000 Math Scale = 0–500 | | State (National) 2000 Science Scale = 0–300 | | State (National) 2000 Reading Scale = 0–500 | |
|---|---|---|---|---|---|---|
| | 4th Grade | 8th Grade | 4th Grade | 8th Grade | 4th Grade | 8th Grade |
| Average Scale Score | 217 (226) | 261 (274) | 144 (148) | 143 (149) | 209 (215) | 256 (261) |
| Advanced | 1% (3%) | 1% (5%) | 2% (3%) | 2% (4%) | 4% (6%) | 1% (2%) |
| Proficient | 12% (23%) | 13% (21%) | 22% (25%) | 21% (26%) | 19% (23%) | 22% (29%) |
| Basic | 43% (43%) | 38% (39%) | 38% (36%) | 31% (29%) | 32% (32%) | 45% (41%) |
| Below Basic | 44% (31%) | 48% (35%) | 38% (36%) | 46% (41%) | 45% (39%) | 32 % (28%) |

- SAT weighted rank (2001): N/A
- ACT weighted rank (2001): 19th out of 26 states
- ALEC Academic Achievement Ranking: 44th out of 50 states and the District of Columbia

## Summary

Arkansas offers limited public school choice. Although the state's charter school law has been amended several times, it remains weak. Eligible high school students may enroll in higher education courses for high school and postsecondary credit. Low-income students may apply for privately funded vouchers provided by private scholarship foundations.

## Background

The Arkansas Public School Choice Act of 1989 declares that

> parents will become more informed about and involved in the public educational system if…provided greater freedom to determine the most effective school…. There is no right school for every student, and permitting students to choose from among different schools with differing assets will increase the likelihood that some marginal students will stay in school and that other, more motivated students will find their full academic potential…. [G]iving more options to parents and students with respect to where they attend public school will increase the responsiveness and effectiveness of the state's schools….[36]

The law enables students to apply for transfer to a school in another district as long as the transfer does not affect desegregation efforts. Students who have been denied a transfer may receive a hearing before the Arkansas State Board of Education. Students may also transfer to other schools within their district.[37]

In 1995, then-Governor Jim Guy Tucker, a Democrat, signed Act 1126, which allowed any local school to become a charter school, but with several stipulations: The charter could not remove existing collective bargaining requirements; it had to be approved by the local board of education; at least two-thirds of the school's employees and two-thirds of the students' parents had to support the transition to a charter school; and the school had to accept the state board's regulations. These strict requirements discouraged teachers and parents at public schools from seeking charters.[38]

The Charter Schools Act of 1999 (Senate Bill 562), signed by Governor Tucker's successor, Mike Huckabee, a Republican, reduced the burden on charters. The law allows any university, private non-sectarian institution, or government entity to apply to open one of 12 open-enrollment charter schools. In addition, an unlimited number of existing public schools can convert to charter schools.[39] Two years later, Governor Huckabee signed into law Act 1311, which amended the charter school law's process of public school conversion.[40]

In 1998, the state became a Children's Scholarship Fund (CSF) partner, and CEO of Central Arkansas, the state's existing private scholarship program, became CSF–Arkansas. The CSF, a $100 million foundation, has matched funds raised by Arkansans to underwrite private scholarships that enable low-income children in elementary school (K–8) to attend a school of choice.[41]

One tax credit bill, House Bill 2159, and one voucher bill, H.B. 2275, were introduced in 1999. H.B. 2159 would have created tax credits for tuition and other educational expenses, and H.B. 2275 would have created "child-centered scholarships" for private school tuition. Both bills died in committee. In 2001, H.B.1071, which would have offered tuition assistance ("learning endowments") for children in low-performing school districts, and S.B. 901, which would have provided a $100 ($500 for joint

---

36. See Arkansas code at *http://arkedu.state.ar.us/pdf/student_laws_2002.pdf*.
37. *Ibid.*
38. Kathleen M. McGree and Sue E. Mutchler, "Variations on Autonomy: Charter School Laws in the Southwestern Region," Southwest Educational Development Laboratory, 1998.
39. See *www.arkleg.state.ar.us/ftproot/bills/1999/WinWord/SB562.rtf*.
40. See *www.arkleg.state.ar.us/ftproot/acts/2001/htm/act1311.pdf*.
41. See Children's Scholarship Fund Web site at *www.scholarshipfund.org*.

filers) income tax credit for contributions to nonprofit scholarship providers, were also introduced. Both of these bills also died in committee.[42]

## Developments in 2002 and 2003

In July 2002, when the U.S. Department of Education announced the number of failing schools throughout the nation, only two states—Arkansas and Wyoming—had no schools among the 8,652 that were so designated.[43] In August 2002, the Arkansas Department of Education identified nearly 200 schools as "needing improvement"; several months later, the department revised its count to 25 schools in 14 districts.[44]

In January 2003, State Representative Jeremy Hutchinson (R–Little Rock) introduced H.B. 1031, under which disabled students could have received vouchers to help them attend a private or public school of choice. The bill died in the Arkansas House of Representatives on April 17, 2003.[45]

## Position of the Governor / Composition of the State Legislature

Governor Mike Huckabee, a Republican, supports charter schools. Democrats control both houses of the legislature.

## State Contacts

### Arkansans for School Choice
Oscar Stilley, Chairman
Central Mall, Suite 520
5111 Rogers Avenue
Fort Smith, AR 72903-2041
Phone: (479) 996-4109
Fax: (479) 996-3409
Web site: www.ostilley.com
E-mail: oscar@ostilley.com

### Arkansas Department of Education
Charter School Liaison
4 Capitol Mall, Room 404-A
Little Rock, AR 72201

Phone: (501) 682-4475
Fax: (501) 682-2534
Web site: http://arkedu.state.ar.us

### Arkansas Policy Foundation
Greg Kaza, Executive Director
111 Center Street, Suite 1610
Little Rock, AR 72201
Phone: (501) 537-0825
Web site: www.reformarkansas.org
E-mail: kaza@reformarkansas.org

### Children First America
John Kirtley, President
P.O. 29928
Austin, TX 78755
Phone: (512) 345-1083
Fax: (512) 345-1280
Web site: www.childrenfirstamerica.org
E-mail: childrenfirstamerica@
childrenfirstamerica.org

### Children's Scholarship Fund–Arkansas
Lawrence Gunnells, Executive Director
Libby Davis, Program Administrator
P.O. Box 3060
Little Rock, AR 72203
Phone: (501) 907-0044
Fax: (501) 907-0047
E-mail: lgunnells@alltel.net
E-mail: libbydavis@alltel.net

### Education Alliance
Jerry Cox, Executive Director
414 South Pulaski, Suite 2
Little Rock, AR 72201
Phone: (501) 375-7000
Fax: (501) 375-7040
Web site: www.familycouncil.org
E-mail: edu@familycouncil.org

## State School Report Card

### Arkansas Department of Education
Web site: www.as-is.org/reportcard/

### Greatschools.net
Web site: www.greatschools.net/modperl/go/AR

---

42. See National School Boards Association Web site at *www.nsba.org/novouchers*.
43. Michael Cardman, "Public School Choice in Store for 8,600 Schools," *Education Daily*, July 2, 2002, p. 1.
44. "135 Students Get Nod to Transfer in the LR District," *Arkansas Democrat-Gazette*, January 7, 2003.
45. Arkansas Legislature, 2003 Regular Session, H.B. 1031. See also Associated Press, "Bill Would Offer School Vouchers to Disabled Children," January 2, 2003.

# CALIFORNIA

## State Profile (Updated May 2003)

### School Choice Status
- Public school choice: Interdistrict/voluntary and intradistrict/mandatory
- State constitution: Blaine amendment
  Charter school law: Established 1992
  - Strength of law: Strong
  - Number of charter schools in operation (fall 2002): 428
  - Number of students enrolled in charter schools (fall 2002): 153,935
- Publicly funded private school choice: No
- Privately funded school choice: Yes
- Home-school law: Low regulation
- Ranking on the Education Freedom Index (2001): 14th out of 50 states

### K–12 Public Schools and Students (2001–2002)
- Public school enrollment: 6,247,889
- Students enrolled per teacher: 20.5
- Number of schools (2000–2001): 8,757
- Number of districts: 989
- Current expenditures: $42,972,693,000
- Current per-pupil expenditure: $6,878
- Amount of revenue from the federal government: 10.6%

### K–12 Public School Teachers (2001–2002)
- Number of teachers: 304,598
- Average salary: $53,870

### K–12 Private Schools (1999–2000)
- Private school enrollment: 619,067
- Number of schools: 3,318
- Number of teachers: 43,159

### K–12 Public and Private School Student Academic Performance
- NAEP test results:

| NAEP Tests California Student Performance | State (National) 2000 Math Scale = 0–500 | | State (National) 2000 Science Scale = 0–300 | | State (National) 2000 Reading Scale = 0–500 | |
|---|---|---|---|---|---|---|
| | 4th Grade | 8th Grade | 4th Grade | 8th Grade | 4th Grade | 8th Grade |
| Average Scale Score | 214 (226) | 262 (274) | 131 (148) | 132 (149) | 202 (215) | 253 (261) |
| Advanced | 1% (3%) | 3% (5%) | 1% (3%) | 1% (4%) | 4% (6%) | 1% (2%) |
| Proficient | 14% (23%) | 15% (21%) | 13% (25%) | 14% (26%) | 16% (23%) | 21% (29%) |
| Basic | 37% (43%) | 34% (39%) | 33% (36%) | 25% (29%) | 28% (32%) | 42% (41%) |
| Below Basic | 48% (31%) | 48% (35%) | 53% (36%) | 60% (41%) | 52% (39%) | 36% (28%) |

- SAT weighted rank (2001): 10th out of 24 states and the District of Columbia
- ACT weighted rank (2001): N/A
- ALEC Academic Achievement Ranking: 35th out of 50 states and the District of Columbia

## Summary

California offers intradistrict open enrollment, allowing students to enroll in a public school of choice within their district. With permission from the school board and principal, a high school student may enroll in college courses for high school and postsecondary credit.[46] Low-income children can attend a school of choice with the help of tuition scholarships provided by several private scholarship foundations.

## Background

In the early 1970s, the U.S. Office of Economic Opportunity implemented a voucher program in Alum Rock, California. Designed by Harvard University professor Christopher Jencks, the program would have given students in Alum Rock's predominately low-income, minority schools a voucher to attend any participating public or private school. To participate, schools would have had to take the voucher as full funding and provide parents with information about the school's academic performance and programs. Because of fierce opposition by the teachers unions, the program was reduced to a program of limited public school choice and eventually abandoned.[47]

In 1992, then-Governor Pete Wilson, a Republican, signed Senate Bill 1448, the Charter School Act.[48] The law was amended in 1998, 1999, and 2002.[49] As it stands, the act permits the establishment of 550 charter schools and raises the cap by 100 schools for each subsequent academic year. Local school boards and the California State Board of Education may authorize a charter. Charter schools receive 100 percent of the public schools' per-pupil funding. Teachers in charter schools must be certified.[50]

Under a pair of bills passed in 1993—Assembly Bill 1114 and A.B. 19—parents have the right to transfer their children to other public schools within the district and outside of the district, subject to limitations of space or racial balance policies. Interdistrict transfers are limited to districts that elect to participate.[51]

Publicly funded private school choice became a major political issue in 1993 when Proposition 174 was placed on the ballot. This proposition would have amended the state constitution to provide vouchers for families to enroll their children in public, private, or parochial schools.[52] The initiative faced stiff opposition from the California Teachers Association, which spent $12.4 million in a successful effort to defeat it.[53]

During the 1999 legislative session, S.B. 882 was introduced to provide vouchers to students in poorly performing schools. Another bill, Assembly Constitutional Amendment 20, would have allowed students to receive vouchers for private school tuition. Both bills died in committee.[54]

In 2000, San Juan Capistrano District Administrator Margaret LaRoe sought the authority to turn the entire district into a charter school district. LaRoe argued that independence from

46. Education Commission of the States, "Postsecondary Options: Dual/Concurrent Enrollment," July 2001.
47. Isabel V. Sawhill with Shannon L. Smith, "Vouchers for Elementary and Secondary Education," Brookings Institution, August 5, 1998.
48. EdSource, "Charter Schools in California: Public Education by a New Set of Rules," November 1999, at www.edsource.org/pdf/charter.pdf.
49. Ibid. See also California Department of Education, "Update of Recent Charter School Legislation," at www.cde.ca.gov/charter/legislation/prgrmbillsum2002.pdf.
50. Center for Education Reform, "Charter School Legislation: Profile of California's Charter School Law," 2001, at http://edreform.com/charter_schools/laws/California.htm.
51. Kristi Hein, "Getting the Public School You Want: School Choice and the Law," School Wise Press, 1997, at www.schoolwisepress.com/smart/browse/hein3.html.
52. Marquette University, Virgil C. Blum Center for Parental Freedom in Education, Educational Freedom Report, Trial Issue No. 2, September 20, 1993.
53. Sandy Banks and Stephanie Chavez, "NEWS ANALYSIS: School Voucher Threat Gives Impetus for Reform Education," Los Angeles Times, November 8, 1993, p. A1.
54. See National School Boards Association Web site at www.nsba.org/novouchers.

state regulations would enable districts to use their funds in the way that best meets their needs and would allow superintendents and school boards to focus on monitoring and supporting charter schools.[55] The Capistrano proposal received support from an unusual alliance that included Republican State Senator Bill Morrow and the California Teachers Association, which supported the effort because it guaranteed that the district would remain unionized.[56] Nevertheless, legislation to implement the proposal died in committee.[57]

In 2000, Silicon Valley venture capitalist Tim Draper sponsored Proposition 38, a voter initiative to provide parents, regardless of income, with universal vouchers worth $4,000 per child for use at any public or private school. As many as 6.6 million children would have been eligible for these vouchers. Draper spent $23 million to gain support for the measure. The California State Board of Education contributed $26.3 million in opposition.[58] A June poll found public opinion to be split, with 39 percent of respondents in favor of the initiative and 39 percent against it.[59] On election day, the proposition was defeated.

Private scholarships continue to attract parents. In 1998, the Children's Scholarship Fund (CSF), a $100 million foundation, selected Los Angeles and San Francisco as two of 40 "partner cities" that would receive matching donations for private scholarships to help low-income students attend a school of choice.[60]

In 1999, the Independent Institute began offering need-based and merit-based tuition scholarships to students in Alameda and Contra Costa Counties in amounts of up to 75 percent of tuition or a maximum of $1,500.[61] The institute awarded 238 scholarships for the 2002–2003 school year.[62]

In 2000, the Catholic Education Foundation announced that it would award $4.5 million in scholarships to nearly 4,700 children from disadvantaged families enrolled in Roman Catholic schools in the fall of 2001.[63]

S.B. 740, signed by the governor on October 14, 2001, reduced funding for charter schools offering home-based instruction. The law created the Charter School Facility Grant Program, providing funds for rent and lease costs for charter schools in low-income areas.[64]

Then-Senator Ray Haynes (R) sponsored S.B. 715, which would have required teachers in public schools to send their children to public schools. A poll conducted by the teachers association found that a third of teachers who have school-age children send their children to private schools.[65] Nevertheless, the bill was strongly criticized by the state's largest teachers union. "In their campaign to defeat school vouchers for all California families," noted Haynes, "the teachers' union argued that vouchers would destroy the public school system." Haynes's bill failed to move out of committee.

During the 2001 session, a tax credit bill, A.B.1625, was introduced to allow individuals to receive a dollar-for-dollar credit for donations to a nonprofit scholarship organization that supports low-income children. The bill died in committee.[66]

---

55. Dion Haynes, "Districts Seek to Join Charter School Movement," *Chicago Tribune*, June 2, 2000, p. 4.

56. Hanh Kim Quach, "An Unusual Alliance Could Help Capistrano Become a Charter District," *Orange County Register*, August 1, 2000, p. B1.

57. Hanh Kim Quach and Keith Sharon, "Speedy Charter-District Bill Fails," *Orange County Register*, August 25, 2000, p. B1.

58. "Election 2000: Californians Take Initiative(s)," *USA Today*, November 8, 2000, at *www.usatoday.com/news/vote2000/ca/ballot01.htm*.

59. Chris Burnett, "Voters Are Indecisive on Voucher Initiative," *Contra Costa Times*, June 30, 2000, p. A11.

60. Press release, Children's Scholarship Fund, September 28, 1998.

61. See Independent Institute Web site at *www.independent.org/tii/students/isf.html*.

62. *Ibid.*

63. Catholic Education Foundation, "Foundation Announces $4.5 Million in Scholarships," May 31, 2000, at *www.cefdn.org/articles/catholicscholarships.pdf*.

64. Education Commission of the States, "Charter School Legislation, 2001," at *www.ecs.org/clearinghouse/22/79/2279.htm*.

65. Wyatt Haupt, "Teachers' Association Blasts Proposal by Haynes," *Californian North County Times*, March 22, 2001.

In May 2001, the Pacific Legal Foundation filed a lawsuit against the California Department of Education for instituting regulations on charter schools that were not in the law and that violate the intent of the Charter Schools Act. The suit contended that the department forced charter schools to discard their own accounting systems and use the more costly and inefficient reporting systems used by the public schools. On April 11, 2002, a Sacramento County Superior Court struck down the regulations instituted by the Department of Education.[67]

## Developments in 2002 and 2003

The Charter School Facility Grant Program was amended in 2002 by S.B. 2039. The state now provides funds for facilities, rent, and lease costs to charter schools where 70 percent or more of the students are eligible for the free lunch program.[68]

According to a 2002 California State University study, *California Charter Schools Serving Low SES Students: An Analysis of the Academic Performance Index*, the state's charter schools were more effective than traditional public schools in increasing academic achievement for low-income and at-risk students. Charter schools with at least half of their students participating in the federal free and reduced-price lunch program improved at a rate of 22 percent, while traditional public schools improved at a 19 percent rate. Charter schools with 75 percent participation improved at a rate of 28 percent, compared with 24 percent in the other public schools.[69]

Parents of homeschoolers in Sonoma County were notified in April 2002 that their children would be deemed truant if they were not enrolled in a public or private school and that the Sonoma County Office of Education would stop providing the form that parents must file to homeschool their children.[70] Several months later, the California Department of Education told parents that they could not homeschool their children unless they had a professional teaching credential and that they would have to enroll their children in a school or risk having them considered truant.[71] Delaine Eastin, then-state Superintendent of Public Instruction, declared that homeschooling was illegal and has called for the state legislature to clarify the status of home schools. The law requires only that homeschooling parents submit a form designating their home school as a private school.[72]

A.B. 1625, a tax credit bill from 2001, was modified and reintroduced. The amended bill would have given taxpayers a credit worth 50 percent of their donations to a tuition scholarship organization. The bill died in committee.[73]

A.B.1464, introduced in March 2003, would allow more individuals and organizations to establish charter schools and would permit both universities and nonprofit organizations to approve charter applications. The bill was referred to the Assembly Education Committee.[74]

In April 2003, the Charter Schools Development Center (CSDC) released a report showing that students at five-year-old state charter schools were doing better on average than other public school students on state tests. The average Academic Performance Index base score for charter schools was almost 20 points higher than the public schools' average score.[75]

A.B. 349, a voucher bill introduced in 2003 by Assemblyman Ray Haynes (R–Murrieta), would create the Cal Grant for Kids Pilot Program in

66. See National School Boards Association Web site at *www.nsba.org/novouchers*.
67. "Legal Action," Heritage Foundation *Insider*, May 2, 2002, at *www.heritage.org/about/community/insider/2002/may02/legal_action.pdf*.
68. California State Assembly, 2001–2002 Session, S.B. 2039.
69. Center for Education Reform, "Achievement Gains Found at California Charter Schools: *Disadvantaged Children Benefit More from Charter Schools*," CER Press Alert, March 11, 2002.
70. Barbara Curtis, "County Tries to Limit Home Schooling," *Press Democrat*, April 25, 2002, p. B7.
71. Ellen Sorokin, "California Warns Home Schoolers," *The Washington Times*, August 21, 2002, p. A4.
72. Lance T. Izumi, "California's Attack on Home Schooling," Pacific Research Institute, *Capital Ideas*, Vol. 7, No. 30 (July 31, 2002).
73. See National School Boards Association Web site at *www.nsba.org/novouchers*.
74. California State Assembly, 2003–2004 Session, A.B. 1464.
75. Charter School Development Center, "Veteran Charter Schools Outperform Non-Charters on API," April 2003, at *www.cacharterschools.org/pdf_files/veteran_API.pdf*.

the Compton Unified School District (a similar program exists for college students).[76] Vouchers would be made available for students to attend any school, public or private, in the Compton district. The bill is in the Assembly Education Committee.[77]

## Position of the Governor / Composition of the State Legislature

Governor Joseph Graham (Gray) Davis, Jr., a Democrat, opposes vouchers. Democrats control both houses of the legislature.

## State Contacts

**Archdiocese of Los Angeles**
Catholic Education Foundation
Hugh Ralston, Executive Director
3424 Wilshire Boulevard, 5th Floor
Los Angeles, CA 90010
Phone: (213) 637-7576
Fax: (213) 637-5901
Web site: www.CatholicEd-foundation.org

**The BASIC Fund**
Eileen Murphy, Administrative Director
268 Bush Street, Suite 2717
San Francisco, CA 94104
Phone: (415) 986-7221
Fax: (415) 986-5358
Web site: www.basicfund.org
E-mail: eileen@basicfund.org

**Black Alliance for Educational Options**
Amber Blackwell, Member, Board of Directors
6441 Herzog Street
Oakland, CA 94608
Phone: (510) 658-6454
Web site: www.baeo.org

**California Charter Schools Development Center**
Institute for Education Reform
California State University
Eric Premack
6000 J Street
Sacramento, CA 95819-6018
Phone: (916) 278-4600
Fax: (916) 278-4094
Web site: www.cacharterschools.org
E-mail: epremack@calstate.edu

**California Citizens for a Sound Economy**
Julie Vazquez
101 East Green Street, Suite 9
Pasadena, CA 91105
Phone: (877) 507-3273
E-mail: jvazquez@cse.org

**California Department of Education**
721 Capitol Mall
P.O. Box 944272
Sacramento, CA 94244-2720
Phone: (916) 319-0792
Web site: www.cde.ca.gov

**California Network of Educational Charters**
Susan Steelman Bragato, Executive Director
744 El Camino Real
San Carlos, CA 94070
Phone: (650) 654-6003
Fax: (650) 654-4267
Web site: www.canec.org

**California Parents for Educational Choice**
Peter Hanley, Executive Director
2291 Stockton Street, #407
San Francisco, CA 94133
Phone: (415) 982-6403
Web site: www.CPEConline.org

**California Public Policy Foundation**
John Kurzweil, President
P.O. Box 931
Camarillo, CA 93011
Phone: (805) 445-9183
E-mail: calprev@cppf.org

**Capitol Resource Institute**
Michael Mears, Executive Director
1414 K Street, Suite 200
Sacramento, CA 95814
Phone: (916) 498-1940
Fax: (916) 448-2888
Web site: www.capitolresource.org
E-mail: admin@capitolresource.org

**Center for the Study of Popular Culture**
David Horowitz, President
4401 Wilshire Boulevard, 4th Floor
Los Angeles, CA 90010
Phone: (800) 752-6562
Fax: (323) 556-2559
Web site: www.cspc.org
E-mail: dhorowitz@cspc.org

---

76. George A. Clowes, "School Choice Roundup," Heartland Institute, May 1, 2003, and California State Assembly, 2003–2004 Session, A.B. 349.

77. California State Assembly, 2003–2004 Session, A.B. 349, and Carl Ingram, "Bill Offers Test Run for School Choice," *Los Angeles Times*, March 24, 2003.

---

**CEO Oakland**
Nancy Berg, Program Director
P.O. Box 21456
Oakland, CA 94620
Phone: (510) 483-7971
Fax: (510) 547-0223
Web site: www.childrenfirstamerica.org

**Christian Home Educators Association of California**
P.O. Box 2009
Norwalk, CA 90651-2009
Phone: (800) 564-2432
Fax: (562) 864-3747
Web site: www.cheaofca.org
E-mail: cheaofca@aol.com

**Claremont Institute**
Brian Kennedy, President
937 Foothill Boulevard, Suite E
Claremont, CA 91711
Phone: (909) 621-6825
Fax: (909) 626-8724
Web site: www.claremont.org
E-mail: info@claremont.org

**Golden State Center for Public Policy Studies**
1127 11th Street, Suite 206
Sacramento, CA 95814
Phone: (916) 446-7924
Fax: (916) 446-7990
Web site: www.claremont.org

**The Guardsmen Scholarship Fund**
Kurt King, Chairman, Scholarship Committee
P.O. Box 29330
San Francisco, CA 94129-0330
Phone: (415) 561-2700
Fax: (415) 561-2966
E-mail: kurtkinginsf@yahoo.com

**The Hoover Institution**
Williamson M. Evers, Research Fellow
Terry Moe, Ph.D., Senior Fellow
Eric Hanushek, Ph.D., Senior Fellow
on Education Policy
Stanford University
Stanford, CA 94305-6010
Phone: (650) 723-1754
Toll-free phone: 1-877-466-8374
Fax: (650) 723-1687
Web site: www-hoover.stanford.edu/
E-mail: Moe@Hoover.Stanford.edu
E-mail: hanushek@hoover.stanford.edu

**Independent Institute**
David J. Theroux, President
100 Swan Way

Oakland, CA 94621
Phone: (510) 632-1366
Fax: (510) 568-6040
Web site: www.independent.org
E-mail: info@independent.org

**Los Angeles Children's Scholarship Fund/ CSF West**
Michael Warder, Executive Director
1650 Ximeno Street, Suite 245
Long Beach, CA 90804
Phone: (562) 961-9250
Fax: (562) 961-9240
Web site: www.lacsf.org
E-mail: mwarder@lacsf.org

**National Home Education Network (NHEN)**
P.O. Box 7844
Long Beach, CA 90807
Fax: (413) 581-1463
Web site: www.nhen.org
E-mail: info@nhen.org

**Pacific Research Institute for Public Policy**
Center for School Reform
Lance Izumi, Director
1414 K Street, Suite 200
Sacramento, CA 95814
Phone: (916) 448-1926
Fax: (916) 448-3856
Web site: www.pacificresearch.org
E-mail: Izumi58@aol.com

**Reason Public Policy Institute**
3415 South Sepulveda Boulevard, Suite 400
Los Angeles, CA 90034
Phone: (310) 391-2245
Fax: (310) 391-4395
Web site: www.reason.org

**RPP International**
Paul Berman
901 Grayson Street, Suite 204
Berkeley, CA 94710
Phone: (510) 647-0500
Fax: (510) 647-3504
Web site: www.rppintl.com
E-mail: info@rppintl.com

**San Francisco Independent Scholars Fund**
Ann Fry, Program Manager
755 Sansome Street, Suite 450
San Francisco, CA 94111
Phone: (415) 989-0833
Fax: (415) 989-2411
E-mail: afry@pacificresearch.org

**State Policy Network**
6255 Arlington Boulevard
Richmond, CA 94805
Phone: (510) 965-9700
Fax: (510) 965-9600
Web site: www.spn.org

## State School Report Card
### California Department of Education
Web site: www.cde.ca.gov/ope/sarc

**Education Data Partnership**
Web site: www.ed-data.k12.ca.us

**Greatschool.net**
Web site: www.greatschools.net/modperl/go/CA

**School Wise Press**
Web site: www.schoolwisepress.com

# COLORADO

## State Profile (Updated May 2003)

### School Choice Status

- Public school choice: Intradistrict and interdistrict/mandatory
- State constitution: Blaine amendment and compelled-support language
- Charter school law: Established 1993
    Strength of law: Strong
    Number of charter schools in operation (fall 2002): 93
    Number of students enrolled in charter schools (fall 2002): 25,512
- Publicly funded private school choice: Yes
- Privately funded school choice: Yes
- Home-school law: Moderate regulation
- Ranking on the Education Freedom Index (2001): 12th out of 50 states

### K–12 Public Schools and Students (2001–2002)

- Public school enrollment: 742,065
- Students enrolled per teacher: 17.1
- Number of schools (2000–2001): 1,590
- Number of districts: 178
- Current expenditures: $4,633,739,000
- Current per-pupil expenditure: $6,244
- Amount of revenue from the federal government: 5.1%

### K–12 Public School Teachers (2001–2002)

- Number of teachers: 43,282
- Average salary: $40,222

### K–12 Private Schools (1999–2000)

- Private school enrollment: 52,142
- Number of schools: 339
- Number of teachers: 4,353

### K–12 Public and Private School Student Academic Performance

- NAEP test results:

| NAEP Tests Colorado Student Performance | State (National) 2000 Math Scale = 0–500 | | State (National) 2000 Science Scale = 0–300 | | State (National) 2000 Reading Scale = 0–500 | |
|---|---|---|---|---|---|---|
| | 4th Grade | 8th Grade | 4th Grade | 8th Grade | 4th Grade | 8th Grade |
| Average Scale Score | N/A (226) | N/A (274) | N/A (148) | N/A (149) | 222 (215) | 264 (261) |
| Advanced | N/A (3%) | N/A (5%) | N/A (3%) | N/A (4%) | 7% (6%) | 2% (2%) |
| Proficient | N/A (23%) | N/A (21%) | N/A (25%) | N/A (26%) | 27% (23%) | 28% (29%) |
| Basic | N/A (43%) | N/A (39%) | N/A (36%) | N/A (29%) | 35% (32%) | 46% (41%) |
| Below Basic | N/A (31%) | N/A (35%) | N/A (36%) | N/A (41%) | 31% (39%) | 24% (28%) |

- SAT weighted rank (2001): N/A
- ACT weighted rank (2001): 9th out of 26 states
- ALEC Academic Achievement Ranking: 18th out of 50 states and the District of Columbia

## Summary

Colorado recently adopted a voucher program for poor students in state-designated low-performing school districts. In addition, the state offers parents numerous other choices for the schooling of their children. They may choose from public schools within and outside of their homeschool districts. There are nearly 100 charter schools, supported by a strong charter school law. The state has a thriving community of homeschoolers and offers virtual schooling on-line. Junior and senior high school students may enroll in college courses for high school and postsecondary credit. Low-income children can attend a school of choice with the help of tuition scholarships provided by several private-sector scholarship foundations.

## Background

In 1988, the Colorado General Assembly passed the Postsecondary Enrollment Options Act, which allows junior and senior high school students to enroll in college courses at public and private institutions of higher education. Students receive high school or college credit or both.[78] Under a separate Fast Track Program, a 12th grade student who has completed classes required for graduation may take college courses. The school district pays for the courses if the student passes.[79]

In 1990, the legislature adopted the Public Schools of Choice Act. Students may transfer to other schools within and outside of their home districts, subject to limitations of capacity or desegregation plans. Transfer requests may be denied if the preferred school does not have appropriate services to meet a child's physical or cognitive special needs, if the student has not met eligibility requirements for a particular pro-gram, or if the student has been expelled from his or her former school.[80]

In November 1992, a parental choice ballot initiative was defeated by a margin of 66.8 percent to 33.2 percent. The initiative would have given parents vouchers worth 50 percent of the public schools' per-pupil expenditure in their district to send a child to a public or private school of choice.[81]

In June 1993, the legislature passed the Charter Schools Act, which allows any group or individual to submit an application to open a charter school. Local school districts have the sole authority to grant charters, but rejected applicants may appeal to the Colorado State Board of Education. Charter applicants can seek waivers from specific district policies and state statutes.[82]

In the 1998 general election, by a margin of 59 percent to 41 percent, Colorado voters rejected Initiative 17, which would have given parents up to $2,500 annually per child in state income tax credits for educational expenses, including tuition at private schools.[83]

On March 31, 1999, Governor Bill Owens, a Republican, signed into law House Bill 1113, which requires that school districts must fully fund charter schools at 95 percent of per-pupil revenue. Previously, districts had funded only 80 percent of charter school costs.[84] The bill also allows districts to keep 5 percent of their per-pupil revenues to cover administration costs for the charter schools and to contract with charter schools to provide other support services.

---

78. Colorado Revised Statutes 22-35-101-111.
79. Colorado Revised Statutes 22-34-101.
80. Pamela Benigno, "Colorado Public School Open Enrollment Policies: Not Very Open," Independence Institute, November 28, 2000.
81. Mark Walsh, "Colorado Defeats Voucher Plan, Backs Limits on Taxes," *Education Week*, November 11, 1992.
82. Center for Education Reform, "Charter School Legislation: Profile of Colorado's Charter School Law," 2001, at *http://edreform.com/charter_schools/laws/Colorado.htm*.
83. Robert C. Johnston, "Status Quo Prevails on State Ballots," *Education Week*, November 11, 1998.
84. Dan Luzadder, "With the Stroke of a Pen, Owens Puts More into Education," *Denver Rocky Mountain News*, March 31, 1999, p. A10.

Another bill introduced in 1999, S.B. 100, which would have created state charter school districts that would be governed by the Colorado State Board of Education, did not pass. H.B. 1044, sponsored by Representative Nancy Spence (R–39), which would have allowed local school boards to waive nearly all state regulations—without the need for approval by local accountability boards, parents, teachers, or administrators—was passed by the House but died in the Senate Education Committee.[85]

Two choice bills introduced in 1999 did not make it out of committee. S.B. 162, introduced by Senator John Andrews (R–Arapahoe), then-vice chairman of the Senate Education Committee, would have created a tuition tax credit for preschool tuition. S.B. 55, introduced by Senator Doug Linkhart (D–Denver), would have provided tax credits worth 25 percent of a taxpayer's cash donations to any school in the state, public or private. The Linkhart bill was approved by the Senate Finance Committee but died in the Appropriations Committee.[86]

Colorado NAACP President Willie Breazell was forced to resign his position after voicing his support for publicly funded private school choice in an August 17, 1999, opinion article in the Colorado Springs *Gazette*.[87]

In the state's House of Representatives, two tax credit bills were introduced in 2000. H.B. 1198 would have provided tax credits for educational expenses, and H.B. 1177 would have offered a credit for contributions to scholarship organizations and private schools. Both bills died in committee.[88]

Also during the 2000 legislative session, Senator Andrews introduced S.B. 46, which would have created a statewide voucher program through the School Guarantee Act. Parents dissatisfied with their child's academic, moral, or physical well-being would have been eligible to receive a voucher to enroll their child in a school of choice. The legislation set the voucher amount at either 80 percent of the per-pupil expenditure of the school from which the child transferred or a means-tested percentage of private-school tuition. S.B. 46 died in committee.[89]

In February 2000, the Alliance for Choice in Education (ACE) launched a private scholarship program to award scholarships annually to low-income Denver students to attend a school of choice. ACE pays for half of the tuition at a private school, up to $2,000 per year for elementary and middle school students and up to $3,000 per year for high school students.[90] Since its inception, ACE has granted scholarships to 917 students. Three-quarters of the ACE-sponsored high school graduates have gone on to college.[91] The Children's Tuition Fund, Parents Challenge, and Educational Options for Children also provide scholarships for children.[92]

In April 2000, under the leadership of Governor Bill Owens, the Colorado legislature established an accountability system that graded schools according to their students' performance on state tests. Public schools that were designated as "failing" and did not improve after three years could be converted to charter schools.[93] In 2001, Governor Owens approved a bill that changed the grading system of schools and required, rather than letter grades of A through F, school rankings of "excellent," "high," "average," "low," or "unsatisfactory."[94]

In May 2000, the Colorado Department of Education released a report on the 1998–1999 school year that included information on the 51 charter schools that had been in operation for at least two years. The report revealed that the charter schools were outpacing the traditional

85. Michelle Dally Johnston, "House OK's GOP School Bills," *The Denver Post*, January 30, 1999.

86. See Colorado General Assembly Web site at *www.state.co.us/gov_dir/stateleg.html*.

87. Eric Gorski, "NAACP Head Steps Down," *The Gazette*, September 8, 1999, p. A1. See also editorial, "Free Willie," *The Wall Street Journal*, September 17, 1999.

88. See National School Boards Association Web site at *www.nsba.org/novouchers*.

89. See National School Boards Association Web site at *www.nsba.org/novouchers*.

90. See Alliance for Choice in Education Web site at *www.acescholarships.net/program.ivnu*.

91. Phone conversation with Norton Rainey, Alliance for Choice in Education, February 19, 2003.

92. See Children First America Web site at *www.childrenfirstamerica.org/*.

93. Milton and Rose D. Friedman Foundation, *The Friedman Report*, No. 3 (2000).

94. John Sanko, "Governor Signs School Report Bill Measure Gives Rating for Accountability in Place of Letter Grades," *Rocky Mountain News*, June 9, 2001, p. A1.

public schools. On average, charter school students scored 10 to 16 percentage points above statewide public school averages, and 75 percent of the charter schools scored higher than schools in their home districts with similar demographics.[95]

Three school choice bills were introduced in the 2001 legislature. S.B. 64, which would have authorized a statewide universal voucher program, died in committee.[96] H.B. 1219, which would have created tax credits for donations to organizations that award tuition scholarships for private schools, was passed by the House but died in a Senate committee.[97] H.B. 1180, which would have established a refundable K–12 tuition tax credit of up to $3,000 per child for tuition expenses and up to $1,000 for home-schooling expenses for one child and $500 per child for additional children, also died in committee.[98]

## Developments in 2002 and 2003

On June 7, 2002, Governor Owens signed H.B. 1349, which made several changes in Colorado's charter school law. The law permits charter schools to have on-line programs and makes it easier for them to gain access to capital funds.[99]

During the 2002 legislative session, two bills were introduced to authorize education tax credits. S.B. 163 would have provided a tax credit against property taxes for contributions to tuition scholarship organizations. H.B. 1309 offered individuals an income tax credit of up to 65 percent of the amount contributed to a scholarship organization. For the first year, the maximum amount of the credits would have been capped at $5 million. By 2006, the cap would have risen to $20 million.[100] H.B. 1309 was passed by the House but died in the Senate. S.B. 163 also died in the Senate.[101]

On April 16, 2003, Governor Owens signed into law the Colorado Opportunity Contract

Pilot Program, H.B. 1160. Sponsored by State Representative Nancy Spence (R–39), this program will provide vouchers to low-income students in state-designated poor-performing school districts. The vouchers will be worth 37.5 percent of the district's per-pupil costs for kindergarten, 75 percent for elementary and junior high school, and 85 percent for high school. Only students who participate in the federal free and reduced-price lunch program and were enrolled in a Colorado public school the previous year will be eligible to participate. Students in grades 4–12 must have failed the state assessment or college entrance exam. Participation is capped at 1 percent of the district's enrollment in 2004–2005, rising yearly to 6 percent in 2007–2008 and subsequent years.[102]

In other legislation, S.B. 99, introduced by Senator John Evans (R–30), would have allowed school boards to set up voucher programs with the approval of district voters. District citizens also could have petitioned to place the issue on the ballot. The bill was passed by the Senate but died in the House. S.B. 77, introduced by Senator Ed Jones (R–11), would have established a pilot voucher program for low-income students in three school districts. Scholarships would have been worth the cost of tuition, the district per-pupil expenditure, or $5,200, whichever was least. S.B. 1, introduced by Senator Bruce Cairns (R–28), would have provided tax credits against property taxes to individuals who donate to scholarship organizations. Both of these bills died in the Senate.[103]

In the Colorado House of Representatives, H.B. 1137, introduced by Representative Keith King (R–21), would have given a tax credit for contributions to organizations that provide scholarships to poor children to attend a school of choice. The credit would have been equal to 50 percent of a donation of up to $25,000 ($50,000 for married couples filing jointly). The state would have been able to grant up to $3

---

95. Robert Holland, "In Colorado, Fulfillment of the Charter-School Dream," *School Reform News*, May 2000.

96. See National School Boards Association Web site at *www.nsba.org/novouchers*.

97. See Colorado General Assembly Web site at *www.state.co.us/gov_dir/stateleg.html*.

98. "Tax Credit Proposals Proliferate," *School Reform News*, April 2001.

99. See Colorado General Assembly Web site at *www.state.co.us/gov_dir/stateleg.html*.

100. See National School Boards Association Web site at *www.nsba.org/novouchers*.

101. See Colorado General Assembly Web site at *www.state.co.us/gov_dir/stateleg.html*.

102. *Ibid.*

103. See Colorado General Assembly Web site at *www.state.co.us/gov_dir/stateleg.html*.

million in tax relief in 2003, with this relief increasing yearly to $10 million by 2010. The bill was passed by the House but died in the Senate.[104]

## Position of the Governor / Composition of the State Legislature

Governor Bill F. Owens, a Republican, is a strong supporter of parental choice in education. Republicans control both the House and Senate.

## State Contacts

**Alliance for Choice in Education (ACE)**
Kathy Porter, Program Director
511 16th Street, Suite 300
Denver, CO 80202
Phone: (303) 573-1603
Fax: (303) 573-7340
Web site: www.acescholarships.net
E-mail: acescholarship@yahoo.com

**Association of Christian Schools International**
Ken Smitherman, President
Burt Carney, Director, Legal/Legislative Issues
P.O. Box 35097
Colorado Springs, CO 80935-3509
Phone: (719) 528-6906
Fax: (719) 531-0631
Web site: www.acsi.org
E-mail: burt_carney@acsi.org

**Black Alliance for Educational Options**
Dale Sadler
Ledbetter & Thomas
5251 DTC Parkway, Suite 690
Greenwood Village, CO 80111
Phone: (303) 799-3501
Fax: (303) 799-3503
Web site: www.baeo.org

**Children's Tuition Fund**
Evelyn Allen, Coordinator
Association of Christian Schools International
P.O. Box 35097
Colorado Springs, CO 80935-3509
Phone: (719) 528-6906, ext. 251
Fax: (719) 531-0631
Web site: www.acsi.org
E-mail: evelyn_allen@acsi.org

**Christian Home Educators of Colorado**
10431 South Parker Road
Parker, CO 80134
Phone: (720) 842-4852
Fax: (720) 842-4854
Web site: www.chec.org
E-mail: office@chec.org

**Colorado Alliance for Reform in Education**
Bob Schaffer
5027 Alder Court
Fort Collins, CO 80525
Phone: (970) 223-7805
Fax: (970) 282-3540
E-mail: bobschaffer@comcast.net

**Colorado Children's Campaign**
Barbara O'Brien, President
1120 Lincoln Street, Suite 125
Denver, CO 80203
Phone: (303) 839-1580
Fax: (303) 839-1354
Web site: www.coloradokids.org
E-mail: barbara@coloradokids.org

**Colorado Department of Education**
Cindy Howerter, Assistant to the Commissioner
201 East Colfax Avenue
Denver, CO 80203-1799
Phone: (303) 866-6646
Fax: (303) 830-0793
Web site: www.cde.state.co.us
E-mail: Howerter_C@cde.state.co.us

**Colorado League of Charter Schools**
Jim Griffin, Executive Director
1601 Vine Street
Denver, CO 80206
Phone: (303) 989-5356
Fax: (303) 984-9345
Web site: www.coloradoleague.org
E-mail: info@coloradoleague.org

**Education Commission of the States**
Todd Ziebarth, Program Director, Governance
National Center on Governing America's Schools
700 Broadway, Suite 1200
Denver, CO 80203-3460
Phone: (303) 299-3652
Fax: (303) 296-8332
Web site: www.ecs.org
E-mail: tziebarth@ecs.org

---

104. *Ibid.*

**Educational Options for Children**
Sheryl Glaser, Program Administrator
PMB 226
11757 West Ken Caryl Avenue, Suite F
Littleton, CO 80127
Phone: (720) 981-2557
Fax: (303) 948-5923

**Independence Institute**
Jon Caldara, President
Pamela Benigno, Director,
Education Policy Center
14142 Denver West Parkway, Suite185
Golden, CO 80401
Phone: (303) 279-6536
Fax: (303) 279-4176
Web site: www.i2i.org
E-mail: nina@i2i.org

**National Conference of State Legislatures**
William Pound, Executive Director
7700 East First Place
Denver, CO 80230
Phone: (303) 364-7700
Fax: (303) 364-7800
Web site: www.ncsl.org
E-mail: info@ncsl.org

**Parents Challenge**
Evelyn Taylor, Director
Sue Forsythe, Project Manager
2 North Cascade Avenue, Suite 1280
Colorado Springs, CO 80903
Phone: (719) 327-5817
Fax: (719) 633-6258
Web site: www.parentschallenge.org
E-mail: edt@theschuckcorporation.com

**Save Our Youth**
Luis Villarreal
3443 West 23rd Avenue
Denver, CO 80211
Phone 303-455-1126
Fax 303-480-1397
Web site: www.saveouryouth.org
E-mail: info@saveouryouth.org

## State School Report Card
**Colorado Department of Education**
Web site: http://reportcard.cde.state.co.us/
reportcard/CommandHandler.jsp

**Denver Public Schools**
Web site: www.dpsk12.org/schools

**Greatschools.net**
Web site: www.greatschools.net/modperl/go/
CO

**Jefferson County Public Schools**
Web site: http://jeffcoweb.jeffco.k12.co.us/
profiles/

# CONNECTICUT

## State Profile (Updated May 2003)

### School Choice Status
- Public school choice: Intradistrict and interdistrict/voluntary
- State constitution: Compelled-support language
- Charter school law: Established 1996
  Strength of Law: Weak
  Number of charter schools in operation (fall 2002): 16
  Number of students enrolled in charter schools (fall 2002): 2,526
- Publicly funded private school choice: No
- Privately funded school choice: Yes
- Home-school law: Moderate regulation
- Ranking on the Education Freedom Index (2001): 24th out of 50 states

### K–12 Public Schools and Students (2001)
- Public school enrollment: 570,145
- Students enrolled per teacher: 13.8
- Number of schools (2000–2001): 1,073
- Number of districts: 193
- Current expenditures: $5,996,000,000
- Current per-pupil expenditure: $10,517
- Amount of revenue from the federal government: 4.9%

### K–12 Public School Teachers (2001–2002)
- Number of teachers: 41,263
- Average salary: $54,300

### K–12 Private Schools (1999–2000)
- Private school enrollment: 70,058
- Number of schools: 348
- Number of teachers: 6,879

### K–12 Public and Private School Student Academic Performance
- NAEP Test Results:

| NAEP Tests Connecticut Student Performance | State (National) 2000 Math Scale = 0–500 | | State (National) 2000 Science Scale = 0–300 | | State (National) 2000 Reading Scale = 0–500 | |
|---|---|---|---|---|---|---|
| | 4th Grade | 8th Grade | 4th Grade | 8th Grade | 4th Grade | 8th Grade |
| Average Scale Score | 234 (226) | 282 (274) | 156 (148) | 154 (149) | 232 (215) | 272 (261) |
| Advanced | 3% (3%) | 6% (5%) | 3% (3%) | 4% (4%) | 11% (6%) | 4% (2%) |
| Proficient | 29% (23%) | 28% (21%) | 32% (25%) | 31% (26%) | 35% (23%) | 38% (29%) |
| Basic | 45% (43%) | 38% (39%) | 40% (36%) | 30% (29%) | 32% (32%) | 40% (41%) |
| Below Basic | 23% (31%) | 28% (35%) | 25% (36%) | 35% (41%) | 22% (39%) | 18% (28%) |

- SAT weighted rank (2001): 7th out of 24 states and the District of Columbia
- ACT weighted rank (2001): N/A
- ALEC Academic Achievement Ranking: 13th out of 50 states and the District of Columbia

## Summary

Connecticut offers charter schools and some choice among traditional public schools. The Open Choice program provides interdistrict choice for students in large urban systems. Community colleges and the University of Connecticut offer dual enrollment for high school students.[105] Tuition scholarships provided by a private foundation enable low-income children to attend a school of choice. Public school districts provide transportation for private school students, and private school students may borrow textbooks used in the public schools without charge.[106]

## Background

In 1996, Governor John Rowland signed a charter school bill authorizing the creation of 24 charter schools. Under the law, the Connecticut State Board of Education can set up state charter schools, while local boards may authorize local charter schools with the state board's approval. The law stipulates that half of the teachers in charter schools must be certified, although the state also allows alternative certification.[107]

In 1996, the Connecticut Supreme Court ruled in *Sheff* v. *O'Neill* that students in the Hartford public schools were racially and economically isolated and that the school system did not provide all students equal educational opportunity as stipulated by the state constitution. In response, Governor Rowland created the Education Improvement Panel to "explore, identify, and report on a broad range of options for reducing racial isolation in our state's public schools, improving teaching and learning, enhancing a sense of community, and encouraging parental involvement."[108]

Responding to the Education Improvement Panel report, the state legislature passed Public Act 97–290, An Act Enhancing Educational Choices and Opportunities. To increase the integration, the law encouraged school boards to initiate magnet schools, charter schools, and intradistrict and interdistrict public school choice programs. The law instituted interdistrict school choice in Bridgeport, New Haven, and Hartford in 1998 and statewide in 1999 with the intent "to: (1) Improve academic achievement; (2) reduce racial, ethnic and economic isolation or preserve racial and ethnic balance; and (3) provide a choice of educational programs for students."[109]

In 1995, CEO Connecticut began providing scholarships to students in Bridgeport. The organization now serves students in Bridgeport, Hartford, and New Haven.[110]

In his State of the State address in February 2000, Governor Rowland called for increased funding for the existing school choice program and a tuition tax credit of up to $500 for the cost of tuition at private or religious schools.[111] Several school bills were introduced during the 2000 session. Senate Bill 144 would have created a state personal income tax credit for primary and secondary education tuition expenses.[112] House Bill 5098 and S.B. 42 would have established a credit against the personal income tax for educational expenses.[113] All of these bills died in committee.

---

105. Education Commission of the States, "Postsecondary Options: Dual/Concurrent Enrollment," July 2001.

106. U.S. Department of Education, Office of Non-Public Education, "State Regulation of Private Schools," June 2000, at *www.ed.gov/pubs/RegPrivSchl/conn.html*.

107. Center for Education Reform, "Charter School Legislation: Profile of Connecticut's Charter School Law," 2001, at *http://edreform.com/charter_schools/laws/Connecticut.htm*.

108. Summarized in Memorandum of Decision, Judge Julia L. Aurigemma, Connecticut Superior Court, March 3, 1999, at *www.state.ct.us/sde/sheff.htm*. For the text of the Connecticut Supreme Court's original decision, see *Sheff* v. *O'Neill*, 238 Conn. 1, 678 A.2d 1267 (1996).

109. *Ibid.*

110. "Just Doing It," National Scholarship Center, Inc., 1994, p. 22; "Directory of Private Scholarship Programs Affiliated with CEO America," *School Reform News*, January 2000.

111. Jeff Archer, "Rowland Proposing Tuition Tax Credits for Connecticut," *Education Week*, February 16, 2000, p. 19.

112. See National School Boards Association Web site at *www.nsba.org/novouchers*.

In 2001, Governor Rowland proposed that $10 million of the state's $538 million budget surplus be used to provide scholarships for children in failing schools. Under this five-year pilot program, parents in the state's poorest districts would have received vouchers of up to $2,000 a year to send their children to private schools.[114] The proposal never came to a vote.

Two voucher bills were introduced during the 2001 session. H.B. 5255 would have created a one-year pilot program to give parents of children in failing schools vouchers equal to half the average per-pupil expenditure in the district. H.B. 5174 also would have provided vouchers to students in failing public schools. In the Senate, the Education Committee rejected an amendment to the education funding bill that would have provided $2,500 vouchers for low-income students in specified school districts.[115]

Four tax-credit bills were also introduced during the 2001 session. S.B. 390 would have given parents a $250 tax credit for public or private school expenses. H.B. 5189 and H.B. 5263 would have offered tax credits for tuition. H.B. 5190 would have provided a tax credit of up to $500 for education expenses to parents of K–12 students with incomes under $50,000 ($100,000 for joint filers). All of these bills died in committee.[116]

## Developments in 2002 and 2003

A poll commissioned in October 2002 by the University of Connecticut found that 51 percent of respondents favored giving parents education tax credits or vouchers for tuition at a private or religious school.[117]

In 2003, Representative Marie Kirkley-Bey (D–5) introduced H.B. 5741 to provide scholarships to students with disabilities. Representative Reginald Beamon (D–72) introduced H.B. 5423 to provide a tax credit for educational expenses not including tuition. Both bills remain in committee.[118]

## Position of the Governor / Composition of the State Legislature

Governor John Rowland, a Republican, strongly supports parental choice in education. Democrats control both houses of the legislature.

## State Contacts

### CEO of Connecticut
Don Wilson, Executive Director
210 Ann Street
Hartford, CT 06103
Phone: (860) 251-6650
Fax: (860) 251-6649
Web site: www.childrenfirstamerica.org
E-mail: dwilson465@aol.com

### Connecticut Charter Schools Network
Clair Howard, Director
55 Walnut Street, Unit 1
New Haven, CT 06511
Phone: (203) 624-4552
Fax: (203) 752-1558
Web site: www.ctcharterschools.org
E-mail: info@ctcharterschools.org

### Connecticut Federation of Catholic School Parents
Matthew T. Boyle, Executive Director
238 Jewett Avenue
Bridgeport, CT 06606
Phone: (203) 372-4301
Fax: (203) 371-8698
Web site: www.bridgeportdiocese.com

### Connecticut State Department of Education
165 Capitol Avenue
Hartford, CT 06145
Phone: (860) 713-6548
Web site: www.state.ct.us/sde

### Education Association of Christian Home-schoolers
363 Carriage Drive
Southbury, CT 06488
Phone: (860) 793-9968
Web site: www.teachCT.org
E-mail: teach.info@pobox.com

---

113. See Connecticut General Assembly Web site at *www.cga.state.ct.us*.

114. Lisa Chedekel, "Rowland to Make Pitch for Vouchers," *The Hartford Courant*, February 3, 2001.

115. See National School Boards Association Web site at *www.nsba.org/novouchers*.

116. *Ibid.*

117. Connecticut State and Community Public Education Poll—October 2002, at *http://www.news.uconn.edu/02107pll.htm*.

118. See Connecticut General Assembly Web site at *www.cga.state.ct.us/*.

**Family Institute of Connecticut**
Kenneth Von Kohorn, Chairman
P.O. Box 260210
Hartford, CT 06126
Phone: (860) 548-0066
Toll Free: 877-33-FAMILY
Fax: (860) 548-9545
Web site: www.ctfamily.org
E-mail: faminst@ibm.net

**Yankee Institute for Public Policy Studies**
Lewis M. Andrews, Executive Director
P.O. Box 260660
Hartford, CT 06126
Phone: (860) 297-4271
Fax: (860) 987-6218
Web site: www.yankeeinstitute.org
E-mail: white-light@att.net

## State School Report Card
**Connecticut State Department of Education**
Web site: www.state.ct.us/sde

**Greatschools.net**
Web site: www.greatschools.net/modperl/go/CT

# DELAWARE

## State Profile (Updated May 2003)

### School Choice Status
- Public school choice: Intradistrict and interdistrict/mandatory
- State constitution: Blaine amendment and compelled-support language
- Charter school law: Established 1995
    Strength of law: Strong
    Number of charter schools in operation (fall 2002): 11
    Number of students enrolled in charter schools (fall 2002): 5,262
- Publicly funded private school choice: No
- Privately funded school choice: No
- Home-school law: Low regulation
- Ranking on the Education Freedom Index (2001): 3rd out of 50 states

### K–12 Public Schools and Students (2001–2002)
- Public school enrollment: 115,486
- Students enrolled per teacher: 15.4
- Number of schools (2000–2001): 191
- Number of districts: 19
- Current expenditures: $1,110,044,000
- Current per-pupil expenditure: $9,612
- Amount of revenue from the federal government: 8.1%

### K–12 Public School Teachers (2001–2002)
- Number of teachers: 7,511
- Average salary: $48,363

### K–12 Private Schools (1999–2000)
- Private school enrollment: 22,779
- Number of schools: 96
- Number of teachers: 1,784

### K–12 Public and Private School Student Academic Performance
- NAEP test results:

| NAEP Tests Delaware Student Performance | State (National) 2000 Math Scale = 0–500 | | State (National) 2000 Science Scale = 0–300 | | State (National) 2000 Reading Scale = 0–500 | |
|---|---|---|---|---|---|---|
| | 4th Grade | 8th Grade | 4th Grade | 8th Grade | 4th Grade | 8th Grade |
| Average Scale Score | N/A (226) | N/A (274) | N/A (148) | N/A (149) | 212 (215) | 256 (261) |
| Advanced | N/A (3%) | N/A (5%) | N/A (3%) | N/A (4%) | 5% (6%) | 2% (2%) |
| Proficient | N/A (23%) | N/A (21%) | N/A (25%) | N/A (26%) | 20% (23%) | 23% (29%) |
| Basic | N/A (43%) | N/A (39%) | N/A (36%) | N/A (29%) | 32% (32%) | 41% (41%) |
| Below Basic | N/A (31%) | N/A (35%) | N/A (36%) | N/A (41%) | 43% (39%) | 34% (28%) |

- SAT weighted rank (2001): 15th out of 24 states and the District of Columbia
- ACT weighted rank (2001): N/A
- ALEC Academic Achievement Ranking: 33rd out of 50 states and the District of Columbia

## Summary

Delaware offers statewide public school choice and a strong charter school law. Parents may enroll their children in any public school in the state, subject only to limitations of space and racial balance.

## Background

Charter schools became an option in 1995 when then-Governor Thomas Carper, a Democrat, signed into law the Charter School Act of 1995. The law has been amended several times. During the first three years, the number of charters was limited to five per year; since then, there has been no limit on the number of schools that can be chartered. Both the state and local boards may charter schools. The initial chartering period is three years, and 65 percent of teachers must be certified.[119]

Since July 1996, Delaware parents have been able to enroll their children in any public school in the state if there is room. Transportation is provided for low-income students.[120]

In 1997, then-State Representative Deborah H. Capano (R–12) introduced House Bill 367 to create a private school choice program. The bill would have provided annual scholarship grants to the parents or guardians of students attending an accredited non-public school in participating school districts; would have allowed a school district to opt into the program by vote of the school board or by referendum; and would have provided scholarships of up to $2,700, based on family income. The bill died in the Education Committee.[121]

In 1999, H.B. 362 was introduced to provide a tax credit for education expenses, including tuition, book fees, transportation, computer software, and extracurricular activities fees. Credits would have been available for families earning under $100,000. Depending on annual income, families would have received a credit

ranging from $1,000 to $3,000 per year. The bill died in committee.[122]

## Developments in 2002 and 2003

In 2002, the governor signed three bills—Senate Bill 291, S.B. 298, and S.B. 168—that amended the charter school law. S.B. 291 requires schools to keep students for at least one year, requires the Delaware Department of Education to review and possibly sanction a management company that fails to open a school as planned, and sets deadlines for application and for obtaining a certificate of occupancy prior to opening the school. S.B. 298 reduced the length of a leave of absence teachers may take from a traditional public school to teach in a charter school. S.B. 168 clarified the roles and responsibilities of chartering authorities.[123]

## Position of the Governor / Composition of the State Legislature

Governor Ruth Ann Minner, a Democrat, has expressed support for charter schools. Republicans control the Delaware House; Democrats control the Senate.

## State Contacts

**Delaware Charter Schools Network**
Martha Manning, Executive Director
100 West 10th Street, Suite 704
Wilmington DE 19801
Phone: (302) 778-5999
Fax: (302) 778-5998
E-mail: Martha@focuskids.org

**Delaware Department of Education**
Dr. Larry Gabbert, Charter Schools Administrator
P.O. Box 1402
401 Federal Street
Dover, DE 19903-1402
Phone: (302) 739-4629
Fax: (302) 739-4654

---

119. Center for Education Reform, "Charter School Legislation: Profile of Delaware's Charter School Law," 2001, at *http://edreform.com/charter_schools/laws/Delaware.htm*. See also *www.uscharterschools.org/pub/sp/18*.
120. See Delaware Code at *www.delcode.state.de.us/title14/chapter04.htm#TopOfPage*.
121. See *www.legis.state.de.us/Legislature.nsf/fsLISArchives?openframeset*.
122. See National School Boards Association Web site at *www.nsba.org/novouchers*.
123. See Delaware General Assembly Web site at *www.legis.state.de.us/*.

Fax: (302) 739-7768
Web site: www.doe.state.de.us
E-mail: lgabbert@doe.k12.de.us

**Delaware Home Education Association**
P.O. Box 268
Hartly, DE 19953
Web site: www.dheaonline.org
E-mail: info@dheaonline.org

**Delaware Public Policy Institute**
Pete Du Pont, Board of Trustees
Michael Strine, Executive Director
1201 North Orange Street, Suite 200
Wilmington, DE 19899
Phone: (302) 655-7908
Fax: (302) 654-0691
Web site: www.dscc.com/dppi
E-mail: petedupont@att.net

**Focus on the Kids, Inc.**
Martha Manning, Executive Director
100 West 10th Street, Suite 704
Wilmington, DE 19801

Phone: (302) 778-5999
Fax: (302) 778-5998
Web site: www.focuskids.org
E-mail: MarthMLM@aol.com

**Rodel Charitable Foundation of Delaware**
Stephanie Clark Fitzgerald, President and CEO
100 West 10th Street Suite 704
Wilmington, Delaware 19801
Phone: (302) 571-1535
E-mail: fitzgeraldstephaniec@yahoo.com

## State School Report Card

**Delaware Department of Education**
Web site: www.doe.state.de.us/del_schools/
school_information.htm

**Greatschools.net**
Web site: www.greatschools.net/modperl/go/DE

# DISTRICT OF COLUMBIA

## District Profile (Updated May 2003)

### School Choice Status
- Public school choice: Citywide
- Charter school law: Established 1996
    Strength of law: Strong
    Number of charter schools in operation (fall 2002): 39
    Number of students enrolled in charter schools (fall 2002): 11,530
- Publicly funded private school choice: No
- Privately funded school choice: Yes
- Home-school law: Low regulation
- Ranking on the Education Freedom Index: N/A

### K–12 Public Schools and Students (2001–2002)
- Public school enrollment: 68,449
- Students enrolled per teacher: 13.1
- Number of schools (2000–2001): 165
- Number of districts: 37
- Current expenditures: $753,562,000
- Current per-pupil expenditure: $11,009
- Amount of revenue from the federal government: 14.6%

### K–12 Public School Teachers (2001–2002)
- Number of teachers: 5,235
- Average salary: $47,049

### K–12 Private Schools (1999–2000)
- Private School Enrollment: 16,690
- Number of Schools: 89
- Number of Teachers: 1,898

### K–12 Public and Private School Student Academic Performance
- NAEP test results:

| NAEP Tests D.C. Student Performance | State (National) 2000 Math Scale = 0–500 | | State (National) 2000 Science Scale = 0–300 | | State (National) 2000 Reading Scale = 0–500 | |
|---|---|---|---|---|---|---|
| | 4th Grade | 8th Grade | 4th Grade | 8th Grade | 4th Grade | 8th Grade |
| Average Scale Score | 193 (226) | 234 (274) | N/A (148) | N/A (149) | 182 (215) | 236 (261) |
| Advanced | 1% (3%) | 1% (5%) | N/A (3%) | N/A (4%) | 3% (6%) | 1% (2%) |
| Proficient | 5% (23%) | 5% (21%) | N/A (25%) | N/A (26%) | 7% (23%) | 10% (29%) |
| Basic | 18% (43%) | 17% (39%) | N/A (36%) | N/A (29%) | 18% (32%) | 32% (41%) |
| Below Basic | 76% (31%) | 77% (35%) | N/A (36%) | N/A (41%) | 72% (39%) | 56% (28%) |

- SAT weighted rank (2001): 25th out of 24 states and the District of Columbia
- ACT weighted rank (2001): N/A
- ALEC Academic Achievement Ranking: 50th out of 50 states and the District of Columbia[124]

## Summary

The District of Columbia has a strong charter school law and offers public school choice.[125] Support for choice has grown substantially since D.C. residents voted down a tax credit referendum in 1981.[126] Low-income students may apply for vouchers provided by private scholarship foundations.

## Background

On November 2, 1995, the U.S. House of Representatives passed a voucher proposal for students in the District of Columbia as an amendment to the fiscal year (FY) 1996 D.C. appropriations bill (H.R. 2546). The amendment, proposed by then-Representative Steve Gunderson (R–WI), would have provided funding for charter schools, would have given $3,000 vouchers to students whose family income fell below the poverty level, and would have provided $1,500 vouchers to students whose family incomes did not exceed 180 percent of the poverty level. The vouchers would have been redeemable at a public, private, or religious school in the District or surrounding counties in Virginia and Maryland.[127]

Representative Gunderson's voucher proposal died in the U.S. Senate following a filibuster led by Senator Edward Kennedy (D–MA), but a charter school plan that Gunderson sponsored was passed. The strong law set up two chartering authorities, the D.C. Board of Education and a Public Charter School Board, which could approve as many as 20 charter schools each year. Any entity interested in opening a charter school could submit an application, and the school, if its application was approved, would receive an automatic waiver from most District education laws.[128]

Consideration of a D.C. school choice plan was revived when then-Senator Dan Coats (R–IN) and Senators Sam Brownback (R–KS), Joseph Lieberman (D–CT), Mary Landrieu (D–LA), and Judd Gregg (R–NH) introduced the D.C. Student Opportunity Scholarship Act of 1997 (then-Representative Richard Armey (R–TX) introduced similar legislation in the House). The legislation would have provided scholarships of up to $3,200 for the District's poorest students in kindergarten through 12th grade to attend a public, private, or religious school of choice in the metropolitan area. The Senate approved the bill by voice vote on November 9, 1997, and the House passed it by a vote of 214 to 206 on April 30, 1998. However, President Bill Clinton vetoed the measure in May 1998.[129]

Three days after the President's veto, *The Washington Post* published the results of a May 1998 poll of District residents that found significant support for using federal dollars to send children to private or religious schools: 65 percent of the District's African–Americans surveyed who had incomes under $50,000 favored the option. Overall, 56 percent of District residents supported school choice.[130]

A 1999 Heritage Foundation analysis of African–American students in Catholic and public schools in the District found that, when demographic and socioeconomic factors were held constant, the children in Catholic schools performed better in mathematics on the national

---

124. D.C. and Mississippi tie for 50th place on the ALEC Academic Achievement Ranking.

125. In order to transfer to another public school, students must receive permission from the principal of the new school. See District of Columbia Public Schools Web site at *www.k12.dc.us/deps/policyfaq.html#transfers*.

126. E. G. West, "An Analysis of The District of Columbia: Education Tax Credit Initiative," Cato Institute *Policy Analysis*, October 27, 1981.

127. Mark Pitsch and Peter Schmidt, "D.C. Bill Stirs Debate Over Federal Policy," *Education Week*, November 15, 1995.

128. Center for Education Reform, "Charter School Legislation: Profile of the District of Columbia's Charter School Law," 2001, at *http://edreform.com/charter_schools/laws/District.htm*.

129. S. 1502, the District of Columbia Student Opportunity Scholarship Act of 1997, sponsored by Senator Daniel Coats, was vetoed on May 20, 1998.

130. Sari Horwitz, "Poll Finds Backing for D.C. School Vouchers: Blacks Support Idea More Than Whites," *The Washington Post*, May 23, 1998, pp. F1, F7.

assessments than did their public school counterparts. In fact, the performance gap increased considerably as higher grade levels were considered: While 4th grade students in Catholic schools scored 6.5 percent higher than their public school peers, 8th grade students in Catholic schools scored more than 8.2 percent higher than their public school counterparts. The average 8th grade black Catholic-school student outscored 72 percent of students in public schools.[131]

In 1993, Douglas D. Dewey and George A. Pieler founded the Washington Scholarship Fund to provide low-income students with partial scholarships to attend private schools. In 1994, 30 children received scholarships averaging $850. Currently, the WSF provides nearly 1,400 students with scholarships averaging $1,380.[132] The WSF has partnered with the Children's Scholarship Fund (CSF).[133]

Also in 1993, Ambassador Henry D. Owen and Theodore A. Schwab founded Capital Partners for Education (CPE), which provides scholarships and mentoring for low-income high school students. CPE has grown from serving six students in its first year to supporting more than 60 young people at 14 partner schools. Mentors are drawn from the local professional community.[134]

A 2000 study of 810 students who received the Washington Scholarship Fund scholarships found that, after one year, African–American students in grades 2 to 5 who transferred to private schools outperformed their public school counterparts by 7 percentage points on math tests and 3 points on reading tests. The study also found that, while nearly half of private school parents gave their children's schools an "A," only 15 percent of public school parents did.[135]

A 2000 Harvard University study of students in grades 2 to 8 reported that African–American students in the District of Columbia, New York City, and Dayton, Ohio, had outscored their public school classmates since transferring to private schools with the help of privately funded vouchers. The report compared public and private school students who had similar family backgrounds. D.C. students who had transferred showed the greatest advances, moving 9 percentile points ahead of their public school peers in combined reading and math test scores.[136]

In October 2001, the D.C. Board of Education considered opening charter schools for students with special needs to rein in special education costs. Throughout the preceding school year, the District had educated 1,830 special-needs children in private schools at an average public expense of $36,000 per pupil per year.[137]

## Developments in 2002 and 2003

Within days of the U.S. Supreme Court's decision supporting the use of vouchers in Cleveland, Ohio, U.S. Senator Judd Gregg (R–NH) and then-U.S. Representative Richard Armey (R–TX) introduced the D.C. Student Opportunity Scholarship Act of 2002 (H.R. 5033/S. 2866) to provide vouchers worth up to $5,000 for students to enroll in a public, private, or parochial school. "The Supreme Court has spoken on educational choice," Representative Armey declared when he introduced his bill. "Now it's time for Congress to do its part on behalf of low-income parents that simply want a better education for their children. Needy children in the District and across the country have waited long enough."[138] The bills were referred to committee but progressed no further. Senator Joseph Lieberman (D–CT) supported the initiative, saying that "I remain convinced that private

131. Kirk A. Johnson, "Comparing Math Scores of Black Students in D.C.'s Public and Catholic Schools," Heritage Foundation *Center for Data Analysis Report* No. 99–08, October 7, 1999.
132. "WSF History," Washington Scholarship Fund, at *www.wsf-dc.org/info/history.html*.
133. See Children's Scholarship Fund Web site at *www.scholarshipfund.org*.
134. See Capital Partners for Education Web site at *www.cpfe.org/index.htm*.
135. Paul Peterson, William Howell, and Patrick Wolfe, "School Choice in Washington, D.C.: An Evaluation After One Year," February 2000; prepared for Conference on Vouchers, Charters, and Public Education, sponsored by the Program on Education Policy and Governance, Harvard University, March 2000.
136. Paul Peterson, "Test-Score Effects of School Vouchers in Dayton, Ohio, New York City, and Washington, D.C.: Evidence from Randomized Field Trials," Harvard University and Brookings Institution, August 2000.
137. Vaishali Honawar, "D.C. Seeks Charters for Special Education," *The Washington Times*, October 1, 2001.
138. Editorial, "Vouchers for D.C.," *The Washington Times*, July 14, 2002.

school choice, while clearly not the solution to what ails our public schools, is a reform idea worth testing, particularly while we are waiting for the No Child Left Behind Act to take hold, and could be a temporary lifeline for poor students who would otherwise be trapped in chronically failing schools."[139]

Charter school leaders have had difficulty finding adequate space for schools and have accused the city of offering them unsafe buildings that needed millions of dollars worth of repairs. By law, unless the District can make a significantly larger profit by selling a property to another buyer, it must give charter schools the first option to buy surplus buildings. According to Friends of Choice in Urban Schools (FOCUS), of the 60 school buildings declared "surplus" over the past few years, charter schools have received only 10. The per-pupil facilities allocation for charter schools was reduced from $1,422 in 2001 to $1,237 for fall 2002.[140]

According to a study released in October 2002 by New American Schools, students at the KIPP DC:KEY Academy—one of the country's Knowledge Is Power Program (KIPP) charter schools—achieved significant gains in academic achievement in 2001. The KIPP DC:Key Academy, which was opened in 2001, serves predominantly low-income children in Southeast D.C. Students at this school improved their Stanford 9 reading scores by 12 points and their math scores by 24 points. The first KIPP school opened in 1994 in Houston, Texas. In 2002, 10 KIPP schools were in operation, and plans were underway to open 19 more in 2003. Hallmarks of these schools are a longer school day, rigorous academic standards, and strong discipline.[141]

In December 2002, a task force recommended that the D.C. Board of Education make it more difficult for students to make out-of-boundary transfers to other public schools. The task force recommended that the District replace the first-come, first-served open enrollment system with a lottery. Siblings would be given priority, and

principals could reject applicants who had a history of academic or disciplinary problems.[142]

In early 2003, President George W. Bush proposed that funds be included in the FY 2004 budget for a pilot voucher program in the District. Several prominent D.C. leaders have voiced their support, including D.C. Mayor Anthony A. Williams (D) and D.C. School Board President Peggy Cooper Cafritz. In an interview with *The Washington Post*, the mayor explained, "We've got a model we've been using for 140 years. I think it's time to try something else." Kevin P. Chavous (D), D.C. Council member and chairman of the Committee on Education, Libraries, and Recreation, backs vouchers as part of a proposal to increase support for charter and traditional schools. According to Chavous, "No school bureaucracy will reform itself internally. It only comes through pressure. And the most effective form of pressure is choice."[143]

D.C. voucher legislation has been introduced by Representative Jeff Flake (R–AZ) and Senator Gregg. The bills (H.B. 684 and S. 4, respectively) would provide low-income students with vouchers to attend a public or private school of choice. Families with incomes no higher than 185 percent of the national poverty level would be eligible for the vouchers. H.B. 684 has been referred to the House Committee on Government Reform, and S. 4 has been referred to the Senate Committee on Health, Education, Labor, and Pensions.[144]

## Position of the Mayor

Mayor Anthony Williams, a Democrat, is in favor of parental choice in education.

## District Contacts

**American Enterprise Institute (AEI)**
Fredrick M. Hess, Resident Scholar
1150 17th Street, NW
Washington, DC 20036
Phone: (202) 862-5800
Fax: (202) 862-7178

139. Center for Education Reform *Newswire*, July 3, 2002, at *www.edreform.com*.

140. Vaishali Honawar, "Charter Schools in 'Crisis'," *The Washington Times*, July 22, 2002, p. A1.

141. Jay Matthews, "Test Scores Are Up at KIPP Schools," *The Washington Post*, October 21, 2002, p. B4.

142. Editorial, "Free D.C. Schoolchildren," *The Washington Times*, December 8, 2002.

143. Craig Timberg, "Williams Sheds Light On Vouchers Stance," *The Washington Post*, May 3, 2003; Page B01.

144. See Library of Congress Web site, 108th Congress, H.B. 684 and S. 4, at *http://thomas.loc.gov/bss/d108query.html*.

Web site: www.aei.org
E-mail: info@aei.org

## American Legislative Exchange Council (ALEC)
Trent Barton, Director, Education Task Force
1129 20th Street, NW, Suite 500
Washington, DC 20036
Phone: (202) 466-3800
Fax: (202) 466-3801
Web site: www.alec.org
E-mail: tbarton@alec.org

## AppleTree Institute for Education Innovation
Jack McCarthy, Managing Director
101 D Street, SE, 2nd Floor
Washington, DC 20003
Phone: (202) 544-8650
Fax: (202) 544-8678
Web site: www.appletreeinstitute.org
E-mail: lextowle@aol.com

## Black Alliance for Educational Options
Lawrence C. Patrick III, President and CEO
501 C Street, NE, Suite 3
Washington, DC 20002
Phone: (202) 544-9870
Fax: (202) 544-7680
Web site: www.baeo.org
E-mail: lawrence@baeo.org

## Bolling Area Home Educators
P.O. Box 8401
Washington, DC 20336
Phone: (202) 562-3952
Web site: http://members.truepath.com/bahe
E-mail: bahewelcome@earthlink.net

## Brookings Institution
Tom Loveless, Ph.D.
Director, Brown Center on Education Policy
1775 Massachusetts Avenue, NW
Washington, DC 20036
Phone: (202) 797-6000
Fax: (202) 797-6004

## Capital Partners in Education
Khari Brown, Executive Director
1524 35th Street, NW
Washington, DC 20007
Phone: (202) 338-1330
Fax: (202) 338-1877
Web site: www.cpfe.org

## Cato Institute
David Salisbury, Director,
Center for Educational Freedom
Casey Lartigue, Education Policy Analyst
1000 Massachusetts Avenue, NW

Washington, DC 20001
Phone: (202) 842-0200
Fax: (202) 842-3490
Web site: www.cato.org
E-mail: cjl@cato.org
E-mail: dsalisbury@cato.org

## Center for Education Reform
Jeanne Allen, President
1001 Connecticut Avenue, NW, Suite 204
Washington, DC 20036
Phone: (202) 822-9000
Fax: (202) 822-5077
Web site: www.edreform.com
E-mail: cer@edreform.com

## Citizens for a Sound Economy (CSE)
Paul Hilliar, Director of Governmental Affairs
1900 M Street, NW, Suite 500
Washington, DC 20036
Phone: (202) 783-3870
Fax: (202) 783-4687
Web site: www.cse.org
E-mail: philliar@cse.org

## D.C. Public Charter School Resource Center
Shirley Monastra, Executive Director
1156 15th Street, NW, Suite 610
Washington, DC 20005
Phone: (202) 835-9011
Fax: (202) 659-8621
Web site: www.dcchartercenter.org
E-mail: smonastra@dcchartercenter.org

## D.C. Public Schools
Dr. Paul Vance, Superintendent
825 North Capitol Street, 9th Floor
Washington, DC 20002
Phone: (202) 442-5635
Web site: www.k12.dc.us/dcps/home.html

## Education Leaders Council
Lisa Graham Keegan, Chief Executive Officer
1225 19th Street, NW, Suite 400
Washington, DC 20036
Phone: (202) 261-2600
Fax: (202) 261-2638
Web site: www.educationleaders.org
E-mail: lmb@educationleaders.org

## Education Policy Institute
Myron Lieberman, Chairman
Charlene Haar, President
4401-A Connecticut Avenue, NW, Box 294
Washington, DC 20008
Phone: (202) 244-7535
Fax: (202) 244-7584
Web site: www.educationpolicy.org
E-mail: lieberman@educationpolicy.org

**Empower America**
Andrew Porter, Education Policy Analyst
1801 K Street, NW, Suite 410
Washington, DC 20006-5805
Phone: (202) 452-8200
Fax: (202) 833-0388
Web site: www.empoweramerica.org
E-mail: aporter@empower.org

**Family Research Council**
Bridget Maher, Policy Analyst
801 G Street, NW
Washington, DC 20001
Phone: (202) 393-2100
Fax: (202) 393-2134
Web site: www.frc.org
E-mail: bem@frc.org

**Fight for the Children**
Joseph E. Robert, Jr., Chairman
Kaleem Caire, Project Director
8133 Leesburg Pike, Suite 410
Vienna, VA 22182
Phone: (703) 245-3560
Fax: (703) 245-3570
Web site: www.fightforchildren.org

**Friends of Choice in Urban Schools (FOCUS)**
Robert Cane, Executive Director
1530 16th Street, NW
Washington, DC 20036
Phone: (202) 387-0405
Fax: (202) 667-3798
Web site: www.focus-dccharter.org
E-mail: rcane@focus-dccharter.org

**Graham Williams Group**
Armstrong Williams, President and CEO
201 Massachusetts Avenue, NE, Suite C3
Washington, DC 20002
Phone: (202) 546-5400
Fax: (202) 546-1218
Web site: www.ArmstrongWilliams.com
E-mail: arightside@aol.com

**The Heritage Foundation**
Krista Kafer, Senior Policy Analyst for Education
214 Massachusetts Avenue, NE
Washington, DC 20002-4999
Phone: (202) 546-4400
Fax: (202) 546-8328
Web site: www.heritage.org/schools
E-mail: Krista.Kafer@heritage.org

**Institute for Justice**
Richard D. Komer, Senior Litigation Attorney
1717 Pennsylvania Avenue, NW, Suite 200
Washington, DC 20006
Phone: (202) 955-1300
Fax: (202) 955-1329
Web site: www.instituteforjustice.org
E-mail: rkomer@ij.org

**National Center for Neighborhood Enterprise**
1424 16th Street, NW
Washington, DC 20036
Phone: (202) 518-6500
Fax: (202) 588-0314
Web site: www.ncne.com
E-mail: info@ncne.com

**Thomas B. Fordham Foundation**
Chester Finn, President
1627 K Street, NW, Suite 600
Washington, DC 20006
Phone: (202) 223-5452
Fax: (202) 223-9226
Web site: www.edexcellence.net
E-mail: cefinnjr@aol.com

**Washington Scholarship Fund**
Ethel Morgan, Program Director
1133 15th Street, NW, Suite 550
Washington, DC 20005
Phone: (202) 293-5560
Application Line: (202) 824-6673
Fax: (202) 293-7893
Web site: www.washingtonscholarshipfund.org

## State Report Card

**D.C. Department of Education**
Web site: www.k12.dc.us/dcps/data/dcdata-home.html

**DC School Search**
Web site: www.dcschoolsearch.com/shopping

**Greatschools.net**
Web site: www.greatschools.net/modperl/go/DC

**Metropolitan Area Boards of Education**
Web site: www.fcps.edu/DFnS/OBS/MABE2001.PDF

***The Washington Post***
Web Site: www.washingtonpost.com/wp-dyn/education/metroschools

# FLORIDA

## State Profile (Updated May 2003)

### School Choice Status
- Public school choice: Interdistrict/voluntary
- State constitution: Blaine amendment
- Charter school law: Established 1996
  - Strength of law: Strong
  - Number of charter schools in operation (fall 2002): 227
  - Number of students enrolled in charter schools (fall 2002): 53,350
- Publicly funded private school choice: Yes
- Privately funded school choice: Yes
- Home-school law: Moderate regulation
- Ranking on the Education Freedom Index (2001): 4th out of 50 states

### K–12 Public Schools and Students (2001–2002)
- Public school enrollment: 2,500,161
- Students enrolled per teacher: 18.4
- Number of schools (2000–2001): 3,231
- Number of Districts: 67
- Current expenditures: $15,581,937,000
- Current per-pupil expenditure: $6,232
- Amount of revenue from the federal government: 9.6%

### K–12 Public School Teachers (2001–2002)
- Number of teachers: 135,866
- Average salary: $38,719

### K–12 Private Schools (1999–2000)
- Private school enrollment: 290,872
- Number of schools: 1,545
- Number of teachers: 22,929

### K–12 Public and Private School Student Academic Performance
- NAEP test results:

| NAEP Tests Florida Student Performance | State (National) 2000 Math Scale = 0–500 | | State (National) 2000 Science Scale = 0–300 | | State (National) 2000 Reading Scale = 0–500 | |
|---|---|---|---|---|---|---|
| | 4th Grade | 8th Grade | 4th Grade | 8th Grade | 4th Grade | 8th Grade |
| Average Scale Score | N/A (226) | N/A (274) | N/A (148) | N/A (149) | 207 (215) | 253 (261) |
| Advanced | N/A (3%) | N/A (5%) | N/A (3%) | N/A (4%) | 5% (6%) | 1% (2%) |
| Proficient | N/A (23%) | N/A (21%) | N/A (25%) | N/A (26%) | 18% (23%) | 22% (29%) |
| Basic | N/A (43%) | N/A (39%) | N/A (36%) | N/A (29%) | 31% (32%) | 42% (41%) |
| Below Basic | N/A (31%) | N/A (35%) | N/A (36%) | N/A (41%) | 46% (39%) | 35% (28%) |

- SAT weighted rank (2001): 20th out of 24 states and the District of Columbia
- ACT weighted rank (2001): N/A
- ALEC Academic Achievement Ranking: 42nd out of 50 states and the District of Columbia

## Summary

Florida leads the country in providing education choices for children. The state provides A+ scholarships for students in failing schools, McKay Scholarships for students with disabilities, tax credits for donations to scholarship organizations, and over 200 charter schools. Eligible high school students may take college courses for high school and postsecondary credit.[145]

## Background

In 1973, the Florida legislature enacted a dual enrollment law allowing eligible high school students to enroll in free college or vocational classes for high school and college credit.[146]

School choice did not become a significant issue until 1996, when the state enacted a charter school law. House Bill 403 allowed for the creation of three to seven charter schools per district, depending on the size of the district. It also required school districts to develop limited open enrollment among their public schools.[147] The plan was subject to desegregation plans. The state did not require the districts to implement their school choice plans.[148]

Subsequent reauthorizations have strengthened the law. Each school district may open 12–28 new charter schools, depending on the size of the districts. An unlimited number of traditional public schools may convert to charter schools. Each school receives 100 percent of the funding minus administrative services fees, not to exceed 5 percent of the total funding. Teachers do not have to be certified.[149]

In June 1999, Governor Jeb Bush signed the A+ Plan for Education, which offers state-paid tuition scholarships to children in failing public schools to attend a public, private, or religious school of choice. The Florida House approved the A+ plan by a vote of 70 to 48, and the Senate approved it by a vote of 25 to 15.[150] The legislation set up a grading system for Florida's public schools based on test scores on the Florida Comprehensive Assessment Test (FCAT). Students at schools receiving a grade of "F" for two years in a four-year period can transfer to a higher-scoring public school or a private school with an Opportunity Scholarship, valued at the state per-pupil expenditure or the tuition and fees of the private school, whichever is less.[151]

The day after the governor signed the A+ plan into law, People for the American Way, teachers unions, the American Civil Liberties Union (ACLU), and others filed suit, claiming the program violates both the state constitution and the U.S. Constitution. A month later, the American Federation of Teachers filed a second lawsuit against the plan. The Institute for Justice represented the five Pensacola families participating in the program and the Urban League of Greater Miami. A state judge struck down the private school choice provision of the program on March 14, 2000. The court ruled that the Florida scholarship program violated the constitutional mandate that the state "provide a free education through a system of public schools."[152]

In October 2000, the Florida First District Court of Appeals ruled that the school voucher program was constitutional and may remain in effect. The decision reversed the March ruling by the Leon County Circuit Court judge that the Opportunity Scholarships violated the state constitution, which bars aid to sectarian

---

145. Education Commission of the States, "Postsecondary Options: Dual/Concurrent Enrollment," July 2001.

146. See Florida Statute 240.116.

147. *The Blum Center's Educational Freedom Report* No. 35, May 24, 1996, at *www.marquette.edu/blum/efr35.html.*

148. FloridaChild, "Public School Choice," at *http://www.floridachild.org/aapubscochoice.html.*

149. Center for Education Reform, "Charter School Legislation: Profile of Florida's Charter School Law," 2001, at *http://edreform.com/charter_schools/laws/Florida.htm.*

150. Jessica L. Sandham, "Florida OKs 1st Statewide Voucher Plan," *Education Week*, May 5, 1999.

151. See Florida Department of Education Web site at *www.myflorida.com/myflorida/education/learn/aplusplan/you-Know.html.*

152. Institute for Justice, "Florida School Choice Case," at *www.ij.org/cases/index.html;* "Private School Choice Target in New Round of Court Challenges," *Education Week*, August 4, 1999.

institutions. The appellate court found that lawmakers experiment with different ways of working "for the common good" and that the state constitution "does not unalterably hitch the requirement to make adequate provision for education to a single, specified engine, that being the public school system."[153]

No other schools received a failing grade during the 1999–2000 school year; all of the schools that had received an "F" the prior year had made substantial progress on the writing part of the Florida Comprehensive Assessment Test.[154]

A 2000 survey of more than 750 public school teachers found significant support for the possibility that the availability of vouchers caused a dramatic improvement in test scores at some of Florida's worst-performing public schools. Of the teachers surveyed, 65 percent responded that the A+ plan played a "minor" or "major" role in the test score changes. Only 17 percent said that the plan played "no role."[155]

In late October 2000, the Pinellas School Board approved a public school choice plan. According to the plan, students entering the district's schools for the first time in fall 2003 will have to choose a school within the attendance area. Some students will be "grandfathered" into the system and allowed to attend their original neighborhood school. Black students who have been bused will be able to choose a school closer to their homes.[156]

On the private scholarship front, in 1998, Miami and Tampa Bay became Florida's first two Children's Scholarship Fund (CSF) "partner cities." The CSF matches the funds raised by residents in these cities to offer four-year scholarships to low-income children entering kindergarten through 8th grade to attend a school of choice.[157]

In April 2000, Tampa businessman John Kirtley announced that he would donate $2 million to private inner-city schools that agree to accept students using Opportunity Scholarships. Grants from Kirtley's nonprofit School Choice Fund could be used for books, computers, transportation, building expansion and renovation, or other needs, excluding tuition. At least 35 private schools in Florida applied for the grants.[158] Kirtley was the founder of the Florida Children's Fund, a private voucher program. In 2002, he became the president of Children First America, a national organization that provides scholarships, information to the public, and support for new choice organizations.[159]

During the 2000 legislative session, H.B. 1127 was introduced to give tax credits for contributions to scholarship organizations or public schools. Individuals would have received a credit of 65 percent of their contribution. The bill died in committee.[160]

In 2001, Jay P. Greene, Ph.D., released an analysis of the Florida A+ program. He found that during 1999–2000, the 76 failing schools had improved an average of 17.59 points in reading and 25.66 points in math on the state assessment (the FCAT), which uses a scale of 100 to 500, compared with 10.02 points in reading and 16.06 points in math for schools that had received a "D" rating.[161]

In July 2000, Volusia County became the state's first charter school district. The plan, approved by the governor, allows the district freedom from certain state regulations and laws in exchange for improved academic achievement. Volusia County is now the nation's largest charter district, with 65 schools serving roughly 60,000 students.[162]

In 2001, the governor signed into law Senate Bill 1180, which expanded a pilot voucher

153. George A. Clowes, "Court Upholds Florida Voucher Program," *School Reform News*, November 2000.

154. Analisa Nazareno, "School Voucher Storm Settles into a Lull," *The Miami Herald*, June 21, 2000, p. B1.

155. Chris Prawdzik, "Florida Teachers Concede Vouchers Spurred Improvement," Alexis de Tocqueville Institution, August 30, 2000.

156. Kelly Ryan, "School Choice Debate Goes Into Morning," *The St. Petersburg Times*, October 25, 2000.

157. See Children's Scholarship Fund Web site at *www.scholarshipfund.org*.

158. Jacqueline Charles, "Schools Offered $2 Million to Accept Voucher Students," *The Miami Herald*, April 21, 2000.

159. Florida Council of Independent Schools, *Independents*, Vol. 6, No. 2 (November/December 2002).

160. See National School Boards Association Web site at *www.nsba.org/novouchers*.

161. Scott S. Greenberger, "Voucher Backers Tout Fla. Scores," *The Boston Globe*, February 16, 2001, p. B3.

162. Diane Rado, "Florida Approves Charter District," *The St. Petersburg Times*, July 12, 2000.

program enacted in 1999. Under the original pilot program, two disabled students received vouchers to attend private schools. The new law made all special-needs students eligible. Parents who are dissatisfied with their children's academic progress may transfer their children to another public or private school using a publicly funded McKay Scholarship.[163] The McKay Scholarship was named after the bill's sponsor, then-State Senator John McKay, who has a child with a disability. In 2001, 4,000 students participated at an average cost of $6,000 per student; in 2002, 8,082 students participated.[164]

The governor also signed a bill to provide tax credits to corporations that donate to organizations that award scholarships to children from low-income families. A corporation can receive a dollar-for-dollar tax credit up to 75 percent of its state income tax liability. The state may award a maximum of $50 million in credits a year.[165] The scholarships, available to recipients who meet income eligibility thresholds, are worth $3,500 or the cost of tuition plus books and transportation, whichever is less. As of December 2002, 14,520 students had received scholarships funded through the tax credit program.[166]

Finally, the School Crowding Relief Intervention for Parents and Teachers Act, H.B. 303 and its companion bill (S.B. 504), was introduced to give each student in schools where enrollment exceeds 120 percent of capacity a $3,000 grant to use toward tuition at a private school. The House passed H.B. 303 by a vote of 63 to 54 on March 22, 2001. The Senate bill died in committee.[167]

On April 26, 2001, the Florida Supreme Court declined to review the October 2000 appeals court ruling to allow public funds to flow to private schools under the Opportunity Scholarship Program. The case was sent back to the Leon County Circuit Court, to consider the union's other claims.[168]

## Developments in 2002 and 2003

During the 2002 legislative session, H.B. 1587, the No Strings Attached Act, was introduced to enable all students to participate in the state's voucher program. Under the program, a school district could have opted to have more flexibility within the state accountability plan in exchange for offering its students Freedom Scholarships. The bill died in committee.[169]

The number of students using Opportunity Scholarships jumped from 45 in 2001 to 575 in 2002. In 2002, 80 schools received failing grades; for 10 of these schools, it was their second "F." Of 9,000 students affected, 900 have transferred to other public schools, and 577 have transferred to private schools. The number of students receiving McKay Scholarships surged to 9,000.[170]

The state's accountability plan has also produced systemwide improvements. On September 6, 2002, Governor Bush held a press conference to announce the release of four-year student FCAT gains in reading. Since implementation of the A+ plan in 1999, reading scores have improved significantly in three grade levels and among African–American, Hispanic, and white students. Steady gains were also noted for students in exceptional education programs.[171]

In July 2002, opponents of vouchers urged Leon County Circuit Judge P. Kevin Davey to rule against the Opportunity Scholarship program because they believe it violates the Florida constitution's Blaine amendment prohibiting tax money from aiding religious institutions. Barry Richard, attorney for Governor Bush, argued that funds do not go to aid religious institutions; rather, they go to parents who decide their destination. Under the opponents' argument, he

163. See National School Boards Association Web site at *www.nsba.org/novouchers*.

164. Lisa Goldstein, "Election Results Boost Special Ed. Vouchers," *Education Week*, December 4, 2002.

165. See National School Boards Association Web site at *www.nsba.org/novouchers*.

166. Kimberly Miller, "Corporate Tax Breaks Are Voucher Boon," *Palm Beach Post*, December 26, 2002, p. A1.

167. See National School Boards Association Web site at *www.nsba.org/novouchers*.

168. *Ibid.*

169. *Ibid.*

170. Alan Richard, "Florida Sees Surge in Use of Vouchers," *Education Week*, September 4, 2002.

171. Press release, "Governor Bush Announces Latest FCAT Reading Scores Show Rising Student Achievement," MyFlorida.com, September 6, 2002.

said, the Florida constitution would prohibit students from using state scholarships to attend religiously affiliated colleges and universities.[172]

In June, the Supreme Court of the United States upheld a similar program in Cleveland, Ohio, in *Zelman* v. *Simmons-Harris*. The Court ruled that it did not matter that government indirectly aided a religious institution. Nor did it matter what percentage of parents might ultimately choose a religious school as long as the program involved "true parental choice" and the choice plan was enacted for a valid secular purpose, such as improving educational opportunities for poor children.

On August 5, 2002, Judge Davey struck down the Opportunity Scholarship program, saying that the state constitution is "clear and unambiguous" in prohibiting the state from sending public funds to sectarian institutions.[173] The state has appealed the decision, and the judge has allowed the program to continue while the case makes its way through the courts.[174]

Higher courts could reverse the decision on federal constitutional grounds, finding that the exclusion of religious institutions in a publicly funded voucher program violates the First Amendment. Even if the Florida Supreme Court supports the circuit court's ruling, the decision could be appealed to the U.S. Supreme Court. According to Eugene Volokh, a University of California constitutional law expert, the result would be a ruling against a state law that excludes religious schools from voucher programs. A challenge to the Florida constitution in federal court would have a similar result.[175]

In 2003, several voucher and tax credit proposals were introduced. At the beginning of the year, Governor Bush proposed vouchers as a way to meet the mandate for smaller class sizes that was passed by referendum in November 2002. The cost of enabling students to transfer from overcrowded public schools to private

schools would be lower than the cost of building additional public school capacity. In a statement to the *Miami Herald*, Governor Bush said, "It's a cost-effective way of dealing with this issue. Many [districts] won't take it, but so what? That option should be there for them to consider."[176]

The legislature reacted with the introduction of several bills. S.B. 1646 would have allowed public school districts to implement vouchers to lower class sizes. Under the program, interested parents would have received a Florida Learning Access Grant to send their child to a school of choice. On March 13, an Appropriations Subcommittee removed the grants from the bill. S.B. 2532 and H.B. 213 would have created the Reduce Class Size Scholarship Opportunity Program, which would have provided vouchers for low-income children. H.B. 45 would have provided scholarships to students to attend a private school if their public school district did not comply with the class size mandate. The bills died in committee.[177]

Other efforts were directed at expanding Florida's current parental choice programs. S.B. 2062 would have increased the cap on the corporate tax credit for donations to scholarship organizations from $50 million to $75 million. The bill passed the Senate on April 15 but died in the House. H.B. 805 would have enabled military families to participate in the tax credit scholarship program; $10 million of credits would have been set aside for this purpose. The bill was passed by the House on March 25 and approved by the Senate Military and Veteran's Affairs Committee on May 2 but died in the Senate Committee on Education. H.B. 703 would have provided students a Florida Learning Access Grant of $3,500 for use at an eligible private school. The bill stalled after passing several committee votes.[178]

172. Jim Saunders, "Voucher Uproar Rages On," *The Florida Times–Union*, July 10, 2002.
173. Michael A. Fletcher, "Florida's Voucher Law Is Struck Down," *The Washington Post*, August 6, 2002, p. A7.
174. Richard, "Florida Sees Surge in Use of Vouchers."
175. Christine Hall, "Florida Voucher Decision Could Be Reversed on Constitutional Grounds," *CNS News*, August 7, 2002.
176. Joni James and Steve Harrison, "Vouchers Proposed to Reduce Class Sizes: Governor Says It's Cost Effective," *The Miami Herald*, January 24, 2003, p. 1.
177. See Florida Legislature Web site at *www.leg.state.fl.us/*.
178. *Ibid.*

# School Choice 2003

## Position of the Governor / Composition of the State Legislature

Governor Jeb Bush, a Republican, strongly supports parental choice in education. Republicans control both houses of the legislature.

## State Contacts

### Children First Central Florida
Sally Simmons, Executive Director
1101 North Lake Destiny Road, Suite 375
Maitland, FL 32751
Phone: (407) 629-8787
Fax: (407) 629-1319
Web site: www.childrenfirstcf.org
E-mail: ceocenfla@aol.com

### Children's Scholarship Fund–Florida
Administered by Children's Scholarship Fund National (Southeast)
8 West 38th Street, 9th Floor
New York, NY 10018
Phone: (888) 239-9350
Fax: (212) 515-7124
Web site: www.scholarshipfund.org
E-mail: neworleans@scholarshipfund.org

### Family First
Mark Merrill, President
101 East Kennedy Boulevard, Suite 1070
Tampa, FL 33602
Phone: (813) 222-8300
Fax: (813) 222-8301
Web site: www.familyfirst.net
E-mail: info@familyfirst.net

### Florida Catholic Conference
Larry Keough, Associate for Education
313 South Calhoun Street
Tallahassee, FL 32301-1807
Phone: (850) 222-3803
Fax: (850) 681-9548
Web site: www.flacathconf.org
E-mail: lkeough@flacathconf.org

### Florida Charter School Resource Center
Dr. Cathy Wooley-Brown, Director
University of South Florida
Tampa, FL 33260
Phone: (813) 974-8350
Fax: (813) 974-7823
Web site: www.charterschools.usf.edu
E-mail: emily@iirp.coedu.usf.edu

### FloridaChild
Dr. Patrick Heffernan, President
Dr. Tina Dupree, Director
1000 Brickell Avenue, Suite 920
Miami, FL 33131
Phone: (800) 805-4485
Fax: (305) 702-5580
Web site: www.floridachild.org
E-mail: heff@floridians.org
E-mail: tdupree@floridachild.org

### Florida Citizens for a Sound Economy (CSE)
Slade O'Brien, Director
110 East Atlantic Avenue, Suite 340
Delray Beach, FL 33444
Phone: (561) 266-8876
Web site: www.cse.org
E-mail: cse@cse.org

### Florida Coalition of Christian Private Schools Association
P.O. Box 13227
Fort Pierce, FL 34979-3227
Phone: (772) 461-9776
Web site: www.flhomeschooling.com
E-mail: FCCPSA@flhomeschooling.com

### Florida Consortium of Charter Schools
Bob Haig, President/CEO
1217 SE 3rd Avenue
Fort Lauderdale, FL 33316
Phone: (954) 522-2997
Fax: (954) 522-3159
Web site: www.floridacharters.org
E-mail: joanne.nelson@tampa.yfcs.com

### Florida Department of Education
Office of School Choice
J. C. Bowman, Director
Robert Metty, Ed.D.,
Director, Scholarship Programs
Turlington Building
325 West Gaines Street, Suite 532
Tallahassee, FL 32399-0400
Phone: (850) 488-5011
Fax: (850) 414-0783
Web site: www.firn.edu/doe/doehome.htm
E-mail: JC.Bowman@FLDOE.org
E-mail: Robert.Metty@fldoe.org

### Florida Federation of Catholic Parents
Joe Magri, President
5510 West Cypress Avenue
Tampa, FL 33607
Phone: (813) 281-9000
Fax: (813) 281-2223
E-mail: merklemagri@cs.com

### Florida Parent–Educators Association Inc.
9951 Atlantic Boulevard, Suite 102
Jacksonville, FL 32225
Phone: (877) 275-3732
Fax: (904) 338-9859

Web site: www.fpea.com
E-mail: office@fpea.com

**Helping Educate Responsible, Outstanding and Enlightened Students, Inc. (HEROES)**
Greg Forster, Executive Director
424 B, South 3rd Street
Jacksonville Beach, FL 32250
Phone: (904) 247-6033
Fax: (904) 247-6034
Web site: www.forheroes.com
E-mail: jaxheroes@aol.com

**The Honorable Jim Horne**
State Commissioner of Education
325 West Gaines Street, Suite 1514
Tallahassee, FL 32399
Phone: (850) 487-1785
Fax: (850) 413-0378

**Independent Voices for Better Education**
Shelley Nelson, President
95 Carmen Street
Melbourne Beach, FL 32951
Phone: (321) 952-1793
Web site: www.ivbe.org
E-mail: sjnelson@aol.com

**James Madison Institute**
J. Stanley Marshall, Chairman
James C. McDowell, President
Curtis C. Leonard, Executive Vice President
P.O. Box 37460
Tallahassee, FL 32315
Phone: (850) 386-3131
Fax: (850) 386-1807

Web site: www.jamesmadison.org
E-mail: jmi@jamesmadison.org

**Miami Inner City Angels (MICA)**
Michael Carricarte, President
Christina Ingelmo, Director
7001 SW 97th Avenue
Miami, FL 33173
Phone: (305) 275-1412
Fax: (305) 275-1454
E-mail: mica@amedex.com

**Urban League of Greater Miami**
T. Willard Fair, President
8500 NW 25th Avenue
Miami, FL 33147
Phone: (305) 696-4450
Fax: (305) 696-4455
E-mail: twfair@msn.com

## State School Report Card

**Florida Department of Education**
Web site: www.firn.edu/doe/bin00005/menus/statistics.html

**Florida Times Union**
Web site: www.jacksonville.com/community/school_frame.html

**Greatschools.net**
Web site: www.greatschools.net/modperl/go/FL

**Jacksonville School Match**
Web site: www.jacksonville.com/schoolmatch

**Palm Beach County Schools**
Web site: www.palmbeach.k12.fl.us/schools

# GEORGIA

## State Profile (Updated May 2003)

### School Choice Status
- Public school choice: Interdistrict/voluntary
- State constitution: Blaine amendment
- Charter school law: Established in 1993
    Strength of law: Weak
    Number of charter schools in operation (fall 2002): 35
    Number of students enrolled in charter schools (fall 2002): 15,117
- Publicly funded private school choice: No
- Privately funded school choice: Yes
- Home-school law: Moderate regulation
- Ranking on the Education Freedom Index (2001): 35th out of 50 states

### K–12 Public Schools and Students (2000–2001)
- Public school enrollment: 1,470,634
- Students enrolled per teacher: 15.1
- Number of schools (2000–2001): 1,946
- Number of districts: 180
- Current expenditures: $11,225,320,000
- Current per-pupil expenditure: $7,633
- Amount of revenue from the federal government: 6.4%

### K–12 Public School Teachers (2001–2002)
- Number of teachers: 97,563
- Average salary: $44,073

### K–12 Private Schools (1999–2000)
- Private school enrollment: 116,407
- Number of schools: 592
- Number of teachers: 10,677
- K–12 Public and Private School Student Academic Performance

### NAEP test results:

| NAEP Tests Georgia Student Performance | State (National) 2000 Math Scale = 0–500 | | State (National) 2000 Science Scale = 0–300 | | State (National) 2000 Reading Scale = 0–500 | |
|---|---|---|---|---|---|---|
| | 4th Grade | 8th Grade | 4th Grade | 8th Grade | 4th Grade | 8th Grade |
| Average Scale Score | 220 (226) | 266 (274) | 143 (148) | 144 (149) | 210 (215) | 257 (261) |
| Advanced | 1% (3%) | 3% (5%) | 3% (3%) | 2% (4%) | 5% (6%) | 1% (2%) |
| Proficient | 17% (23%) | 16% (21%) | 20% (25%) | 21% (26%) | 19% (23%) | 24% (29%) |
| Basic | 40% (43%) | 36% (39%) | 35% (36%) | 29% (29%) | 31% (32%) | 43% (41%) |
| Below Basic | 42% (31%) | 45% (35%) | 42% (36%) | 48% (41%) | 45% (39%) | 32% (28%) |

- SAT weighted rank (2001): 23rd out of 24 states and the District of Columbia
- ACT weighted rank (2001): N/A
- ALEC Academic Achievement Ranking: 45th out of 50 states and the District of Columbia

## Summary

Georgia offers limited public school choice and has a weak charter school law.[179] Eligible junior and senior high school students may take college courses for high school and postsecondary credit.[180] Low-income students may apply for scholarships provided by private scholarship foundations.

## Background

In 1993, then-Governor Zell Miller signed a charter school law allowing an unlimited number of existing public schools to convert to charter schools upon the approval of two-thirds of the teachers, two-thirds of the parents, and the local and state school boards.[181]

Vouchers gained attention in 1993 when attorney Glenn Delk, president of Georgia Parents for Better Education, publicized a 1961 law that provided education grants to help families avoid desegregated public schools and attend a public or private school of choice. Section 20-2-640-650 of the Georgia Code specifies that

> Every child between the ages of six and 19 years residing in this state…who is otherwise eligible and qualified to attend the elementary and secondary public schools of the local school system wherein such child resides shall, in lieu of attending the public schools of such local school system be eligible to receive an education grant to be

expended for the purpose of paying or otherwise defraying the cost of tuition at a nonsectarian private school….[182]

Delk declared that the law "may have been passed for the wrong reasons, but we hope to use it for the right reasons. I think all parents should have a choice about whether they send their children to public or private schools. The people who can benefit the most are those who don't have a choice—low income black parents."[183] State officials deemed the law "unusable," but strong public interest encouraged then-Lieutenant Governor Pierre Howard, a Democrat, to call for special public hearings.[184] In 1997, the Georgia Supreme Court ruled that there was no funding mechanism available to provide the vouchers under the old law.[185]

In 1995, Governor Miller signed legislation to facilitate the process of forming or renewing a charter by changing the requirement for teacher support from a two-thirds vote to a simple majority. Another amendment to the charter school law extended the length of the charters from three to five years.[186]

A 1995 law enables junior and senior high school students to take selected higher education courses. Under the program, students may receive both secondary and postsecondary credit and graduate early from high school.[187]

During the 1998 legislative session, the legislature further amended the charter school law. Under the revised law, local schools, private

---

179. Students in state-designated poor-performing schools may transfer to higher-performing schools within the district. If a student lives closer to another school, has a parent who is a teacher or administrator, or is in an overcrowded school, he or she can transfer to another school. Otherwise, students may transfer out of the district with district permission. See Georgia Code, Sec. 20-14-41, 20-2-293, 20-2-294; Sec. 160-5-4-09.

180. Education Commission of the States, "Postsecondary Options: Dual/Concurrent Enrollment," July 2001.

181. Georgia Department of Education, "Georgia Charter Schools Statistics at a Glance," February 2003, at *www.doe.k12.ga.us/_documents/schools/charterschools/cs_stats.pdf*.

182. Susan Stevenot Sullivan, "School Choice Advocates Press for Voucher Funds," *Georgia Bulletin*, Archdiocese of Atlanta, October 21, 1993.

183. *Ibid.*

184. The Blum Center's *Educational Freedom Report* No. 3, November 24, 1993, at *www.marquette.edu/blum/efr3.html*.

185. Susan Laccetti Meyers, "School Vouchers: Multiple Choice U.S. High Court Ruling Rekindles Debate that Has Raged for Decades," *Atlanta Journal–Constitution*, June 30, 2002.

186. Georgia Department of Education, "Georgia Charter Schools Statistics at a Glance," February 2003, at *www.doe.k12.ga.us/_documents/schools/charterschools/cs_stats.pdf*.

187. Education Commission of the States, "Postsecondary Options: Dual/Concurrent Enrollment," July 2001.

individuals and organizations, or state or local entities can operate a charter school. A majority of the governing board of a charter school must be composed of parents whose children attend the school.[188]

In 1999, then-Senator Clay Land introduced an Early HOPE Scholarship bill, Senate Bill 68, designed to award state-funded scholarships to low-income families whose children attended poor-performing public schools. These vouchers would have been worth the cost of tuition at a private school or 90 percent of the state's expenditure per public school pupil, whichever was less. When Senator Land introduced the bill as a floor amendment to another education bill, a lengthy debate on choice ensued. The bill failed by a vote along party lines.[189]

Another school choice bill, S.B. 517, that was introduced during the 1999–2000 legislative session would have provided tax credits of up to $500 for donations to the Georgia Elementary and Secondary Education Assistance Corporation, which would have provided financial assistance for students enrolled in both public and private schools. The bill died in committee.[190]

In 2000, the legislature adopted House Bill 1187, which requires annual testing in core subjects and the establishment of an accountability office to monitor school performance. Under the law, the Georgia State Board of Education may grant parents of children in failing schools the option to transfer to another public school within their district.[191] In addition to allowing intradistrict transfers, H.B. 1187 also allows charter school applicants who have been rejected by the local school board to appeal to the state board and requires all charter schools to participate in the state's accountability system.[192]

The Georgia Public Policy Foundation (GPPF) established the Charter School Resource Center to help groups maneuver through the daunting legal and financial challenges involved in opening a charter school.[193] The GPPF also releases rankings of every public school in the state and encourages parents to learn more about their children's schools and to compare their school's performance against the performance of other schools.[194] Meanwhile, charter school petitioners and operators formed the Georgia Charter Schools Association to network, to lobby for changes in the state's charter school laws and policies, and to educate the public about charter schools.[195]

In 2001, three school choice bills were introduced in the state legislature. S.B. 200 would have established the Early HOPE Scholarship Program through which low-income students in failing schools could have received vouchers. These vouchers would have been worth the cost of tuition at a private school or 90 percent of the funding per public school pupil, whichever was less. S.B. 201 would have required the Georgia State Board of Education to implement a pilot voucher for poor children in three failing public schools throughout the state. As with S.B. 200, these vouchers would have been worth the cost of tuition at the private school of choice or 90 percent of the funding per public school pupil, whichever was less. H.B. 588 would have given taxpayers an income tax credit of up to $1,000 for education expenses, including private school tuition. All three bills failed to pass.[196]

## Developments in 2002 and 2003
The voucher and tax credit bills introduced during the 2001 legislative session (S.B. 200, S.B. 201, and H.B. 588) were carried over into the 2002 session, but no further action was taken.[197]

188. Ibid.
189. Georgia School Superintendents Association, Current News, February 2, 1999, at www.gssanet.org/new9900/n35336.html.
190. See National School Boards Association Web site at www.nsba.org/novouchers.
191. Milton and Rose D. Friedman Foundation, The Friedman Report, Issue 1, 2000.
192. Georgia Department of Education, "Georgia Charter Schools Statistics at a Glance," October 2002, at www.doe.k12.ga.us/charterschools/cs_stats.pdf.
193. See Charter School Resource Center Web site at www.gppf.org/education/charters.htm.
194. See Georgia Public Policy Foundation Web site at www.gppf.org/.
195. See Georgia Charter Schools Association Web site at www.gacharters.org/.
196. See National School Boards Association Web site at www.nsba.org/novouchers.
197. Ibid.

The legislature passed H.B. 1200, which made several changes in the charter school law. Local boards are now required to provide a written rationale for the rejection of a charter school plan. This law removed the blanket exemption provided by the 1998 law and requires applicants to list the specific laws and rules for which they request a waiver. It also removed the requirement that a majority of the governing board be composed of parents.[198]

Less than 1 percent of the 70,000 students attending failing schools in the Atlanta metropolitan area transferred to better schools under the federal No Child Left Behind Act, although the law requires districts to give students in poor-performing schools the option to transfer to other schools within the district. Among the factors contributing to their failure to transfer children from nonperforming schools, parents cited a lack of alternative higher-performing schools, unavailability of test scores to compare schools, and dissuasion by school officials.[199]

The Georgia Department of Education released a report showing that the state's charter schools are outpacing their traditional counterparts. Specifically, 93 percent of charter school students passed the state's standardized tests in all five subjects, in contrast to 85 percent of students in traditional public schools. Fewer charter school students repeat grades or drop out of school, yet Georgia charter schools serve a higher percentage of English-as-a-second-language learners and special education students.[200]

Representative Chip Rogers introduced H.B. 337 to provide a tax credit of up to $250 for home-schooling families and H.B. 985 to enable private and home-schooled students to participate in the dual enrollment program. No action was taken on either bill.

## Position of the Governor / Composition of the State Legislature

Governor Sonny Perdue, a Republican, has expressed support for charter schools but has stated no position on other forms of school choice. Republicans control the Senate, and Democrats control the House.

## State Contacts

### Children's Scholarship Fund–Atlanta
Administered by Louisiana CSF
Faith Sweeney, Executive Director
Sil Boria, Program Coordinator
7611 Maple Street, Suite F
New Orleans, LA 70118
Phone: (504) 862-6992
Fax: (504) 821-5271
Fax: (504) 862-6993
Web site: www.scholarshipfund.org
E-mail: csfsb@bellsouth.net

### Georgia Charter Schools Association
Phil Andrews, Executive Director
2606 Alston Drive, SE
Atlanta, GA 30317
Phone: (404) 371-9992
Fax: (404) 373-4354
Web site: www.gacharters.org

### Georgia Department of Education
Kathy Cox, Superintendent of Schools
Beverly Schrenger, Coordinator
Office of Charter Schools Compliance
205 Butler Street, 1770 Twin Towers East
Atlanta, GA 30334
Phone: (404) 656-2800
Fax: (404) 651-8984
Web site: www.doe.k12.ga.us/index.asp
E-mail: kcox@doe.k12.ga.us

### Georgia Family Council
Randall Hicks, President
5380 Peachtree Industrial Boulevard, Suite 100
Norcross, GA 30071-1565
Phone: (770) 242-0001
Fax: (770) 242-0501

### Georgia Home Education Association
1856 Pearl Way
Lilburn, GA 30047
Fax: (770) 461-9053
Web site: www.ghea.org
E-mail: info@ghea.org

---

198. Georgia Department of Education, "Georgia Charter Schools Statistics at a Glance," February 2003, at *www.doe.k12.ga.us/_documents/schools/charterschools/cs_stats.pdf.*

199. Jen Sansbury, "Obstacles Hold Kids in Bad Schools: No Child Left Behind Fails to Deliver Results," *Atlanta Journal–Constitution*, September 15, 2002, p. A1.

200. Center for Education Reform, *Education Reform Newswire*, November 19, 2002, at *www.edreform.com.*

**Georgia Parents for Better Education**
Glenn Delk, President
1355 Peachtree Street, NE, Suite 1150
Atlanta, GA 30309
Phone: (404) 876-3335
Fax: (404) 876-3338
E-mail: glenndelk@mindspring.com

**Georgia Public Policy Foundation**
Holly Robinson, Vice President
Charter School Resource Center
6100 Lake Forest Drive, Suite 110
Atlanta, GA 30328
Phone: (404) 256-4050
Fax: (404) 256-9909
Web site: www.gppf.org
E-mail: hrobinson@gppf.org

**Georgians for Freedom in Education**
209 Cobb Street
Palmetto, GA 30268
Phone: (770) 982-9828
Fax: (770) 982-9828

**North Georgia Home Education Association**
200 West Crest Road
Rossville, GA 30741-1410
Phone: (706) 861-1795
E-mail: Tdrennan@juno.com

**Southeastern Legal Foundation**
Phil Kent, President
Valle Dutcher, General Counsel
3340 Peachtree Road, NE, Suite 2515
Atlanta, GA 30326
Phone: (404) 365-8500
Fax: (404) 365-0017
Web site: www.southeasternlegal.org
E-mail: info@southeasternlegal.org

## State School Report Card
**Atlanta Digital City**
Web site: www.digitalcity.com/atlanta/
public_schools/?page=elem&state=ga

*Gainesville Times*
Web site: www.gainesvilletimes.com/communi-
ties/schools/index.html

**Georgia Department of Education**
Web site: http://accountability.doe.k12.ga.us/
report01/

**Georgia Public Policy Foundation**
Web site: www.gppf.org

**Greatschools.net**
Web site: www.greatschools.net/modperl/go/GA

**Savannah Morning News**
Web site: www.savannahnow.com/features/
ourschools

# HAWAII

## State Profile (Updated May 2003)

### School Choice Status
- Public school choice: Intradistrict/voluntary
- State constitution: Blaine amendment
- Charter school law: Established in 1994
    - Strength of law: Weak
    - Number of charter schools in operation (fall 2002): 25
    - Number of students enrolled (fall 2002): 3,301
- Publicly funded private school choice: No
- Privately funded school choice: No
- Home-school law: Moderate regulation
- Ranking on the Education Freedom Index (2001): 50th out of 50 states

### K–12 Public Schools and Students (2002–2002)
- Public school enrollment: 184,546
- Students enrolled per teacher: 16.9
- Number of schools (2000–2001): 261
- Number of districts: 1
- Current expenditures: $1,250,379,000
- Current per-pupil expenditure: $6,775
- Amount of revenue from the federal government: 8.4%

### K–12 Public School Teachers (2001–2002)
- Number of teachers: 10,943
- Average salary: $41,951

### K–12 Private Schools (1999–2000)
- Private school enrollment: 32,193
- Number of schools: 130
- Number of teachers: 2,475

### K–12 Public and Private School Student Academic Performance
- NAEP test results:

| NAEP Tests Hawaii Student Performance | State (National) 2000 Math Scale = 0–500 | | State (National) 2000 Science Scale = 0–300 | | State (National) 2000 Reading Scale = 0–500 | |
|---|---|---|---|---|---|---|
| | 4th Grade | 8th Grade | 4th Grade | 8th Grade | 4th Grade | 8th Grade |
| Average Scale Score | 216 (226) | 263 (274) | 136 (148) | 132 (149) | 200 (215) | 250 (261) |
| Advanced | 1% (3%) | 2% (5%) | 1% (3%) | 1% (4%) | 3% (6%) | 1% (2%) |
| Proficient | 13% (23%) | 14% (21%) | 15% (25%) | 14% (26%) | 14% (23%) | 18% (29%) |
| Basic | 41% (43%) | 36% (39%) | 35% (36%) | 25% (29%) | 28% (32%) | 41% (41%) |
| Below Basic | 45% (31%) | 48% (35%) | 49% (36%) | 60% (41%) | 55% (39%) | 40% (28%) |

- SAT weighted rank (2001): 14th out of 24 states and the District of Columbia
- ACT weighted rank (2001): N/A
- ALEC Academic Achievement Ranking: 38th out of 50 states and the District of Columbia

## Summary

Hawaii offers little public school choice. The state has a weak charter school law. It also has the nation's highest percentage of students in private schools, with one in five students attending private schools.[201]

## Background

In 1994, the Hawaii legislature passed a weak charter school bill, Act 272, which allowed up to 25 public schools to convert to charter schools. The bill refers to the charter schools as "student-centered" schools.[202]

In 1999, the legislature amended the law to allow new charter schools and changed their designation from "student-centered" to "New Century" schools.[203] Two years later, the law was again amended to grant an appeals process for rejected charters.[204]

Despite these improvements, the law earned a "C" in the Center for Education Reform's 2003 ranking. The law remains highly prescriptive. Each charter school's governing board must be composed of one or more of each of the following: a principal, a teacher, a support staff member, a parent, a student, and a citizen from the community. Although charter schools receive an automatic waiver from most district and state laws, they enjoy limited legal autonomy and no fiscal autonomy.[205]

During the 1999 legislative session, House Bill 2702 was introduced to give corporations income tax credits for contributions to private organizations that provide scholarships for pri-

vate school tuition. The bill died in committee.[206]

Several parental choice bills were introduced during the 2001 session. H.B. 1678 and a companion bill, Senate Bill 512, would have provided disabled children with "service vouchers" from the Hawaii Department of Education. The vouchers could have been used to purchase educational and support services. The House passed H.B. 1678 on March 6, 2001. The bill was approved by a Senate committee and was then carried over into the 2002 session.[207]

H.B. 1634 and S.B. 1290 would have amended the state constitution to allow children to receive public funds to attend nonprofit private schools. H.B. 802 would have given individuals a dollar-for-dollar tax credit for donations to scholarship organizations; in addition, such donations could have been designated for a specific student, including the donor's own child. No action was taken on these bills in 2001.[208]

## Developments in 2002 and 2003

Two charter school bills were signed into law in 2002. Act 262 allows charter school students to participate in team sports with conventional public schools, specifies that charter schools may not sue the state, establishes transitional funding for conversion charter schools, and adds new criteria for audits. Act 002 allows nonprofit organizations to manage and operate a New Century conversion charter school and specifies that the charter school's local school board may consist of the board of directors of the nonprofit organization.[209]

---

201. Jacques Steinberg, "In Hawaii, Public Schools Feel a Long Way from Paradise," *The New York Times*, October 12, 2001.

202. University of Hawaii, "State of Hawaii Act 272 Student-Centered Schools Summary," at *http://kalama.doe.hawaii.edu/~lanikai/School_act.html*.

203. See Hawaii Charter School Information, updated December 4, 2002, at *www.uscharterschools.org/pub/sp/24*.

204. Center for Education Reform, "Charter Schools in Hawaii," at *http://edreform.com/charter_schools/states/hawaii.htm*.

205. Center for Education Reform, "Charter School Legislation: Profile of Hawaii's Charter School Law," 2001, at *http://edreform.com/charter_schools/laws/Hawaii.htm*.

206. See National School Boards Association Web site at *www.nsba.org/novouchers*.

207. See Hawaii State Legislature Archives Web site at *www.capitol.hawaii.gov/site1/archives/archives.asp?press1=archives*.

208. *Ibid.*

209. *Ibid.*

Four 2001 school choice bills were reintroduced during the 2002 legislative session. H.B. 1634 and S.B. 1290 called for a constitutional amendment to allow vouchers; H.B. 802 would have provided tax credits for contributions to scholarship funds; and H.B. 1678 would have offered "service vouchers" for disabled students. No action was taken on any of these bills.[210]

During her 2003 State of the State address, Governor Linda Lingle advocated breaking up Hawaii's single school district into seven districts with locally elected boards. She intends to take her case to the voters with a referendum. Governor Lingle has also called for more charter schools, home schooling, magnet schools, and on-line schooling.[211] "No other state, other than Hawaii, has a statewide school system. None. Not even one," she said. "The reason they don't is because it doesn't work."

Several tax credit proposals were introduced during the session. S.B. 1486 would have given individuals a credit of up to $500 and corporations a credit of up to $10,000 for donations to tuition scholarship organizations. Up to $15 million in tax credits could have been granted in a given year. H.B. 442 also would have provided a tax credit for such donations, and S.B. 292 would have provided a credit for home schooling; however, the amounts were not specified in the legislation. H.B. 441 would have given parents a tax credit of up to $3,500 per child for tuition. A constitutional amendment was proposed (S.B. 428) to enable children with disabilities to enroll in private elementary and secondary schools. All of these bills died in committee.[212]

## Position of the Governor / Composition of the State Legislature

Governor Linda Lingle, a Republican, supports charter schools. Democrats control both houses of the legislature.

## State Contacts

**Christian Homeschoolers of Hawaii**
91824 Oama Street
Ewa Beach, HI 96706
Phone: (808) 689-6398
Web site: www.christianhomeschoolersof
hawaii.org
E-mail: chohinfo@aol.com

**Grassroot Institute of Hawaii**
Dick Rowland, Director
1314 South King Street, Suite 1163
Aiea, HI 96841
Phone: (808) 487-4959
Fax: (808) 484-0117
Web site: www.grassrootinstitute.org
E-mail: grassroot@hawaii.rr.com

**Hawaii Department of Education**
Patricia Hamamoto, Ph.D., Superintendent
Charles Higgins,
Public Charter Schools Specialist
P.O. Box 2360
Honolulu, HI 96804
Phone: (808) 586-3570
Fax: (808) 586-3577
Web site: http://doe.k12.hi.us/
charterschools.htm
E-mail: chuck_higgins@notes.k12.hi.us

**University of Hawaii Charter Schools Resource Center**
Nina Buchanan, Director
Robert Fox, Director
University of Hawaii at Hilo
200 West Kawili Street
Hilo, HI 96720-4091
Phone (808) 974-7583
Fax: (808) 974-7737
Web site: www.uhh.hawaii.edu/~charter
E-mail: ninab@hawaii.edu

## State School Report Card

**Greatschools.net**
Web site: www.greatschools.net/modperl/go/HI

**Hawaii Department of Education**
Web site: http://arch.k12.hi.us/school/nclb/
default.html

210. *Ibid.*
211. Mark Walsh, "State of the States," *Education Week*, January 29, 2003.
212. See Hawaii State Legislature Web site at *www.capitol.hawaii.gov/*.

# IDAHO

## State Profile (Updated May 2003)

### School Choice Status
- Public school choice: Intradistrict and interdistrict/voluntary
- State constitution: Blaine amendment and compelled-support language
- Charter school law: Established in 1998
  Strength of law: Weak
  Number of charter schools in operation (fall 2002): 13
  Number of students enrolled (fall 2002): 2,694
- Publicly funded private school choice: No
- Privately funded school choice: No
- Home-school law: No notice required
- Ranking on the Education Freedom Index (2001): 11th out of 50 states

### K-12 Public Schools and Students (2001–2002)
- Public school enrollment: 246,000
- Students enrolled per teacher: 17.8
- Number of schools (2000–2001): 653
- Number of districts: 113
- Current expenditures: $1,424,116,000
- Current per-pupil expenditure: $5,789
- Amount of revenue from the federal government: 7.3%

### K-12 Public School Teachers (2001–2002)
- Number of teachers: 13,800
- Average salary: $37,482

### K-12 Private Schools (1999–2000)
- Private school enrollment: 10,209
- Number of schools: 94
- Number of teachers: 790

### K-12 Public and Private School Student Academic Performance
- NAEP test results:

| NAEP Tests Idaho Student Performance | State (National) 2000 Math Scale = 0–500 | | State (National) 2000 Science Scale = 0–300 | | State (National) 2000 Reading Scale = 0–500 | |
|---|---|---|---|---|---|---|
| | 4th Grade | 8th Grade | 4th Grade | 8th Grade | 4th Grade | 8th Grade |
| Average Scale Score | 227 (226) | 278 (274) | 153 (148) | 159 (149) | N/A (215) | N/A (261) |
| Advanced | 1% (3%) | 3% (5%) | 3% (3%) | 4% (4%) | N/A (6%) | N/A (2%) |
| Proficient | 20% (23%) | 24% (21%) | 27% (25%) | 34% (26%) | N/A (23%) | N/A (29%) |
| Basic | 50% (43%) | 44% (39%) | 42% (36%) | 35% (29%) | N/A (32%) | N/A (41%) |
| Below Basic | 29% (31%) | 29% (35%) | 28% (36%) | 27% (41%) | N/A (39%) | N/A (28%) |

- SAT weighted rank (2001): N/A
- ACT weighted rank (2001): 14th out of 26 states
- ALEC Academic Achievement Ranking: 28th out of 50 states and the District of Columbia

## Summary

Students may attend any participating public school within or outside the district, provided certain conditions are met. The state has a weak charter school law. Junior and senior high school students may take college courses for high school and postsecondary credit.[213]

## Background

In 1998, with passage of House Bill 517, Idaho became the 30th state to enact a charter school law.[214] The measure authorized chartering for as many as 12 new schools per year for the first five years following the legislation's enactment. The law stipulates that teachers in charter schools must be certified and that a traditional public school may convert to charter status if such a transition has the approval of 60 percent of the parents, 60 percent of the teachers, and the local school board.[215]

In 2000, H.B. 686 was introduced to provide tax credits to individuals and corporations that donated funds to help support students in private schools. Individuals would have received a credit of up to $250 in the first year after the bill was enacted, and the maximum credit for individuals would have increased to $1,000 by 2006. Corporations would have received an initial credit of up to $1,000 per year, which would have risen to a maximum of $10,000 by 2006. The bill died in committee.[216]

In 2001, the Idaho House of Representatives passed H.B. 311, which would have provided tax credits of up to $1,000 for individuals and $10,000 for corporations for donations to support students attending a private school. The bill died in the State Senate.[217]

Governor Dirk Kempthorne signed Senate Bill 1132, which allows charter schools to appeal a local school board's decision not to approve the revision of a school's charter.[218]

## Developments in 2002 and 2003

In 2003, the House passed H.B. 346 to allow community colleges, universities, and other nonprofit entities to charter schools. Currently, the local school board is the only chartering authority. The bill, however, did not proceed in the Senate. H.B. 255, which exempts charter school property from taxation, was signed into law.[219]

## Position of the Governor / Composition of the State Legislature

Governor Dirk Kempthorne, a Republican, has not declared a position on school choice. Republicans control both houses of the legislature.

## State Contacts

**Center for School Improvement**
Bill Parret, Director
Boise State University
1910 University Drive
Boise, ID 83725-1745
Phone: (208) 426-4343
Web site: http://www.boisestate.edu
E-mail: csicee@boisestate.edu

**Christian Homeschoolers of Idaho State**
P.O. Box 45062
Boise, ID 83711-5062
Phone: (208) 424-6685
Web site: www.chois.org
E-mail: linda@chois.org

---

213. Education Commission of the States, "Postsecondary Options: Dual/Concurrent Enrollment," July 2001.

214. National Conference of State Legislators, "Charter Schools," June 3, 1998, at *www.ncsl.org/programs/educ/c1schls.htm*.

215. Center for Education Reform, "Charter School Legislation: Profile of Idaho's Charter School Law," 2001, at *http://edreform.com/charter_schools/laws/Idaho.htm*.

216. See National School Boards Association Web site at *www.nsba.org/novouchers*.

217. *Ibid.*

218. Education Commission of the States, "ECS State Notes: Charter School Legislation, 2001," at *www.ecs.org/clearinghouse/22/79/2279.htm*.

219. See Idaho Legislature Web site at *www2.state.id.us/legislat/legislat.html*.

**Idaho Coalition of Home Educators**
5415 Kendall Street
Boise, ID 83706
Web site: www.iche-idaho.org
E-mail: listkeeper@iche-idaho.org

**Idaho Department of Education**
Marilyn Howard, Superintendent
P.O. Box 83720
Boise, ID 83720-0027
Phone: (208) 332-6800, 6863
Fax: (208) 334-2228
Web site: www.sde.state.id.us/Dept

**Idahoans for Tax Reform**
Laird Maxwell, Chairman
702 West Hays, Suite 16

Boise, ID 83702
Phone: (208) 426-0358
Fax: (208) 426-0363
Web site: www.idtaxreform.com
E-mail: taxcut@idtaxreform.com

## State School Report Card[220]
**Greatschools.net**
Web site: www.greatschools.net/modperl/go/ID

**Idaho State Department of Education**
Web site: www.sde.state.id.us/Finance/
profiles99-00/default.htm

---

220. Idaho provides district-level information.

# ILLINOIS

## State Profile (Updated May 2003)

### School Choice Status
- Public school choice: Intradistrict/mandatory
- State constitution: Blaine amendment and compelled-support language
- Charter school law: Established 1996
  Strength of law: Weak
  Number of charter schools in operation (fall 2002): 29
  Number of students enrolled (fall 2002): 10,309
- Publicly funded private school choice: Yes
- Privately funded school choice: Yes
- Home-school law: No notice required
- Ranking on the Education Freedom Index (2001): 21st out of 50 states

### K–12 Public Schools and Students (2001–2002)
- Public school enrollment: 2,068,182
- Students enrolled per teacher: 16.5
- Number of schools (2000–2001): 4,282
- Number of districts: 898
- Current expenditures: $15,713,240,000
- Current per-pupil expenditure: $7,598
- Amount of revenue from the federal government: 8.5%

### K–12 Public School Teachers (2001–2002)
- Number of teachers: 125,130
- Average salary: $50,000

### K–12 Private Schools (1999–2000)
- Private school enrollment: 299,871
- Number of schools: 1,354
- Number of teachers: 19,589

### K–12 Public and Private School Student Academic Performance
- NAEP test results:

| NAEP Tests Illinois Student Performance | State (National) 2000 Math Scale = 0–500 | | State (National) 2000 Science Scale = 0–300 | | State (National) 2000 Reading Scale = 0–500 | |
|---|---|---|---|---|---|---|
| | 4th Grade | 8th Grade | 4th Grade | 8th Grade | 4th Grade | 8th Grade |
| Average Scale Score | 225 (226) | 277 (274) | 151 (148) | 150 (149) | N/A (215) | N/A (261) |
| Advanced | 2% (3%) | 4% (5%) | 4% (3%) | 3% (4%) | N/A (6%) | N/A (2%) |
| Proficient | 19% (23%) | 25% (21%) | 27% (25%) | 27% (26%) | N/A (23%) | N/A (29%) |
| Basic | 45% (43%) | 41% (39%) | 37% (36%) | 32% (29%) | N/A (32%) | N/A (41%) |
| Below Basic | 34% (31%) | 32% (35%) | 32% (36%) | 38% (41%) | N/A (39%) | N/A (28%) |

- SAT weighted rank (2001): N/A
- ACT weighted rank (2001): 9th out of 26 states
- ALEC Academic Achievement Ranking: 21st out of 50 states and the District of Columbia

## Summary

Illinois has a weak charter school law and limited public school choice. Families may take advantage of the state's education tax credit, which has survived several legal challenges. Low-income children may apply for vouchers provided by private scholarship foundations.

## Background

Charter schools became an option in 1996, when the legislature passed a bill allowing for the creation of up to 45 schools: 15 in Chicago, 15 in Chicago's suburbs, and 15 in the rest of the state. Any not-for-profit organization, including a school district, can sponsor a charter school.[221]

In 1996, then-Representative Peter Roskam (R–48) introduced the Educational Choice Act (House Bill 3533), a pilot school voucher program that would have provided vouchers worth up to $2,500 to low-income students.[222] The bill was approved in committee but did not receive a vote in the House.[223]

The following year, another Educational Choice Act (H.B. 991) was introduced to start a pilot choice program in Chicago. The voucher would have been worth the lesser of the cost of private school tuition or $2,500, and the program would have cost $5 million a year. The bill died in committee.[224]

Chicago first became a Children's Scholarship Fund (CSF) "partner city" in 1998. The CSF matches funds raised by residents to fund private scholarships for low-income students to attend a school of choice.[225]

In 1997, Representative Kevin McCarthy (D–37) introduced H. B. 999, which would have provided parents a tax credit of up to $500 for education expenses, including tuition, books, and lab fees, for classes at public, private, or parochial schools. The legislature approved the bill, but then-Governor Jim Edgar, a Republican, vetoed it on January 2, 1998.[226]

A two-year study released in 1998 by the Special Task Force on Catholic Schools found that the Archdiocese of Chicago, which educates many poor children who are not Catholic, would have to close or downsize some of its 270 elementary schools in Cook and Lake Counties within a year unless it found new funding. The Archdiocese hoped, among other things, to find funds to increase teacher salaries to 75 percent of market value. At the time, teachers in Catholic schools earned about half as much as teachers in public schools. The Archdiocese had called on then-Governor-elect George Ryan to approve a voucher or tax credit program to help offset the costs of educating children.[227] In 2000, the Catholic Conference of Illinois estimated that were 594 Catholic schools educating 212,285 children. These schools save Illinois $1.4 billion annually, which is what it costs to educate those students in public schools.[228]

In 1999, the state House and Senate approved the Educational Expenses Tax Credit plan (Senate Bill 1075). Signed into law on June 3, 1999, this law provides an annual tax credit of up to 25 percent of education-related expenses (including tuition, book fees, and lab fees) that exceed $250, up to a maximum of $500 per family.[229]

221. Center for Education Reform, "Charter School Legislation: Profile of Illinois' Charter School Law," 2001, at *http://edreform.com/charter_schools/laws/Illinois.htm*.
222. *The Blum Center's Educational Freedom Report*, No. 35, May 24, 1996.
223. Illinois Association of School Boards, "The Education Year in Review July 1, 1995 to June 30, 1996," at *www.iasb.com/files/year.htm*.
224. See National School Boards Association Web site at *www.nsba.org/novouchers*.
225. *Ibid.*
226. "Illinois Legislature Approves Tuition Tax Credit," *School Reform News*, January 1998, and "News in Brief: A State Capitals Roundup," *Education Week*, January 14, 1998.
227. Steve Kloehn and Rick Pearson, "Catholic School Alarm," *Chicago Tribune*, December 16, 1998.
228. News release, "Superintendent Elaine Schuster Reports on the State of Catholic Schools in the Archdiocese of Chicago," Archdiocese of Chicago, January 28, 2000, at *www.archdiocese-chgo.org/news_releases/news_2000/news_012800.shtm*.

A poll of 1,000 Illinois residents commissioned by the Illinois Family Institute before adoption of the tax credit program found that 77 percent of respondents supported allowing parents and students to choose their schools. Over half believed that families should be able to use their per-student tax dollars at a school of choice. One-third said that tax money should be spent only at public schools authorized by the school board. A 1998 Metro Chicago Information Center survey found that 62 percent of respondents in Chicago supported vouchers for poor children. Over half supported authorizing students to use vouchers at religious schools.[230]

Nevertheless, a voucher plan (S.B. 329) introduced by Senator Dan Cronin (R–21) in 1999 was voted down in committee. The bill would have provided Educational Opportunity Grants of $2,000 to $3,000 for students in Chicago, East St. Louis, Joliet, Peoria, and Rockford to use at a school of choice, including religious schools.[231]

In 1999, the legislature enacted two charter school laws. S.B. 648 establishes a process by which 5 percent or more of the voters can present a petition to the Illinois State Board of Education, which would then direct the local board to allow a referendum. It also grants funds to school districts for the first three years after the establishment of a charter school and provides grants and loans to cover start-up costs for charter schools. The second bill, H.B. 230, allows school districts to enter into partnerships to set up charter schools.[232]

In July 1999, the local chapter of the American Federation of Teachers filed a lawsuit in the Circuit Court of Franklin County, alleging that the tax credit law violated the state prohibition against the establishment of religion. On December 7, 1999, Judge Loren P. Lewis dis-

missed the suit. Opponents of choice appealed the decision to the Appellate Court of the Fifth Judicial District, which upheld the Circuit Court's decision.[233] On April 4, 2001, the Appellate Court of Illinois for the Fifth Judicial District unanimously upheld the constitutionality of the Illinois educational expenses tax credit law.[234]

A second lawsuit was filed in Sangamon County Circuit Court by a coalition of groups led by the Illinois Education Association, also challenging the program on state constitutional grounds. In April 2000, the circuit court judge dismissed the suit, emphasizing that the tax credit allows Illinois parents to keep more of their own money to spend on their children's education and does not involve the expenditure of public money.[235] Opponents appealed this decision to the Appellate Court of the Fourth Judicial District.

On April 21, 2001, the Appellate Court for the Fourth Judicial District also unanimously upheld the constitutionality of the state's 1999 tax credit law. "By creating the credit," Justice Rita Garman wrote for the three-judge panel, "the legislature has recognized that parents who send their children to private schools often do so at considerable expense to themselves and that they provide a benefit to the State treasury by relieving the State and local taxpayers of the expense of educating their children."[236]

In two separate decisions in June 2001, the Illinois Supreme Court refused to reconsider the two district appeals court rulings. Since the plaintiffs did not raise First Amendment claims in either case, no appeal to the U.S. Supreme Court was possible.[237]

Two choice bills were introduced during the 2001 legislative session. H.B. 3550, the Educational Choice Act, would have provided

229. State of Illinois, 91st General Assembly Public Acts, at *www.legis.state.il.us/legislation/publicacts/pubact91/acts/91-0009.html.*
230. "Poll Finds Illinoisans Support Choice," *School Reform News*, July 1999.
231. See Illinois Association of School Boards, *School Board News Bulletin*, April 1999.
232. State of Illinois, 91st General Assembly Public Acts, at *www.legis.state.il.us/legislation/publicacts/pubact91/pa91group5.html.*
233. George A. Clowes, "Challenge to Illinois Tax Credit Dismissed," *School Reform News*, June 2000.
234. *Griffith v. Bower,* 747 N.E.2d 423 (Ill. App. Ct. 2001).
235. See Institute for Justice, "2nd Illinois Court Dismisses Case Against Tuition Tax Credit, Resounding Victory for School Choice, Teachers' Union Argument Branded 'Absurd,'" April 21, 2000.
236. *Toney v. Bower,* 744 N.E.2d 351, 363 (Ill. App. Ct. 2001).
237. George A. Clowes, "Other Court Action on School Choice," *School Reform News*, August 2001.

vouchers for educational expenses. H.B. 1010 would have amended the state's education tax credit program to mandate that the taxpayer provide the name of the school. The school also would have been subject to the testing, reporting, disciplinary, and enrollment rules of the local school board. Neither bill was passed.[238]

Two charter school bills were voted down by the legislature in early June 2001. S.B. 78 would have allowed Chicago to open an additional 15 schools above the current cap of 15. S.B. 36 would have increased the amount of charter grants and start-up loans.[239]

## Developments in 2002 and 2003

Several choice bills were introduced during the 2002 legislative session. H.B. 3550, first introduced in 2001, would have allowed vouchers for educational expenses. H.B. 1010 would have amended the existing tuition tax credit program by adding a provision that the taxpayer must state the name of the school for which the expense credit is claimed. The bill also would have subjected private schools to local school board requirements on testing, academic standards, reporting, graduation requirements, suspensions and expulsions, and student enrollment. Both bills died in a House committee.[240]

State Representative Joseph Lyons (D–19) and then-Representative Mary Lou Cowlishaw (R–41) introduced the Educational Improvement Tax Credit bill, H.B. 4077, which would have authorized state income tax credits of up to $100,000 for corporations donating to scholarship organizations. Students from families with an income of less than $50,000 a year would have been eligible for the vouchers to attend a private school of choice. After debate and amendment, the bill died in committee.[241]

Another bill, S.B. 1240, would have raised the charter school cap in Chicago from 15 to 30. The addition of 15 schools would have come at a price, however, since the bill would have placed a two-year moratorium on contracting with for-profit management companies. It also would have required half of the teachers in urban charter schools to be certified by the 2006–2007 school year. [242] S.B. 1240 was passed by the Senate and House but died in conference.[243]

As required by the federal No Child Left Behind Act, Illinois identified 179 elementary schools in Chicago that were not meeting state standards. The federal law requires that the district give each of the 125,000 students in the failing schools the option to transfer to a higher-performing school.

Chicago public school authorities planned to permit 29,000 students in only 50 of the schools to move into one of 90 higher-performing schools with about 2,900 open seats, leaving students at the remaining 129 failing schools eligible for after-school programs or tutoring. In 70 of the 90 transfer-eligible schools, however, a majority of students had failed state tests during the previous year.[244] In the end, 1,900 students asked to be transferred.[245]

In 2003, State Senator Donne E. Trotter (D–17) introduced S.B.1135, which would eliminate the state's educational tax credit law at the end of the year. The bill has been referred to the Rules Committee.[246]

Illinois's charter school law was revised in April 2003 with the signing of S.B. 19, the Chicago Education Reform Act of 2003.[247] The law

---

238. See National School Boards Association Web site at *www.nsba.org/novouchers*.

239. Center for Education Reform, *Education Reform Newswire*, June 5, 2001, at *www.edreform.com*.

240. State of Illinois, 92nd General Assembly, Legislation (2001–2002), at *www.legis.state.il.us/legislation/legisnet92/92gatoc.html*.

241. *Ibid*.

242. Center for Education Reform, *Education Reform Newswire*, November 26, 2002, at *www.edreform.com*.

243. State of Illinois, 92nd General Assembly, Legislation (2001–2002), at *www.legis.state.il.us/legislation/legisnet92/92gatoc.html*.

244. Stephanie Banchero and Diane Rado, "Chicago Restricts Transfer Options: Choice Program Limited to Pupils in 50 Schools," *Chicago Tribune*, July 30, 2002.

245. Stephanie Banchero and Ana Beatriz Cholo, "Only 7% Seek to Transfer to a Better School: Despite U.S. Plan, Most City Pupils Not About to Move," *Chicago Tribune*, August 20, 2002.

246. State of Illinois, 93rd General Assembly, Senate Bill 1135.

247. State of Illinois, 93rd General Assembly, Senate Bill 19.

provides for the creation of 15 new charter schools in the city, but it also gives teachers more bargaining rights—making charter school advocates wary of the measure.[248]

## Position of the Governor / Composition of the State Legislature

Governor Rod Blagojevich, a Democrat, has no stated position on charter schools or vouchers. Democrats control both houses of the legislature.

## State Contacts

**Big Shoulders Fund**
Heidi Waltner-Pepper,
Acting Executive Director
309 West Washington, Suite 550
Chicago, IL 60606
Phone: (312) 751-8394
Fax: (312) 751-5235
Web site: www.bigshouldersfund.org
E-mail: information@bigshoulders.org

**Catholic Conference of Illinois**
Robert Gilligan, Executive Director
65 East Wacker Place
Chicago, IL 60610
Phone: (312) 368-1066
Fax: (312) 368-1090
Zach Wichmann, Education Expert
108 East Cook Street
Springfield, IL 62704
Phone: (217) 528-9200
Fax: (217) 528-7214
Web site: www.catholicconferenceofillinois.org
E-mail: zwichmanncci@aol.com

**Charter Consultants**
Governor French Academy
Paul Seibert, Director
219 West Main Street
Belleville, IL 62220
Phone: (618) 233-0428
Fax: (618) 233-7416
Web site: www.gfacademy.com/charter.htm
E-mail: chrsch@gfacademy.com

**Chicago Charter School Foundation**
Heidi McDermott
228 South Wabash, Suite 600
Chicago, IL 60604
Phone: (312) 455-7890

Fax: (312) 455-7891
E-mail: ccsfbrowdy@aol.com

**Chicago Public Schools**
Arnie Duncan, CEO
125 South Clark Street
Chicago, IL 60603
Phone: (773) 553-1500
Fax: (773) 553-1501
E-mail: aduncan@csc.k12.il.us

**Charter School Office**
Greg Richmond, Director
125 South Clark Street, 12th Floor
Chicago, IL 60603
Phone: (773) 553-1535
Fax: (773) 553-1559
Web site: www.cps.k12.il.us
E-mail: grichmond@csc.cps.k12.il.us

**Children's Scholarship Fund–Chicago**
Gale Byrnes, Executive Director
55 West Superior, Suite 300
Chicago, IL 60610
Phone: (312) 960-0205
Fax: (312) 377-1837
Web site: www.scholarshipfund.org
E-mail: gbyrnes@csfchicago.org

**Christian Home Educators Coalition of Illinois**
P.O. Box 47322
Chicago, IL 60647
Phone: (773) 278-0673
Fax: (773) 278-0673
Web site: www.chec.cc
E-mail: chec@chec.cc

**Daniel Murphy Scholarship Foundation**
Candace A. Browdy, Executive Director
228 South Wabash, Suite 600
Chicago, IL 60604
Phone: (312) 455-7800
Fax: (312) 455-7801
Web site: www.dmsf.org
E-mail: dmsf@dmsf.org

**Family Taxpayers Foundation**
Jack Roeser, Chairman
8 East Main Street
Carpentersville, IL 60110
Phone: (847) 428-0212
Fax: (847) 428-9206
Web site: www.thechampion.org
E-mail: mail@thechampion.org

---

248. Center for Education Reform, *Education Reform Newswire*, Vol. 5, No. 17 (April 22, 2003), and Ana Beatriz Colo and Christi Parsons, "City Gets 15 More Charter Schools," *Chicago Tribune*, April 17, 2003, p. 1.

**Heartland Institute**
George A. Clowes, Education Specialist
19 South LaSalle, Suite 903
Chicago, IL 60603-1405
Phone: (312) 377-4000
Fax: (312) 377-5000
Web site: www.heartland.org
E-mail: Clowesga@aol.com

**Illinois Christian Home Educators**
P.O. Box 775
Harvard, IL 60033
Phone: (815) 943-7882
Fax: (815) 943-7883
Web site: www.iche.org
E-mail: info@iche.org

**Illinois Family Institute**
Dr. John Koehler, Chairman
799 West Roosevelt Road
Building 3, Suite 218
Glen Ellyn, IL 60137
Phone: (630) 790-8370
Fax: (630) 790-8390
Web site: www.ilfaminst.com
E-mail: ilfaminst@aol.com

**Illinois State Board of Education**
100 North First Street
Springfield, IL 62777
Phone: (217) 782-4321
Chicago: (217) 524-8585
Web site: www.isbe.state.il.us

**Leadership for Quality Education**
John Ayers, Director
Bank One Plaza, #3120
Chicago, IL 60603
Phone: (312) 853-1206
Fax: (312) 853-1214
Web site: www.lqe.org
E-mail: jayers@lqe.org

**Link Unlimited**
Virgil Jones, Executive Director
7759 South Eberhart Avenue
Chicago, IL 60619
Phone: (773) 487-5465
Fax: (773) 487-8626
Web site: www.linkunlimited.org

**Partnership to Educate and Advance Kids**
(PEAK)
Walter Bledsoe, Executive Director
P.O. Box 353
559 West Diversey Parkway
Chicago, IL 60614
Phone: (773) 975-6540
E-mail: walterbledsoe@msn.net

**TEACH America**
Patrick J. Keleher, President
Joan M. Ferdinand, Vice President, Operations
Georgetown Square
522 Fourth Street
Wilmette, IL 60091
Phone: (847) 256-8476
Fax: (847) 256-8482
E-mail: TEACH522@aol.com

## State School Report Card
**Catalyst Chicago**
Web site: www.catalyst-chicago.org/quickreference/data.htm#ChicagoSchoolBoard

**Consortium on Chicago School Improvement**
Web site: www.consortium-chicago.org/Va2/ValueAdd.html

**Greatschools.net**
Web site: www.greatschools.net/modperl/go/IL

**Illinois State Board of Education**
Web site: http://206.166.105.128/ReportCard/rchome.asp

# INDIANA

## State Profile (Updated May 2003)

### School Choice Status
- Public school choice: Interdistrict/voluntary
- State constitution: Blaine amendment and compelled-support language
- Charter school law: Established 2001
    Strength of law: Strong
    Number of charter schools in operation: 10
    Number of students enrolled: 1,275
- Publicly funded private school choice: No
- Privately funded school choice: Yes
- Home-school law: No notice required
- Ranking on the Education Freedom Index (2001): 13th out of 50 states

### K–12 Public Schools and Students (2001–2002)
- Public school enrollment: 994,545
- Students enrolled per teacher: 16.6
- Number of schools (2000–2001): 1,882
- Number of districts: 294
- Current expenditures: $7,990,000,000
- Current per-pupil expenditure: $8,034
- Amount of revenue from the federal government: 5.6%

### K–12 Public School Teachers (2001–2002)
- Number of teachers: 59,832
- Average salary: $44,195

### K–12 Private Schools (1999–2000)
- Private school enrollment: 105,533
- Number of schools: 677
- Number of teachers: 7,362

### K–12 Public and Private School Student Academic Performance
- NAEP test results:

| NAEP Tests Indiana Student Performance | State (National) 2000 Math Scale = 0–500 | | State (National) 2000 Science Scale = 0–300 | | State (National) 2000 Reading Scale = 0–500 | |
|---|---|---|---|---|---|---|
| | 4th Grade | 8th Grade | 4th Grade | 8th Grade | 4th Grade | 8th Grade |
| Average Scale Score | 234 (226) | 283 (274) | 155 (148) | 156 (149) | N/A (215) | N/A (261) |
| Advanced | 3% (3%) | 5% (5%) | 3% (3%) | 3% (4%) | N/A (6%) | N/A (2%) |
| Proficient | 28% (23%) | 26% (21%) | 29% (25%) | 32% (26%) | N/A (23%) | N/A (29%) |
| Basic | 47% (43%) | 45% (39%) | 43% (36%) | 33% (29%) | N/A (32%) | N/A (41%) |
| Below Basic | 22% (31%) | 24% (35%) | 25% (36%) | 32% (41%) | N/A (39%) | N/A (28%) |

- SAT weighted rank (2001): 15th out of 24 states and the District of Columbia
- ACT weighted rank (2001): N/A
- ALEC Academic Achievement Ranking: 20 out of 50 states and the District of Columbia

## Summary

Indiana offers limited public school choice.[249] In 2001, the state legislature passed a strong charter school law. Low-income students may apply for privately funded vouchers provided by several private scholarship foundations.

## Background

Indiana is home to the nation's first privately funded scholarship organization: the Educational CHOICE Charitable Trust created by J. Patrick Rooney, then-chairman of the Golden Rule Insurance Company in Indianapolis.[250] In 1991, its first year of operation, the organization gave scholarships to 746 children. Since then, more than 2,300 children in grades K–8 have received $1,000 scholarships toward their private school education.[251] Other organizations that have joined the Educational CHOICE Charitable Trust in serving Indiana's children include the Northwest Indiana Children's Scholarship Fund in Gary and the Guardian Angel Society in Fort Wayne.

In 1997, the legislature enacted the Postsecondary Enrollment Options Act, which allows 9th and 10th grade "gifted and talented" students and junior and senior high school students to enroll in higher education courses for both secondary and college credit. Tuition is the responsibility of the student.[252]

Several choice bills were introduced in 1999. Senate Bill 89 would have provided vouchers to students in Indianapolis to attend another public school or an accredited private school. The vouchers would have been equal to the state's per-pupil funding. House Bill 1877 would have

established tax credits for charitable donations to education foundations or public schools, as well as for personal expenses of students enrolled in public, private, or home schools. H.B. 2015, H.B. 2016, and H.B. 2017 would have provided tax credits for charitable donations to accredited private schools and public schools. All of these bills died in committee.[253]

In May 2001, Governor Frank O'Bannon signed S.B. 165, the state's charter school bill.[254] Under this legislation, local school boards and universities may authorize an unlimited number of charter schools, including both new schools and conversions from existing schools. The mayor of Indianapolis may sponsor up to five charter schools a year. Charter schools receive an automatic waiver from most state and local rules and regulations.[255] Most of Indiana's charter schools have been authorized by Ball State University and the mayor of Indianapolis.[256]

In 2001, S.B. 105 was introduced to provide students with vouchers to attend another public school or an accredited private school within the Indianapolis school district. The voucher would have been equal to the per-pupil cost of educating the student in the Indianapolis school system. Parents would have been responsible for the transportation, fees, and tuition not covered by the voucher. The bill died in committee.[257]

## Developments in 2002 and 2003

Introduced during the 2002 session, the Education Improvement Tax Credit (H.B. 1389) would have provided tax credits for donations to organizations providing tuition scholarships or public-school support organizations. The taxpayer would have received a credit for

---

249. By law, the Indianapolis school district must offer intradistrict school choice.

250. Clearinghouse on Educational Management, College of Education, University of Oregon, "Trends and Issues: School Choice," at *http://eric.uoregon.edu/trends_issues/choice/abstracts.html.*

251. Joseph P. Viteritti, "Vouchers on Trial," *Education Next,* Summer 2002.

252. Education Commission of the States, "Postsecondary Options: Dual/Concurrent Enrollment," July 2001.

253. See National School Boards Association Web site at *www.nsba.org/novouchers.*

254. "Education Issues: Legislature 2001," *Indianapolis Star,* at *www.indystar.com/library/factfiles/gov/legislature/2001/issues/education.html.*

255. Center for Education Reform, "Charter School Legislation: Profile of Indiana's Charter School Law," 2001, at *http://edreform.com/charter_schools/laws/Indiana.htm.*

256. See Charter School Resource Center of Indiana Web site at *www.indianacharters.org/contactapproved.asp.*

257. See National School Boards Association Web site at *www.nsba.org/novouchers.*

contributions worth up to 75 percent of his or her tax liability or $1,000, whichever was less. For joint filers, the maximum credit would have been $2,000. A corporation would have received a credit for donations worth up to 75 percent of its tax liability or $100,000, whichever was less. Organizations receiving those donations could have provided scholarships of up to $3,300 to students. Public-school support organizations could have used the contributions to provide grants of up to $500 per student to public schools to help pay for textbooks, computers, or tutors. The aggregate amount of tax credits could not have exceeded $30 million in one year.[258] The bill died in committee.

The Indiana Department of Education delayed the release of start-up funds for charter schools for six months and finally allocated approximately $392,000 to the charter schools in July 2002 after Indiana Attorney General Steve Carter ruled that the state must release the funds.[259]

Three tax credit bills were introduced in 2003, but no action was taken on them before adjournment. H.B. 2002 would have created tax credits for donations to scholarship organizations. Single individuals would have received a credit of up to $500, those filing jointly would have received a credit of up to $1,000, and corporations would have received the lesser of 10 percent of their adjusted gross income tax liability or $500. H.B. 1846 would have created a pilot tax credit program for 2004 and 2005. The maximum credit for families with household incomes under $35,000 would have been $2,000, and the maximum credit for those with incomes over $35,000 would have been $1,000. H.B. 1706 would have phased in tax credits over three years for contributions to scholarship organizations, donations to public schools, tuition expenses, and home-school expenses.[260]

S.B. 501 was signed into law in April 2003, revising Indiana's charter school law. Charters will now be funded as a school district is funded: 35 percent will come from local property tax, and 65 percent will come from the state. Under S.B. 501 (now Act 501) charters are allowed to borrow money from the state for their first semester of operation or if the school has an increase in enrollment of at least 15 percent. The state can only have five charters approved by universities, and the mayor of Indianapolis can approve up to five charters. However, a mayor cannot save his or her unused charter approvals from year to year.[261]

## Position of the Governor / Composition of the State Legislature

Governor Frank O'Bannon, a Democrat, supports public charter schools. Democrats control the Indiana House, and Republicans control the Senate.

## State Contacts

### Black Alliance for Educational Options
Jacqueline Joyner Cissell,
Member, Board of Directors
2423 East McLeay Drive
Indianapolis, IN 46220
Web site: www.baeo.org

### Charter School Association of Indiana, Inc.
10 West Market Street, Suite 1990
Indianapolis, IN 46204
Phone: (317) 464-2679
Fax: (317) 464-2039

### Educational CHOICE Charitable Trust
Robert L. Hoy, Executive Director
7440 Woodland Drive
Indianapolis, IN 46278-1719
Phone: (317) 293-7600, ext. 7378
Fax: (317) 715-7036
E-mail: rhoy@choicetrust.org

### Greater Educational Opportunities Foundation
Kevin Teasley, President
Connie Lee Pulliam, Director of Parent Services
302 South Meridian Street, Suite 201
Indianapolis, IN 46225
Phone: (317) 524-3770
Fax: (317) 524-3773
Web site: www.geofoundation.org
E-mail: Connie@geofoundation.org

---

258. *Ibid.*

259. Center for Education Reform, *Education Reform Newswire*, Vol. 4, No. 30 (July 30, 2002).

260. Indiana General Assembly, House Bills 2002, 1846, and 1706.

261. Indiana General Assembly, Senate Bill 501, and Charter School Resource Center of Indiana, "Summary of SB 501," at *www.indianacharters.org/UsefulResources/Summary%20of%20SB%20501%20 (passed%20April%2027%202003).pdf.*

**Guardian Angel Society**
William "Bill" Dotterweich, Director
2010 Prestwick Lane
Fort Wayne, IN 46814
Phone: (219) 625-3122
Fax: (219) 625-3125
E-mail: bill@dotterweich.com

**Hudson Institute**
Herman Kahn Center
Derek Redelman, Director,
Education Policy Center
5395 Emerson Way
Indianapolis, IN 46226
Phone: (317) 545-1000
Fax: (317) 545-9639
Web site: www.hudson.org
E-mail: derek@hudson.org

**Indiana Association of Home Educators**
8106 Madison Avenue
Indianapolis, IN 46227
Phone: (317) 859-1202
Fax: (317) 859-1204
Web site: www.inhomeeducators.org
E-mail: iahe@inhomeeducators.org

**Indiana Chamber of Commerce**
David Holt, Director of Education Policy and
Congressional Affairs
115 West Washington, Suite 850 South
Indianapolis, IN 46204-3407
Phone: (317) 264-6883
Fax: (317) 264-6855
E-mail: dholt@indianachamber.com

**Indiana Department of Education**
Suellen Reed, Superintendent
Room 229, State House
Indianapolis, IN 46204-2798
Phone: (317) 232-6665
Fax: (317) 232-8004
Web site: www.doe.state.in.us
E-mail: sreed@doe.state.in.us

**Indiana Family Institute**
Curt Smith, President
55 Monument Circle, Suite 322
Indianapolis, IN 46204
Phone: (317) 423-9178
Fax: (317) 423-9421
Web site: www.hoosierfamily.org
E-mail: ifi@hoosier.org

**Indiana Non-Public Education Association**
Glen Tebbe, Executive Director
1400 North Meridian Street
Indianapolis, IN 46202-2367
Phone: (317) 236-7329
Fax: (317) 236-7328
Web site: www.inpea.org
E-mail: inpea@archindy.org

**Milton and Rose D. Friedman Foundation**
Robert Enlow, Vice President,
Programs and Development
P.O. Box 82078
One American Square, Suite 1750
Indianapolis, IN 46282
Phone: (317) 681-0745
Fax: (317) 681-0945
Web site: www.friedmanfoundation.org
E-mail: rcenlow@friedmanfoundation.org

**Northwest Indiana Children's Scholarship Fund–Gary**
Kim Pryzbylski, Executive Director
9292 Broadway
Merriville, IN 46410
Phone: (219) 769-9292, ext. 23
Fax: (219) 738-9034

## State School Report Card
**Greatschools.net**
Web site: www.greatschools.net/modperl/go/IN

**Indiana Department of Education**
Web site: http://doe.state.in.us/htmls/education.html

# IOWA

## State Profile (Updated May 2003)

### School Choice Status
- Public school choice: Interdistrict/mandatory
- State constitution: Compelled-support language
- Charter school law: Established 2002
  Strength of law: Weak
  Number of charter schools in operation: 0
  Number of students attending charter schools: 0
- Publicly funded private school choice: Yes
- Privately funded school choice: Yes
- Home-school law: Moderate regulation
- Ranking on the Education Freedom Index (2001): 33rd out of 50 states

### K–12 Public Schools and Students (2001–2002)
- Public school enrollment: 491,169
- Students enrolled per teacher: 14.2
- Number of schools (2000–2001): 1,529
- Number of districts: 371
- Current expenditures: $3,500,200,000
- Current per-pupil expenditure: $7,126
- Amount of revenue from the federal government: 4.7%

### K–12 Public School Teachers (2001–2002)
- Number of teachers: 34,702
- Average salary: $38,230

### K–12 Private Schools (1999–2000)
- Private school enrollment: 49,565
- Number of schools: 265
- Number of teachers: 3,545

### K–12 Public and Private School Student Academic Performance
- NAEP test results:

| NAEP Tests Iowa Student Performance | State (National) 2000 Math Scale = 0–500 | | State (National) 2000 Science Scale = 0–300 | | State (National) 2000 Reading Scale = 0–500 | |
|---|---|---|---|---|---|---|
| | 4th Grade | 8th Grade | 4th Grade | 8th Grade | 4th Grade | 8th Grade |
| Average Scale Score | 233 (226) | N/A (274) | 160 (148) | N/A (149) | 223 (215) | N/A (261) |
| Advanced | 2% (3%) | N/A (5%) | 4% (3%) | N/A (4%) | 7% (6%) | N/A (2%) |
| Proficient | 26% (23%) | N/A (21%) | 33% (25%) | N/A (26%) | 28% (23%) | N/A (29%) |
| Basic | 50% (43%) | N/A (39%) | 44% (36%) | N/A (29%) | 35% (32%) | N/A (41%) |
| Below Basic | 22% (31%) | N/A (35%) | 19% (36%) | N/A (41%) | 30% (39%) | N/A (28%) |

- SAT weighted rank (2001): N/A
- ACT weighted rank (2001): 3rd out of 26 states
- ALEC Academic Achievement Ranking: 4th out of 50 states and the District of Columbia

## Summary

Since 1987, parents have been able to take a tax deduction or credit for education expenses. Iowa has a limited public school choice law and a weak charter school law. Eligible high school students may take college courses for high school and postsecondary credit. The state also has a dual-enrollment policy that allows both private and home-school students to attend classes at a public school or participate in public school athletic activities.

## Background

In 1987, the legislature enacted the Postsecondary Enrollment Options Act to allow junior and senior high school students to take nonsectarian college courses. The district pays for the courses if the student passes.[262]

During the same year, Iowa enacted legislation that allowed parents with household incomes under $45,000 to deduct up to $1,000 per child for education-related expenses. If using the standard deduction, parents could take a credit equal to 5 percent of $1,000 ($50) for each child.[263] In 1996, the credit was raised to 10 percent and the income eligibility limit was removed.[264]

In 1998, then-Governor Terry E. Branstad signed House File 2513, which increased the tax credit from 10 percent to 25 percent of the first $1,000. This revision stipulated that "materials for extracurricular activities" were also eligible for the tax credit.[265]

In 1999, H.F. 12 was introduced to increase the tuition tax credit to 50 percent of the first

$1,000. House Study Bill 776 similarly would have increased the tuition tax credit and provided tax credits to individuals and corporations that donated to scholarship organizations. Neither bill was passed. A similar attempt was made during the 2001–2002 session in Senate File 86 to raise the tuition tax credit to 50 percent, but no action was taken on the bill.[266]

Iowa offers interdistrict public school choice. Parents are responsible for transporting students to regularly scheduled bus routes. Sending districts reimburse low-income parents for this cost.[267] The superintendent can deny student transfers if they upset the racial quotas. This authority was used in 1992 when Iowa's largest school district, Des Moines, denied more than 100 white students the right to transfer while granting six minority student transfers. The school board determined that the white students' transfers would have hindered desegregation efforts in the district. Des Moines' then-Superintendent of Schools Gary L. Wegenke stated that the transfers would have cost the district state funds used for at-risk student programs.[268]

The district revised its desegregation standards in 1993, and the standards were upheld in a district court decision in 1995. Under the revised standards, which are currently in effect, student transfers will be denied "if [they] would cause the minority enrollment percentage in either the sending or receiving school to exceed the District's minority enrollment percentage" by more than 15 percentage points.[269]

Iowa's open enrollment law allows both private school students and home-school students to

262. Education Commission of the States, "Postsecondary Options: Dual/Concurrent Enrollment," July 2001.

263. Tom Mirga, "Tuition Tax Credits Are Challenged in Iowa," *Education Week*, October 28, 1987.

264. "Legislative Update," *Education Week*, June 5, 1996.

265. Iowa Legislature, "1998 Iowa Tax-Related Legislative Summaries," at *www.state.ia.us/tax/taxlaw/98legsum.html*.

266. Heartland Institute, *School Reform News*, excerpts from *Friedman–Blum Educational Freedom Report* No. 71, May 21,1999, at *www.heartland.org/archives/education/jul99/blum.htm*. See also National School Boards Association, "Voucher Strategy Center," at *www.nsba.org/novouchers/vsc_search.cfm*.

267. Education Commission of the States, "Open Enrollment," August 2001, at *www.ecs.org/clearinghouse/28/73/2873.htm*.

268. Peter Schmidt, "Des Moines Board Refuses to Let White Students Transfer," *Education Week*, December 16, 1992.

269. Des Moines Public Schools, "Board Policy Series 600," at *www.des-moines.k12.ia.us/schoolboard/5policy600.htm#639*.

participate in classes or extracurricular activities that are paid for with state funds at public schools. For each student in this dual-enrollment program, public schools receive one-tenth of the state funds that are given for each full-time public school student. In March 2001, the Ankeny school district in Polk County approved a measure preventing students who are 16 and older (those no longer "compelled" to be in school) from participating in this dual-enrollment program. This restriction was designed to save district funds by not providing tuition for dual-enrollment students who are eligible to take college classes. Parents protested the decision, which had the additional effect of preventing students from participating in public school athletic programs.[270] Faced with legislation that would have nullified its age restrictions, the board decided to defer action regarding dual-enrollment participation in 2002 until after the legislature adjourned for the year. In 2001, there were more than 3,000 dual-enrollment students in Iowa, 65 of whom were in the Ankeny District.[271]

### Developments in 2002 and 2003

Governor Tom Vilsack signed Iowa's charter school law (S.F. 348) in April 2002. S.F. 348 provides for a pilot program allowing 10 charters, but provisions in the bill stipulate that the law will be effective only after the state receives federal funding.[272] Further, charter schools are given little flexibility and cannot waive most regulations.[273] Because of the bill's funding provision, the federal government did not recognize the statute as a true charter school law, and federal money was not granted under the federal charter school program in the No Child Left

Behind Act. In 2003, H.F. 13 and S.F. 172 were introduced to require the Iowa State Board of Education to apply for a federal grant. S.F. 172 was signed into law.[274]

On April 26, 2002, Governor Vilsack signed S.F. 2259, overruling the Ankeny district's dual-enrollment policy. The bill allows both private school students and home-school students to attend classes or participate in athletics at public schools throughout their high school years.[275]

In August 2002, even though 26 Iowa schools did not meet improvement standards under the No Child Left Behind Act, which mandates that students in such schools must be given the option to transfer, fewer than 7 percent of students in those low-performing schools exercised this option. Waterloo District's Logan Middle School had the most transfer requests, but due to space limitations, fewer than half of those 163 requests were granted.[276]

In February 2003, Representative Carmine Boal (R–70) introduced H.F. 268, which would have expanded the tax credit to include the costs of books and other materials used for supplemental education services.[277] Representative Dwayne Alons (R–5) introduced H.F. 474 to create a tax credit worth 25 percent of the first $1,000 spent on books or tuition fees.[278] The bills did not progress.

### Position of the Governor / Composition of the State Legislature

Governor Tom Vilsack, a Democrat, supports charter schools but opposes full parental choice policies such as vouchers. Republicans control both houses of the legislature.

270. Dave DeValois, "Policy Bans Private Students," *The Des Moines Register*, March 23, 2001, and "Bill Would Outlaw Student Policy in Ankeny," *The Des Moines Register*, May 11, 2001.

271. DeValois, "Bill Would Outlaw Student Policy in Ankeny."

272. Iowa Senate File 348 at *www.legis.state.ia.us/GA/79GA/Legislation/SF/00300/SF00348/Current.html*.

273. Center for Education Reform, "Charter Schools in Iowa," at *http://edreform.com/charter_schools/states/iowa.htm*.

274. Iowa Senate File 172 at *http://coolice.legis.state.ia.us/Cool-ICE/default.asp?category=Matt&Service=Billbook&hbill=SF172*; telephone interview with State Representative Philip Wise, April 11, 2003.

275. Iowa Senate File 2259, at *www.legis.state.ia.us/GA/79GA/Legislation/SF/02200/SF02259/Current.html*.

276. Kathy Bolten, "Most Parents Keep Children in Iowa's 'Failing' Schools," *The Des Moines Register*, August 30, 2002.

277. Iowa House File 268, at *www.legis.state.ia.us/GA/80GA/BillHistory/HF/00200/HF00268.html*.

278. Iowa House File 474, at *http://coolice.legis.state.ia.us/Cool-ICE/default.asp?Category=Matt&Service=Billbook&frame=1&hbill=HF474%20%20%20%20%20%20&cham=House*.

## State Contacts

### Iowa Department of Education

Grimes State Office Building
Des Moines, IA 50319-0146
Phone: (515) 281-5294
Fax: (515) 242-5988
Web site: www.state.ia.us/educate

### Iowa Family Policy Center

Chuck Hurley, President
1100 North Hickory Boulevard, Suite 105
Pleasant Hill, IA 50327
Phone (515) 263-3495
Web site: www.ifpc.org
E-mail: info@ifpc.org

### Network of Iowa Christian Home Educators

P.O. Box 158
Dexter, IA 50070
Phone: (515) 830-1614
Fax: (515) 285-7468

Web site: www.the-NICHE.org
E-mail: info@the-niche.org

### Public Interest Institute

Dr. Don Racheter, President
600 North Jackson Street
Mount Pleasant, IA 52641
Phone: (319) 385-3462
Fax: (319) 385-3799
Web site: www.limitedgovernment.org
E-mail: public.interest.institute@limitedgovernment.org

## State School Report Card

### Greatschools.net

Web site: www.greatschools.net/modperl/go/IA

### Iowa Department of Education[279]

Web site: http://www.state.ia.us/educate/fis/pre/eddata/schooltestresults.html

---

279. Iowa provides district-level information.

# KANSAS

## State Profile (Updated May 2003)

### School Choice Status
- Public school choice: Interdistrict/voluntary
- State constitution: Blaine amendment and compelled-support language
- Charter school law: Established 1994
    Strength of law: Weak
    Number of charter schools in operation (fall 2002): 30
    Number of students enrolled in charter schools (fall 2002): 2,568
- Publicly funded private school choice: No
- Privately funded school choice: Yes
- Home-school law: Low regulation
- Ranking on the Education Freedom Index (2001): 20th out of 50 states

### K–12 Public Schools and Students (2001–2002)
- Public school enrollment: 468,140
- Students enrolled per teacher: 14.4
- Number of schools (2000–2001): 1,426
- Number of districts: 304
- Current expenditures: $3,232,852,000
- Current per-pupil expenditure: $6,906
- Amount of revenue from the federal government: 6.2%

### K–12 Public School Teachers (2001–2002)
- Number of teachers: 32,519
- Average salary: $36,673

### K–12 Private Schools (1999–2000)
- Private school enrollment: 43,113
- Number of schools: 237
- Number of teachers: 3,166

### K–12 Public and Private School Student Academic Performance
- NAEP test results:

| NAEP Tests Kansas Student Performance | State (National) 2000 Math Scale = 0–500 | | State (National) 2000 Science Scale = 0–300 | | State (National) 2000 Reading Scale = 0–500 | |
|---|---|---|---|---|---|---|
| | 4th Grade | 8th Grade | 4th Grade | 8th Grade | 4th Grade | 8th Grade |
| Average Scale Score | 232 (226) | 284 (274) | N/A (148) | N/A (149) | 222 (215) | 268 (261) |
| Advanced | 3% (3%) | 4% (5%) | N/A (3%) | N/A (4%) | 6% (6%) | 2% (2%) |
| Proficient | 27% (23%) | 30% (21%) | N/A (25%) | N/A (26%) | 28% (23%) | 33% (29%) |
| Basic | 45% (43%) | 43% (39%) | N/A (36%) | N/A (29%) | 37% (32%) | 46% (41%) |
| Below Basic | 25% (31%) | 23% (35%) | N/A (36%) | N/A (41%) | 2% (39%) | 19% (28%) |

- SAT weighted rank (2001): N/A
- ACT weighted rank (2001): 6th out of 26 states
- ALEC Academic Achievement Ranking: 6th out of 50 states and the District of Columbia

## Summary

Kansas offers little public school choice and has a weak charter school law. Private scholarship foundations help low-income students attend schools of choice.

## Background

In 1993, the legislature enacted the Kansas Challenge to Secondary Schools Pupils Act to allow junior and senior high school students to take higher education courses approved by the Kansas State Department of Education. The student may receive both high school and postsecondary credit.[280]

In 1994, Kansas enacted a charter school law that allowed for the creation of 15 charters statewide.[281] In 2000, the law was amended to allow 30 charters. Under current law, any group that is not affiliated with a religious organization may apply for a charter by submitting a petition to the local school board. Once the charter application is approved by the local board, it is sent to the state board of education for approval. Upon approval, the charter school may apply to the local and state boards for a waiver from the rules and regulations that apply to conventional public schools.[282]

In 1994, then-Representative Kay O'Connor introduced House Bill 2754, an initiative that would have phased in a voucher program over a five-year period. The bill died in committee.[283] Another voucher bill introduced that year, Senate Bill 184, would have provided parents a $3,600 voucher to enroll a child in a public or private school of choice.[284] Neither bill was passed.

In 1995, Representative O'Connor introduced H.B. 2217, a voucher initiative known as the Kansas G.I. Bill for Kids. A companion bill, S.B. 182, was introduced by then-Senators Phil Martin and Michael Harris. The bills would have provided vouchers for children to attend a school of choice, with any amount that was more than the cost of tuition to be held in an account for the child's future college tuition.[285] H.B. 2217 was defeated on the floor by a vote of 23 to 98.[286] S.B. 182 died committee.[287]

In 1997, Representative O'Connor introduced the Parents in Control of Education Act (H.B. 2379), which would have established a K–12 choice program to be phased in throughout a six-year period. By the sixth year, all grades would have been served and the voucher would have been worth the public schools' per-pupil expenditure. The bill died in committee.[288] Another bill, H.B. 2466, introduced by Representative Brenda Landwehr, would have created a pilot voucher program for poor students in Sedgwick and Wyandotte Counties. This bill also died in committee.[289]

In 1998, Kansas City became one of 40 Children's Scholarship Fund (CSF) "partner cities." The CSF, a $100 million foundation, gave the Kansas City metropolitan area a $2.5 million, four-year challenge grant to be matched by local donations. In 1999, the CSF announced the first recipients of the scholarships, students in grades K–8 who had been selected randomly by a computer-generated lottery from 11,000 applications. The CSF currently provides tuition assistance to 968 students in the Kansas City area.[290]

---

280. Education Commission of the States, "Postsecondary Options: Dual/Concurrent Enrollment," July 2001.

281. "Legislative Update," *Education Week*, November 9, 1994.

282. Kansas Statute 72-1906, at *www.ksbe.state.ks.us/charter/law.htm*. See also "Kansas Charter School Information," at *www.uscharterschools.org/pub/sp/27*.

283. Blum Center for Parental Freedom in Education, *Educational Freedom Report* No. 18, February 17, 1995.

284. Blum Center for Parental Freedom in Education, *Educational Freedom Report* No. 5, January 21, 1994.

285. *Educational Freedom Report* No. 18.

286. Blum Center for Parental Freedom in Education, *Educational Freedom Report* No. 31, January 19, 1996.

287. Blum Center for Parental Freedom in Education, *Educational Freedom Report* No. 30, January 30, 1995.

288. Blum Center for Parental Freedom in Education, *Educational Freedom Report* No. 54, December 19, 1997.

289. See National School Boards Association Web site at *www.nsba.org/novouchers*.

290. See Children's Scholarship Fund of Kansas City Web site at *www.csf-kc.org/default.aspx*.

Several parental choice education bills were introduced in 1999. Representative O'Connor resubmitted the Parents in Control of Education Act as H.B. 2462. The Kansas Educational Opportunities Certificate Pilot Program Act, H.B. 2504 and S.B. 295, would have provided a voucher to low-income students in four counties for tuition costs at an accredited private school. The certificate would have been worth 80 percent of the base state per-pupil public school allocation.[291]

The Kansas Opportunity Scholarship Research Experiment Act (H.B. 2913) would have established a three-year research project to test "whether there is a positive, negative or neutral correlation between vouchers which provide availability of choice in the selection of schools and successful pupil learning." Under this proposal, the Kansas State Board of Education would have contracted with a researcher to design and conduct an experiment in which the academic achievement of scholarship recipients was compared to that of a control group that remained in the public school system. All of these bills died in committee.[292]

A 2000 survey commissioned by the Emporia State University Teachers College and funded in part by the Kansas National Education Association (NEA) found that 60 percent of respondents favored school vouchers. In a similar survey taken in February 1994, 53 percent of respondents had favored vouchers.[293]

Also in 2000, Wichita education activist Cindy Duckett launched CEO Kansas, a program that gives poor families privately funded vouchers to send their children to private schools. CEO Kansas followed the model of programs throughout the nation that operate under the umbrella organization Children First America.[294]

In June 2000, Kansas Attorney General Carla Stovall issued a non-binding legal opinion that school vouchers were unconstitutional according to the state's bill of rights and the state constitution.[295]

On-line education made strides in 2000. Educators in the Basehor–Linwood School District created a virtual charter school, designed to appeal to homeschoolers, which allows students to complete coursework on the Internet at their own pace, though students must take state standardized tests to evaluate their progress.[296] The Wichita Public School District created an "eschool" to attract local home-schooling parents to the state's largest school district. The school's mission statement declares that "Wichita School's mission is to eliminate barriers between home school and traditional school-based learning by offering lessons, resources, and teaching support."[297]

During the 2001 legislative session, the Kansas Opportunity Scholarship Research Experiment Act (H.B. 2496 and S.B. 199) was reintroduced. This legislation would have granted funding for a pilot program to study the effects of vouchers on the academic achievement of low-income students. Two tax credit bills, H.B. 2255 and H.B. 2407, were also introduced. H.B. 2255 would have given parents a tax credit of up to $500 for education expenses, such as textbooks and fees, and a tax credit of up to $2,000 for tuition. H.B. 2407 would have provided up to $1 million worth of tax credits to businesses that contributed to organizations that give scholarships to children who are in special-education classes or from low-income families. Additionally, Senator Kay O'Connor reintroduced the Parents in Control of Education Act as S.B. 238 to establish a phased-in choice program for students in grades K–12. All of these bills died in committee.[298]

---

291. See Kansas Legislature Web site at *www.kslegislature.org/*.

292. *Ibid.*

293. George A. Clowes, "Polls Show Majority Support for Vouchers," *School Reform News*, July 2000.

294. Julie Mah, "A New Twist for School Vouchers: Private Funding," *The Wichita Eagle*, May 30, 2000, p. A1.

295. Philip Brownlee, "Don't Read Vouchers Their Last Rites," *The Wichita Eagle*, June 10, 2000, p. A9.

296. See Basehor–Linwood Virtual Charter School Web site, at *http://vcs.usd458.k12.ks.us/*, and Rebecca Weiner, "Kansas Educators Turn to the Web to Create a Unique 'Virtual' School," *The New York Times*, August 16, 2000.

297. See Wichita eSchool at *www.usd259.com/eschool/*.

298. See Kansas Legislature Web site at *www.kslegislature.org/*.

## Developments in 2002 and 2003

H.B. 2255, which would have provided tax credits to parents for private school expenses, and H.B. 2407, which would have given corporations tax credits for donations to scholarship organizations, were carried over into the 2002 session. S.B.199 and H.B. 2496, which would have initiated an experiment to research the effects of vouchers, were also carried over. None of these bills was passed.[299]

The Kansas Parent Control of Education Act was introduced again in 2003, this time as S.B. 211. Under this program, vouchers would be available to students in any grade who are eligible for the free lunch program. The vouchers would be worth a percentage of the state per-pupil allocation, and the voucher amount would increase annually over six years. No action was taken on the bill before adjournment.[300]

## Position of the Governor / Composition of the State Legislature

Governor Kathleen Sebelius, a Democrat, has no stated position on parental choice in education. Republicans control both houses of the legislature.

## State Contacts

**Children First CEO Kansas**
Cindy Duckett, Executive Director
Kim Potochnik, Assistant Director
3410 South Kessler
Wichita, KS 67217
Phone: (316) 942-4545
Fax: (316) 681-3667
Web site: www.ceokansas.com
E-mail: CEOKansas@cox.net

**Children's Scholarship Fund–Kansas City**
Dr. Carl Herbster, President
Mark Brainbridge, Director
4500 Little Blue Parkway
Independence, MO 64057
Phone: (816) 795-8643
Fax: (816) 795-8096

Web site: www.csf-kc.org
E-mail: info@csf-kc.org

**Christian Home Educators Confederation of Kansas**
P.O. Box 1332
Topeka, KS 66601
Phone: (785) 272-6655
Fax: (316) 685-1617
Web site: www.kansashomeschool.org
E-mail: info@kansashomeschool.org

**Flint Hills Center for Public Policy**
Scott Kaye, Executive Director
P.O. Box 782317
Wichita, KS 67278-2317
Phone: (316) 634-0218
Fax: (316) 683-0219
Web site: www.flinthills.org
E-mail: kaye@flinthills.org

**Kansas State Department of Education**
John A. Tompkins, Commissioner
120 Southeast 10th Avenue
Topeka, KS 66612
Phone: (785) 296-3201
Fax: (785) 296-7933
Web site: www.ksbe.state.ks.us
E-mail: atompkins@ksde.org

**Kansas Taxpayers Network**
Karl Peterjohn, Executive Director
P.O. Box 20050
Wichita, KS 67208
Phone: (316) 684-0082
Fax: (316) 684-7527
E-mail: KPeterjohn@prodigy.net
Web site: www.kansastaxpayers.com

## State School Report Card

**Greatschools.net**
Web site: www.greatschools.net/modperl/go/KS

**Kansas State Department of Education**
Web site: www.ksbe.state.ks.us/Welcome.html

**Lawrence Public Schools**
Web site: www.usd497.org/schools

---

299. See National School Boards Association Web site at *www.nsba.org/novouchers*.
300. See Kansas Legislature Web site at *www.kslegislature.org/bills/2004/211.pdf*.

# KENTUCKY

## State Profile (Updated May 2003)

### School Choice Status
- Public school choice: Limited
- State constitution: Blaine amendment and compelled-support language
- Charter school law: No
- Publicly funded private school choice: No
- Privately funded school choice: Yes
- Home-school law: Low regulation
- Ranking on the Education Freedom Index (2001: 43rd out of 50 states

### K–12 Public Schools and Students (2001–2002)
- Public school enrollment: 630,461
- Students enrolled per teacher: 15.6
- Number of schools (2000–2001): 1,376
- Number of districts: 176
- Current expenditures: $4,066,102,000
- Current per-pupil expenditure: $6,449
- Amount of revenue from the federal government: 8.5%

### K–12 Public School Teachers (2001–2002)
- Number of teachers: 40,374
- Average salary: $37,847

### K–12 Private Schools (1999–2000)
- Private school enrollment: 75,084
- Number of schools: 368
- Number of teachers: 5,478

### K–12 Public and Private School Student Academic Performance
- NAEP test results:

| NAEP Tests Kentucky Student Performance | State (National) 2000 Math Scale = 0–500 | | State (National) 2000 Science Scale = 0–300 | | State (National) 2000 Reading Scale = 0–500 | |
|---|---|---|---|---|---|---|
| | 4th Grade | 8th Grade | 4th Grade | 8th Grade | 4th Grade | 8th Grade |
| Average Scale Score | 221 (226) | 272 (274) | 152 (148) | 152 (149) | 218 (215) | 262 (261) |
| Advanced | 1% (3%) | 3% (5%) | 3% (3%) | 3% (4%) | 6% (6%) | 2% (2%) |
| Proficient | 16% (23%) | 18% (21%) | 26% (25%) | 26% (26%) | 23% (23%) | 27% (29%) |
| Basic | 43% (43%) | 42% (39%) | 41% (36%) | 33% (29%) | 34% (32%) | 45% (41%) |
| Below Basic | 40% (31%) | 37% (35%) | 30% (36%) | 38% (41%) | 37% (39%) | 26% (28%) |

- SAT weighted rank (2001): N/A
- ACT weighted rank (2001): 22nd out of 26 states
- ALEC Academic Achievement Ranking: 40th out of 50 states and the District of Columbia

## Summary

Kentucky has limited public school choice and no charter schools.[301] Scholarships are available in the Louisville area through a private foundation. Eligible high school students may take community college courses for high school and postsecondary credit. The number of students being educated in home and private schools has grown rapidly over the past 10 years.

## Background

Section 189 of the Kentucky constitution states that public school funds must "be appropriated to the public schools and to no other purpose." The Kentucky Supreme Court applied this provision in 1983 when it declared that public school textbooks may not be given to private schools.[302] However, another provision in the constitution allows for greater flexibility in the use of public funds: Section 184 stipulates that taxes may be used in areas "other than in common schools" if "the majority of the votes cast at said election shall be in favor of such taxation."[303]

In 1998, House Bill 683 was introduced to provide scholarships to students from families earning less than $42,000. Schools would have been subject to annual performance and financial audits by the Office of Education Accountability. Voucher students could not exceed 65 percent of a private school's enrollment. Another bill, H.B. 533, would have given parents with an adjusted income of $75,000 or less a $500 tax credit for private school expenses. Both bills died in committee.[304]

School CHOICE Scholarships (SCS) began in 1998 and serves Kentucky's largest city, Louisville (Jefferson County). Scholarships of amounts up to $1,000 are awarded each year for up to three years to students from low-income families.[305]

Kentucky has a growing contingent of home-schooling families. According to a report in the *Lexington Herald–Leader*, the number of home schools in Kentucky increased at a rate of "nearly 10 percent a year" from 1991 to 2001, and "the actual number could be much higher."[306]

H.B. 455, a bill similar to H.B. 683 from the 1998 session, was introduced in 2000 to initiate a voucher program. A tax credit bill, H.B. 442, was introduced to give parents a credit for private school expenses. Both bills died in committee.[307]

In 2001, a state circuit court judge declared home schooling "a fundamental right" in a case involving a student whose parents undertook to homeschool her when health problems made it difficult for her to attend a public school. The case, in which the Home School Legal Defense Foundation represented the defendants, was an appeal of a previous decision in which a court had ruled that the student was truant. The circuit court judge ruled that the student could finish her high school studies at home.[308]

## Developments in 2002 and 2003

In September 2002, student transfers from failing Kentucky schools were postponed until the

---

301. Students in state-designated low-performing schools may transfer to another school within or outside of their district.

302. U.S. Department of Education, *State Regulation of Private Schools*, June 2000, at *www.ed.gov/pubs/RegPrivSchl/kentucky.html*.

303. Kentucky Constitution, Sect. 184, at *www.lrc.state.ky.us/Legresou/Constitu/184.htm*.

304. See National School Boards Association Web site at *www.nsba.org/novouchers*.

305. School CHOICE Scholarships, "What is School CHOICE Scholarships?" at *www.schoolchoiceky.com/what.htm* (April 4, 2003). For more information about the Jefferson County enrollment system, see Barbara Myerson Katz, "County Schools: Definitions of Choice," *Louisville Magazine*, January 2002, at *www.louisville.com/loumag/loumagdisplay.html?article=8132*.

306. Linda B. Blackford and Linda J. Johnson, "Private School Figures Jump: Some Areas Eclipse Fayette Gain of 76% Since 1990," *Lexington Herald–Leader*, August 20, 2002, p. A1.

307. See National School Boards Association Web site at *www.nsba.org/novouchers*.

308. Julie Foster, "Kentucky Home-Schooler Wins Victory," *WorldNetDaily*, June 6, 2001, at *www.worldnetdaily.com/news/article.asp?ARTICLE_ID=23116*.

second semester of the school year because state test scores were not released until September 19.[309] Under the federal No Child Left Behind Act, enacted in January 2002, schools that have failed to meet state standards for two consecutive years must inform parents that they may transfer their children to higher-performing schools. On the basis of test scores from the 2000–2001 and 2001–2002 school years, students in 28 schools should have been given the option to transfer to higher-performing schools.[310]

Difficulties arose in informing parents of their new options, and there was conflict regarding the duration for which transferring students would remain at their new schools. News reports indicated that the Fayette school district limited parents' choices, citing reasons of capacity and distance.[311] It was further reported that parents had indicated dissatisfaction with available choices and that limited options prevented many parents from changing their child's school.[312] The transfers were also made less appealing by the fact that students would have to change schools in the middle of the school year,[313] and Kentucky law states that it is the prerogative of the district, rather than the parents, to decide the schools to which students will be transferred.[314]

In 2002, then-Representative Barbara White Colter (R–90) introduced H.B. 54, which would have required that homeschooling parents give "a declaration of intent" before the school year begins; that students take annual norm-refer-enced tests; and that parents who homeschool must have a high school diploma or its equivalent.[315] Currently, home schools are subject to the same laws as private schools, and parents intending to homeschool their children must "first establish a bona fide school, notify the local superintendent…and report the names, ages, and place of residence for each pupil in attendance."[316] H.B. 54 died in committee.[317]

At the end of the summer of 2002, numbers from the 2000 U.S. Census showed a striking increase in the number of students in private schools. Throughout the past decade, for example, private school enrollment has grown by 76 percent in Fayette County, 267 percent in Scott County, and 258 percent in Bourbon County. During the same period, there was a 53.2 percent increase in Kentucky's overall private school enrollment.[318]

In December 2002, the American Center for Law and Justice (ACLJ) filed a lawsuit against Kentucky for "prohibiting state scholarship funds [from being] used by students who pursue a degree in religious studies." The case involved a student at Cumberland College whose state scholarship was revoked when he declared philosophy/religion as his major. The ACLJ, which has dealt successfully with cases of this kind, argued that "[Kentucky's policy] is not only unfair; it is unconstitutional as well."[319] In January 2003, state officials reversed the policy and will no longer discriminate against students who choose a religious

309. Linda B. Blackford, "Student Transfer Option Is Put Off," *Lexington Herald–Leader*, September 5, 2002, p. B1.

310. Mark Pitsch, "28 Kentucky Schools Must Offer Chance to Transfer," *The Courier–Journal*, September 21, 2002, p. A6.

311. Lisa Deffendall, "Fayette District Limits Choices in Schools Taking Transfers; Few Parents Expected to Move Students from Schools that Missed Goals; Parents Can Get Details at 2 Meetings This Week," *Lexington Herald–Leader*, October 28, 2002, p. A7.

312. Lisa Deffendall, "Failing Schools Expect Few to Transfer: Parents' Fears Likely to Prevent Exodus," *Lexington Herald–Leader*, October 28, 2002, p. A1.

313. *Ibid.*

314. Linda B. Blackford, "'Failing' Schools Report Criticized: Kentucky Educators Call It Misleading; Some on List Improved," *Lexington Herald–Leader*, July 3, 2002, p. A1.

315. Home School Legal Defense Association, "House Bill 54: An Act Relating to Nonpublic Schools," April 15, 2002, at *www.hslda.org/legislation/state/ky/2002/kyhb54/default.asp?PrinterFriendly=True*.

316. U.S. Department of Education, *State Regulation of Private Schools*.

317. Home School Legal Defense Association, "House Bill 54: An Act Relating to Nonpublic Schools."

318. Blackford and Johnson, "Private School Figures Jump."

319. American Center for Law and Justice, "ACLJ Files Federal Suit Against Kentucky for Denying Scholarship Funds to Students Who Study Religion," December 6, 2002, at *www.aclj.org/news/pressreleases/021206_nash.asp*.

course of study. In response, the ACLJ filed a motion to dismiss the lawsuit.[320]

## Position of the Governor / Composition of the State Legislature

Governor Paul Patton, a Democrat, has no stated position on school choice. Democrats control the House, and Republicans control the Senate.

## State Contacts

**Kentucky Association of Professional Educators**
Ruth Green, Director
3499 Lansdowne Drive
Lexington, KY 40524
Phone: (888) 438-7179

**Thomas and Katie Stephens**
1014 Tilley Drive
Carrolton, KY 41008
Phone: (502) 732-5957
Web site: www.kentuckyteachers.org
E-mail: tskape@yahoo.com or ktbugstep@yahoo.com

**Kentucky Department of Education**
Lisa Gross
Capitol Plaza Tower, 19th Floor
Frankfort, KY 40601
Phone: (502) 564-4770
Fax: (502) 564-6470
Web site: www.kde.state.ky.us
E-mail: lgross@kde.state.ky.us

**Kentucky Home Education Association**
P.O. Box 51591
Bowling Green, KY 42102
Phone: (859) 737-3338
Fax: (859) 745-4466
Web site: www.khea.8k.com
E-mail: katy@mis.net

**Kentucky League for Educational Alternatives**
Harry Borders, Executive Director
1042 Burlington Lane
Frankfort, KY 40601
Phone: (502) 875-8010
Fax: (502) 875-2841
Web site: www.kleaonline.org

**School CHOICE Scholarships, Inc.**
Diane Cowne, Executive Director
P.O. Box 221546
Louisville, KY 40252-1546
Phone: (502) 254-7274
Fax: (502) 245-4792
Web site: www.schoolchoiceky.com
E-mail: diane@pattco.net

## State School Report Card

**Greatschools.net**
Web site: www.greatschools.net/modperl/go/KY

**Kentucky Department of Education**
Web site: http://apps.kde.state.ky.us/report_card

---

320. Alana Keynes, "Faced With Lawsuit, Ky. Changes Scholarship Policy," *Education Daily*, January 29, 2003.

# LOUISIANA

## State Profile (Updated May 2003)

### School Choice Status
- Public school choice: Interdistrict/voluntary
- State constitution: No prohibitive language
- Charter school law: Established 1995
    Strength of law: Weak
    Number of charter schools in operation (fall 2002): 20
    Number of students enrolled (fall 2002): 4,631
- Publicly funded private school choice: No
- Privately funded school choice: Yes
- Home-school law: Moderate regulation
- Ranking on the Education Freedom Index (2001): 23rd out of 50 states

### K–12 Public Schools and Students (2001–2002)
- Public school enrollment: 731,474
- Students enrolled per teacher: 14.7
- Number of schools (2000–2001): 1,508
- Number of districts: 87
- Current expenditures: $4,586,237,000
- Current per-pupil expenditure: $6,270
- Amount of revenue from the federal government: 11.7%

### K–12 Public School Teachers (2001–2002)
- Number of teachers: 49,915
- Average salary: $35,437

### K–12 Private Schools (1999–2000)
- Private school enrollment: 138,135
- Number of schools: 434
- Number of teachers: 9,206

### K–12 Public and Private School Student Academic Performance
- NAEP test results:

| NAEP Tests Louisiana Student Performance | State (National) 2000 Math Scale = 0–500 | | State (National) 2000 Science Scale = 0–300 | | State (National) 2000 Reading Scale = 0–500 | |
|---|---|---|---|---|---|---|
| | 4th Grade | 8th Grade | 4th Grade | 8th Grade | 4th Grade | 8th Grade |
| Average Scale Score | 218 (226) | 259 (274) | 139 (148) | 136 (149) | 204 (215) | 252 (261) |
| Advanced | 1% (3%) | 1% (5%) | 2% (3%) | 2% (4%) | 3% (6%) | 1% (2%) |
| Proficient | 13% (23%) | 11% (21%) | 17% (25%) | 16% (26%) | 16% (23%) | 17% (29%) |
| Basic | 43% (43%) | 36% (39%) | 34% (36%) | 27% (29%) | 29% (32%) | 46% (41%) |
| Below Basic | 43% (31%) | 52% (35%) | 47% (36%) | 55% (41%) | 52% (39%) | 36% (28%) |

- SAT weighted rank (2001): N/A
- ACT weighted rank (2001): 25th out of 26 states
- ALEC Academic Achievement Ranking: 49th out of 50 states and the District of Columbia

## Summary

The Louisiana constitution contains neither a Blaine amendment nor compelled-support language. The state has funded vouchers for pre-kindergarten students since 2001. Louisiana has a weak charter school law and limited public school choice.[321]

## Background

In 1995, then-Governor Edwin Edwards, a Democrat, signed a weak charter school bill (Act 192), which allowed eight districts to participate in a pilot charter school program. The law was substantially enhanced in 1997 by Act 477, which allowed all 66 school districts to participate in the program. However, the number of charter schools statewide was capped at 42.[322] In addition, Act 477 enabled charter applicants to re-apply for a charter from the Louisiana School Chartering Authority, part of the Louisiana Board of Elementary and Secondary Education (BESE), if the local district denied the initial application. The law also provides a $5 million no-interest loan fund to help new schools with initial costs.[323] Minor logistical changes were made in the state's charter school law in 1999 through Acts 14, 757, 821, 1210, and 1339.

The Louisiana Department of Education classifies the state's charter schools into four categories, which determine whether schools can enroll students outside of the district, how they are funded, their degree of independence from the district, and the percentage of low-income students they are required to enroll.[324]

In May 1997, the Louisiana Senate Education Committee defeated a $300 million voucher bill, Senate Bill 343, by a vote of 4 to 3.[325] This bill would have created state vouchers to be used toward tuition at private schools, including schools with a religious affiliation. On the basis of the state's per-pupil expenditure for public schools, approximately $2,500 would have followed a student to a school of choice.[326]

Voucher legislation was stymied again in 1999 with the failure of House Bill 725, which died in committee. The bill would have authorized tuition vouchers for amounts up to $1,500 for students who qualify for the free lunch program. The program would have phased in students in grades K–3 over three years, starting with kindergarten and 1st grade students in the 2000–2001 school year. The vouchers would have been administered through a Right to Learn program that would have been supervised by a five-member commission.[327] Two other bills, H.B. 1652 and S.B. 299, would have created the Education Voucher Program, a private-school voucher program that would have been implemented over a 13-year period. Kindergarten students would have been eligible in the program's first year, 1st grade students in the second year, and students in higher grades in subsequent years. Both of these bills also died in committee.[328]

S.B. 964, which would have created the Louisiana Opportunity Scholarship Program, was also introduced in 1999. This bill would have made it possible for students in grades 1–7 in schools that had been declared "academically unacceptable" by the district to receive scholarships to attend a private school until 8th grade. The bill was passed in committee but was tabled on the Senate floor by a vote of 22 to 14.[329]

---

321. Students in state-designated low-performing schools may attend another public school within or outside of the district.

322. Louisiana Department of Education, "Charter Schools," at *www.lcet.doe.state.la.us/doe/bese/charter.asp*.

323. Louisiana State Legislature, "Governor Foster's K–12 Legislative Package: Key 1997 Education Reform Items," February 26, 1997, at *www.gov.state.la.us/educ/1997/over2.html*.

324. Louisiana Department of Education, "Charter Schools."

325. Littice Bacon-Blood, "School Voucher Plan Rejected in Close Vote," *The New Orleans Times–Picayune*, May 2, 1997, A4.

326. *Ibid.*

327. Louisiana State Legislature, Regular Session, 1999, House Bill No. 725.

328. Louisiana State Legislature, Regular Session, 1999, House Bill No. 1652 and Senate Bill No. 299.

329. Louisiana State Legislature, Regular Session, 1999, Senate Bill No. 964.

It was not until 2001 that state-funded vouchers became a reality in Louisiana. In 2001, $3 million was included in the state budget to help low-income families pay tuition for all-day pre-kindergarten at private schools or religious schools as part of a one-year pilot program. The American Civil Liberties Union immediately challenged the measure, arguing that money from the state budget had been appropriated without legislation that would determine its use. To quell the opposition and give evidence that a clear plan accompanied the money, Governor Mike Foster, a Republican, made public the program's outline, including the draft of a contract with Catholic Charities of the Archdiocese of New Orleans, which would administer the project. The Louisiana Board of Elementary and Secondary Education compiled a list of approved nonpublic schools that students could attend.[330] For the 2001–2002 school year, the program provided approximately $4,700 per recipient.[331]

There are two privately funded scholarship organizations in Louisiana: CSF–Baton Rouge and CSF–New Orleans. Both programs operate in conjunction with the Children's Scholarship Fund, the privately funded national scholarship organization that matches parents' expenditures for their children's education.[332] CSF–Baton Rouge awarded 93 scholarships in 1988 (its first year) and 77 scholarships in 2002–2003.[333]

On June 28, 2000, in a 6 to 3 decision, the Supreme Court of the United States upheld the practice of lending educational equipment, including computers and books, to private schools for nonreligious purposes.[334] Under Chapter 2 of the federal Elementary and Secondary Education Act of 1965, funds were provided to public and private schools based on enrollment. Parents in Jefferson Parish, Louisiana, filed suit against the state, arguing that the practice of lending equipment to private schools violated the Establishment Clause of the U.S. Constitution. In 1985, a federal appeals court struck down the aid program.

The 2000 Supreme Court ruling reversed this decision and agreed with the parents of private school children who had appealed the 1985 ruling, arguing that such aid was constitutional as long as it was dispersed to schools on a neutral basis. "[I]f numerous private choices, rather than the single choice of a government, determine the distribution of aid pursuant to neutral eligibility criteria," wrote Associate Justice Clarence Thomas, "then a government cannot, or at least cannot easily, grant special favors that might lead to a religious establishment."[335] Currently, districts receive funds on the basis of the total number of students in a district, not just the number of public school students, and the funds must be shared with nonpublic schools.[336]

## Developments in 2002 and 2003

In 2003, Governor Mike Foster proposed providing vouchers to students attending the state's academically troubled public schools. State Representative Carl Crane (R–70) then introduced H.B. 1337 to provide vouchers to low-income students. The bill required private schools in the program to have two years of nationally recognized testing data. It also mandated state testing for all students, even those not on state scholarship. The bill's author gave up when three similar bills were voted down in committee on April 30.[337]

H.B. 1771 would have established the Louisiana Parental Choice in Education Program to provide scholarships or tutorial grants to low-income students in poor-performing schools.

330. Erik W. Robelen, "Louisiana Plan to Subsidize Pre-K in Religious Schools Draws Fire," *Education Week*, August 8, 2001, and George A. Clowes, "Voucher Proposals Flourish Nationwide," *School Reform News*, Heartland Institute, October 2001.

331. Clowes, "Voucher Proposals Flourish Nationwide."

332. For more information, see Children's Scholarship Fund Web site at *www.scholarshipfund.org/index.asp*.

333. Phone interview with Sylvia Mangum, CSF–Baton Rouge, April 14, 2003.

334. *Mitchell v. Helms* 530 U.S. 793 (2000).

335. *Ibid.* See also National Center for Policy Analysis, "School Choice in the Courts," *Policy Backgrounder* No. 153, August 7, 2000, at *www.ncpa.org/bg/bg153/bg153.html*.

336. George A. Clowes, "Court OKs Neutral Aid to Religious Schools," *School Reform News*, Heartland Institute, August 2000.

337. Scott Dyer, "'No Chance of Passing,' House Panel Kills Bill Offering Vouchers for Private Schools," *The Advocate*, May 1, 2003, and Louisiana Legislature, 2003 Regular Session, at *www.legis.state.la.us/*.

Students in grades K–8 would have been able to use the scholarship at another public, charter, or eligible private school or for tutoring. The scholarship would have been worth the state share of public school funding or private school tuition, whichever was less. To be eligible to participate, private schools would have had to meet certain requirements such as minimum enrollment and approval by the Louisiana Board of Elementary and Secondary Education. The bill was defeated in committee by a vote of 14 to 3.[338]

H.B. 854 would have phased in vouchers starting with kindergarten students in 2004, adding vouchers for students in the next higher grade each year until 2016. Any student would have been eligible to participate in the program, and the vouchers could have been used for tuition at any state-approved nonpublic school. The bill was killed in committee by a vote of 13 to 4.[339]

H.B. 1739 would have provided vouchers to poor students in low-performing schools in parishes with a population of at least 475,000 persons (New Orleans). The bill required private schools in the program to have five years of testing data using a nationally recognized test. It also required schools to give all students, both private pay and voucher students, the state math and reading tests. This bill also lost in committee by a vote of 13 to 4.[340]

On May 8, the Senate Education Committee, by a margin of 3 to 2, voted to shelve one voucher bill (S.B. 1037) and set aside two others (S.B. 985 and S.B. 943). S.B. 1037 would have provided scholarships to low-income children for preschool or K–3 education. Under S.B. 985, poor students in grades K–8 would have been able to use a state-funded scholarship at another public, charter, or eligible private school or for tutoring. S.B. 943 would have enabled students in grades 1–7 who attend a poor-performing public school to transfer to an approved private school. Students on state scholarship would

have had to participate in the state testing program.[341]

## Position of the Governor / Composition of the State Legislature

Governor M. J. "Mike" Foster, Jr., a Republican, supports parental choice in education, including vouchers. Democrats control both houses of the legislature.

## State Contacts

**Children's Scholarship Fund–Baton Rouge**
Pat Van Burkleo, Director
P.O. Box 2013
Baton Rouge, LA 70821
Phone: (225) 387-6840
Fax: (225) 344-2582

**Children's Scholarship Fund–
New Orleans/Southeast**
Virginia Soileau, Program Coordinator
7611 Maple Street, Suite F
New Orleans, LA 70118
Phone: (504) 862-6992
Fax: (504) 862-6993
Web site: www.scholarshipfund.org
E-mail: csfsb@bellsouth.net

**Jacklyn Ducote & Associates–
Empowerment Resources**
Jackie Ducote, President
P.O. Box 14588
Baton Rouge, LA 70898
Phone: (225) 343-7020
Fax: (225) 383-1967
E-mail: Jhducote@aol.com

**Louisiana Department of Education**
Cecil J. Picard
State Superintendent of Education
P.O. Box 94064
Baton Rouge, LA 70804-9064
Phone: (225) 342-3602
Web site: www.doe.state.la.us
E-mail: cpicard@doe.state.la.us

---

338. *Ibid.*.
339. *Ibid.*
340. *Ibid.*
341. Will Sentell, "Senate panel kills 3 bills to create voucher plans," *The Advocate*, May 9, 2003 and Louisiana Legislature, 2003 Regular Session, at *www.legis.state.la.us*.

**Public Affairs Research Council**
Jim Brandt, President
4664 Jamestown Avenue, Suite 300
P.O. Box 14776
Baton Rouge, LA 70898-4776
Phone: (225) 926-8414
Fax: (225) 926-8417
Web site: www.la-par.org
E-mail: staff@la-par.org

## State School Report Card

**Greatschools.net**
Web site: www.greatschools.net/modperl/go/LA

**Louisiana Department of Education**
Web site: www.doe.state.la.us/DOE/asps/
home.asp?I=TESTS

# MAINE

## State Profile (Updated May 2003)

### School Choice Status
- Public school choice: Interdistrict/voluntary
- State constitution: No prohibitive language
- Charter school law: No
- Publicly funded private school choice: Yes
- Privately funded school choice: Yes
- Home-school law: High regulation
- Ranking on the Education Freedom Index (2001): 15th out of 50 states

### K–12 Public Schools and Students (2001–2002)
- Public school enrollment: 211,461
- Students enrolled per teacher: 12.4
- Number of schools (2000–2001): 686
- Number of districts: 285
- Current expenditures: $1,725,472,000
- Current per-pupil expenditure: $8,160
- Amount of revenue from the federal government: 7.3%

### K–12 Public School Teachers (2001–2002)
- Number of teachers: 17,040
- Average salary: $37,100

### K–12 Private Schools (1999–2000)
- Private school enrollment: 18,287
- Number of schools: 139
- Number of teachers: 1,760

### K–12 Public and Private School Student Academic Performance
- NAEP test results:

| NAEP Tests Maine Student Performance | State (National) 2000 Math Scale = 0–500 | | State (National) 2000 Science Scale = 0–300 | | State (National) 2000 Reading Scale = 0–500 | |
|---|---|---|---|---|---|---|
| | 4th Grade | 8th Grade | 4th Grade | 8th Grade | 4th Grade | 8th Grade |
| Average Scale Score | 231 (226) | 284 (274) | 161 (148) | 160 (149) | 225 (215) | 273 (261) |
| Advanced | 2% (3%) | 6% (5%) | 4% (3%) | 3% (4%) | 8% (6%) | 4% (2%) |
| Proficient | 23% (23%) | 26% (21%) | 34% (25%) | 34% (26%) | 28% (23%) | 38% (29%) |
| Basic | 49% (43%) | 44% (39%) | 44% (36%) | 38% (29%) | 37% (32%) | 42% (41%) |
| Below Basic | 26% (31%) | 24% (35%) | 18% (36%) | 25% (41%) | 27% (39%) | 16% (28%) |

- SAT weighted rank (2001): 13th out 24 states and the District of Columbia
- ACT weighted rank (2001): N/A
- ALEC Academic Achievement Ranking: 14th out of 50 states and the District of Columbia

## Summary

Maine has been paying for students to attend private schools since colonial times. A century ago, the state enacted the town "tuitioning" law that still serves students today. Under the law, school districts without public schools allow students to attend nonsectarian private or public schools in other districts.[342] High school students may take college courses with district approval for high school and postsecondary credit.[343] Private scholarship funds provide vouchers to low-income students to attend a school of choice.

## Background

State "town tuitioning" for education predates statehood in Maine. In the 18th and 19th centuries, many towns made provision for the education of children, but few operated schools. Instead, they contracted with religious organizations and ministers to provide an elementary school education for all children. Some students also received public funds for secondary education at a private religiously affiliated academy.[344]

The demand for secondary education increased significantly throughout the 19th century. In 1873, Maine adopted the Free High School Act, which encouraged towns to make a free secondary education available to students by building public schools or paying their tuition at private academies. In 1909, the legislature began requiring towns without a secondary school to pay tuition for students to attend a private or public school in another town.[345]

Families could choose religiously affiliated schools under the tuitioning program until 1981, when the Maine legislature passed a law that restricted school choice to nonsectarian schools. The new law was a response to a 1980 decision by Maine Attorney General Joseph Brennan (himself a graduate of a private school) that tuition payments to religious schools were in violation of the Establishment Clause of the U.S. Constitution.[346]

By the late 1990s, 140 school districts with public schools were paying tuition for roughly 13,000 students with tuition fees averaging $6,000. Approximately 40 percent of the students were enrolled in nonsectarian private schools.[347] The towns' tuition expenditures were reimbursed partially or completely by the state.[348]

In 1997, the Institute for Justice, a public-interest law firm based in Washington, D.C., filed a lawsuit in the case of *Bagley* v. *Town of Raymond* on behalf of Maine parents living in tuitioning towns who wished to send their children to a religious school and receive the same subsidy as parents who send their children to secular private schools. The lawsuit argued that excluding religious schools violates the U.S. Constitution, which guarantees both the free exercise of religion and equal protection under the law.[349] The Cumberland County Superior Court in Portland ruled against the parents in 1998.[350] The Maine Supreme Court upheld that decision in April 1999, and the First Circuit Court of Appeals upheld the Maine law in a similar case brought by the American Center for Law and Justice (ACLJ). In October 1999, the Supreme Court of the United States declined to review either decision.[351]

---

342. Institute for Justice, "The Case for School Choice: Raymond, Maine Litigation Backgrounder," at *www.ij.org/cases/index.html*.

343. Education Commission of the States, "Postsecondary Options: Dual/Concurrent Enrollment," July 2001.

344. Institute for Justice, "The Case for School Choice."

345. Frank Heller, "Lessons from Maine: Education Vouchers for Students Since 1873," Cato Institute *Briefing Paper* No. 66, September 10, 2001.

346. Institute for Justice, "The Case for School Choice."

347. *Ibid.*

348. Heller, "Lessons from Maine."

349. Institute for Justice, "The Case for School Choice."

350. Correspondence from Maureen Blum, Institute for Justice, December 16, 1998.

In 1995, the Maine Legislature established its first "charter school"—the Maine School of Science and Mathematics (MSSM). Although it is funded by the legislature and receives more flexibility than other schools, the MSSM is essentially a magnet school that serves students in grades 10–12 who enroll from districts throughout the state. Like magnet schools, the MSSM has admissions requirements.[352]

In 1996, several bills to authorize the creation of public charter schools were introduced but died in committee. Between 1997 and 1998, the Maine State Board of Education undertook a study of charter schools. In 1999, Legislative Document 2027, An Act to Enable the Formation of Public Charter Schools, was introduced. After being significantly weakened during the amendment process, the proposed legislation was withdrawn by its sponsor. The committee chairman proposed new language, making it easier for students to transfer to another public school within a region, and L.D. 2027 (now titled "An Act to Encourage Educational Options") was passed. One provision in the bill required that a "Charter School Stakeholders' Group" be created by the Maine Department of Education in 2000 to discuss how Maine could meet the criteria to participate in the federal charter school grant program.[353]

Two choice-related bills were introduced in 1999. H.B. 560 would have required the Maine State Department of Education to implement a voucher program. If the amount of the voucher was greater than the amount for tuition, parents could have used the funds for additional education-related costs such as athletics, transportation, or school supplies. Another bill, Senate Bill 621, would have established a $500 tax credit for parents with incomes under $50,000 who enroll their children in private schools. Neither bill passed.[354]

In 2000, Betsy Chapman and Frank Heller launched the Maine Children's Scholarship Fund. This organization (which has no affiliation with the nationwide Children's Scholarship Fund) offers partial tuition scholarships for low-income K–12 students in public and private schools and reimburses expenses for home schooling. It provides up to 75 percent of tuition costs, up to $1,700.[355] During the 2002–2003 school year, the Maine Children's Scholarship Fund provided assistance to 77 students. During the previous year, 50 students received scholarships.[356]

L.D. 1531, introduced in 2001, would have allowed the local school district, the state board, or nonsectarian higher education institutions to sponsor charter schools and would have allowed any existing public school to convert to charter status with sufficient approval by teachers and parents. Under this legislation, rejected charters could have appealed to the state board. L.D. 1531 was amended in committee to allow only existing public schools to convert to charter schools. It also would have directed the state board of education to propose rules for creation of new charter schools. This version was passed by the Senate but was defeated in the House of Representatives by a vote of 89 to 49.[357]

L.D. 311, also introduced in 2001, would have provided an income tax credit for educational expenses associated with public, private, or home schooling for K–12 students. The credit would have been equal to 33 percent of a student's education expenses, up to $750 per dependent child. The bill died in committee.[358]

In February 2001, approximately 500 home-schooling parents attended a hearing to oppose L.D. 405, a bill that would have required their children to take the Maine Educational Assessment Test. In addition, the bill would have provided state funds to local districts for every student who was homeschooled, despite the fact

---

351. Institute for Justice, "Maine School Choice," at *www.ij.org/cases/index.html.*

352. Maine Association for Charter Schools, "Frequently Asked Questions," at *www.mainecharterschools.org/Faqs.cfm.* See also Maine School of Science and Mathematics Web site at *www.mssm.org/about/index.htm.*

353. Maine Association for Charter Schools, "Brief History of Charter School Efforts in Maine," at *www.mainecharterschools.org/MaineStatus.cfm.*

354. See National School Boards Association Web site at *www.nsba.org/novouchers.*

355. See Maine Children's Scholarship Fund Web site at *www.mecsf.org/Homex.html.*

356. Phone conversation with Betsy Chapman, President, MCSF Board of Directors, April 22, 2003.

357. Maine Association for Charter Schools, "Brief History of Charter School Efforts in Maine."

358. See Maine Legislature Web site at *http://janus.state.me.us/legis/.*

that few students use public school services. (At that time, over 4,000 Maine students were home-schooled).[359] L.D. 405 did not make it out of committee.

## Developments in 2002 and 2003

On November 26, 2002, the Maine Principals' Association, the organization that regulates high school interscholastic extracurricular activities, sent a memorandum to private schools stating that they would be ineligible to compete with other teams if they allowed home-schooled students to play on their teams. A 1995 Maine statute allows home schoolers to play on local public school teams; since then, home-schooled students have participated in sports activities through both public and private schools. In response to the Maine Principals' Association memorandum, the Home School Legal Defense Association filed a complaint in court in March 2003, requesting a preliminary injunction.[360] On May 12, 2003, a federal district court ruled that if home-schooled students wished to participate in sports, they would have to do so through the public school system.[361]

Six Maine families, represented by the Institute for Justice, are challenging the law that prevents them from choosing religious schools under the state's tuitioning program. The families live in three small rural towns—Durham, Minot, and Raymond—where the school districts do not maintain a public high school and instead pay for tuition to attend private schools or public schools in other districts. According to Institute

for Justice senior attorney Richard Komer, lead counsel for the litigation, "Maine offers school choice to everyone except those who choose religious schools. Under the Constitution, that's religious discrimination, and we intend to restore our clients' religious liberty."[362] In October 2002, the ACLJ filed a similar suit against the Maine Department of Education on behalf of families in Minot.[363]

During the 2003 legislative session, Representative Kevin Glynn (R–South Portland) introduced a bill that would repeal this state law prohibiting state-funded tuition to religious schools (L.D. 182). The bill was defeated in the House by a vote of 89 to 56.[364]

Senator Carol Weston (R–Montville) introduced charter school legislation, L.D. 1391, in 2003. The bill was defeated in the Senate by a vote of 22 to 13.[365]

In 2003, Senator Weston also introduced L.D. 160 to ease restrictions on home-school students; allow parents to notify officials of their intent to homeschool rather than applying for permission to do so, as they are currently mandated to do; and reduce paperwork for home-schooling parents. This bill was passed and signed into law.[366]

In early 2003, Representative Roger L. Sherman (R–Hodgdon) introduced L.D. 756, which would have provided tax credits for private school tuition payments. The bill died in the Senate Committee on Taxation.[367]

359. Tess Nacelewicz, "Schooling at Home: Advocates Rise to Test," *Portland Press Herald*, February 22, 2001.

360. Home School Legal Defense Association, "Maine Homeschoolers Denied Access to Private School Sports," March 18, 2003, at *www.hslda.org/docs/news/hslda/200303/200303200.asp*.

361. Home School Legal Defense Association, "Judge Rules Against Maine Family in Sports Case," May 13, 2003, at *www.hslda.org/hs/state/me/200305130.asp*.

362. Institute for Justice, "Institute for Justice Launches School Choice Offensive With Nation's First Choice Lawsuit After U.S. Supreme Court Victory," Web release, September 18, 2002.

363. American Center for Law and Justice, "ACLJ Files Suit Against Maine Dept. of Education for Discriminating Against Religious Schools by Denying Tuition Payments," October 18, 2002, at *www.aclj.org/news/pressreleases/021018_maine_school.asp*.

364. Maine Legislature, 2003 Session, L.D. 182, at *http://janus.state.me.us/legis/LawMakerWeb/summary.asp?ID=280008196*.

365. Maine Legislature, 2003 Session, L.D. 1391, at *http://janus.state.me.us/legis/LawMakerWeb/dockets.asp?ID=280010056*.

366. Home School Legal Defense Association, "Maine Homeschoolers Pack Hearing Room for LD 160," May 9, 2003, at *www.hslda.org/hs/state/me/200305090.asp*.

367. Maine Legislature, 2003, L.D. 756, at *http://janus.state.me.us/legis/LawMakerWeb/summary.asp?ID=280008994*.

## Position of the Governor / Composition of the State Legislature

Governor John Baldacci, a Democrat, has no stated position on school choice. Democrats control both houses of the legislature.

## State Contacts

**Homeschoolers of Maine**
Ed Green, President
P.O. Box 159
Camden, ME 04843
Phone: (207) 763-2880
Web site: www.homeschoolersofmaine.org
E-mail: homeschl@midcoast.com

**Maine Association for Charter Schools**
Judith Jones, Chair
199 Hatchet Mountain Road
Hope, ME 04847
Phone: (207) 763-3576
Fax: (207) 763-4552
Web site: www.mainecharterschools.org
E-mail: macs@mainecharterschools.org

**Maine Children's Scholarship Fund**
Kari Picard, Program Director
27 State Street, Suite 64A
Bangor, ME 04401

Phone: (207) 945-6893
Fax: (207) 945-6583
Web site: www.mecsf.org
E-mail: mecsf@midmaine.com

**Maine School Choice Coalition**
Frank Heller, State Coordinator
12 Belmont Street
Brunswick, ME 04011-3004
Phone: (207) 729-1590
Fax: (207) 729-1590
E-mail: global1@gwi.net

## State School Report Card

**Greatschools.net**
Web site: www.greatschools.net/modperl/go/ME

**Independent Schools Association of Northern New England**
Web site: www.isanne.org/frame_isanne.asp?x=choose

**Maine State Department of Education**
Web site: www.state.me.us/education/profiles/profilehome.htm

# MARYLAND

## State Profile (Updated May 2003)

### School Choice Status
- Public school choice: Limited
- State constitution: Compelled-support language
- Charter school law: Yes
- Publicly funded private school choice: No
- Privately funded school choice: Yes
- Home-school law: Moderate regulation
- Ranking on the Education Freedom Index (2001): 46th out of 50 states

### K–12 Public Schools and Students (2001–2002)
- Public school enrollment: 860,890
- Students enrolled per teacher: 15.8
- Number of schools (2000–2001): 1,342
- Number of districts: 24
- Current expenditures: $6,755,070,000
- Current per-pupil expenditure: $7,847
- Amount of revenue from the federal government: 5.0%

### K–12 Public School Teachers (2001–2002)
- Number of teachers: 54,360
- Average salary: $46,200

### K–12 Private Schools (1999–2000)
- Private school enrollment: 144,131
- Number of schools: 701
- Number of teachers: 12,152

### K–12 Public and Private School Student Academic Performance
- NAEP test results:

| NAEP Tests Maryland Student Performance | State (National) 2000 Math Scale = 0–500 | | State (National) 2000 Science Scale = 0–300 | | State (National) 2000 Reading Scale = 0–500 | |
|---|---|---|---|---|---|---|
| | 4th Grade | 8th Grade | 4th Grade | 8th Grade | 4th Grade | 8th Grade |
| Average Scale Score | 231 (226) | 284 (274) | 146 (148) | 149 (149) | 225 (215) | 273 (261) |
| Advanced | 2% (3%) | 6% (5%) | 3% (3%) | 3% (4%) | 7% (6%) | 4% (2%) |
| Proficient | 20% (23%) | 23% (21%) | 23% (25%) | 25% (26%) | 22% (23%) | 27% (29%) |
| Basic | 39% (43%) | 36% (39%) | 35% (36%) | 31% (29%) | 32% (32%) | 41% (41%) |
| Below Basic | 39% (31%) | 35% (35%) | 39% (36%) | 41% (41%) | 39% (39%) | 28% (28%) |

For updates go to: *heritage.org*

101

- SAT weighted rank (2001): 8th out of 24 states and the District of Columbia
- ACT weighted rank (2001): N/A
- ALEC Academic Achievement Ranking: 22nd out of 50 states and the District of Columbia

## Summary

Maryland offers little public school choice. Governor Robert Ehrlich signed a charter law for the state on May 22, 2003. Low-income children can attend a school of choice with the help of privately funded tuition scholarships.

## Background

In a 1972 ballot referendum, Maryland residents voted against a statewide voucher program by a margin of 55 percent to 45 percent.[368]

Baltimore became one of 40 Children's Scholarship Fund (CSF) "partner cities" in 1998. A lottery in April 1999 awarded four-year scholarships to 430 of more than 20,000 applicants who were entering kindergarten through 8th grade. Baltimore residents raised $1 million to complement the fund.[369]

The Take Credit for Learning Act (House Bill 564) was introduced in 1999 to provide tax deductions of up to $1,500 per child in grades K–6 for education expenses, including tuition, and up to $2,500 for students in grades 7–12. For parents earning less than $33,500, the bill would have granted a tax credit of $1,000 per child (maximum of $2,000) for education expenses. The bill was killed in committee.[370]

Nearly one-third of Baltimore City's elementary school students failed to meet promotion standards at the end of the 2000–2001 school year. Approximately half of the city's 8th graders also failed to meet the standards.[371] It was later discovered that students who had failed to meet the standards were promoted to the next grade by some of the city's principals.[372] A 2001 statewide poll found that Maryland voters were not satisfied with their public schools. On average,

respondents gave their schools a "C+," with Baltimore voters assigning their schools even lower grades.[373]

In 2001, under a federal law that took effect in July of that year, Maryland notified parents of children in its 141 worst-performing public schools that they could transfer to another public school of choice. A provision included in the November 1999 federal education appropriations bill granted districts additional funds if they allowed students at failing schools the opportunity to transfer to another public school. However, the legislation allowed higher-performing schools to turn down transfers if space was not available. Howard County was exempted because it had a policy prohibiting transfers.[374]

In 2001, Senate Bill 722 and H.B. 1089 were introduced to allow school boards to give students enrolled in reconstituted schools the opportunity to attend other public schools, a charter school, or a private school. Private schools would have received tuition subsidies equal to the per-pupil expenditure of the public schools. Students would have been able to attend a private school through the highest grade taught at the school even if their original public school was later removed from the reconstitution list. Both bills died in committee.[375]

Also in 2001, two charter school bills (H.B. 29, the Public Charter School Act of 2001, and S.B. 604, bearing the same title) were passed by their respective houses, but legislators were unable to agree on the language of the final bill.[376]

In Calvert County, there was a legal battle over home-schooled children's use of public facilities. The county refused to let home-schooled students use its community centers for

---

368. National Education Association, "Vouchers," at *www.nea.org/issues/vouchers/*.

369. See Children's Scholarship Fund–Baltimore Web site at *www.csfbaltimore.org/*.

370. See Maryland General Assembly Web site at *http://mlis.state.md.us/1999rs/billfile/hb0564.htm*.

371. Liz Bowie, "30,000 Facing Summer School," *The Baltimore Sun*, June 7, 2001, p. A1.

372. Erika Niedowski and Liz Bowie, "Pupil Passing Rules Broken," *The Baltimore Sun*, December 13, 2001, p. B1.

373. Howard Libit and Thomas Waldron, "Baltimoreans Least Happy with Schools," *The Baltimore Sun*, January 10, 2001, p. A14.

374. JoAnna Daemmrich, "State Offers School Choice," *The Baltimore Sun*, April 25, 2001, p. B1.

375. See Maryland General Assembly Web site at *http://mlis.state.md.us/2001rs/bills/hb/hb1089f.rtf*.

376. See Maryland General Assembly Web site at *http://mlis.state.md.us/2001rs/billfile/sb0604.htm*.

organized recreation and classes, even though the centers were available to all community residents for similar activities. In August 2002, the U.S. District Court for Maryland held that the community facility at the center of the fight had violated neither the homeschoolers' Fourteenth Amendment equal protection rights nor their right to free speech. The Home School Legal Defense Association, which is representing the families, has appealed to the U.S. Court of Appeals for the Fourth Circuit in Richmond, Virginia. A decision is expected by the end of 2003.[377]

## Developments in 2002 and 2003

The Maryland House of Delegates passed H.B. 131, the Public Charter School Act of 2002, and the Senate passed S.B. 213 with the same name. However, as with other charter school legislation, the two chambers were not able to agree on the final bill.[378]

In the absence of a state law, Maryland school boards may approve charter schools and determine the rules under which they will operate. Frederick and Montgomery Counties have adopted charter school policies, although only Frederick County has approved a charter.[379]

On March 13, 2002, the Frederick County Board of Education gave final approval for the Monocacy Valley Montessori School, provided that it met the requirements set by the board—including 70 percent enrollment, securing a building, and recruiting a principal and staff of teachers who must eventually be certified.[380] The school opened in September 2002 with 157 students. Montgomery County had rejected the application of the Jaime Escalante Public Char-

ter School one day before Frederick County approved the state's first charter school.[381]

Under the federal No Child Left Behind Act, students in failing schools have the right to transfer to better-performing schools. In Baltimore, 30,000 students were eligible to transfer out of 83 schools; but in July 2002, city officials announced that the opportunity to transfer would be available to only 194 students because of a lack of space.[382]

On December 4, the Maryland State Board of Education voted to delay a decision on a proposal that would have required parents to notify their local district every year of their intention to homeschool. Currently, parents are required to notify the district only when they first begin to homeschool. The home-school community protested the proposed change.[383]

In 2003, the State Board of Education decided not to require home-school students to complete an official registration form and send it to the board every year; however, new rules are being considered that, among other things, will require parents to notify (by phone or mail) their local superintendent of their intent to homeschool.[384]

On May 22, 2003, Governor Robert Ehrlich signed into law S.B. 75, the Maryland Public Charter School Program. The bill, passed by votes of 33 to 4 in the Senate and 98 to 30 in the House,[385] was significantly weakened during the legislative process; under the law, only school districts can approve charters, and the appeals process is cumbersome for applicants.[386]

377. Home School Legal Defense Association, "Goulart and Travers v. Calvert County," September 12, 2002.
378. See Maryland General Assembly Web site at *http://mlis.state.md.us/2002rs/billfile/sb0213.htm.*
379. David Snyder, "Charter School a Fit for Frederick," *The Washington Post*, April 4, 2002, p. B6.
380. Julia Robb, "Charter School Gets OK," *The Frederick News–Post*, March 14, 2002.
381. Snyder, "Charter School a Fit for Frederick."
382. Liz Bowie, "Schools Setting Limit on Transfers," *The Baltimore Sun*, July 10, 2002, p. B1.
383. See Home School Legal Defense Association, "New Maryland Homeschool Regulations Delayed," November 14, 2002, at *www.hslda.org/hs/state/md/20021140.asp.*
384. Home School Legal Defense Association, "Proposed Change to Homeschooling Regulations," March 12, 2003, at *www.hslda.org/Legislation/State/md/2002/MDDOERegs/default.asp.*
385. See Maryland General Assembly Web site at *http://mlis.state.md.us/2003rs/billfile/SB0075.htm.*
386. Center for Education Reform, *Education Reform Newswire*, Vol. 5, No. 15 (April 8, 2003), at *http://207.201.191.212/update/2003/8april.html.*

## Position of the Governor / Composition of the State Legislature

Governor Robert Ehrlich, a Republican, supports all forms of parental choice in education. Democrats control both houses of the legislature.

## State Contacts

**Trevor Bothwell**
*The Right Report*
P.O. Box 472
California, MD 20619
Phone: (240) 298-8862
Web site: www.therightreport.com
E-mail: bothwell@therightreport.com

**Calvert Institute for Policy Research**
Gene Liebman, Executive Director
8 West Hamilton Street
Baltimore, MD 21201
Phone: (410) 662-7252
Fax: (410) 539-3973
Web site: www.calvertinstitute.org
E-mail: info@calvertinstitute.org

**Center for Charter Schools in Frederick County**
Leslie Mansfield, Co-Director
P.O. Box 24
Braddock Heights, MD 21714
Phone: (301) 473-9716
Web site: www.geocities.com/centerforcharterschools
E-mail: ccsfredco@cs.com

**Charles J. O'Malley & Associates**
Charles O'Malley, President
442 Cranes Roost Court
Annapolis, MD 21401
Phone: (410) 349-0139
Fax: (410) 349-0140
Web site: cjoainc.home.mindspring.com
E-mail: cjoainc@mindspring.com

**Children's Scholarship Fund–Baltimore**
Paul Ellis, Executive Director
2315 St. Paul Street
Baltimore, MD 21218
Phone: (410) 243-2510
Fax: (410) 243-8629
Web site: www.csfbaltimore.org
E-mail: pelliscsfb@msn.com

**Christian Home Educators Network (CHEN)**
P.O. Box 2010
Ellicott City, MD 21043
Phone: (301) 474-9055

Web site: www.chenmd.org
E-mail: chenwbal@chenmd.org

**Education Resource Center**
2604 Sisson Street
Baltimore, MD 21211
Phone: (410) 243-9333
Fax: (410) 366-5416
E-mail: suzannad@harborduvall.com

**Maryland Association of Christian Home Educators (MACHE)**
P.O. Box 417
Clarksburg, MD 20871
Phone: (301) 607-4284
Web site: www.machemd.org
E-mail: info@machemd.org

**Maryland Charter School Network**
Joni Gardner, President
6152 Silver Arrows Way
Columbia, MD 21045
Phone: (410) 707-2676
Fax: (410) 312-1664
Web site: http://groups.yahoo.com/group/marylandcharterschoolnetwork
E-mail: jonigardner@comcast.net

**Maryland Parents for Better Education**
Barbara Davidson
P.O. Box 432
Barnesville, MD 20838
Phone: (301) 428-8548
E-mail: marylandcharters@aol.com

**Maryland Public Policy Institute**
Christopher B. Summers, President
P.O. Box 195
Germantown, MD 20875-0195
Phone: (240) 686-3510
Fax: (240) 686-3511
Web site: www.mdpolicy.org
E-mail: csummers@mdpolicy.org

**+TEACH Maryland**
John Schiavone, President
P.O. Box 43573
Baltimore, MD 21234
Phone: (410) 592-3390
Fax: (410) 592-5265
E-mail: JDSchiavo@aol.com

## State School Report Card

**Greatschools.net**
Web site: www.greatschools.net/modperl/go/MD

**Maryland State Department of Education**
Web site: www.msde.state.md.us

# MASSACHUSETTS

## State Profile (Updated May 2003)

### School Choice Status
- Public school choice: Interdistrict/voluntary
- State constitution: Blaine amendment
- Charter schools: Established 1993
  Strength of law: Strong
  Number in operation (fall 2002): 46
  Number of students enrolled (fall 2002): 14,013
- Publicly funded private school choice: No
- Privately funded school choice: Yes
- Home-school law: High regulation
- Ranking on the Education Freedom Index (2001): 36th out of 50 states

### K–12 Public Schools and Students (2001–2002)
- Public school enrollment: 979,593
- Students enrolled per teacher: 14.2
- Number of schools (2000–2001): 1,898
- Number of districts: 481
- Current expenditures: $9,681,713,000
- Current per-pupil expenditure: $9,883
- Amount of revenue from the federal government: 5.4%

### K–12 Public School Teachers (2001–2002)
- Number of teachers: 69,000
- Average salary: $49,054

### K–12 Private Schools (1999–2000)
- Private school enrollment: 132,154
- Number of schools: 694
- Number of teachers: 12,497

### K–12 Public and Private School Student Academic Performance
- NAEP test results:

| NAEP Tests Massachusetts Student Performance | State (National) 2000 Math Scale = 0–500 | | State (National) 2000 Science Scale = 0–300 | | State (National) 2000 Reading Scale = 0–500 | |
|---|---|---|---|---|---|---|
| | 4th Grade | 8th Grade | 4th Grade | 8th Grade | 4th Grade | 8th Grade |
| Average Scale Score | 235 (226) | 283 (274) | 162 (148) | 161 (149) | 225 (215) | 269 (261) |
| Advanced | 3% (3%) | 6% (5%) | 6% (3%) | 5% (4%) | 8% (6%) | 3% (2%) |
| Proficient | 30% (23%) | 26% (21%) | 37% (25%) | 37% (26%) | 29% (23%) | 33% (29%) |
| Basic | 46% (43%) | 44% (39%) | 38% (36%) | 32% (29%) | 36% (32%) | 44% (41%) |
| Below Basic | 21% (31%) | 24% (35%) | 19% (36%) | 26% (41%) | 27% (39%) | 20% (28%) |

- SAT weighted rank (2002): 5th out of 24 states and the District of Columbia
- ACT score (2002): N/A
- Academic Achievement Ranking: 8th out of 50 states and the District of Columbia

## Summary

Massachusetts has a strong charter school law. Juniors and seniors at public and private high schools may enroll in college courses for high school and postsecondary credit.[387] Private scholarship foundations make it possible for low-income students to attend private and religious schools of choice.

## Background

Massachusetts has several intradistrict choice programs. In 1981, Cambridge launched an intradistrict K–8 program. In this program, families choose four schools and rank them according to preference. The district then assigns the student to a school based on preference, school capacity, and racial composition.[388] Since 1989, the Boston school district had been divided into three school zones for kindergarten through 8th grade. Families choose a school and alternates within their zone. Student assignments are made to achieve racial integration at each school.[389]

In 1991, then-Governor William Weld, a Republican, signed the Massachusetts interdistrict school choice law, allowing students to transfer to schools in other participating districts. The law specified that a student's former district must pay the tuition in the receiving district. In 1993, the law was amended to require districts that choose not to participate to opt out of the program through an annual vote of the local school committee.[390] The Massachusetts Board of Education established an information system to help parents choose from among schools within participating districts. Transportation assistance is provided for low-income children.[391]

A 1997 study of the interdistrict programs by the Boston-based Pioneer Institute found that those districts that lost large numbers of students at the outset of the program responded by improving their policies and programs to encourage students to return and to attract transfer students from other districts. Conversely, districts that initially lost only a small number of students made few improvements and lost more students in subsequent years. These findings provide evidence that a competitive market can have positive effects on the quality of public education.[392]

On the charter school front, Governor Weld signed the Education Reform Act in 1993. The law authorized the establishment of up to 25 charter schools for the 1995–1996 school year, with the stipulation that schools must be open to all students and could not charge tuition.[393]

In 1997, Massachusetts amended its 1993 charter school law, raising the cap on charter schools from 25 to 50. Half of the new schools were designated as Horace Mann Schools—schools that had converted from traditional public schools with the approval of the district, the teachers union, and the Massachusetts Board of Education.[394] The cap was raised again in 2000 to allow for the creation of 72 commonwealth charters and 48 Horace Mann charters.[395]

Since 1996, several studies of charter schools conducted by the Pioneer Institute have found

387. Education Commission of the States, "Postsecondary Options: Dual/Concurrent Enrollment," July 2001.
388. Peter W. Cookson, Jr., and Sonali M. Shroff, "School Choice and Urban School Reform," *ERIC Digest*, No. 110, 1997, at *http://eric-web.tc.columbia.edu/mono/UDS110.pdf*.
389. Tyler Weaver, "Controlled Choice: An Alternative School Choice Plan," *ERIC Digest*, No. 70, 1992, at *www.ericfacility.net/ericdigests/ed344342.html*.
390. David J. Armor and Brett Peiser, *Competition in Education: A Case Study of Interdistrict Choice* (Boston: Pioneer Institute for Public Policy Research, 1997).
391. See *www.state.ma.us/legis/laws/mgl/76%2D12b.htm*.
392. Armor and Peiser, *Competition in Education: A Case Study of Interdistrict Choice*.
393. Massachusetts Department of Education, "The Education Reform Act of 1993, Section 55, P. 76 Charter Schools (SUMMARY)," at *www.ed.psu.edu/insys/ESD/charter/MACharter.html*; capitalization and punctuation as in original.
394. Massachusetts Department of Education, "Massachusetts Charter Schools Overview," at *www.doe.mass.edu/charter/reports/1998/overview.html*.

that, compared with conventional public schools, the charter schools are more effective in meeting the needs of traditionally underserved student populations, serving a higher percentage of low-income, bilingual, and minority children. The institute also has found that most charter students had been average or below average in academic achievement at their previous schools.[396]

A 1998 Pioneer Institute poll found high parental satisfaction with charter schools: 60 percent of parents whose children were in charter schools gave their schools an "A," compared to 37 percent of parents whose children were in traditional public schools. Nearly two-thirds of the parents whose children had transferred to charter schools said that their child's academic performance had improved.[397] In addition, 78 percent of the parents of students in charter schools but only 50 percent of parents with children in traditional schools said that they would like to keep their children in their current schools. Charter school parents also reported twice as many meetings with their children's teachers, as well as more communication by phone and more written correspondence, and indicated greater confidence that their children could readily obtain supplementary academic assistance if needed.[398]

In 1998, the Home School Legal Defense Foundation won a major victory in the Massachusetts Supreme Judicial Court, ending a seven-year legal battle between parents and the Lynn School District. The judges ruled unanimously that school officials could not impose home inspections on homeschooling families.[399]

An October 2000 survey commissioned by the Pioneer Institute found widespread support for school vouchers: 58 percent of residents (including 64 percent of minorities and 57 percent of self-described liberals) favored vouchers.[400]

In 1998, a group of citizens filed a lawsuit challenging provisions in the Massachusetts constitution that prohibited citizens from petitioning the legislature to fund private schools. Later that year, a federal judge signed an order to allow a petition drive for signatures while this case was pending. The proponents of funding private schools did not acquire the requisite number of signatures on their first petition, but in 1999, they collected more than enough signatures and delivered the petition to Attorney General Thomas Reilly for certification so they could present it to the legislature.[401]

Attorney General Reilly refused to certify the petition on the grounds that the state constitution prohibited such voter initiatives on this subject. In 2000, the Becket Fund, which represented the plaintiffs, requested that a federal district court order the Attorney General to certify the petition before the May 10 deadline so that it could be considered by the legislature. U.S. District Court Judge George O'Toole denied the motion.[402]

In 2001, Judge O'Toole dismissed a portion of the challenge to the state's constitutional provision prohibiting any referenda to change or eliminate the ban on aid to religious schools, but he also allowed the case to continue.[403]

The Massachusetts Department of Education ordered inspections of each of the state's charter schools using a consulting firm, SchoolWorks. The firm's findings indicated that the schools were generally well-run and well-staffed and that they had met education standards.[404] An October 2000 Pioneer Institute poll indicated that 84 percent of parents with children in charter schools gave their schools "A"s and "B"s.

395. Center for Education Reform, "Charter School Legislation: Profile of Massachusetts's Charter School Law," 2001, at *http://edreform.com/charter_schools/laws/Massachusetts.htm*.
396. Pioneer Institute for Public Policy Research, *Massachusetts Charter School Profiles, 1995–96 School Year*, July 1996, and *Massachusetts Charter School Profiles, Interim 1996–1997*, 1997.
397. Massachusetts Charter School Resource Center, "Poll Finds Higher Satisfaction Rate Among Charter School Parents," Pioneer Institute for Public Policy Research, *Policy Directions* No. 3, June 1998.
398. *Ibid.*
399. David Bresnahan, "Massachusetts at War with Home Schoolers," *The Massachusetts News*, May 3, 2001.
400. Pioneer Institute for Public Policy Research, "Survey Finds Majority Support for School Vouchers," at *www.pioneerinstitute.org/research/policy/piodrct8.cfm*.
401. Becket Fund, "Litigation Activities: *Boyette v. Galvin*," at *www.becketfund.org/*.
402. *Ibid.*
403. *Ibid.*

Even though parents' ratings of conventional public schools had improved since a previous poll that was conducted in 1998, charter school parents were still more satisfied with their children's school experience.[405]

Private scholarships make it possible for low-income students in Massachusetts to attend private or parochial schools. The Catholic Schools Foundation has offered scholarships to low-income children to attend Catholic schools in Boston since 1983.[406] Both Give a Child a Choice and the Children's Scholarship Fund operate scholarship programs in Boston.[407]

Three choice bills were introduced during the 2001 session of the legislature. House Bill 1429 would have eliminated the provision in the state constitution that prevents public funding of religious institutions. The bill failed to pass in a committee vote. H.B. 1581 would have created a voucher program for students in failing schools in Boston, Holyoke, and Lawrence but excluded private religious schools from participating. H.B. 1699 proposed a private tuition tax deduction of up to 25 percent of the cost of tuition, not to exceed $5,000. Both H.B. 1581 and H.B. 1699 died in committee.[408]

## Developments in 2002 and 2003

According to an analysis by the Beacon Hill Institute, the state's $1 billion infusion of funding for its public schools has not improved student test scores. State reforms such as raising teacher salaries and reducing class size have likewise failed to boost student achievement. The report recommended vouchers as a more effective investment of funds to improve academic performance.[409]

In September 2002, the Newton Public School Committee voted to end the practice of granting diplomas to home-schooled students as of May 2003 unless they pass the state's 10th grade exam. Massachusetts state legislation does not require home-school students to take state tests.[410]

A bill proposing tax deductions for tuition payments, H.B. 851, was introduced in 2003. This bill would allow parents to deduct the full amount paid toward their child's tuition from their taxable income. The bill is in committee.[411]

## Position of the Governor / Composition of the State Legislature

Governor Mitt Romney, a Republican, has stated no position on vouchers but supports charter schools. Democrats control both houses of the legislature.

## State Contacts

**Beacon Hill Institute for Public Policy Research**
David Tuerck, Executive Director
Suffolk University
8 Ashburton Place
Boston, MA 02108-2770
Phone: (617) 573-8750
Fax: (617) 720-4272
Web site: www.beaconhill.org
E-mail: bhi@beaconhill.org

**Black Alliance for Educational Options**
Judy Burnette, Member, Board of Directors
Urban Law and Public Policy Institute
Northeastern University
716 Columbus Avenue, Suite 212
Boston, MA 02120
Phone: (617) 373-8235
Fax: (617) 373-8236
Web site: www.baeo.org
E-mail: j.burnette@neu.edu

**Caroline Hoxby, Ph.D.**
Professor of Economics
Department of Economics

---

404. Kathryn Ciffolo and Charles Chieppo, "Early Grades Good for Charter Schools," *The Boston Herald*, June 5, 2000.

405. "Poll Finds High Satisfaction Rate Among Charter School Parents," Pioneer Institute for Public Policy Research, *Policy Directions* No. 9, October 2000.

406. See Catholic Schools Foundation, Inc., Web site at *www.csfboston.org*.

407. See Children First America Web site at *www.childrenfirstamerica.org/*.

408. See National School Boards Association Web site at *www.nsba.org/novouchers*.

409. Beacon Hill Institute, "Getting Less for More: Lessons in Massachusetts Education Reform," August 2002, at *www.beaconhill.org/BHIStudies/BHIEdReformMCAS702a.pdf*.

410. Valentina Zic, "Home-Schoolers to Be Denied Diplomas," *Newton TAB*, September 25, 2002.

411. See Massachusetts General Court Web site at *www.state.ma.us/legis/legis.htm*.

Harvard University
Cambridge, MA 02138
Phone: (617) 496-3588
Fax: (617) 495-8570
Web site: www.economics.harvard.edu/
~choxby

**Catholic Schools Foundation, Inc.**
Sean P. Dunlavy, Executive Director
260 Franklin Street, Suite 630
Boston, MA 02110
Phone: (617) 778-5981
Fax: (617) 778-5980
Web site: www.csfboston.org
E-mail: sdunlavy@csfboston.org

**Children's Scholarship Fund Midwest/Northeast**
Gael Byrnes, Executive Director
55 West Superior, Suite 3N
Chicago, IL 60610
Phone: (312) 960-0205
Fax: (312) 377-1837
E-mail: gbyrnes@csfchicago.org

**Coalition for Parental Choice in Education (CPCE)**
Con Chapman, President
P.O. Box 846
Boston, MA 02103
Phone: (617) 345-3838
Fax: (617) 345-3299
Web site: www.massparentschoice.org
E-mail: CChapman@B-L.com

**Massachusetts Charter School Association**
Marc Kenen, Executive Director
11 Beacon Street, Suite 430
Boston, MA 02108
Phone: (617) 973-6655
E-mail: Kenen@masscharterschools.org

**Massachusetts Department of Education**
Rebecca Homes, Charter School Office
350 Main Street
Malden, MA 02148
Phone: (781) 338-3227
Fax: (781) 338-6565
Web site: www.doe.mass.edu
E-mail: charterschools@doe.mass.edu

**Massachusetts Homeschool Organization of Parents (MassHOPE)**
5 Atwood Road
Cherry Valley, MA 01611-3332
Phone: (508) 829-2959

Web site: www.masshope.org
E-mail: info@masshope.org

**Parents' Alliance for Catholic Education (PACE)**
Steve Perla, Executive Director
124 Summer Street
Fitchburg, MA 01420
Phone: (978) 665-9890
Fax: (978) 665-9885
Web site: www.pacesite.org
E-mail: sperla@paceorg.net

**Paul Peterson, Ph.D.**
Henry Lee Shattuck Professor of Government
Program on Education Policy and Governance
Harvard University
Cambridge, MA 02138
Phone: (617) 495-8312
Fax: (617) 496-4428
Web site: www.ksg.harvard.edu/pepg/

**Pioneer Institute for Public Policy Research**
Steve Adams, Executive Director
Charter School Resource Center
85 Devonshire Street, 8th Floor
Boston, MA 02109-3504
Phone: (617) 723-2277
Fax: (617) 723- 0782
Web site: www.pioneerinstitute.org
E-mail: sdadams@pioneerinstitute.org

**Worcester Regional Research Bureau**
Dr. Roberta R. Schaefer, Ph.D.,
Executive Director
319 Main Street
Worcester, MA 01608
Phone: (508) 799-7169
Fax: (508) 799-4720
Web site: www.wrrb.org
E-mail: info@wrrb.org

## State School Report Card

**Greatschools.net**
Web site: www.greatschools.net/modperl/go/MA

**Massachusetts Department of Education**
Web site: www.doe.mass.edu/ata/sda.html

**Pioneer Institute Charter School Research Center**
Web site: www.pioneerinstitute.org/csrc/cshb/profiles.cfm

# MICHIGAN

## State Profile (Updated May 2003)

### School Choice Status
- Public school choice: Interdistrict/voluntary
- State constitution: Blaine amendment and compelled-support language
- Charter school law: Established 1993
    Strength of law: Strong
    Number of charter schools in operation (fall 2002): 196
    Number of students enrolled in charter schools (fall 2002): 60,236
- Publicly funded private school choice: No
- Privately funded school choice: Yes
- Home-school law: No notice required
- Ranking on the Education Freedom Index (2001): 9th out of 50 states

### K–12 Public Schools and Students (2001–2002)
- Public school enrollment: 1,733,900
- Students enrolled per teacher: 17.9
- Number of schools (2000–2001): 3,743
- Number of districts: 783
- Current expenditures: $14,930,266,000
- Current per-pupil expenditure: $8,611
- Amount of revenue from the federal government: 4.5%

### K–12 Public School Teachers (2001–2002)
- Number of teachers: 96,900
- Average salary: $52,037

### K–12 Private Schools (1999–2000)
- Private school enrollment: 179,579
- Number of schools: 1,012
- Number of teachers: 11,771

### K–12 Public and Private School Student Academic Performance
- NAEP test results:

| NAEP Tests Michigan Student Performance | State (National) 2000 Math Scale = 0–500 | | State (National) 2000 Science Scale = 0–300 | | State (National) 2000 Reading Scale = 0–500 | |
|---|---|---|---|---|---|---|
| | 4th Grade | 8th Grade | 4th Grade | 8th Grade | 4th Grade | 8th Grade |
| Average Scale Score | 231 (226) | 278 (274) | 154 (148) | 156 (149) | 217 (215) | N/A (261) |
| Advanced | 3% (3%) | 5% (5%) | 3% (3%) | 4% (4%) | 5% (6%) | N/A (2%) |
| Proficient | 26% (23%) | 23% (21%) | 30% (25%) | 33% (26%) | 23% (23%) | N/A (29%) |
| Basic | 43% (43%) | 42% (39%) | 38% (36%) | 32% (29%) | 35% (32%) | N/A (41%) |
| Below Basic | 28% (31%) | 30% (35%) | 29% (36%) | 31% (41%) | 37% (39%) | N/A (28%) |

- SAT weighted rank (2001): N/A
- ACT weighted rank (2001): 17th out of 26 states
- ALEC Academic Achievement Ranking: 29th out of 50 states and the District of Columbia

## Summary

Michigan offers charter schools and statewide public school choice to children residing in districts that opt to participate in the state's Schools of Choice program. Eligible high school students may enroll in college courses for high school or postsecondary credit. Private scholarship foundations help low-income students attend private schools.

## Background

The first of two ballot initiatives on vouchers in Michigan was held in 1978. Seventy-four percent of state residents voted against a proposed statewide voucher program, and 26 percent favored it.[412]

The state passed a charter school law in 1993. Shortly thereafter, however, the teachers unions and the American Civil Liberties Union filed a lawsuit, claiming that charter schools were unconstitutional because they would use state funds but would not be regulated by the Michigan State Board of Education. On November 1, 1994, Ingham County Circuit Judge William Collette ruled that charter schools could not receive public funds.[413] The decision was appealed, and the Michigan Supreme Court upheld the state's charter legislation in 1997.[414]

Under then-Governor John Engler, the law was revised in 1994. Current law allows state public universities, community colleges, and local school districts to create public-school academies. Teachers in district charter schools must be certified and are covered by district collective bargaining agreements. Universities may charter up to 150 schools, and there is no limit on the number of schools districts may charter.[415]

In 1996, the legislature established interdistrict school choice through the enactment of Public Act 180. Under this legislation, students may transfer to other participating districts within the Intermediate School District (ISD), which is composed of several school districts within a county. Students may attend schools outside their ISD with the permission of the receiving district superintendent. If the sending district chooses not to pay the receiving district, the parents must pay tuition.[416]

Also in 1996, the Postsecondary Enrollment Options Program (Public Act 160) went into effect. The program allows qualified high school students to enroll in college courses for high school or postsecondary credit or both.[417]

In 1999, Senate Bill 31 was introduced to give vouchers to students in cities with a population exceeding 750,000. Students from families earning less than 150 percent of the federal poverty level would have been eligible. The bill died in committee.[418]

Under the leadership of Amway co-founder and former Michigan Board of Education member Richard DeVos, school choice activists and civic and business leaders formed Kids First! Yes!, which sought to amend the Michigan constitution to give parents whose children attend schools in districts with poor academic performance a publicly funded voucher worth one-half of the public per-pupil expenditure to attend a school of choice. At that time, about 30 of the state's hundreds of districts failed to graduate two-thirds of their students. Proposal 1 would have guaranteed that public school spending would never fall below the current level and would have required teacher testing in academic subject areas.[419]

412. Nick Penning, "Vouchers: What Now?" American Association of School Administrators, July 11, 2002, at *www.aasa.org/government_relations/nick's_notes/July11_2002.htm*.

413. Mark Walsh, "Charter Ruling Sends Schools in Michigan Reeling," *Education Week*, November 30, 1994.

414. Center for Education Reform, "News Alert: Unions Lose Again! Michigan Charter School Law Determined Constitutional," July 30, 1997.

415. Center for Education Reform, "Charter School Legislation: Profile of Michigan's Charter School Law," 2001, at *http://edreform.com/charter_schools/laws/Michigan.htm*.

416. Matthew J. Brouillette, "School Choice in Michigan: A Primer for Freedom in Education," Mackinac Center for Public Policy, July 1999.

417. Education Commission of the States, "Postsecondary Options: Dual/Concurrent Enrollment," July 2001.

418. See National School Boards Association Web site at *www.nsba.org/novouchers*.

A January 2000 *Detroit News* poll indicated that 53 percent of voters favored the Kids First! Yes! proposal, while 23 percent opposed it.[420] Michigan's Catholic bishops called expanded educational choice "not an option [but] a requirement of social justice."[421] Proposal 1 also enjoyed the support of many Protestant religious leaders.[422]

Opponents included teachers unions and a coalition of 30 anti–parental choice groups organized under the name All Kids First! Three school districts broke the state's election laws by distributing materials opposing the measure to parents, prompting the Secretary of State to issue a warning to all of the state's districts.[423]

Ultimately, Proposal 1 was defeated by a margin of more than 2 to 1 on November 7, 2000. Since then, school choice supporter Betsy DeVos has created a Grand Rapids–based think tank, Choices for Children, and a political action committee called the Great Lakes Education Project.[424]

Since 1991, the Education Freedom Fund, a privately funded scholarship organization, has awarded scholarships to children in grades K–8. Students who qualify for the federal free and reduced-price lunch program are eligible to receive these scholarships. Recipients are chosen by lottery and receive a maximum of $1,000. The number of participants in this program has skyrocketed, increasing from three in 1991 to more than 3,700 in 2001.[425] In addition, two other private organizations, the Educational Choice Project in Battle Creek and the Children's Scholarship Fund of Detroit, also provide scholarships for Michigan students.

## Developments in 2002 and 2003

Interdistict school programs are popular and currently involve two-thirds of all Michigan school districts. An estimated 33,200 children statewide attended school in a district other than the their own in 2002.[426]

On April 10, 2002, the Commission on Charter Schools, created by the Michigan legislature, issued its final report, *Charter Schools in Michigan*. Chaired by Michigan State University President Peter McPherson, members included the Superintendent of Public Instruction and representatives of the governor and legislature. The commission recommended, among other things, creating a statewide accountability structure, increasing the authority of the state superintendent over charter authorizers, holding authorizers responsible for oversight, and raising the cap on university-sponsored charter schools while limiting the number of new charters to one per year in Detroit and two per year in other districts through 2007.[427]

A Center for Education Reform (CER) analysis of the report pointed to inconsistencies. According to CER President Jeanne Allen, the commission "ignored the facts" and "neglected to look at the growth in state test scores in many of the charter schools, or why parents—who are taxpayers and deserved their attention—want to send their children to charter schools. And they chose to ignore the evidence in Michigan that charter schools have spurred public school districts to improve."[428]

House Bill 4800, which incorporated many of the commission's recommendations, was defeated by a vote of 54 to 52 on May 1, 2002.[429]

419. See Kids First! Yes! Web site at *http://209.153.134.223/index.asp.*

420. Michael Cardman, "Michigan: School Vouchers Popular in Newspaper Poll," *Education Daily*, January 21, 2000.

421. Cecil Angel, "Bishops Pitch School Vouchers," *Detroit Free Press*, June 28, 2000.

422. See Kids First! Yes! Web site at *http://209.153.134.223/index.asp.*

423. Milton and Rose D. Friedman Foundation, *The Friedman Report*, Issue 7 (2000).

424. Cami Reister, "Voucher Backers Hopes Are Rekindled," *Grand Rapids Press*, June 17, 2002.

425. See Education Freedom Fund Web site at *www.educationfreedomfund.org.*

426. Julie Ross, "School Choice Gets Competitive," *Detroit Free Press*, March 1, 2002.

427. See Commission on Charter Schools Web site at *www.charterschools.msu.edu/index.htm.*

428. Center for Education Reform, "Michigan Commission Does Hatchet-Job on Charter Schools; Conclusions Appease Education Establishment, Charter Opponents," *CER Analysis*, at *http://207.201.191.212/ charter_schools/micommission.htm.*

429. Center for Education Reform, "Proposed Negative Changes to Michigan's Charter School Law," *CER Analysis*, June 2002, and Michigan Legislature, H.B. 4800, at *www.michiganlegislature.org/mileg.asp?page=Bills.*

According to an EPIC/MRA poll commissioned by the Mackinac Center for Public Policy prior to the 2002 Supreme Court decision upholding vouchers, 43 percent of respondents said they would support a voucher program for Michigan, 67 percent said they would support an education tax credit similar to the one developed by the Mackinac Center, and 22 percent indicated that a favorable decision by the court would make them more likely to support a voucher program.[430] In December 2002, the Institute for Public Policy and Social Research at Michigan State University released a survey showing that 72 percent of those polled support charter schools.[431]

A September 2002 study by the Mackinac Center found that, while charter school students in Michigan score below their traditional public school counterparts, they are making stronger academic gains on the Michigan Educational Assessment Program (MEAP). During the 2000–2001 school year, charter school students improved 43 percent on the 4th grade MEAP reading test compared to a 10.1 percent improvement among students in traditional public schools; 4th grade math and 7th grade reading test improvements showed a similar trend.[432]

Enrollment in Detroit's traditional public schools dropped 5 percent between 1990 and 2000, while enrollment in Detroit's charter schools increased by 7 percent. By the 2001–2002 school year, charter enrollment in Detroit had increased to 19,000. Reacting to the competition posed by charter schools, administrators of Detroit public schools are working to improve. According to a district spokeswoman, "We know that it's a competitive market. We are implementing a comprehensive, no-excuses school improvement plan with the objective and belief that every child can learn."[433]

On February 3, 2003, a student at the University of Michigan filed suit against the state because the state stopped funding her scholarship when she declared theology as her major. The student, Teresa Becker, was receiving a scholarship under the Michigan Competitive Scholarship Program, but after she declared her major in her sophomore year, the state cancelled the award.[434]

In April 2003, Standard & Poor's School Evaluation Services published a review of the 57 charter schools operated by Central Michigan University (CMU).[435] The study found that the charter schools served students who were more likely to be from lower-income families, and the schools themselves operated with less money than other public schools. Although the average passing rates on state tests for CMU charter school students were lower than the state average, 14 of the schools performed better on state tests than other schools in their district.[436]

In May 2003, a study released by the Michigan Chamber of Commerce refuted claims that charter schools are more expensive to taxpayers than other public schools. The study revealed that, on average, the per-student expenditure of charter schools is $1,036 less than that of conventional public schools. In some districts, the disparity is even greater; for example, due to operating costs, the public schools in the Ann Arbor and Southfield districts cost taxpayers over $2,000 more per pupil than charter schools.[437]

430. Joseph Lehman, "Historic Supreme Court Voucher Decision Imminent," Mackinac Center for Public Policy, June 26, 2002.

431. Lori Higgins, "Educational Preferences: Charters Graded High in Survey," *Detroit Free Press*, December 5, 2002.

432. Lori Higgins, "Charter Students Gaining on Tests," *Detroit Free Press*, September 5, 2002; see also Kirk Johnson, Ph.D. "Michigan's Public Charter Schools See MEAP Scores Rise Faster than Regular Public Schools," Mackinac Center for Public Policy, September 4, 2002, at *www.mackinac.org/4581*.

433. Peggy Walsh-Sarnecki, "Charter Schools Growing," *Detroit Free Press*, September 10, 2002.

434. Associated Press, "Michigan Theology Student Sues After State Cuts Her Aid," February 7, 2003.

435. See Standard & Poor's Web site at *www.ses.standardandpoors.com*.

436. Thomas B. Fordham Foundation, *The Education Gadfly*, Vol. 3, No. 15 (May 1, 2003), at *www.edexcellence.net/gadfly/v03/gadfly15.html*.

437. Michigan Chamber of Commerce, "Michigan Chamber Foundation Study Finds Public School Academy Funding Gap," May 5, 2003, at *www.michamber.com/chamnews/index.asp#school*.

## Position of the Governor / Composition of the State Legislature

Governor Jennifer Granholm, a Democrat, does not support school choice. Republicans control both houses of the legislature.

## State Contacts

### Black Alliance for Educational Options
Detroit Chapter
DeAmo Murphy, President/CEO
11000 West McNichols, Suite 313
Detroit, MI 48221
Phone: (313) 727-3763
Web site: www.baeo.org

### Cornerstone Schools
Ernestine Sanders, President
6861 East Nevada
Detroit, MI 48234
Phone: (313) 892-1860
Fax: (313) 892-1861
Web site: www.cornerstoneschools.com

### Crossroads Charter Academy
David VanderGoot, Principal
215 North State Street
Big Rapids, MI 49307
Phone: (231) 796-9041
Fax: (616) 796-9790

### Education Freedom Fund
Kevin Stotts, Executive Director
Sandy Hankiewicz, Program Administrator
201 Monroe Avenue, Suite 350
Grand Rapids, MI 49503
Phone: (616) 459-2222
Phone: (800) 866-8141
Fax: (616) 459-2198
Web site: www.educationfreedomfund.org

### Educational Choice Project
Kelly Boles Chapman, Program Director
Battle Creek Community Foundation
34 West Jackson
One River Walk Center
Battle Creek, MI 49017
Phone: (616) 962-2181
Fax: (616) 962-2182

### Information Network for Christian Homes
4934 Cannonsburg Road
Belmont, MI 49306
Phone: (616) 874-5656
Fax: (616) 874-5577
Web site: www.inch.org
E-mail: inforequest@inch.org

### Mackinac Center for Public Policy
Lawrence Reed, President
Joe Overton, Senior Vice President
Brian Carpenter, Director of
Leadership Development
140 West Main Street
P.O. Box 568
Midland, MI 48640
Phone: (517) 631-0900
Fax: (989) 631-0964
Web site: www.mackinac.org
E-mail: mcpp@mackinac.org

### Michigan Association for Public School Academies (MAPSA)
Daniel L. Quisenberry, President
215 South Washington Square, Suite 210
Lansing, MI 48933
Phone: (517) 374-9167
Fax: (517) 374-9197
Web site: www.charterschools.org
E-mail: mapsa@charterschools.org

### Michigan Department of Education
608 West Allegan Street
Lansing, MI 48933
Phone: (517) 373-3324
Web site: www.michigan.gov/mde
E-mail: mdeweb@michigan.gov

### *Michigan Education Report*
Elizabeth Moser, Managing Editor
140 West Main Street
P.O. Box 568
Midland, MI 48640
Phone: (989) 631-0900
Fax: (989) 631-0964
Web site: www.educationreport.org
E-mail: letters@educationreport.org

### Michigan Family Forum
Dan Jarvis, Research and Policy Director
P.O. Box 15216
Lansing, MI 48901-5216
Phone: (517) 374-1171
Fax: (517) 374-6112
Web site: www.michiganfamily.org

### Michigan School Board Leaders Association
Web site: www.msbla.org
E-mail: info@msbla.org

### National Charter School Development and Performance Institute
Central Michigan University
Teresa Staten, Director
2520 South University Park, Suite 11
Mount Pleasant, MI 48859
Phone: (989) 774-2999

Fax: (989) 774-2591
Web site: www.nationalcharterschools.org/
charter.nsf

**National Heritage Academies**
Peter Ruppert, Chairman
989 Spaulding Avenue, SE
Grand Rapids, MI 49546
Phone: (616) 222-1700
Phone: (800) 699-9235
Fax: (616) 222-1701
Web site: www.heritageacademies.com
E-mail: jc@superschools.com

## State School Report Card

**Greatschools.net**
Web site: www.greatschools.net/modperl/go/MI

**Michigan Department of Education**
Web site: www.michigan.gov/mde/0,1607,7-
140-5233_5978---,00.html

**Standard & Poors**
Web site: www.ses.standardandpoors.com

# MINNESOTA

## State Profile (Updated May 2003)

### School Choice Status
- Public school choice: Interdistrict/mandatory
- State constitution: Blaine amendment and compelled-support language
- Charter school law: Established 1991
    Strength of law: Strong
    Number of charter schools in operation (fall 2002): 87
    Number of students enrolled in charter schools (fall 2002): 12,269
- Publicly funded private school choice: Yes
- Privately funded school choice: Yes
- Home-school law: High regulation
- Ranking on the Education Freedom Index (2001): 5th out of 50 states

### K–12 Public Schools and Students (2001–2002)
- Public school enrollment: 845,700
- Students enrolled per teacher: 15.8
- Number of schools (2000–2001): 2,105
- Number of districts: 341
- Current expenditures: $6,623,305,000
- Current per-pupil expenditure: $7,832
- Amount of revenue from the federal government: 4.9%

### K–12 Public School Teachers (2001–2002)
- Number of teachers: 53,450
- Average salary: $43,330

### K–12 Private Schools (1999–2000)
- Private school enrollment: 92,795
- Number of schools: 530
- Number of teachers: 6,467

### K–12 Public and Private School Student Academic Performance
- NAEP test results:

| NAEP Tests Minnesota Student Performance | State (National) 2000 Math Scale = 0–500 | | State (National) 2000 Science Scale = 0–300 | | State (National) 2000 Reading Scale = 0–500 | |
|---|---|---|---|---|---|---|
| | 4th Grade | 8th Grade | 4th Grade | 8th Grade | 4th Grade | 8th Grade |
| Average Scale Score | 235 (226) | 288 (274) | 157 (148) | 160 (149) | 222 (215) | 267 (261) |
| Advanced | 3% (3%) | 7% (5%) | 3% (3%) | 5% (4%) | 8% (6%) | 2% (2%) |
| Proficient | 31% (23%) | 33% (21%) | 32% (25%) | 37% (26%) | 28% (23%) | 35% (29%) |
| Basic | 44% (43%) | 40% (39%) | 43% (36%) | 31% (29%) | 33% (32%) | 44% (41%) |
| Below Basic | 22% (31%) | 20% (35%) | 22% (36%) | 27% (41%) | 31% (39%) | 19% (28%) |

- SAT weighted rank (2001): N/A
- ACT weighted rank (2001): 2nd out of 26 states
- ALEC Academic Achievement Ranking: 3rd out of 50 states and the District of Columbia

## Summary

Minnesota has been at the forefront of the school choice movement. It was the first state to offer tax deductions for education expenses, the first to enact interdistrict school choice, and the first to create charter schools.

## Background

Since 1955, Minnesota families have been able to deduct their education expenditures from their state taxes.[438] Twenty-five years after enactment of the statute that allowed the deductions, a group of Minnesota taxpayers sued in a federal district court contending that the state education tax deduction violated the Establishment Clause of the U.S. Constitution by providing funds to sectarian institutions. In 1981, the district court held that the statute was "neutral on its face and in its application and does not have a primary effect of either advancing or inhibiting religion." The Eighth Circuit Court of Appeals affirmed the district court's opinion in 1982. On June 29, 1983, the Supreme Court of the United States upheld the Minnesota tax deduction in *Mueller* v. *Allen*, ruling that the program met a three-part constitutional test established by a previous Supreme Court decision in *Lemon* v. *Kurtzman*.[439] The test standards stipulate: "First, the statute must have a secular legislative purpose; second, its principal or primary effect must be one that neither advances nor inhibits religion…. [F]inally, the statute must not foster 'an excessive government entanglement with religion.'"[440]

The *Mueller* case has been a controlling precedent in several other pivotal school choice cases, including the recent *Zelman* v. *Simmons-Harris*

decision that upheld voucher programs as constitutional. In *Zelman*, writing for the majority, Chief Justice William Rehnquist stated, "We believe that the program challenged here is a program of true private choice, consistent with *Mueller*, *Witters*, and *Zobrest*, and thus constitutional. As was true in those cases, the Ohio program is neutral in all respects toward religion."[441]

In 1985, Minnesota enacted the Post-Secondary Enrollment Options Act, which enabled public, private, or home-schooled junior and senior high school students to take college courses, with the state's Department of Children, Families, and Learning paying for the tuition and books.[442]

Since 1987, the state has offered a High-School Graduation Incentive Program, which is a "second chance" program for students who are at risk of dropping out or who have dropped out of school. Students enrolled in this program may attend a public school or a nonsectarian private school that has an approved program designed to meet their special needs.[443]

In 1988, Minnesota became the first state to enact statewide interdistrict public school choice for all students.[444] In 1991, it became the first to enact a charter school law, permitting teachers to create and operate up to eight new charter schools.[445]

In his 1996 State of the State address, then-Governor Arne Carlson proposed a voucher program for students from low- and middle-income families in Minneapolis, St. Paul, and Brooklyn Center, a nearby suburb. The vouchers' value would have ranged from $500

---

438. See Minnesota House of Representatives, Research Department, "Minnesota's Public School Fee Law and Education Tax Credit and Deduction," *Information Brief*, January 2003, at *www.house.leg.state.mn.us/hrd/pubs/feelaw.pdf*.

439. *Mueller* v. *Allen*, 463 U.S. 388, (1983).

440. *Lemon* v. *Kurtzman*, 403 U.S. 602, at 612–613 (1971).

441. *Zelman* v. *Simmons-Harris*, 122 S.Ct. 2460 at 2467 (2002).

442. See Minnesota Office of the Revisor of Statutes Web site at *www.revisor.leg.state.mn.us/stats/124D/09.html*.

443. Peter W. Cookson, Jr., and Sonali M. Shroff, "School Choice and Urban School Reform," Columbia University, Teachers College, ERIC Clearinghouse on Urban Education Institute for Urban and Minority Education, *Urban Diversity Series* No. 110, December 1997.

444. *Ibid.*

445. Lynn Olson, "Nation's First 'Charter' School Clears a Key Hurdle," *Education Week*, November 27, 1991.

to $3,000, varying with the families' incomes. The Senate Education Committee defeated the proposal by a voice vote in February 1996.[446]

In 1997, the legislature enacted House File 1, giving Minnesota families with incomes of $33,500 or less a refundable tax credit of up to $1,000 per student, up to $2,000 per family, for education expenses, excluding tuition. The law increased the maximum tax deduction to $1,625 for expenses associated with elementary school education, including tuition, and $2,500 for junior and senior high school expenses.[447] In addition, it eliminated the charter school cap and allocated a $50,000 fund to help charter schools with start-up costs.[448]

Minnesota's charter school law has been amended three times—in 1997, 1999, and 2001. Under current law, local school boards and colleges and universities may charter schools. The initial term of a charter is up to three years. The Minnesota State Board of Education must approve the charter and serves as an appeals body when a charter is rejected at the local level. Teachers in charter schools must be certified.[449]

In 1998, benefactors Ronald and Laurie Eibensteiner established the KidsFirst Scholarship Fund of Minnesota, which enables low-income students in Minneapolis and St. Paul to attend a school of choice. KidsFirst pays up to 75 percent of tuition expenses, up to $1,200, for students in grades K–8. Funds are matched by Children First America, a $100 million foundation that matches funds raised by residents of the Twin Cities.[450]

In 2001, 300 Minneapolis students applied to attend public schools in suburban districts through a program known as The Choice Is Yours—a voluntary desegregation program that was the result of a lawsuit in which the NAACP argued that students in Minneapolis were not receiving an adequate education as guaranteed by the state constitution. In this program, the state pays for transportation to the schools of choice.[451]

## Developments in 2002 and 2003

During the 2002 legislative session, H.F. 2586 was introduced to provide vouchers that would have enabled low-income students in schools that had performed poorly for three consecutive years to attend a private school of choice. The vouchers would have been worth the cost of the private school's tuition or the state's average per-pupil expenditure, whichever was less. The bill died in committee.[452]

In 2002, according to a report from the University of Minnesota, 30 percent of the state's secondary students were participating in one of its four public-school choice programs—open enrollment, college dual-enrollment, Second Chance programs, and charter schools. The study found that "Minnesota's public school choice plans have produced many benefits for participating students, as well as for the overall public education system." Researchers recommended both providing more information to families and better oversight.[453]

In February 2003, the Center for School Change at the University of Minnesota's Humphrey Institute hired Mason–Dixon Polling to conduct a review of state residents' opinions on school choice programs. More than 600 residents were polled, and strong support was found for school choice, charter schools, and open enrollment. Of those polled, 75 percent believed "families should have the right to select among various public schools;" 56 percent supported open

446. "News in Brief: School-Finance Suit Is Dismissed in N.M.," *Education Week*, February 14, 1996.

447. Minnesota House of Representatives, Research Department, "Minnesota's Public School Fee Law and Education Tax Credit and Deduction."

448. Ann Bradley, "Minn. Expands Tax Breaks Tied to Education," *Education Week*, July 9, 1997.

449. Center for Education Reform, "Charter School Legislation: Profile of Minnesota's Charter School Law," 2001, at *http://edreform.com/charter_schools/laws/Minnesota.htm*.

450. See KidsFirst Scholarship Fund of Minnesota Web site at *www.kidsfirstmn.org*. See also Children's Scholarship Fund Web site at *www.scholarshipfund.org*.

451. Allie Shah, "Interest Growing in Expanded School-Choice Program," *Minneapolis Star Tribune*, January 19, 2001.

452. See National School Boards Association Web site at *www.nsba.org/novouchers*.

453. William Lowe Boyd, Debra Hare, and Joe Nathan, "What Really Happened?" Center for School Change, Hubert H. Humphry Institute of Public Affairs, University of Minnesota, May 2002, at *www.hhh.umn.edu/centers/school-change/docs/wrhc.pdf*.

For updates go to: *heritage.org*

119

enrollment (while 32 percent opposed it); and 52 percent supported Minnesota's charter school law (while 21 percent opposed it).[454] The report reveals a shift in public opinion: A 1985 study had found that residents opposed a statewide open enrollment plan by a margin of nearly 2 to 1.[455]

Companion bills to institute educational tax credit legislation, H.F. 301 and Senate File 1419, were introduced in 2003. These bills would allow individuals to take a credit of up to $1,000 for 75 percent of a donation to an organization that awards scholarships to low-income families. No action was taken prior to adjournment.[456]

Another set of companion bills would allow for more state control over private schools. S.F. 760, introduced in 2003 by State Senator Ellen R. Anderson (D–66), and its companion, H.F. 743, introduced by Assistant House Minority Leader Mindy Greiling (D–54A), would require private schools that accept students whose parents claim a tax deduction for educational expenses to adhere to state graduation requirements. No action was taken this session.[457]

State Representative Barbara Sykora (R–33B) introduced H.F. 1266 to create a state-funded scholarship program for students with disabilities. These "Learning Scholarships" would be worth a district's average per-pupil expenditure or the costs of tuition and transportation to the receiving school, whichever is less. No action was taken on this bill prior to adjournment.[458]

## Position of the Governor / Composition of the State Legislature

Governor Tim Pawlenty, a Republican, supports charter schools. Republicans control the Minnesota House, and Democrats control the Senate.

## State Contacts

### Center for School Change
Hubert Humphrey Institute of Public Affairs
University of Minnesota, Room 230
Joe Nathan, Director
301 19th Avenue South, Room 234

Minneapolis, MN 55455
Phone: (612) 626-1834
Fax: (612) 625-0104
Web site: www.centerforschoolchange.org
E-mail: csc@hhh.umn.edu

### Center of the American Experiment
Mitchell B. Pearlstein, President
12 South 6th Street, Suite 1024
Minneapolis, MN 55402
Phone: (612) 338-3605
Fax: (612) 338-3621
Web site: www.amexp.org
E-mail: amexp@amexp.org

### KidsFirst Scholarship Fund of Minnesota
Ron and Laurie Eibensteiner, Founders
Margie Lauer, Executive Director
800 Nicollet Mall, Suite 2680
Minneapolis, MN 55402
Phone: (612) 573-2020
Fax: (612) 573-2021
Web site: www.kidsfirstmn.org
E-mail: kids1st@visi.com

### Minneapolis Public Schools
807 NE Broadway
Minneapolis, MN 55413
Phone: (612) 668-0000
Web site: www.mpls.k12.mn.us
*For school choice questions, contact:*
Student Placement Services
910 West Broadway
Minneapolis, MN 55411
Phone: (612) 668-1840
E-mail: sps.department@mpls.k12.mn.us

### Minnesota Association of Charter Schools
Steve Dess, Executive Director
1295 Bandana Boulevard, Suite 165
St. Paul, MN 55108
Phone: (651) 644-0031
Fax: (651) 644-0433
Web site: www.mncharterschools.org
E-mail: stevedess@mncharterschools.org

### Minnesota Association of Christian Home Educators
P.O. Box 32308
Fridley, MN 55432-0308
Phone: (763) 717-9070

---

454. University of Minnesota, Humphrey Institute of Public Affairs, Center for School Change, "CSC Public School Choice Poll Summary," at *www.hhh.umn.edu/centers/school-change/*.
455. Paul Tosto, "Minnesotans Back Public School Choice," *Pioneer Press*, March 13, 2003.
456. See Minnesota Office of the Revisor of Statutes at *www.revisor.leg.state.mn.us/*.
457. *Ibid.*
458. *Ibid.*

Web site: www.mache.org
E-mail: MACHE@ISD.NET

### Minnesota Department of Children, Families, and Learning
1500 Highway 36 West
Roseville, MN 55113
Phone: (651) 582-8200
Web site: http://cfl.state.mn.us
E-mail: children@state.mn.us

### Minnesota Family Council
Tom Prichard, President
2855 Anthony Lane South, Suite 150
Minneapolis, MN 55418-3265
Phone: (612) 789-8811
Fax: (612) 789-8858
Web site: www.mfc.org
E-mail: mail@mfc.org

### New Twin Cities Charter School Project
Hubert H. Humphrey Institute of Public Affairs
University of Minnesota
301 19th Avenue South
Minneapolis, MN 55455
Phone: (612) 626-1834
E-mail: csc@hhh.umn.edu

### Partnership for Choice in Education
Elizabeth Mische, Executive Director
46 East 4th Street, Suite 900
St. Paul, MN 55101
Phone: (651) 293-9196
Fax: (651) 293-9285

Web site: www.pcemn.org
E-mail: pcemail@pcemn.org

### Public Strategies Group, Inc.
Peter Hutchinson, President
275 East 4th Street, Suite 710
St. Paul, MN 55101
Phone: (651) 227-9774
Fax: (651) 292-1482
Web site: www.psgrp.com
E-mail: peter@psgrp.com

### Republican School Choice Task Force
Cory Miltimore, Executive Director
480 Cedar Street, Suite 560
St. Paul, MN 55101
Phone: (651) 222-0022
Web site: www.mngop.com

## State School Report Card

### Greatschools.net
Web site: www.greatschools.net/modperl/go/MN

### Minneapolis Public Schools
Web site: http://services.mpls.k12.mn.us/schoolinfo

### St. Paul Public Schools
Web site: www.stpaul.k12.mn.us/schools/select_school.html

# MISSISSIPPI

## State Profile (Updated May 2003)

### School Choice Status
- Public school choice: Interdistrict/voluntary
- State constitution: Blaine amendment
- Charter school law: Established 1997
   Strength of law: Weak
   Number of charter schools in operation (fall 2002): 1
   Number of students enrolled in charter schools (fall 2002): 334
- Publicly funded private school choice: No
- Privately funded school choice: Yes
- Home-school law: Low regulation
- Ranking on the Education Freedom Index (2001): 37th out of 50 states

### K–12 Public Schools and Students (2001–2002)
- Public school enrollment: 491,686
- Students enrolled per teacher: 15
- Number of schools (2000–2001): 884
- Number of districts: 152
- Current expenditures: $2,573,778,000
- Current per-pupil expenditure: $5,235
- Amount of revenue from the federal government: 14.4%

### K–12 Public School Teachers (2001–2002)
- Number of teachers: 32,757
- Average salary: $32,800

### K–12 Private Schools (1999–2000)
- Private school enrollment: 51,369
- Number of schools: 207
- Number of teachers: 3,884

### K–12 Public and Private School Student Academic Performance
- NAEP test results:

| NAEP Tests Mississippi Student Performance | State (National) 2000 Math Scale = 0–500 | | State (National) 2000 Science Scale = 0–300 | | State (National) 2000 Reading Scale = 0–500 | |
|---|---|---|---|---|---|---|
| | 4th Grade | 8th Grade | 4th Grade | 8th Grade | 4th Grade | 8th Grade |
| Average Scale Score | 211 (226) | 254 (274) | 133 (148) | 134 (149) | 204 (215) | 251 (261) |
| Advanced | 0% (3%) | 1% (5%) | 1% (3%) | 1% (4%) | 3% (6%) | 1% (2%) |
| Proficient | 9% (23%) | 7% (21%) | 13% (25%) | 14% (26%) | 15% (23%) | 18% (29%) |
| Basic | 36% (43%) | 33% (39%) | 33% (36%) | 27% (29%) | 30% (32%) | 42% (41%) |
| Below Basic | 55% (31%) | 59% (35%) | 53% (36%) | 58% (41%) | 52% (39%) | 39% (28%) |

- SAT weighted rank (2001): N/A
- ACT weighted rank (2001): 26th out of 26 states
- ALEC Academic Achievement Ranking: 50th out of 50 states and the District of Columbia

## Summary

Mississippi offers little public school choice and has only one charter school. Eligible high school students may take community college courses for high school and postsecondary credit.[459] Low-income students may apply for privately funded scholarships to attend a private school of choice.

## Background

On April 24, 1997, then-Governor Kirk Fordice signed Mississippi's charter school law (House Bill 1672). The law allows any public school to convert to a charter school.[460] Schools may not be managed by for-profit organizations, and the conversion schools will receive no additional funding over what they received before conversion. The conversion must be supported by a majority of the students' parents, school staff, and school faculty. Charter contracts last for four years, and the state has a limit of six charter schools.[461]

In 1999, two voucher bills, H.B. 500 and H.B. 437, died in committee. H.B. 500 would have established a program providing vouchers worth up to $3,350 per recipient for use at either a public or private school.[462] H.B. 437 would have provided vouchers worth up to $2,500 for students whose families met certain income requirements (married couples who earned less than $30,000 per year and single parents who earned less than $20,000).

CEO Metro Jackson provides scholarships to low-income students. In 1998, Jackson became a Children's Scholarship Fund (CSF) "partner city." The CSF is a foundation that provides privately funded vouchers.[463] Parents must submit an application, and voucher recipients are selected by lottery. In 1999, CEO Metro Jackson received nearly 5,000 applications and awarded 325 scholarships.[464]

In January 2001, Representative Joseph L. Warren (D–90) introduced H.B. 924, which would have allowed the creation of new charter schools as well as the conversion of conventional public schools. The legislation would have enabled the Mississippi State Board of Education to grant charters for schools and would have required the state to provide students with transportation to charter schools. H.B. 924 died in committee.[465]

Voucher legislation similar to that which was proposed in 1999 was introduced again in 2001. H.B. 71 would have established a program to provide vouchers worth up to $3,350 for students to attend participating private schools.[466] Like H.B. 437 from 1999, H.B. 1398 would have established a program offering vouchers worth up to $2,500 to parents who met certain income requirements.[467] Both H.B. 71 and H.B. 1398 died in committee.

The Mississippi Public School Relief Act, Senate Bill 2122, was also introduced in 2001. The bill would have provided tax credits worth up to $500 for contributions to scholarship organizations.[468] S.B. 2122 died in committee.[469]

---

459. Education Commission of the States, "Postsecondary Options: Dual/Concurrent Enrollment," July 2001.

460. Mississippi Legislature, 1997 Regular Session, H.B. 1672.

461. Center for Education Reform, "Charter School Legislation: Profile of Mississippi's Charter School Law," 2001, at *http://edreform.com/charter_schools/laws/Mississippi.htm.*

462. Mississippi Legislature, 1999 Regular Session, H.B. 500.

463. Children's Scholarship Fund, "Children's Scholarship Fund Announces 40 Cities $140 Million in Scholarships Will Go to Kids," press release, September 28, 1998.

464. Public Education Forum of Mississippi, "School Choice 1999: What's Happening in the States," September 8, 1999, at *www.publiceducationforum.org/miss_99.htm.*

465. Mississippi Legislature, 2001 Session, H.B. 924, at *http://billstatus.ls.state.ms.us/documents/2001/html/HB/0900-0999/HB0924IN.htm.*

466. Mississippi Legislature, 2001 Session, H.B. 71, at *http://billstatus.ls.state.ms.us/documents/2001/html/HB/0001-0099/HB0071IN.htm.*

467. Mississippi Legislature, 2001 Session, H.B. 1398, at *http://billstatus.ls.state.ms.us/documents/2001/html/HB/1300-1399/HB1398IN.htm.*

## Developments in 2002 and 2003

H.B. 100 was introduced in 2002 to provide low-income families with private-school vouchers worth $2,500 for their children. H.B. 100 died in committee.[470] Another bill, H.B. 349, would have established vouchers worth $3,500 for students to use for tuition or educational materials at either a public school or a private school. H.B. 349 also died in committee.[471]

In 2003, three voucher proposals were introduced. H.B. 935 would have established vouchers worth up to $2,500 for use at participating private schools.[472] H.B. 372, introduced by Thomas F. Cameron, III (I–52), would have established vouchers worth $3,350.[473] S.B. 2598 would have created a program similar to Florida's Opportunity Scholarship Program. Students in schools deemed "low-performing" by the state two years out of the past four would have received Opportunity Scholarships. All three bills died in committee.[474]

One tax credit bill was introduced in the Senate in 2003 but died in committee. S.B. 2043 would have created a tax credit for contributions to public schools or scholarship organizations. The credits would have been worth up to $500.[475]

H.B. 164 was introduced as tax credit legislation in the House. This bill would have provided tax credits for the purchase of tutoring services. The bill died in the Ways and Means Committee.[476]

## Position of the Governor / Composition of the State Legislature

Governor Ronnie Musgrove, a Democrat, does not support vouchers. Democrats control both houses of the legislature.

## State Contacts

### Children's Scholarship Fund–Metro Jackson
200 South Lamar Street, Suite 800 South
Jackson, MS 39201
Phone: (601) 985-3510
Fax: (601) 949-8959
Web site: www.scholarshipfund.org
E-mail: csf@irby.com

### Mississippi Department of Education
Central High School
P.O. Box 771
359 North West Street
Jackson, MS 39205
Phone: (601) 359-3513
Web site: www.mde.k12.ms.us

### Mississippi Family Council
Forest Thigpen, President
P.O. Box 13514
Jackson, MS 39236
Phone: (601) 969-1200
Fax: (601) 969-1600
Web site: www.msfamily.org
E-mail: fthigpen@msfamily.org

---

468. See National School Boards Association Web site at *www.nsba.org/novouchers*.

469. Mississippi Legislature, 2001 Session, S.B. 2122, at *http://billstatus.ls.state.ms.us/2001/html/history/SB/SB2122.htm*.

470. Mississippi Legislature, 2002 Session, H.B. 100, at *http://billstatus.ls.state.ms.us/documents/2002/html/HB/0100-0199/HB0100IN.htm*.

471. Mississippi Legislature, 2002 Session, H.B. 349, *http://billstatus.ls.state.ms.us/documents/2002/html/HB/0300-0399/HB0349IN.htm*.

472. Mississippi Legislature, 2003 Session, H.B. 935, at *http://billstatus.ls.state.ms.us/2003/html/history/HB/HB0935.htm*.

473. Mississippi Legislature, 2003 Session, H.B. 372, at *http://billstatus.ls.state.ms.us/2003/html/history/HB/HB0372.htm*.

474. Mississippi Legislature, 2003 Session, S.B. 2598, at *http://billstatus.ls.state.ms.us/2003/html/history/SB/SB2598.htm*.

475. Mississippi Legislature, 2003 Session, S.B. 2043, at *http://billstatus.ls.state.ms.us/2003/html/history/SB/SB2043.htm*.

476. Mississippi Legislature, 2003 Session, H.B. 164, at *http://billstatus.ls.state.ms.us/2003/html/history/HB/HB0164.htm*.

**Mississippi Home Educators Association**
P.O. Box 855
Batesville, MS 38606-0855
Phone: (662) 578-6432
Fax: (662) 563-0041
Web site: www.mhea.net
E-mail: MHEA@mhea.net

## State School Report Card

**GreatSchools.net**
Website: www.greatschools.net/modperl/go/MS

**Mississippi Department of Education**
Web site: www.mde.k12.ms.us/account/report/mrc.htm

# MISSOURI

## State Profile (Updated May 2003)

### School Choice Status
- Public school choice: Interdistrict/voluntary
- State constitution: Blaine amendment and compelled-support language
- Charter school law: Established 1998
  - Strength of law: Strong
  - Number of charter schools in operation (fall 2002): 26
  - Number of students enrolled in charter schools (fall 2002): 12,130
- Publicly funded private school choice: No
- Privately funded school choice: Yes
- Home-school law: No notice required
- Ranking on the Education Freedom Index (2001): 8th out of 50 states

### K–12 Public Schools and Students (2001–2002)
- Public school enrollment: 892,582
- Students enrolled per teacher: 13.9
- Number of schools (2000–2001): 2,266
- Number of Districts: 524
- Current expenditures: $5,867,680,000
- Current per-pupil expenditure: $6,574
- Amount of revenue from the federal government: 7.3%

### K–12 Public School Teachers (2001–2002)
- Number of teachers: 64,000
- Average salary: $37,695

### K–12 Private Schools (1999–2000)
- Private school enrollment: 122,387
- Number of schools: 576
- Number of teachers: 9,105

### K–12 Public and Private School Student Academic Performance
- NAEP test results:

| NAEP Tests Missouri Student Performance | State (National) 2000 Math Scale = 0–500 | | State (National) 2000 Science Scale = 0–300 | | State (National) 2000 Reading Scale = 0–500 | |
|---|---|---|---|---|---|---|
| | 4th Grade | 8th Grade | 4th Grade | 8th Grade | 4th Grade | 8th Grade |
| Average Scale Score | 229 (226) | 274 (274) | 156 (148) | 156 (149) | 216 (215) | 263 (261) |
| Advanced | 2% (3%) | 2% (5%) | 4% (3%) | 4% (4%) | 5% (6%) | 1% (2%) |
| Proficient | 21% (23%) | 20% (21%) | 31% (25%) | 32% (26%) | 24% (23%) | 28% (29%) |
| Basic | 49% (43%) | 45% (39%) | 40% (36%) | 32% (29%) | 34% (32%) | 47% (41%) |
| Below Basic | 28% (31%) | 33% (35%) | 25% (36%) | 32% (41%) | 37% (39%) | 24% (28%) |

- SAT weighted rank (2001): N/A
- ACT weighted rank (2001): 6th out of 26 states
- ALEC Academic Achievement Ranking: 24th out of 50 states and the District of Columbia

## Summary

Missouri offers interdistrict public school choice for students in participating districts. Districts in certain counties and the city of St. Louis are exempt. The state has a strong charter school law. Private scholarship foundations help low-income students attend private schools with the help of privately funded vouchers.

## Background

In January 1998, then-State Representative Rich Chrismer (R–16) introduced the Pilot Project Scholarship Program bill (House Bill 1472) to provide scholarships to students in school districts that were under a federal court desegregation order. Scholarships would have been valued at 75 percent or 90 percent of tuition, depending on the parents' income level, with an additional amount available for students with disabilities. The bill died in committee.[477]

In 1998, the legislature enacted Senate Bill 781 to permit the establishment of an unlimited number of charter schools in the St. Louis and Kansas City school districts. Local school boards or colleges and universities with an approved teacher education program can grant charters. Charter schools receive 100 percent of the per-pupil funding, and 80 percent or more of the teaching staff must hold state certification.[478]

Two tax credit bills were introduced during the 1999 legislative session. S.B. 497 would have provided $5 million worth of tax credits to individuals who donated to organizations that provide scholarships. S.B. 483 would have provided tax credits of up to $500 a year to scholarship organizations. Both bills died in committee.[479]

In early January 2000, a judge dismissed a lawsuit filed by the Missouri School Boards Association challenging the state's charter law. The association had contended that the Missouri Charter School Act was unconstitutional and was in violation of several state laws.[480]

In 2000, then-State Representatives Rich Chrismer (R–16) and Harry Kennedy (D–66) introduced the Pilot Project Challenge Scholarship Program bill (H.B. 1373), which would have established a pilot voucher program in school districts that were under a federal desegregation order. Students would have been able to attend a private school or public school in another district. The bill died in committee.[481]

Senator Anita Yeckel (R–1) introduced S.B. 592 in 2000 to authorize state income tax credits for contributions, not to exceed $500 per year, to a school tuition organization. Another bill, S.B. 656, would have established a tax credit for donations to scholarship charities. The total annual amount of credits would have been limited to $20 million. Both bills died in committee. S.B. 599 would have authorized corporate and individual tax deductions of up to $2,500 for the cost of tuition, supplies, or transportation for students in grades 9–12. The Senate Ways and Means Committee approved the bill, but no further action was taken.[482]

On February 15, 2000, the St. Louis School Choice Scholarship Fund gave some 750 St. Louis students scholarships to escape poorly performing schools. The scholarships, which totaled $3.6 million, were made possible largely by retired St. Louis businessman Eugene Williams and his wife, and by David Farrell, a former chief executive of the May Department Stores Company.[483] The Children's Scholarship Fund of Kansas City also provides scholarships to students in need.

In 2000, enrollment figures indicated that about 45 percent of St. Louis's charter school population came from private schools. Nationally,

477. Missouri General Assembly, House and Senate Joint Bill Tracking, at *www.house.state.mo.us/jointsearch.asp*.
478. See Center for Education Reform, "Charter School Legislation: Profile of Missouri's Charter School Law," 2001, at *http://edreform.com/charter_schools/laws/Missouri.htm*.
479. Missouri General Assembly, House and Senate Joint Bill Tracking, at *www.house.state.mo.us/jointsearch.asp*.
480. Center for Education Reform, *Education Reform Update*, January 10, 2000.
481. Missouri General Assembly, House and Senate Joint Bill Tracking, at *www.house.state.mo.us/jointsearch.asp*.
482. Missouri General Assembly, House and Senate Joint Bill Tracking, at *www.house.state.mo.us/jointsearch.asp*.
483. "New Scholarship Programs Launched in St. Louis and Denver," *School Reform News*, April 2000.

about 11 percent of charter enrollment comes from private schools. Some suggest that the high Catholic school enrollment in St. Louis stems from parents' desire for quality academics rather than religious affiliation. These families switched schools when given a free secular alternative.[484]

Several choice bills to give tax credits for contributions to scholarship programs were introduced during the 2001 legislative session. S.B. 74, S.B. 576, and H.B. 906 would have provided tax credits of up to 50 percent of a contribution to organizations that provide scholarships. No action was taken on the bills. S.B. 177 would have provided a $2,500 income tax deduction for private secondary school expenses. The Senate Ways and Means Committee approved the bill, but no further action was taken.[485]

## Developments in 2002 and 2003

As required by the federal No Child Left Behind Act, Missouri identified 62 failing schools. Missouri districts were required to pay for transportation. Tutoring was not available for students in 2002 because, as a result of changes in the way calculations are made, the state was not able to determine which schools had been failing for three or more years.[486]

During the 2002 session, S.B. 659 (prefiled in late 2001) was introduced to amend the state's charter school law. The legislation would have allowed teachers in charter schools to retain tenure status and seniority rights for three years, would have doubled the number of public schools that could be converted to charter schools, would have created a Charter School Sponsor Oversight Fund, and would have required charter schools to publish audits and financial reports. The bill was approved in committee but never made it to final passage.[487]

S.B. 735 would have provided $5 million worth of tax credits to taxpayers who contribute to scholarship foundations. The credit would have been worth up to 50 percent of the taxpayer's contribution to a scholarship charity, not to exceed $50,000 per taxable year per taxpayer. Eligible students would have had to come from failing schools and qualify for the federal free or reduced-price lunch program. The bill was approved by the Senate Ways and Means Committee but received no other action.[488]

Similarly, H.B. 1278 would have provided tax credits to individuals and corporations that contribute to scholarship organizations. Credits would have been worth up to 50 percent of the donation but not more than $50,000. The bill died in committee.[489]

In 2003, three educational tax credit bills have been introduced. H.B. 398 would create tax credits worth the amount spent on education expenditures, up to $2,500. This bill is with the House Committee on Tax Policy.[490] H.B. 345 would create credits for individuals or corporations that donate to scholarship organizations. The credits would be worth up to 50 percent of donations of $200 or more. This bill was approved in committee.[491] S.B. 497 was introduced to create the Show Me Parental Choice Tax Credit Program, which would provide tax credits for donations made to scholarship organizations in Kansas City or St. Louis serving students eligible for the free or reduced-priced lunch program. The bill would also create Schools of Choice Resource Centers, which would serve to inform parents in these two cities of their children's educational options. Tax credits would also be given for donations to these centers. S.B. 497 has been referred to the Senate Ways and Means Committee.[492]

484. Matthew Franck, "Religious, Independent Schools Here May Lose Students to Charter Schools," *St. Louis Post–Dispatch*, July 19, 2000, p. A1.
485. See National School Boards Association Web site at *www.nsba.org./novouchers*.
486. Diane Carroll, "Federal Education Law Raises Questions for Educators, Parents," *Kansas City Star*, July 18, 2002.
487. Missouri General Assembly, House and Senate Joint Bill Tracking, at *www.house.state.mo.us/jointsearch.asp*.
488. *Ibid.*
489. *Ibid.*
490. Missouri General Assembly, 2003 Session, H.B. 398, at *www.house.state.mo.us/bills03/bills/hb398.htm*.
491. Missouri General Assembly, 2003 Session, H.B. 345, at *www.house.state.mo.us/bills03/bills/hb345.htm*.
492. Missouri General Assembly, 2003 Session, S.B. 497, at *www.house.state.mo.us/bills03/bills/sb497.htm*.

## Position of the Governor / Composition of the State Legislature

Governor Bob Holden, a Democrat, opposes vouchers. Republicans control both houses of the legislature.

## State Contacts

**Children's Scholarship Fund–Kansas City**
Dr. Carl Herbster, President
Mark Bainbridge, Director
4500 Little Blue Parkway
Independence, MO 64057
Phone: (816) 795-8643
Fax: (816) 795-9759
Web site: www.csf-kc.org
E-mail: info@csf-kc.org

**Citizens for Educational Freedom**
Mae Duggan, President
Adrian Brigham, Executive Director
9333 Clayton Road
St. Louis, MO 63124
Phone: (314) 997-6361
Fax: (314) 997-6321
Web site: www.Educational-Freedom.org
E-mail: CitEdFree@aol.com

*Kansas City Chapter*
Ed Burns, President
401 East 106th Street
Kansas City, MO 64131
Phone: (816) 761-0700
Fax: (816) 761-0700

**Hispanic Council for Reform and Educational Options (CREO)**
Sandy Aguirre Mayer, Member
4142 Mercier
Kansas City, MO 64111
Phone: (816) 531-2554
E-mail: SANDYMAYER@msn.com

**Families for Home Education**
P.O. Box 800
Platte City, MO 64079-0800
Phone: (816) 767-9825
Web site: www.fhe-mo.org
E-mail: 1983@fhe-mo.org

**Gateway Educational Trust**
Irene Allen, Executive Director

7716 Forsyth Boulevard
St. Louis, MO 63105-1810
Phone: (314) 771-1998
Fax: (314) 721-1857
E-mail: ager2@aol.com

**Landmark Legal Foundation**
3100 Broadway, Suite 1110
Kansas City, MO 64111
Phone: (816) 931-5559
Fax: (816) 931-1115
Web site: www.landmarklegal.org
E-mail: info@landmarklegal.org

**The Learning Exchange**
Tammy Blossom, President and CEO
3132 Pennsylvania
Kansas City, MO 64111-2776
Phone: (816) 751-4100
Fax: (816) 751-4101
Web site: www.lx.org
E-mail: ebieberly@lx.org

**Missouri Association of Teaching Christian Homes**
2203 Rhonda Drive
West Plains, MO 65775-1615
Phone: (815) 550-8641
Fax: (815) 550-8641
Web site: www.match-inc.org
E-mail: match@match-inc.org

**Missouri Charter School Information Center**
Dave Camden, Executive Director
35 North Central Avenue, Suite 335
St. Louis, MO 63105
Phone: (314) 726-6474
Fax: (314) 721-4729
Web site: www.mocsic.org
E-mail: mocsic@aol.com

**Missouri Department of Elementary and Secondary Education**
D. Kent King, Commissioner
P.O. Box 480
Jefferson City, MO 65102-0480
Phone: (573) 751-4212
Fax: (573) 751-8613
Web site: www.dese.state.mo.us
E-mail: pubinfo@mail.dese.state.mo.us

## Show Me Choices for Kids in Education
Sandy Aguirre Mayer, Chair
4142 Mercier
Kansas City, MO 64111
Phone: (816) 531-2554
E-mail: sandymayer@msn.com

### Josh Schneider, Legislative Chair
4500 Little Blue Parkway
Independence, MO 64057
Phone: (816) 795-8700, ext. 300
Fax: (816) 795-8096
E-mail: jscheiderer@tri-city.org

### Betty Conley-Denton,
Outreaching Committee Chair
4001 Euclid Avenue
Kansas City, MO 64130
Phone: (816) 921-0951
Fax: (816) 668-3381
E-mail: bdenton@kc.rr.com

## State School Report Card

### Greatschools.net
Web site: www.greatschools.net/modperl/go/MO

### Independence Public Schools
Web site: www.indep.k12.mo.us/schools.html

### Kansas City School District
Web site: www.kcmsd.k12.mo.us/schools.asp?b=8&id=4

### Missouri Department of Elementary and Secondary Education
Web site: http://services.dese.state.mo.us/schooldata

# MONTANA

## State Profile (Updated May 2003)

### School Choice Status
- Public school choice: Interdistrict/voluntary
- State constitution: Blaine amendment
- Charter school law: No
- Publicly funded private school choice: No
- Privately funded school choice: No
- Home-school law: Low regulation
- Ranking on the Education Freedom Index (2001): 29th out of 50 states

### K–12 Public Schools and Students (2001–2002)
- Public school enrollment: 151,970
- Students enrolled per teacher: 14.9
- Number of schools (2000–2001): 878
- Number of districts: 449
- Current expenditures: $1,076,000,000
- Current per-pupil expenditure: $7,080
- Amount of revenue from the federal government: 11.8%

### K–12 Public School Teachers (2001–2002)
- Number of teachers: 10,212
- Average salary: $34,379

### K–12 Private Schools (1999–2000)
- Private school enrollment: 8,711
- Number of schools: 90
- Number of teachers: 740

### K–12 Public and Private School Student Academic Performance
- NAEP test results:

| NAEP Tests Montana Student Performance | State (National) 2000 Math Scale = 0–500 | | State (National) 2000 Science Scale = 0–300 | | State (National) 2000 Reading Scale = 0–500 | |
|---|---|---|---|---|---|---|
| | 4th Grade | 8th Grade | 4th Grade | 8th Grade | 4th Grade | 8th Grade |
| Average Scale Score | 230 (226) | 287 (274) | 160 (148) | 165 (149) | 226 (215) | 270 (261) |
| Advanced | 2% (3%) | 6% (5%) | 4% (3%) | 5% (4%) | 8% (6%) | 2% (2%) |
| Proficient | 23% (23%) | 31% (21%) | 33% (25%) | 41% (26%) | 29% (23%) | 36% (29%) |
| Basic | 48% (43%) | 43% (39%) | 44% (36%) | 34% (29%) | 36% (32%) | 45% (41%) |
| Below Basic | 27% (31%) | 20% (35%) | 19% (36%) | 20% (41%) | 27% (39%) | 17% (28%) |

- SAT weighted rank (2001): N/A
- ACT weighted rank (2001): 4th out of 26 states
- ALEC Academic Achievement Ranking: 5th out of 50 states and the District of Columbia

## Summary

Montana offers parents little public school choice and has no charter school law or tuition scholarship organizations.[493]

## Background

Legislation to establish refundable tuition tax credits was defeated in 1995, 1997, and 1999.[494] A tuition tax credit bill, House Bill 433, was introduced in 1997. Under this law, parents would have received a tax credit of up to $1,000 for private school tuition for their first child, a $700 credit for their second child, and a $500 credit for their third child. The bill died in committee.[495] In 1999, then-State Representative Allen Walters (R–60) introduced H.B. 318, which would have provided a refundable tax credit of $1,200 for tuition, fees, and textbooks. This bill also died in committee.[496]

In 1999, a charter school bill, S.B. 204, was introduced by then-State Senator Tom Keating (R–5) but was tabled. The legislation would have established a five-member Board of Charter Schools, appointed by the governor, to authorize charter schools. Charters would have been issued for 15 years and would have received a review every five years.[497]

In 2001, State Representative Joe Balyeat (R–32) introduced H.B. 555, which would have provided a tax credit of up to $375 for tuition and other expenses for 2001, up to $750 in 2002, and up to $1,000 in 2003 and succeeding years. The bill died in committee.[498]

## Developments in 2002 and 2003

Tax credit legislation was introduced in the fall of 2002 and referred to a committee in 2003. H.B. 398 would have created an endowment tax credit for contributions to scholarship organizations or tuition assistance programs.[499]

Legislation to create a charter school law for Montana was also introduced in the fall of 2002. H.B. 704, the Montana Charter Schools Act, would have established a process for the creation of both charter schools and charter school districts, and charters would have been granted for 15 years. Lawmakers adjourned for the session before acting on either H.B. 398 or H.B. 704.[500]

## Position of the Governor / Composition of the State Legislature

Governor Judy Martz, a Republican, has expressed little interest in school choice.. Republicans control both houses of the legislature.

## State Contacts

**Montana Coalition of Home Educators**
P.O. Box 43
Gallatin Gateway, MT 59730
Phone: (406) 587-6163
Fax: (406) 587-5630

---

493. A student may attend a school in another district with approval from the sending and receiving districts. The receiving district may charge the parent or the sending district tuition. In some cases (for example, when a student lives closer to a school in another district), the transfer must be approved. See Montana Statutes 20-5-320, 20-5-321, 20-5-322, and 20-5-324.

494. Information provided by Robert G. Natelson, Professor of Law, University of Montana.

495. See National School Boards Association Web site at *www.nsba.org/novouchers*.

496. See Montana State Legislature Web site at *http://leg.state.mt.us/css/default.asp*.

497. *Ibid.*

498. *Ibid.*

499. *Ibid.*

500. Montana Legislature, 2003 Session, H.B. 398 and H.B. 704.

**Montana Conservatives**
Representative Joe Balyeat, President
6909 Rising Eagle Road
Bozeman, MT 59715
Phone: (406) 586-1838
Fax: (406) 586-1838
E-mail: joecpa@imt.net

**Montana Office of Public Instruction**
Linda McCulloch, Superintendent
P.O. Box 202501
Helena, MT 59620
Phone: (406) 444-3095
Web site: www.opi.state.mt.us/index.html

**Robert G. Natelson**
Professor of Law
University of Montana
Missoula, MT 59802
Phone: (406) 721-2266
Fax: (406) 728-2803
E-mail: natelson@montana.com

## State School Report Card
**Greatschools.net**
Web site: www.greatschools.net/modperl/go/MT

**Montana Office of Public Instruction**
Not available on-line.

# NEBRASKA

## State Profile (Updated May 2003)

### School Choice Status
- Public school choice: Interdistrict/mandatory
- State constitution: Blaine amendment and compelled-support language
- Charter school law: No
- Publicly funded private school choice: No
- Privately funded school choice: Yes
- Home-school law: Low regulation
- Ranking on the Education Freedom Index (2001): 18th out of 50 states

### K–12 Public Schools and Students (2001–2002)
- Public school enrollment: 285,022
- Students enrolled per teacher: 13.6
- Number of schools (2000–2001): 1,296
- Number of districts: 534
- Current expenditures: $2,150,954,000
- Current per-pupil expenditure: $7,547
- Amount of revenue from the federal government: 5.5%

### K–12 Public School Teachers (2001–2002)
- Number of teachers: 21,004
- Average salary: $36,236

### K–12 Private Schools (1999–2000)
- Private school enrollment: 42,141
- Number of schools: 237
- Number of teachers: 2,963

### K–12 Public and Private School Student Academic Performance
- NAEP test results:

| NAEP Tests Nebraska Student Performance | State (National) 2000 Math Scale = 0–500 | | State (National) 2000 Science Scale = 0–300 | | State (National) 2000 Reading Scale = 0–500 | |
|---|---|---|---|---|---|---|
| | 4th Grade | 8th Grade | 4th Grade | 8th Grade | 4th Grade | 8th Grade |
| Average Scale Score | 226 (226) | 281 (274) | 150 (148) | 157 (149) | N/A (215) | N/A (261) |
| Advanced | 2% (3%) | 5% (5%) | 2% (3%) | 4% (4%) | N/A (6%) | N/A (2%) |
| Proficient | 22% (23%) | 26% (21%) | 24% (25%) | 32% (26%) | N/A (23%) | N/A (29%) |
| Basic | 43% (43%) | 43% (39%) | 42% (36%) | 34% (29%) | N/A (32%) | N/A (41%) |
| Below Basic | 33% (31%) | 26% (35%) | 32% (36%) | 30% (41%) | N/A (39%) | N/A (28%) |

- SAT weighted rank (2001): N/A
- ACT weighted rank (2001): 5th out of 26 states
- ALEC Academic Achievement Ranking: 10th out of 50 states and the District of Columbia

## Summary

Nebraska offers statewide public school choice that allows students to attend any school outside of their home district, provided certain conditions are met. State funds for the transportation of students across district lines are available for all low-income children. Low-income students may apply for scholarships provided by private scholarship foundations to attend a private school of choice.

## Background

A Nebraska case was one of two important Supreme Court decisions in the 1920s that affirmed the right of parents to direct their children's schooling. In the first case, *Meyer* v. *State of Nebraska*,[501] a private school teacher was convicted of violating the state law that prohibited elementary school teachers from teaching in any language other than English; conviction brought a monetary fine or time in jail. In 1923, the case was heard by the Supreme Court of the United States, which ruled that the statute conflicted with the Fourteenth Amendment and infringed upon both the teacher's rights and the rights of parents "to control the education of their own."[502]

Two years later, the Court's rationale in *Meyer* v. *State of Nebraska* was used to support a second, equally important decision. In *Pierce* v. *Society of Sisters*,[503] the Court struck down an Oregon law mandating that all children attend public schools. In this decision, Justice James C. McReynolds wrote for the Court that

> Under the doctrine of *Meyer* v. *Nebraska*…we think it entirely plain that the Act of 1922 unreasonably interferes with the liberty of parents and guardians to direct the upbringing and education of children under their control…. The child is not the mere creature of the state; those who nurture him and direct his destiny have the right, coupled with the high duty, to recognize and prepare him for additional obligations.[504]

In 1989, Nebraska adopted an open enrollment law, Legislative Bill 183, which permits parents to choose a school outside their district, subject to restrictions of space and legal requirements for racial balance. Under the law, students may exercise their transfer option only once in their academic career (unless the family moves). The law does not address choice of schools within district boundaries, and each district is free to set its own policy. State funds for the transportation of students across district lines are available for all low-income children who qualify under the national free and reduced-price lunch program or who are disabled. A district may provide transportation for free or for a fee to children who are not poor or disabled.[505]

In 1998, Omaha became one of 40 Children's Scholarship Fund (CSF) "partner cities." The CSF is a $100 million foundation created to promote educational options. In Omaha, it matches the money raised by state residents to fund private scholarships for low-income K–8 students to attend a school of choice.[506]

Several choice bills were introduced in 1999. L.B. 385 would have created vouchers of up to $5,000 for low-income students to attend private or parochial schools. The bill died in committee.[507] L.B. 483, the Parent Education Equitable Reimbursement System Act, would have provided state aid to students in non-public schools. Half of the state's funding per public school pupil would have followed a child to the private school; half would have remained within the public school system. L.B. 484 would have provided a tax credit of up to $100 per child in a private elementary school and up to $200 per

---

501. *Meyer* v. *State of Nebraska*, 262 U.S. 390 (1923).

502. *Ibid.*, at 401.

503. *Pierce* v. *Society of Sisters*, 268 U.S. 510 (1925).

504. *Ibid.*, at 534–35.

505. See Nebraska Legislature Online at *http://statutes.unicam.state.ne.us/*.

506. See Children's Scholarship Fund Web site at *www.scholarshipfund.org*.

507. See National School Boards Association Web site at *www.nsba.org/novouchers*.

child in a private secondary school for education expenses. Both L.B. 483 and L.B. 484 also died in committee.[508]

In 2001, L.B. 271, the Elementary and Secondary Scholarship Assistance Act, was introduced to provide state income tax credits of up to $500 for contributions by individuals and businesses to education scholarship programs. The bill died in committee.[509]

## Developments in 2002 and 2003

State Senator Philip Erdman (District 47) introduced L.B. 534 in 2003 to allow home school students to participate in public school educational activities or athletics. The bill died in Committee.[510]

## Position of the Governor / Composition of the State Legislature

Governor Mike Johanns, a Republican, has supported school choice in the past, although this was not a primary issue in his most recent election. Nebraska has a unicameral, nonpartisan legislature.

## State Contacts

### Children's Scholarship Fund–Omaha

Judy Tamisiea, Executive Director
Judy Krhounek, Program Co-Administrator
Nancy Nielsen, Program Co-Administrator
3212 North 60th Street
P.O. Box 4130
Omaha, NE 68104-0130
Phone: (402) 554-8493
Fax: (402) 551-3426
Web site: www.scholarshipfund.org
E-mail: csfomaha@creighton.edu

### Nebraska Christian Home Educators Association

P.O. Box 57041
Lincoln, NE 68505-7041
Phone: (402) 423-4297
Fax: (402) 420-2610
E-mail: nchea@alltel.net

### Nebraska Department of Education

Doug Christensen, Commissioner
301 Centennial Mall South
Lincoln, NE 68509
Phone: (402) 471-2295
Fax: (402) 471-0117
Web site: www.nde.state.ne.us

## State School Report Card

### Greatschools.net

Web site: www.greatschools.net/modperl/go/NE

### Lincoln Public Schools

Web site: www.lps.org/about/statistics

### Nebraska Department of Education

Web site: http://reportcard.nde.state.ne.us

---

508. See Nebraska Catholic Conference, "Legislative Issues," at *www.nebcathcon.org/ education_leg__issues.htm#choice*.

509. *Ibid.*

510. See Nebraska Legislature Online at *http://statutes.unicam.state.ne.us/*.

# NEVADA

## State Profile (Updated May 2003)

### School Choice Status
- Public school choice: Interdistrict/voluntary
- State constitution: Blaine amendment
- Charter school law: Established 1997
    Strength of law: Weak
    Number of charter schools in operation (fall 2002): 13
    Number of students enrolled in charter schools (fall 2002): 2,851
- Publicly funded private school choice: No
- Privately funded school choice: No
- Home-school law: Low regulation
- Ranking on the Education Freedom Index (2001): 45th out of 50 states

### K–12 Public Schools and Students (2001–2002)
- Public school enrollment: 356,038
- Students enrolled per teacher: 18.5
- Number of schools (2000–2001): 500
- Number of districts: 17
- Current expenditures: $2,183,900,000
- Current per-pupil expenditure: $6,134
- Amount of revenue from the federal government: 5.4%

### K–12 Public School Teachers (2001–2002)
- Number of teachers: 19,255
- Average salary: $41,524

### K–12 Private Schools (1999–2000)
- Private school enrollment: 13,926
- Number of schools: 80
- Number of teachers: 973

### K–12 Public and Private School Student Academic Performance
- NAEP test results:

| NAEP Tests Nevada Student Performance | State (National) 2000 Math Scale = 0–500 | | State (National) 2000 Science Scale = 0–300 | | State (National) 2000 Reading Scale = 0–500 | |
|---|---|---|---|---|---|---|
| | 4th Grade | 8th Grade | 4th Grade | 8th Grade | 4th Grade | 8th Grade |
| Average Scale Score | 220 (226) | 268 (274) | 142 (148) | 143 (149) | 208 (215) | 257 (261) |
| Advanced | 1% (3%) | 2% (5%) | 2% (3%) | 2% (4%) | 4% (6%) | 1% (2%) |
| Proficient | 15% (23%) | 18% (21%) | 17% (25%) | 21% (26%) | 17% (23%) | 23% (29%) |
| Basic | 45% (43%) | 38% (39%) | 39% (36%) | 31% (29%) | 32% (32%) | 45% (41%) |
| Below Basic | 39% (31%) | 42% (35%) | 42% (36%) | 46% (41%) | 47% (39%) | 31% (28%) |

- SAT weighted rank (2001): N/A
- ACT weighted rank (2001): 9th out of 26 states
- ALEC Academic Achievement Ranking: 31st out of 50 states and the District of Columbia

## Summary

Nevada offers little public school choice and few charter schools.

## Background

In 1997, the state enacted Senate Bill 220, a weak charter school bill to create up to 21 charters statewide. The number of charters allowed in each district varies, depending on the population. Districts may have additional charter schools that specifically serve at-risk students. Local school boards may grant charters following an initial review by the state committee on charter schools. Charter schools do not receive an automatic waiver from local and state laws, rules, and regulations.[511]

In 1997, Assembly Bill 571 was introduced to permit the creation of voucher schools. Voucher schools would have been state-certified, private, nonsectarian schools that could not charge tuition or fees beyond the voucher for disabled or low-income students. The bill died in committee. During the 1999 session, choice advocates introduced A.B. 507 and Senate Bill 385, which also would have allowed the establishment of voucher schools. These schools would have had to be certified by the state as in the 1997 legislation; in addition, they could have been sectarian, with students able to opt out of religious activities. Both bills died in committee.[512]

S.B. 235, which would have authorized vouchers for low-income students in failing schools, was introduced during the 2001 legislative session but did not pass. As in earlier legislation, the bill would have established voucher schools authorized by the Nevada Department of Edu-cation. The voucher would have been worth the cost of the private school's tuition or the district's per-pupil expenditure, whichever was less.[513]

In 2001, Governor Kenny Guinn signed S.B. 399, which stipulates that classes offered online by charter schools must be equivalent to what is provided by the district. The bill clarifies that charter schools may not be "for-profit" and that home schools and existing public schools may not convert to charter status. It also guarantees the right of school employees to bargain collectively.[514]

## Developments in 2002 and 2003

Under the criteria of the federal No Child Left Behind Act, Nevada identified 19 schools as "failing."[515] In Clark County, 102 of the 4,700 students at five poorly performing schools transferred to better-performing schools in fall 2002.[516]

Assemblyman Ronald L. Knecht (R–40) introduced legislation in 2003 that would allow home-school students to participate in public-school athletic and scholastic programs. The bill, A.B. 311, was approved by the Committee on Education.[517]

S.B. 376, introduced in the 2003 session, would grant vouchers to students who are living in poverty and attending low-performing schools. No action was taken prior to adjournment.[518]

On April 3, 2003, the Senate passed a school choice bill, S.B. 254, by a vote of 13 to 8. The bill would allow parents to apply to send their child to a public school in another district. No action was taken in the House.[519]

---

511. Center for Education Reform, "Charter School Legislation: Profile of Nevada's Charter School Law," 2001, at *http://edreform.com/charter_schools/laws/Nevada.htm*.

512. See Nevada Legislature Web site at *www.leg.state.nv.us/*.

513. See National School Boards Association Web site at *www.nsba.org/novouchers*.

514. See "Nevada State Education Association Legislative Wrap-Up, 2001 Legislature," at *www.nsea-nv.org/WRAPUP.htm*.

515. "Given a Choice," *Education Week*, July 10, 2002.

516. Lisa Kim Bach, "Few Use School Choice Law," *Las Vegas Review–Journal*, July 11, 2002.

517. Home School Legal Defense Association, "Assembly Bill 311: Authorizes Homeschoolers to Participate in Public School Activities," at *www.hslda.org/Legislation/State/nv/2003/NVAB311/default.asp*, and Nevada Legislature, 72nd Session, A.B. 311, at *www.leg.state.nv.us/72nd/bills/AB/AB311.html*.

518. Nevada Legislature, 72nd Session, S.B. 376, at *www.leg.state.nv.us/72nd/bills/SB/SB376.html*.

## Position of the Governor / Composition of the State Legislature

Governor Kenny Guinn, a Republican, supports charter schools. Democrats control the House, and Republicans control the Senate.

## State Contacts

**Nevada Department of Education**
700 East Fifth Street
Carson City, NV 89701
Phone: (775) 687-9200
Fax: (775) 687-9101
Web site: www.nde.state.nv.us

**Nevada Homeschool Network**
Elissa Wahl, President
2250 East Tropicana, Suite 19, Box 378
Las Vegas, NV 89119
Phone: (888) 842-2606
Web site: www.nevadahomeschoolnet-work.com

**Nevada Policy Research Institute**
Helene Denney, Executive Director
2073 East Sahara Avenue, Suite B
Las Vegas, NV 89104
Phone: (702) 222-0642
Fax: (702) 227-0927
Web site: www.npri.org
E-mail: hd@npri.org
E-mail: info@npri.org

**Northern Nevada Home Schools**
P.O. Box 21323
Reno, NV 89515
Phone: (775) 852-6647
Web site: www.nnhs.org
E-mail: NNHS@aol.com

## State School Report Card

**Clark County Schools**
Web site: www.ccsd.net/schools/acc_reports/index.html

**Greatschools.net**
Web site: www.greatschools.net/modperl/go/NV

---

519. Nevada Legislature, 72nd Session, S.B. 254, at *www.leg.state.nv.us/72nd/bills/SB/SB254.html.*

# NEW HAMPSHIRE

## State Profile (Updated May 2003)

### School Choice Status
- Public school choice: Intradistrict and interdistrict/voluntary
- State constitution: Blaine amendment and compelled-support language
- Charter school law: Established 1995
    Strength of law: Weak
    Number of charter schools in operation (fall 2002): 0
    Number of students enrolled (fall 2002): 0
- Publicly funded private school choice: No
- Privately funded school choice: Yes
- Home-school law: Moderate regulation
- Ranking on the Education Freedom Index (2001): 17th out of 50 states

### K–12 Public Schools and Students (2001–2002)
- Public school enrollment: 211,429
- Students enrolled per teacher: 15.1
- Number of schools (2000–2001): 524
- Number of districts: 177
- Current expenditures: $1,675,871,000
- Current per-pupil expenditure: $7,926
- Amount of revenue from the federal government: 5.1%

### K–12 Public School Teachers (2001–2002)
- Number of teachers: 13,990
- Average salary: $38,911

### K–12 Private Schools (1999–2000)
- Private school enrollment: 23,383
- Number of schools: 171
- Number of teachers: 2,208

### K–12 Public and Private School Student Academic Performance
- NAEP test results:

| NAEP Tests New Hampshire Student Performance | State (National) 2000 Math Scale = 0–500 | | State (National) 2000 Science Scale = 0–300 | | State (National) 2000 Reading Scale = 0–500 | |
|---|---|---|---|---|---|---|
| | 4th Grade | 8th Grade | 4th Grade | 8th Grade | 4th Grade | 8th Grade |
| Average Scale Score | N/A (226) | N/A (274) | N/A (148) | N/A (149) | 226 (215) | N/A (261) |
| Advanced | N/A (3%) | N/A (5%) | N/A (3%) | N/A (4%) | 7% (6%) | N/A (2%) |
| Proficient | N/A (23%) | N/A (21%) | N/A (25%) | N/A (26%) | 31% (23%) | N/A (29%) |
| Basic | N/A (43%) | N/A (39%) | N/A (36%) | N/A (29%) | 37% (32%) | N/A (41%) |
| Below Basic | N/A (31%) | N/A (35%) | N/A (36%) | N/A (41%) | 25% (39%) | N/A (28%) |

# School Choice 2003

- SAT weighted rank (2001): 4th out of 24 states and the District of Columbia
- ACT weighted rank (2001): N/A
- ALEC Academic Achievement Ranking: 7th out of 50 states and the District of Columbia

## Summary

New Hampshire has a weak charter school law. Though the law has been in place for eight years and there is no longer a cap on the number of allowable charters, the state has no charter schools. Over the past six years, New Hampshire has expanded its open enrollment law.

## Background

In 1995, the New Hampshire legislature passed the Act Relative to Charter Schools and Open Enrollment (Senate Bill 9).[520] The state allows for intradistrict and interdistrict open enrollment—a provision that is optional for public schools but mandatory for charter schools.[521]

The local school board is the only institution with chartering authority. Voters can decide by referendum whether their district can charter a school or whether a charter school's funding should be removed from the district's budget.[522] Originally, the state capped the number of allowable charter schools at five, but in 1997, then-Governor Jeanne Shaheen signed S.B. 154, which doubled the cap.[523] The limit was removed in 2000.[524]

Charters are granted for five-year terms. A for-profit company may manage a charter school but may not be granted a charter directly. For each student, a charter receives 80 percent of the district's average per-pupil expenditure. Half of the teachers at a charter school must have at least three years of teaching experience or a teaching certificate. A charter can be either a new school or a converted public school.[525]

In 1998, House Bill 1476 was introduced to provide reimbursement for public, private, or home-schooling tuition costs. The bill was defeated by a vote of 227 to 109.[526] A companion bill (S.B. 456) would have allowed five districts to implement a parental choice program. This bill was passed in the Senate by a vote of 16 to 8 but died in the House.[527]

In 1998, the entire state of New Hampshire was named as one of 40 Children's Scholarship Fund (CSF) "partner" communities. New Hampshire matches funds that low-income parents spend for their child's tuition.[528]

In 1999, H.B. 514 was introduced to increase public school choice. The bill was approved by the House but was killed in the Senate.[529] H.B. 514 would have authorized superintendents to transfer students, with parental consent, to other schools within or outside of the district and would have limited transfers to a maximum of 1 percent of the students in a district and 5 percent of the students in a school.[530]

520. New Hampshire General Court, 1995 Session, S.B. 9, at *www.gencourt.state.nh.us/legislation/1995/sb0009.html*.

521. New Hampshire Constitution, Chapter 194-B, Section 2, at *http://gencourt.state.nh.us/rsa/html/XV/194-B/194-B-2.htm*.

522. Center for Education Reform, "Charter School Legislation: Profile of New Hampshire's Charter School Law," October 2001, at *http://edreform.com/charter_schools/laws/NewHampshire.htm*.

523. New Hampshire General Court, 1995 Session, S.B. 9, and 1997 Session, S.B. 154, at *www.gencourt.state.nh.us/legislation/1995/SB0009.html*.

524. USCharterSchools.org, "New Hampshire Charter School Information," at *www.uscharterschools.org/pub/sp/30*.

525. Center for Education Reform, "Charter School Legislation: Profile of New Hampshire's Charter School Law," 2001.

526. Blum Center for Parental Freedom in Education, Marquette University, *Educational Freedom Report* No. 56, February 20, 1998, at *www.marquette.edu/blum/efr56.html*. See also New Hampshire General Court, H.B. 1476, at *www.gencourt.state.nh.us/legislation/1998/HB1476.html*.

527. New Hampshire General Court, 1998 Session, S.B.456, at *www.gencourt.state.nh.us/legislation/1998/SB0456.html*.

528. Denis Paiste, "School Voucher Challenge Rejected; NH Students Get Shot at Choice Scholarships," *The Union Leader*, November 10, 1998, p. A1. See also Children's Scholarship Fund Web site at *www.scholarshipfund.org*.

529. New Hampshire General Court, 2000 Session, H.B. 514-L, at *www.gencourt.state.nh.us/legislation/2000/HB0514.html*.

530. New Hampshire General Court, "State of New Hampshire House Record," Vol. 22, December 31, 1999, at *www.gencourt.state.nh.us/hcaljourns/calendars/2000/houcal101.html*.

Also in 1999, Representative Marie Rabideau (R–16) introduced H.B. 633, which would have created a voucher system to help low-income parents fund primary and secondary education for their children. Parents would have been eligible for the scholarship if their child's school had "average scores in the bottom 1/3 on a state-wide basis in the state assessment test" and if their household income was less than 300 percent of the federal poverty level.[531] Scholarships would have been limited to 5 percent of the students in a school. H.B. 633 was passed by the House but was killed in the Senate. H.B. 701, also introduced in 1999, would have offered vouchers to students to use to attend any school, public or private. The vouchers would have been worth 10 percent of the public schools' average per-pupil cost. If the parent received vouchers for more than one child, the vouchers' value could not have exceeded 50 percent of the town's average per-pupil cost. This bill was defeated in the House by a vote of 283 to 78.[532]

In 2000, H.B.1580 was introduced to allow businesses an investment tax credit equal to 75 percent of a contribution made toward charter schools, scholarship organizations, or public schools. H.B.1580 failed to pass.[533]

New Hampshire's open enrollment law was expanded in 2001 by H.B. 726, signed by Governor Shaheen on July 17, 2001. This bill gave superintendents the authority to approve student transfers "where such changes are in the best interests of the pupil." Although the bill limited annual student transfers in a district to 1 percent of the school district's average daily attendance or 5 percent of a participating school's attendance, it allowed the school board to override these stipulations.[534]

In 2001, the *Boston Globe* reported that New Hampshire private schools were very popular among both students and parents. The surge in applications was attributed to public schools' overcrowding and financial instability.[535]

## Developments in 2002 and 2003

The Josiah Bartlett Center for Public Policy, a New Hampshire think tank, published a study in October 2002 to explore why the state has not opened a single charter school since the law was enacted in 1995. The study reported:

In asking what factors in New Hampshire prevented support for their schools, respondents cited misleading and negative information, time-consuming approval procedures, lack of understanding of the charter school concept, and a system that requires the charter school to compete with other local school board improvement initiatives. Time, money, inability to counteract negative information or, as one person interviewed stated—it was just politics, plain and simple local politics that killed their charter school's approval.[536]

H.B. 515 was introduced in 2002 to provide vouchers for low-income students in poorly performing public schools. In November 2002, the bill was killed by a House Finance Committee vote of 18 to 0.[537]

H.B. 1281, signed by Governor Craig Benson in May 2002, established a commission to "study public educational choice initiatives and to develop recommendations." The commission is composed of three members from the House and three from the Senate; the Commissioner of the New Hampshire Department of Education; representatives from the New Hampshire School

531. New Hampshire General Court, 1999 Session, H.B. 633, at *www.gencourt.state.nh.us/legislation/1999/HB0633.html.*

532. New Hampshire General Court, 1999 Session, H.B. 701, at *www.gencourt.state.nh.us/legislation/1999/HB0701.html.*

533. New Hampshire General Court, 2000 Session, H.B. 1580, at *www.gencourt.state.nh.us/legislation/2000/HB1580.html.*

534. New Hampshire General Court, 2001 Session, H.B. 726, at *www.gencourt.state.nh.us/legislation/2001/HB0726.html.*

535. Clare Kittredge, "Private Schools Report Flood of Applications," *Boston Globe*, April 8, 2001, p. 1.

536. Susan D. Hollins, Ph.D., *The Promise of Charter Schools in New Hampshire: What We Know and What We Need to Do*, Josiah Bartlett Center for Public Policy, October 2002.

537. See National School Boards Association Web site at *www.nsba.org/novouchers.* See also New Hampshire General Court, 2002 Session, H.B. 515, at *www.gencourt.state.nh.us/legislation/2002/HB0515.html.*

Administrators Association, New Hampshire School Boards Association, and the state branch of the National Education Association; and an appointee selected by the Commissioner. The commission is to report the feasibility of various public-school choice initiatives in New Hampshire including, but not limited to, charter schools, open enrollment schools, magnet schools, and alternative public schools. It is assigned to determine whether or not such initiatives can be implemented within the existing framework of the New Hampshire public educational system; the effect of public school choice programs on children, schools, and communities in New Hampshire; and any other issues deemed relevant to its purpose.[538] No results from the commission's study have been made available.[539]

In January 2003, Representative John B. Hunt (R–28) introduced H.B.135 to create a pilot charter school program. The bill was passed by the House and has been referred to the Senate. H.B.135 would establish a 10-year pilot program, allowing up to two charters per year to be approved by the state. These schools would be exempt from some of the burdensome approval provisions that are included in the current law.[540]

H.B. 754, also introduced in 2003, proposes education certificates worth $1,000 for use at any nonpublic school or for home schooling. The bill has been referred to committee.[541]

Tax credit legislation was introduced this session. H.B. 756 would provide a credit worth up to $300 for payment of private school tuition. In March 2003, the bill was referred to committee.[542]

H.B. 603, also introduced in 2003, would require that districts reimburse half of the amount that parents spend for private school tuition. The bill was defeated by a vote of 250 to 112.[543]

## Position of the Governor / Composition of the State Legislature

Governor Craig Benson, a Republican, supports all forms of parental choice in education. Republicans control both houses of the legislature.

## State Contacts

### Center for Market-Based Education
Judy Alger, President
P.O. Box 373
Rumney, NH 03266-0373
Phone: (603) 786-9562
Fax: (603) 786-9463
E-mail: judy.alger@eagle1st.com

### Charter School Resource Center
Sue Hollins, Director
P.O. Box 1125
Grantham, NH 03753
Phone: (603) 863-4411
E-mail: suefromNH@aol.com

### Children's Scholarship Fund– New Hampshire
Mercedes Wilson-Barthes, Program Assistant
8 West 38th Street, 9th Floor
New York, NY 10018
Phone: (888) 633-0099
Fax: (212) 750-2840
Web site: www.scholarshipfund.org
E-mail: mwilson-barthes@scholarshipfund.org

### Christian Home Educators of New Hampshire
40 Old Rindge Road
New Ipswich, NH 03071
Phone: (603) 878-5001
Web site: www.chenh.org
E-mail: parison@chenh.org

### Citizens' Education Association
Bob Ouellette, Director
5-B Orchard Street
Franklin, NH 03235

---

538. New Hampshire General Court, 2002 Session, H.B. 1281, at *www.gencourt.state.nh.us/legislation/2002/HB1281.html.*

539. Personal communications with New Hampshire Department of Education, April 17, 2003, and Josiah Bartlett Center for Public Policy, April 17, 2003.

540. See New Hampshire General Court, 2003 Session, at *www.gencourt.state.nh.us/ie/billstatus/quickbill.html.*

541. New Hampshire General Court, 2003 Session, H.B. 754, at *www.gencourt.state.nh.us/legislation/2003/HB0754.html.*

542. New Hampshire General Court, 2003 Session, H.B. 756, at *www.gencourt.state.nh.us/legislation/2003/HB0756.html.*

543. New Hampshire General Court, 2003 Session, H.B. 603, at *www.gencourt.state.nh.us/legislation/2003/HB0603.html.*

Phone: (603) 934-8236

E-mail: bouel1@metrocast.net

**Josiah Bartlett Center for Public Policy**

Charles M. Arlinghaus, President

7 South State Street

P.O. Box 897

Concord, NH 03302

Phone: (603) 224-4450

Fax: (603) 224-4329

Web site: www.jbartlett.org

E-mail: jbartlett@jbartlett.org

## State School Report Card

**GreatSchools.net**

Web site: www.greatschools.net/modperl/go/NH

**Independent Schools Association of Northern New England**

Web site: www.isanne.org/frame_isanne.asp?x=choose

**New Hampshire Department of Education**

Web site: www.ed.state.nh.us/Assessment/assessme(NHEIAP).htm

per-pupil cost for each transferring student. This legislation would have established a five-year pilot program, with 10 districts offering choice in the first year, 15 districts in the second year, and 21 districts in the third year, when the number of districts providing choice would be capped.[554] Both bills died in committee.[555]

S. 1537 was also introduced during the 1998–1999 session to create a pilot voucher program. This legislation would have provided elementary and junior high school students with vouchers worth up to $8,500 and high school students with vouchers worth up to $10,000. The bill died in committee.[556]

On September 1, 1999, the New Jersey State Board of Education approved a pilot program of public school choice. The initiative is in place for five years, and the program is similar to that proposed in A. 2320 and S. 1279, with 10 districts participating during the first year, 15 during the second, and the number capped at 21 in the third year. Transportation is provided for students residing within 20 miles of their school of choice.[557] Districts can receive only students in grades 1 through 10. The state set aside $800,000 for the program's inaugural year, 2000–2001. The New Jersey Department of Education reported that receiving districts opened 700 seats in the program's first year, with 96 students participating.[558] More than 200 students participated in 2001–2002.

In 2000, S. 920 (with companion bill A. 1145) was introduced to establish a pilot voucher program. Elementary and junior high school students would have received vouchers worth $2,500, and high school students would have

received vouchers worth $3,500. The New Jersey Department of Education would have allocated $5.5 million to the program, with some of the funds being used for an evaluation. The bills died in committee.[559]

On June 28, 2000, the New Jersey Supreme Court upheld a school choice provision that allowed charter schools to enroll students from other districts and ruled that the state's charter school law was constitutional. This was the ninth case in the nation challenging the constitutionality of charter schools.[560] The case originated when the Highland Park Board of Education challenged the creation of Greater Brunswick Charter School, which intended to serve students in surrounding districts.[561] The court upheld the application's approval.[562]

In October 2001, then-Commissioner of Education Vito A. Gagliardi, Sr., submitted a five-year review of New Jersey's charter school program to the governor and other state officials.[563] The report found that

> Charter schools, in aggregate, achieved a 12 percentage point increase in the proportion of students who were at or above the proficient level in math on the Elementary School Proficiency Assessment (ESPA). This evidence indicates that charter schools are making discernable progress in their achievement of New Jersey Core Curriculum Content Standards (NJCCCS) in math.[564]

The aggregate progress made by charter students in the math portion of the ESPA was

554. New Jersey Assembly Education Committee, "Statement to Assembly, 2320," December 10, 1998, at *www.njleg.state.nj.us/9899/Bills/A2500/2320_S1.HTM.*

555. New Jersey Legislature, Bills 1998–1999, A2320, at *www.njleg.state.nj.us/9899/Bills/A2500/2320_I1.HTM.*

556. New Jersey Legislature, Bills 1998–1999, S1537, at *www.njleg.state.nj.us/9899/Bills/S2000/1537_I1.HTM.*

557. New Jersey Department of Education, press release, "State Board Approves Interdistrict Public School Choice Pilot Program," September 1, 1999.

558. New Jersey Department of Education, "Interdistrict Public School Choice," at *www.nj.gov/njded/choice/genfo.htm.*

559. See National School Boards Association Web site at *www.nsba.org/novouchers.*

560. Center for Education Reform, "CER News Alert," June 30, 2000, at *www.edreform.com/press/000630sc.htm.*

561. Rutgers School of Law, *In the Matter of the Grant of the Charter School Application of the Greater Brunswick Charter School, Middlesex County,* at *http://lawlibrary.rutgers.edu/courts/supreme/a-35-99.opn.html.*

562. *Ibid.*

563. New Jersey Department of Education, press release, "Commissioner Submits Charter School Evaluation Report," October 2, 2001.

564. New Jersey Department of Education, *Evaluation of New Jersey Charter Schools,* "Executive Summary," p. 2, at *www.nj.gov/njded/chartsch/evaluation/exec_highlights.pdf.*

better than the aggregate progress of students in conventional public schools in the district. Charter schools were popular among parents and students: 76 percent of charter schools had a waiting list in 1999–2000, and a total of 5,178 students throughout the state were waiting for a space at a charter school. Eighteen charter school applications were submitted in 2001, but only two were approved.[565]

In 2001, A. 3475 and A. 3476 were introduced to create education-related tax credits. A. 3475 would have created a tax credit for contributions by businesses and individuals to scholarship organizations. This bill died in the Assembly Education Committee.[566] A. 3476 would have created tax credits for education expenses, including a $500 tax credit for private school tuition or tutoring services and tax credits up to $150 for "computer-related purchases."[567] A. 3476 also died in committee.[568]

The Scholarship Fund for Inner-City Children is a nonsectarian, nonreligious scholarship organization providing scholarships for poor students attending Catholic schools in Essex, Hudson, Bergen, and Union Counties. The fund also operates programs in Jersey City, Newark, and Elizabeth that offer scholarships to any private school in the area. In 2001, the fund awarded 2,347 scholarships.[569] The fund has since partnered with Children's Scholarship Fund, the multimillion-dollar nationwide scholarship foundation that matches the money parents pay for their children's private school tuition.

In November 2001, an Eagleton–Rutgers poll revealed that New Jersey residents favor vouchers. Of the more than 800 residents polled, 60 percent were in favor of vouchers. Urban residents showed the most support for vouchers: 71 percent favored vouchers, and 21 percent opposed them. Support was also found among respondents with annual incomes under $25,000.[570]

## Developments in 2002 and 2003

A. 3475, tuition tax credit legislation from 2001, was reintroduced as A. 1594 during the 2002–2003 session. The bill, which would give individuals or businesses tax credits worth up to 75 percent of their donations to scholarship organizations, is in committee.[571]

On July 25, 2002, in response to the favorable ruling on the Cleveland, Ohio, school voucher program, the Camden City Council unanimously passed a resolution calling on the state legislature to create a voucher program for their city.[572] The Camden District serves more than 18,000 school-age children.[573] The New Jersey legislature and governor have not responded to the request.

## Position of the Governor / Composition of the State Legislature

Governor James E. McGreevey, a Democrat, opposes school vouchers. Democrats control the House, and the Senate is evenly split.

## State Contacts

**Black Alliance for Educational Options**
Dawn Martinez, President
127 South Valley Road
West Orange, NJ 07052
Phone: (973) 243-2758
Web site: www.baeo.org
E-mail: dmart127@aol.com

**Education Network of Christian Home-schoolers of New Jersey**
P.O. Box 308
Atlantic Highlands, NJ 07716
Phone: (732) 291-7800
Fax: (732) 291-5398

565. *Ibid.* and Center for Education Reform, "Charter Schools in New Jersey," at *http://edreform.com/charter_schools/states/newjersey.htm*.

566. New Jersey Legislature, Bills 2000–2001, A3475.

567. See National School Boards Association Web site at *www.nsba.org/novouchers*.

568. New Jersey Legislature, Bills 2000–2001, A3476.

569. Scholarship Fund for Inner-City Children, "About Us," at *www.rcan.org/icsf/aboutus.htm*.

570. Tom Hester, "60 percent of Jerseyans Back Vouchers, Poll Says," *The Star–Ledger*, November 28, 2001.

571. See National School Boards Association Web site at *www.nsba.org/novouchers*.

572. George A. Clowes, "Camden Is First to Call for Vouchers," *School Reform News*, September 2002, at *www.heartland.org/archives/education/sep02/camden.htm*.

573. Melanie Burney, "School Vouchers Sought for Camden Council," *The Philadelphia Inquirer*, July 26, 2002, B1.

Web site: www.enochnj.org
E-mail: office@enochnj.org

**Excellent Education for Everyone (E-3)**
Peter R. Denton, Founder
Dan Gaby, Executive Director
810 Broad Street, 10th Floor
Newark, NJ 07102
Phone: (973) 286-7791
Fax: (973) 286-7822
Web site: www.nje3.org
E-mail: dangaby33@aol.com

**New Jersey Charter Public Schools Association (NJCPSA)**
Sarah Tantillo, Executive Director
10 Washington Place
Newark, NJ 07102
Phone: (973) 642-0101
Fax: (973) 642-5800
Web site: www.njcpsa.org
E-mail: jchsa@aol.com

**New Jersey Department of Education**
Michael Klavon, Office of Innovative Programs and Schools
P.O. Box 500
Trenton, NJ 08625
Phone: (609) 292-5850
Fax: (609) 633-9825
Web site: www.state.nj.us/education

**New Jersey Scholarship Fund**
Bret Schundler, Founder and Chairman

Daniel J. Cassidy, President
P.O. Box 352
Jersey City, NJ 07302-0352
Phone: (800) 563-2244
Fax: (973) 497-4282
Web site: www.njsf.org
E-mail: dncassidy@aol.com

**Newark Student–Partner Alliance**
Frieda Zaffarese, Program Director
P.O. Box 566
Millburn, NJ 07041
Phone: (973) 379 5878
Fax: (973) 467-7544

**Scholarship Fund for Inner-City Children**
Kevin Moriarty, Executive Director
P.O. Box 9500
Newark, NJ 07104-0500
Phone: (973) 497-4279
Fax: (973) 497-4282
Web site: www.rcan.org/icsf
E-mail: moriarke@rcan.org

## State School Report Card

**GreatSchools.net**
Web site: www.greatschools.net/modperl/go/NJ

**New Jersey Department of Education**
Web site: http://nj.evalsoft.com/

# NEW MEXICO

## State Profile (Updated May 2003)

### School Choice Status
- Public school choice: Intradistrict and interdistrict/voluntary
- State constitution: Blaine amendment and compelled-support language
- Charter school law: Established 1993
    Strength of law: Strong
    Number of charter schools in operation (fall 2002): 28
    Number of students enrolled in charter schools (fall 2002): 4,234
- Publicly funded private school choice: No
- Privately funded school choice: Yes
- Home-school law: Low regulation
- Ranking on the Education Freedom Index (2001): 19th out of 50 states

### K–12 Public Schools and Students (2001–2002)
- Public school enrollment: 316,143
- Students enrolled per teacher: 15.8
- Number of schools (2000–2001): 763
- Number of districts: 89
- Current expenditures: $2,242,287,000
- Current per-pupil expenditure: $7,093
- Amount of revenue from the federal government: 12.9%

### K–12 Public School Teachers (2001–2002)
- Number of teachers: 20,000
- Average salary: $36,490

### K–12 Private Schools (1999–2000)
- Private school enrollment: 23,055
- Number of schools: 182
- Number of teachers: 1,992

### K–12 Public and Private School Student Academic Performance
- NAEP test results:

| NAEP Tests New Mexico Student Performance | State (National) 2000 Math Scale = 0–500 | | State (National) 2000 Science Scale = 0–300 | | State (National) 2000 Reading Scale = 0–500 | |
|---|---|---|---|---|---|---|
| | 4th Grade | 8th Grade | 4th Grade | 8th Grade | 4th Grade | 8th Grade |
| Average Scale Score | 214 (226) | 260 (274) | 138 (148) | 140 (149) | 206 (215) | 258 (261) |
| Advanced | 1% (3%) | 1% (5%) | 2% (3%) | 1% (4%) | 4% (6%) | 1% (2%) |
| Proficient | 11% (23%) | 12% (21%) | 16% (25%) | 19% (26%) | 18% (23%) | 23% (29%) |
| Basic | 39% (43%) | 37% (39%) | 36% (36%) | 28% (29%) | 30% (32%) | 46% (41%) |
| Below Basic | 49% (31%) | 50% (35%) | 46% (36%) | 52% (41%) | 48% (39%) | 30% (28%) |

- SAT weighted rank (2001): N/A
- ACT weighted rank (2001): 22nd out of 26 states
- ALEC Academic Achievement Ranking: 48th out of 50 states and the District of Columbia

## Summary

New Mexico has a strong charter school law and offers limited public school choice. High school students may take courses at participating universities for high school and postsecondary credit.[574] Educate New Mexico provides partial scholarships to students to attend private schools of choice.

## Background

In 1993, New Mexico passed the Charter Schools Act, House Bill 888, authorizing the State Board of Education to convert five existing public schools into charter schools. Each charter was granted for a five-year period, after which it would have to pass a review process to be renewed. Charter schools remained under the authority of the local school boards. Waivers from state and local laws and regulations had to be approved by the state board.[575]

In 1997, then-Governor Gary Johnson, a Republican, announced a comprehensive education reform program called "For the Children's Sake." The plan would have increased accountability, funding, and choice for students by providing scholarships that were redeemable at public, private, or religious schools. The proposal failed to garner enough support and was not enacted.[576]

In 1999, the legislature replaced New Mexico's limited charter school law with a strong law, Senate Bill 192. The 1999 law allows for up to 75 start-up and 25 conversion charter schools within any five-year period. Local school boards authorize charter schools, and applicants who are rejected may appeal to the state board. Char-

ter schools receive some automatic waivers from state and local laws and regulations.[577]

Governor Johnson twice vetoed the state budget in 1999 in part because it did not include desired education provisions, such as voucher plans or tax credits. The governor advocated a program that would provide vouchers worth approximately $3,200 for students to attend any public, charter, private, or religious school of choice.[578]

Governor Johnson signed H.B. 753, a charter school amendment, on April 6, 2001. This bill limited the provision of transportation for students to and from charter schools to a radius of 10 miles from the school's location.[579]

Several tax credit bills were introduced during the 2001 session. H.B. 422, the Tuition Scholarship Tax Credit, would have provided tax credits of up to $500 for donations toward tuition scholarships for low-income students (but would not have allowed the donor to designate a particular student as a recipient of the scholarship). H.B. 421 would have established a refundable tax credit for families at or below 185 percent of the federal poverty level. H.B. 420 would have established a tax credit of up to $500 for home-schooling families. All of these bills died in committee.[580]

Voucher legislation was also introduced in 2001. H.B. 503, the Children's Educational Guarantee Act, would have given vouchers to students in failing schools. S.B. 414, the Opportunity Scholarship Act, would have authorized scholarships for children in kindergarten.[581] These bills also died in committee.

---

574. Education Commission of the States, "Postsecondary Options: Dual/Concurrent Enrollment," July 2001.

575. Southwest Educational Development Laboratory, "Charter Schools: Early Learnings Insights," *Insights on Education Policy, Practice, and Research*, No. 5, July 1995.

576. "New Mexico Governor Calls for School Choice," *School Reform News*, January 1998.

577. See "New Mexico Charter School Information" at *www.uscharterschools.org/pub/sp/6*.

578. "Johnson Aims to Sway Public," *Albuquerque Journal*, April 20, 1999, p. D3, and Mary Perea, "Education Groups: Governor's Plan Bad for Students," *Albuquerque Journal*, August 15, 1999, p. B6.

579. New Mexico Legislature, 2001 Regular Session, H.B. 753, at *http://legis.state.nm.us/session01.asp?chamber=H&type=++&number=753&Submit=Search*.

580. See National School Boards Association Web site at *www.nsba.org/novouchers*.

581. *Ibid.*

## Developments in 2002 and 2003

Several school choice bills were introduced in 2002. The Parental Choice Act, H.B. 319, was introduced to establish a school voucher program for low-income students in urban areas with populations of more than 400,000. Under this legislation, students using vouchers would have to take a standardized state proficiency test. S.B. 415 and S.B. 301 would have authorized income tax credits of up to $500 annually for contributions to scholarship organizations.[582] S.B. 301 lost a committee vote, and the other two bills died in committee.

Two bills that would have allowed tax deductions for parents of home and private school students died in 2003. S.B. 97 would have allowed home-schooling parents to take a deduction of up to $3,500.[583] H.B. 868 would have allowed parents of home or private school students to deduct $1,000 from their taxable income.[584] Both bills died in committee.[585]

A tuition tax credit bill, S.B. 237, was introduced in 2003. Under this legislation, individuals contributing to a scholarship organization could have received a tax credit of up to $500 and would have been allowed to earmark their donation so that it directly benefited a specified student, including a dependent. This bill also died in committee.[586]

## Position of the Governor / Composition of the State Legislature

Governor Bill Richardson, a Democrat, does not support vouchers. Democrats control both houses of the legislature.

## State Contacts

**Christian Association of Parent Educators–NM**
P.O. Box 25046
Albuquerque, NM 87125
Phone: (505) 898-8548
Fax: (505) 294-7582

Web site: www.cape-nm.org
E-mail: info@cape-nm.org

**Educate New Mexico**
Troy Williamson, Executive Director
P.O. Box 794
Albuquerque, NM 87703
Phone: (505) 797-4002
Fax: (505) 797-1984
Web site: www.educateNM.org
E-mail: tdwilli@educateNM.org

**Freedom to Choose Foundation**
Steve Ulibarri, Director
P.O. Box 12294
Albuquerque, NM 87195
Phone: (505) 836-6533
Fax: (505) 836-6545
E-mail: ulibarrigeo@aol.com

**New Mexico Department of Education**
Ruth Williams, Public Outreach Director
300 Don Gaspar Avenue
Santa Fe, NM 87501-2786
Phone: (505) 476-0393
Fax: (505) 827-6588
Web site: http://sde.state.nm.us
E-mail: rwilliams@sde.state.nm.us

**New Mexico Foundation Business Roundtable**
Jacki Riggs, President and CEO
20 First Plaza, NW, Suite 303
Albuquerque, NM 87102
Phone: (505) 242-8052
E-mail: DrJPR@aol.com

**New Mexico Independence Research Institute**
Gene Aldridge, President and CEO
2401 Nieve Lane
Las Cruces, NM 88005
Phone: (505) 523-8700
Phone: (505) 268-2030
Web site: www.zianet.com/nmiri
E-mail: gsaldridge@zianet.com

582. Ibid.
583. Home School Legal Defense Association, "Senate Bill 97: Income Tax Deduction for Homeschools," March 21, 2003, at www.hslda.org/Legislation/State/nm/2003/NVSB97/default.asp.
584. Home School Legal Defense Association, "House Bill 868: Income Tax Deduction for Homeschools and Private Schools," March 21, 2003, at www.hslda.org/Legislation/State/nm/2003/NVHB868/default.asp.
585. See New Mexico Legislature Web site at http://legis.state.nm.us/default.asp.
586. New Mexico Legislature, 2003 Regular Session, S.B. 237, at http://legis.state.nm.us/session03.asp?chamber=S&type=++&number=237&Submit=Search.

## State School Report Card

### Albuquerque Public Schools

Web site: http://albuquerquerealestateandrelo-cation.com/albuquerque-new-mexico-schools.htm

### Gadsden District Report Card

Web site: www.gisd.k12.nm.us/DRC

### Greatschools.net

Web site: www.greatschools.net/modperl/go/NM

# NEW YORK

## State Profile (Updated May 2003)

### School Choice Status
- Public school choice: Interdistrict/voluntary
- State constitution: Blaine amendment
- Charter school law: Established 1998
    Strength of law: Strong
    Number of charter schools in operation (fall 2002): 38
    Number of students enrolled in charter schools (fall 2002): 10,954
- Publicly funded private school choice: No
- Privately funded school choice: Yes
- Home-school law: High regulation
- Ranking on the Education Freedom Index (2001): 34th out of 50 states

### K–12 Public Schools and Students (2001–2002)
- Public school enrollment: 2,920,000
- Students enrolled per teacher: 13.5
- Number of schools (2000–2001): 4,292
- Number of districts: 704
- Current expenditures: $31,316,964,000
- Current per-pupil expenditure: $10,725
- Amount of revenue from the federal government: 7.0%

### K–12 Public School Teachers (2001–2002)
- Number of teachers: 215,500
- Average salary: $53,081

### K–12 Private Schools (1999–2000)
- Private school enrollment: 475,942
- Number of schools: 1,981
- Number of teachers: 37,190

### K–12 Public and Private School Student Academic Performance
- NAEP test results:

| NAEP Tests New York Student Performance | State (National) 2000 Math Scale = 0–500 | | State (National) 2000 Science Scale = 0–300 | | State (National) 2000 Reading Scale = 0–500 | |
|---|---|---|---|---|---|---|
| | 4th Grade | 8th Grade | 4th Grade | 8th Grade | 4th Grade | 8th Grade |
| Average Scale Score | 227 (226) | 276 (274) | 149 (148) | 149 (149) | 216 (215) | 266 (261) |
| Advanced | 2% (3%) | 4% (5%) | 2% (3%) | 2% (4%) | 8% (6%) | 3% (2%) |
| Proficient | 20% (23%) | 22% (21%) | 24% (25%) | 28% (26%) | 29% (23%) | 33% (29%) |
| Basic | 45% (43%) | 42% (39%) | 41% (36%) | 31% (29%) | 36% (32%) | 44% (41%) |
| Below Basic | 33% (31%) | 32% (35%) | 33% (36%) | 39% (41%) | 27% (39%) | 20% (28%) |

- SAT weighted rank (2001): 15th out of 24 states and the District of Columbia
- ACT weighted rank (2001): N/A
- ALEC Academic Achievement Ranking: 30th out of 50 states and the District of Columbia

## Summary

New York has a strong charter school law, and its limited open enrollment policies were expanded in 2002. The state also has a limited dual enrollment policy that allows high school students to take courses for college credit. Several private scholarship programs exist to help students attend private school.

## Background

In the early 1970s, New York lawmakers passed legislation assisting private and religious schools serving low-income students with facility maintenance. Lawmakers also created tax deductions and tuition reimbursements for low-income parents who sent their children to non-public schools. The laws were, in part, an effort to prevent overcrowding in public schools by helping poor students attend private school. In 1973, the Supreme Court of the United States ruled against this early form of school choice in *Committee for Public Education* v. *Nyquist*. The Court found that, because most of the schools involved in the New York choice program were religious schools, the state or district-funded assistance promoted religion—therefore violating the First Amendment. Future attempts to create public aid for private schools would have to be clearly "neutral" in nature.[587]

New York legislators created a weak interdistrict enrollment provision in 1993. The law was strengthened after the federal No Child Left Behind Act was passed in 2002, but for the first nine years under the law, few students transferred out of low-performing schools.[588] In 2000, a *New York Post* study found that many parents were not informed of their options and

that the availability of bus services for transferring students was limited. With schools already overcrowded, districts rejected 40 percent of transfer requests in 2000. At that time, nearly one-third (338) of the state's elementary schools were rated as "low performing."[589]

Legislators have been unsuccessful in their attempts to pass legislation on education tax credits. In 1997, Senate 7832 would have provided an investment tax credit worth up to 50 percent of a contribution to a public school, private school, or scholarship organization. The bill died in Senate committee.[590] In 1999, S. 7832 was reintroduced as S. 4176 and again died in Senate committee. Assembly 9644 and S. 6693, introduced in 1999, would have created the Educational Tax Incentives Act to provide income tax credits of up to $500 for donations made in a variety of areas, including contributions to public school districts and tuition scholarship organizations or purchases made for home schooling. Both bills died in committee.[591] A. 3216, introduced in the 2001 session, would have provided tax credits of up to $200 for purchases related to public-school extracurricular activities and tax credits of up to $500 for donations to private-school scholarship funds.[592]

The School Choice Scholarships Foundation began offering scholarships in 1997. Students who qualify for the federal free and reduced-priced lunch program are eligible.[593] Recipients are chosen by lottery, and scholarships awarded in 1997 were worth up to $1,400 each.[594] In 1997, the foundation selected 1,300 scholarship recipients from 20,000 applicants.[595] A study conducted in 1998 found that recipients

587. Clint Bolick, *Voucher Wars: Waging the Legal Battle Over School Choice* (Washington, D.C.: Cato Institute, 2003), pp. 4–5; *Committee for Public Education* v. *Nyquist*, 413 U.S. 756 (1973).

588. Carl Campanile, "School 'Choice' No Choice at All," *The New York Post*, September 25, 2000, p. 19.

589. *Ibid.*

590. See National School Boards Association Web site at *www.nsba.org/novouchers*.

591. *Ibid.*

592. *Ibid.*

593. Mathematica Policy Research and Program on Education Policy and Governance (PEPG) at Harvard, "An Evaluation of the New York City School Choice Scholarships Program: The First Year," October 1998.

594. School Choice New York, "Scholarship Programs," at *www.nyschoolchoice.com/scholarships*.

595. American Association of Christian Schools, "Another School Choice Victory," at *www.aacs.org/pubs/ViewPArticle.aspx?ArticleID=671*.

improved in both math and reading, with students in 4th and 5th grades making the largest gains.[596] In addition, parents of scholarship students reported a high level of satisfaction with their child's school.

A Better Choice (ABC) scholarship program operates in Albany and offers vouchers worth up to $2,000.[597] In 1997, the group offered vouchers to all students of the Giffen Memorial Elementary School, and more than 150 students accepted them. Giffen was selected because of its high poverty rate (96 percent of the students qualified for the federal free-lunch program) and low performance (more than 50 percent of the students could not read at a "minimum competency" level).[598] While the scholarship program allowed students to transfer to a school of choice, Giffen made significant improvements: By 2000, a new principal and 12 new teachers were hired and a mentoring program for new teachers was initiated. A study by Seton Hall reported that changes made at Giffen helped improve the school for the students who remained. Between 1999 and 2000, Giffen's students' scores on the 4th grade language arts exam improved by 14 percent.[599]

Advocates of school choice won an important legal victory in 1997 when the U.S. Supreme Court ruled in *Agostini* v. *Felton* that public school teachers can provide "remedial" services to private or parochial school students without violating the Establishment Clause of the First Amendment—a ruling that overturned the Court's own 1985 decision in *Aguilar* v. *Felton*.[600] Before *Aguilar* v. *Felton*, public school

teachers had offered tutoring services for students in private and religious schools who were underperforming by state standards. Because the aid took place at the school, the Supreme Court had ruled that the practice was unconstitutional because the potential existed for using public funds to promote religion. As a result of that decision, it was necessary either to transport students to a neutral site for tutoring or to create additional facilities that were not a part of the school. The board of a religious New York school asked the Court to reverse its decision in *Aguilar* because it presented a burden for students seeking tutoring. In *Agostini*, the Court ruled that remedial services could take place within a private or religious school because the assistance was available to all eligible students, regardless of their school, and was not used to promote any specific religion.[601]

The BISON Scholarship Fund offers low-income Buffalo students privately funded scholarships. Supported by the Children's Scholarship Fund, BISON awards scholarships by lottery to students who meet income qualifications. The average family income of recipients is approximately $22,000.[602] In 2001, BISON helped more than 1,000 students attend private and parochial schools and had more than 2,000 students on its waiting list. BISON awarded 942 scholarships in 2002.[603]

Governor George Pataki signed New York's charter school law in December 1998.[604] The law allows the formation of up to 100 new schools and the conversion of an unlimited number of public schools to charter status.[605]

596. Mathematica Policy Research and Program on Education Policy and Governance, "An Evaluation of the New York City School Choice Scholarships."

597. Jeff Archer, "Albany Program Puts New Spin on Private Vouchers," *Education Week*, May 28, 1997.

598. Nina Rees, "Public School Benefits of Private School Vouchers," *Policy Review*, No. 93, January–February 1999.

599. Maureen McGuinness, "Voucher Trial Improved Both Schools Involved," *The Evangelist*, August 24, 2000, at *www.evangelist.org/archive/htm2/0824giff.htm*.

600. U.S. Department of Education, "Guidance on the Supreme Court's Decision in Agostini V. Felton," at *www.ed.gov/legislation/ESEA/feltguid.html* (capitalization as in original).

601. Freedom Forum, "Supreme Court Files," *Agostini v. Felton*, at *www.freedomforum.org/fac/96-97/Agos_sum.htm*; *Agostini v. Felton*, 521 U.S. 203 (1997); *Aguilar v. Felton*, 473 U.S. 402 (1985).

602. Peter Simon, "Rethinking Vouchers: President Bush's Education Plan Includes School Vouchers," *Buffalo News*, January 31, 2001, p. A1.

603. Peter Simon, "Vouchers, Buffalo-Style: Bringing the School Choice Debate Close to Home," *Buffalo News*, March 7, 2002, p. A1.

604. New York Charter School Resource Center, "New York State Charter School Law," at *www.nycsrc.org/resources/guide/part%2002--article%2056%205-18.pdf.pdf*.

605. Gregg Birnbaum, "Senate OKs Charter Schools in 38% Pay-Raise Megadeal," *The New York Post*, December 18, 1998, p. 16.

The State Board of Regents and the State University of New York (SUNY) may grant up to 50 new school charters.[606]

In 1999, Governor Pataki vetoed legislation that would have altered the charter law. A. 8835 and S. 3680, passed by the Assembly and the Senate, respectively, would have required teachers to join a union if their charter school initially served more than 250 students. In his veto message, Governor Pataki declared:

> I am proud to say that New York State's legislation has been widely acclaimed as being among the strongest and most innovative in the nation. The bill before me today…would curtail some of the freedom from State mandates conferred by that legislation. New York State cannot and will not retreat from the historic commitment to…choice within the public education system.[607]

In the fall of 2000, then-New York City Mayor and charter school advocate Rudolph Giuliani announced the creation of a $10 million fund for New York City charter schools. The Charter School Improvement Fund awards charter schools annual grants worth up to $250,000 for building construction, maintenance, and educational materials.[608] In April 2001, 14 schools received grants.[609]

Mayor Giuliani promoted vouchers as well as charter schools. In 1999, he proposed an experimental voucher program for one city school district, to be modeled after Milwaukee's program, which had been upheld by the Wisconsin Supreme Court.[610] The plan was not approved for the 1999 budget. However, in August 2000,

a Hunter College survey found that 75 percent of respondents who reported understanding how vouchers work said vouchers should be made available. The survey also revealed strong support for vouchers among minorities: More than 80 percent of African–Americans, Asians, and Hispanics surveyed were in favor of them.[611]

Voucher legislation introduced in the legislature in 2001 included A. 7239 and S. 3725, which would have established the Elementary and Secondary Education Improvement Act. The legislation would have given parents "parental choice certificates" for use at a public or private school of choice. Neither bill was enacted.[612]

## Developments in 2002 and 2003

New York's school choice enrollment provisions were improved in response to the federal No Child Left Behind Act. In 2002, nearly one-third of New York City's schools and 68 percent of the schools in the state were deemed "in need of improvement" and mandated to allow student transfers.[613] In December 2002, Mayor Michael Bloomberg and Chancellor Joel Klein pledged to improve New York City's enrollment and transfer system by "centralizing the process."[614] Under their plan, students can transfer to any school in the city, but transfer requests from students in low-performing schools are given priority.[615] Before the end of 2002, Chancellor Klein was to inform parents of their options for the 2003–2004 school year, giving ample time for applications to be filed and assignments made by June 2003.[616]

In compliance with the No Child Left Behind Act, New York City must allocate at least 5 per-

606. Hartocollis, "Hoping Smaller and Freer Is Better."

607. New York Charter Schools Association, "NYS Charter School Legislation Archives," at *www.nycsa.org/search_form.asp*.

608. Thomas J. Lueck, "$10 Million Fund to Help New York City's Charter Schools Pay for Equipment and Repairs," *The New York Times*, November 1, 2000, B15.

609. New York City Web site, "New York City Charter School Improvement Fund," at *www.nyc.gov/html/dycd/html/charter.html*.

610. Abby Goodnough, "Mayor Proposes Voucher Experiment in Single School District," *The New York Times*, January 15, 1999, p. B10.

611. Carl Campanile, "Nyers Support Vouchers: Poll," *The New York Post*, August 25, 2000, p. 20.

612. See National School Boards Association Web site at *www.nsba.org/novouchers*.

613. Carl Campanile, "1 in 3 City Schools Can't Make Grade," *The New York Post*, September 5, 2002, p. 12.

614. New York City Department of Education, "Mayor Michael R. Bloomberg and Chancellor Joel I. Klein Announce a Citywide Public School Choice Process Under *No Child Left Behind Act*," press release, December 9, 2002, at *www.nycenet.edu/press/02-03/n50_03.htm*.

615. Abby Goodnough, "Policy Eases the Way Out of Bad Schools," *The New York Times*, December 9, 2002, p. B1.

cent of its federal Title I funds for tutoring services. Students in high-poverty areas whose schools have not shown improvement over three years are eligible for tutoring.[617] Due to logistical problems, Chancellor Joel Klein extended the program's 2002 sign-up deadline until the end of November so that more of the 240,000 eligible students could participate.[618] In October, the chancellor disbursed $10 million in tutoring funds to 27 providers.[619] Earlier in the year, State Attorney General Eliot Spitzer drafted a legal opinion supporting the use of public funds to tutor parochial school students. Specifically, Spitzer said that students in religious schools who were struggling with the state's standardized math and reading tests should be offered government-sponsored tutoring services.[620]

In January 2003, parents from Albany and New York City filed a class-action lawsuit against their local school systems, charging that requests for transfers and tutoring requests made in accordance with the No Child Left Behind Act had been unlawfully denied.[621]

Several legislative items were carried over into the 2002 session. A. 3216, proposing $200 tax credits for purchases made for extracurricular activities and $500 tax credits for donations to scholarships, was still with an Assembly committee in early 2002, as were A. 7239 and S. 3725, both of which had been introduced in 2001 to create "parental choice certificates" or vouchers. Neither bill was enacted.[622]

Tax credit legislation was introduced in early 2003. S. 154, would provide a tax credit for tuition and textbook expenses.[623] Another bill, A. 3590, the Educational Tax Incentives Act,

would offer tax credits for donations made to public schools, including charter schools. The credit would be capped at $250 for individuals and $25,000 for businesses. The bills have been referred to committee.[624]

As of fall 2003, parents of pre-kindergarten, kindergarten, and 1st grade students in Buffalo can choose any public school for their child. The new school choice options are part of a larger initiative by Buffalo school officials to improve their school system and respond to opinion polls indicating that parents want their children to attend school closer to home. Now that a court desegregation order has been lifted, parents are no longer obligated to send their children on long bus rides—sometimes across the city—to school. Bus service will be provided for students living more than a half-mile from their school of choice. The first phase of the plan began in the 2002–2003 school year and allowed 9th grade students to attend a public school of choice.[625]

## Position of the Governor / Composition of the State Legislature

Governor George Pataki, a Republican, supports charter schools. Democrats control the Assembly, and Republicans control the Senate.

## State Contacts

**Alliance for Parental Involvement in Education**
P.O. Box 59
East Chatham, NY 12060
Phone: (518) 392-6900
Web site: www.croton.com/allpie
E-mail: allpie@taconic.net

616. New York City Department of Education, "Mayor Michael R. Bloomberg and Chancellor Joel I. Klein Announce a Citywide Public School Choice Process Under *No Child Left Behind Act*."

617. Abby Goodnough, "Free Tutoring Fails to Draw Many Students," *The New York Times*, November 15, 2002, p. B1.

618. Abby Goodnough, "Schools Chief Extends Date to Sign up for Tutoring," *The New York Times*, November 16, 2002, p. B1.

619. Carl Campanile, "Klein's $10M Outlaw for Private Tutors," *The New York Post*, October 23, 2002, p. 8.

620. Carl Campanile, "Spitzer Supports Tutoring for Failing Parochial Kids," *The New York Post*, May 30, 2002, p. 2.

621. Michael A. Fletcher, "N.Y. Suit Claims Denial of Rights in School Law," *The Washington Post*, January 28, 2003, p. A4.

622. See National School Boards Association Web site at *www.nsba.org/novouchers*.

623. New York State Assembly, 2003–2004 Session, at *http://assembly.state.ny.us/*.

624. New York State Assembly, 2003–2004 Session, and George A. Clowes, "The Friedman Report: School Choice Roundup," Heartland Institute, April 2003.

625. Peter Simon, "Pupils Set for School Choice in Fall Term," *Buffalo News*, January 2, 2003, p. A1.

# School Choice 2003

**American Family Association of New York**
Frank Russo, State Director
P.O. Box 203
Port Washington, NY 11050
Phone: (516) 767-9179
Fax: (516) 944-3544
Web site: www.afany.org
E-mail: fjrussojr@cs.com

**Archdiocese of New York**
Dr. Catherine Hickey, Superintendent of
Schools
1011 First Avenue
New York, NY 10022-4134
Phone: (212) 371-1000
Fax: (212) 371-9236
Web site: www.nycatholicschools.org
E-mail: supt@adnyschools.org

**BISON Scholarship Fund**
Christopher L. Jacobs, President
Kathleen Christy, Executive Director
Cindy MacDonald, Program Director
220 Theater Place
Buffalo, NY 14202
Phone: (716) 854-0869
Fax: (716) 854-0877
Web site: www.bisonfund.com
E-mail: info@bisonfund.com

**Black Alliance for Educational Options**
Floyd Flake, Member, Board of Directors
Greater Allen Cathedral of New York
110-31 Merrick Boulevard
Jamaica, NY 11433
Phone: (718) 206-4600
Fax: (718) 526-1311
Web site: www.baeo.org
E-mail: cmenital@aol.com

**The Brighter Choice Foundation**
Thomas Carroll, Chairman
Christian Bender, Executive Director
250 Central Avenue
Albany, NY 12206
Phone: (518) 694-4114
Fax: (518) 694-4281
Web site: www.Brighterchoice.org
E-mail: info@brighterchoice.org

**Buffalo Niagara Partnership**
Dr. Andrew Rudnick, President and CEO
665 Main Street, Suite 200
Buffalo, NY 14203
Phone: (716) 852-7100
Fax: (716) 852-2761
Web site: www.thepartnership.org
E-mail: arudnick@thepartnership.org

**Center for Educational Innovation–
Public Education Association (CEI–PEA)**
Colman Genn, Executive Director
28 West 44th Street, Suite 914
New York, NY 10036
Phone: (212) 302-8800
Fax: (212) 302-0088
Web site: www.cei-pea.org
E-mail: vsilva@cei-pea.org

**Children's Scholarship Fund New York**
8 West 38th Street, 9th Floor
New York, NY 10018
Phone: (212) 515-7100
Fax: (212) 515-7111
Web site: www.scholarshipfund.org/nyc
E-mail: stephen_esposito@scholarshipfund.org

**Edison Schools, Inc.**
521 5th Avenue, 11th Floor
New York, NY 10175
Phone: (212) 419-1600
Fax: (212) 419-1604
E-mail: geninfo@edisonschools.com

**Foundation for Education Reform
and Accountability**
4 Chelsea Park, 2nd Floor
Clifton Park, NY 12065
Phone: (518) 383-2598
Fax: (518) 383-0650
Web site: www.nyfera.org
E-mail: info@nyfera.org

**Loving Education at Home**
P.O. Box 438
Fayetteville, NY 13066-0438
Phone: (315) 637-4525
Fax: (315) 637-4525
Web site: www.leah.org
E-mail: info@leah.org

**Manhattan Institute for Policy Research**
Henry Olsen, Executive Director, Center for
Civic Innovation
52 Vanderbilt Avenue, 2nd Floor
New York, NY 10017
Phone: (212) 599-7000
Fax: (212) 599-3494
Web site: www.manhattan-institute.org
E-mail: holsen@manhattan-institute.org

**Jay P. Greene, Ph.D. Senior Fellow**
Manhattan Institute for Policy Research
4801 South University Drive, Suite 2070
Davie, FL 33328
Phone: (954) 680-8083
Alt. Phone: (954) 349-2322

Fax: (954) 680-8981
Web site: www.miedresearchoffice.org

**Mosaica Education, Inc.**
Kenneth Campbell, Vice President,
Business Division
61 Broadway, Suite 2924
New York, NY 10006
Phone: (212) 232-0305
Fax: (212) 232-0309
Web site: www.mosaicaeducation.com
E-mail: Kcampbell@MosaicaEducation.com

**National Home Education Network (NHEN)**
Linda Dobson, Director
R.R. 1, Box 368
Trudeau Road
Saranac Lake, NY 12983
Phone: (518) 891-4714
Web site: www.nhen.org
E-mail: ldobson@aldus.northnet.org

**New York Charter Schools Association**
Bill Phillips, President
18 Corporate Woods Boulevard
Albany, NY 12211
Phone: (518) 465-4400
Fax: (518) 465-3383
Web site: www.nycsa.org
E-mail: bphillips@nycsa.org

**New York Charter School Resource Center**
Gerry Vazquez, President
Peter Murphy, Vice President
One Penn Plaza, 36th Floor
250 West 34th Street
New York, NY 10119
Phone (NYC, Long Island): (800) 519-6362
Phone (Upstate): (888) 248-5326
Fax (NYC, Long Island): (212) 849-6901
Fax (Upstate): (877) 248-5326
Web site: www.nycharterschools.org
E-mail: nycharters@yahoo.com or
charters@capital.net

**New York City Board of Education**
Charter Schools Office
Jonathon Gyurko, Director
52 Chambers Street, Room 405
New York, NY 10007
Phone: (212) 374-6500
Fax: (212) 374-5581
Web site: www.nycenet.edu/charterschools

**New Yorkers for Constitutional Freedoms**
Rev. Duane Motley, Executive Director
P.O. Box 107
Spencerport, NY 14559
Phone: (585) 225-2340

Fax: (585) 225-2810
Web site: www.nyfrf.org
E-mail: family@nyfrf.org

**New York State Conservative Party**
Michael Long, Chairman
486 78th Street
Brooklyn, NY 11209
Phone: (718) 921-2158
Fax: (718) 921-5268
E-mail: nyscp@aol.com

**New York State Education Department**
James A. Kadamos, Deputy Commissioner
89 Washington Avenue, Room 875 EBA
Albany, New York 12234
Phone: (518) 474-5915
Web site: www.emsc.nysed.gov
E-mail: emscgen@mail.nysed.gov

**School Choice Scholarships Foundation**
Stephen Esposito, Executive Director
8 West 38th Street, 9th Floor
New York, NY 10018
Phone: (800) 310-5164
Fax: (212) 750-4064

**Student Sponsor Partners**
Chris O'Malley, Executive Director
21 East 40th Street, Suite 1601
New York, NY 10016
Phone: (212) 986-9575
Fax: (212) 986-9570
E-mail: comalley@sspnyc.org

**Toussaint Institute Fund**
Gail Foster
2565 Broadway, Box 326
New York, NY 10025
Phone: (212) 422-5338
Web site: www.toussaint.org
E-mail: tfund@ix.netcom.com

**United New Yorkers for Choice in Education**
Timothy Mulhearn, President
P.O. Box 4096
Hempstead, NY 11551-4096
Phone: (516) 292-1224
Fax: (516) 292-9019
E-mail: unyce@earthlink.net

**Victory Schools, Inc.**
Ethel Adu
720 5th Avenue, 3rd Floor
New York, NY 10019
Phone: (212) 720-0310
Fax: (212) 582-1816
Web site: www.victoryschools.com
E-mail: eadu@victoryschools.com

## State School Report Card

**GreatSchools.net**
Web site: www.greatschools.net/modperl/go/NY

**New York City Department of Education**
Web site: www.nycenet.edu/daa/SchoolReports

**New York State Education Department**
Web site: http://usny.nysed.gov/
publications.html

# NORTH CAROLINA

## State Profile (Updated May 2003)

### School Choice Status
- Public school choice: No
- State constitution: No prohibitive language
- Charter school law: Established 1996
    Strength of law: Strong
    Number of charter schools in operation: 99
    Number of students enrolled in charter schools (fall 2002): 21,030
- Publicly funded private school choice: No
- Privately funded school choice: Yes
- Home-school law: Moderate regulation
- Ranking on the Education Freedom Index (2001): 27th out of 50 states

### K–12 Public Schools and Students (2001–2002)
- Public school enrollment: 1,303,928
- Students enrolled per teacher: 15.6
- Number of schools (2000–2001): 2,192
- Number of districts: 117
- Current expenditures: $8,577,066,000
- Current per-pupil expenditure: $6,578
- Amount of revenue from the federal government: 7.7%

### K–12 Public School Teachers (2001–2002)
- Number of teachers: 83,526
- Average salary: $42,959

### K–12 Private Schools (1999–2000)
- Private school enrollment: 96,262
- Number of schools: 588
- Number of teachers: 8,962

### K–12 Public and Private School Student Academic Performance
- NAEP test results:

| NAEP Tests North Carolina Student Performance | State (National) 2000 Math Scale = 0–500 | | State (National) 2000 Science Scale = 0–300 | | State (National) 2000 Reading Scale = 0–500 | |
|---|---|---|---|---|---|---|
| | 4th Grade | 8th Grade | 4th Grade | 8th Grade | 4th Grade | 8th Grade |
| Average Scale Score | 232 (226) | 280 (274) | 148 (148) | 147 (149) | 217 (215) | 264 (261) |
| Advanced | 3% (3%) | 6% (5%) | 2% (3%) | 3% (4%) | 6% (6%) | 2% (2%) |
| Proficient | 25% (23%) | 24% (21%) | 22% (25%) | 24% (26%) | 22% (23%) | 29% (29%) |
| Basic | 48% (43%) | 40% (39%) | 40% (36%) | 29% (29%) | 34% (32%) | 45% (41%) |
| Below Basic | 24% (31%) | 30% (35%) | 36% (36%) | 44% (41%) | 38% (39%) | 24% (28%) |

- SAT weighted rank (2001): 21st out of 24 states
- ACT weighted rank (2001): N/A
- ALEC Academic Achievement Ranking: 32nd out of 50 states and the District of Columbia

## Summary

For most North Carolina students, school choice is limited to charter schools. High school students may take courses at community colleges for high school and postsecondary credit.[626] Recently, the Charlotte–Mecklenburg school district adopted a public school choice program. Two private scholarship organizations help students to attend a school of choice.

## Background

North Carolina's charter school law was passed in 1996.[627] Under this legislation, any individual, group, or nonprofit corporation can apply to open a charter school. The state and local boards of education may grant charters. A public school may convert to a charter school if a majority of teachers and parents in the school favor conversion. The number of five-year charters is capped at five per district per year, with a maximum of 100 charter schools allowed in the state.[628]

A Manhattan Institute study released in 2000 compared the academic achievement of recipients of privately funded vouchers in Charlotte with that of students who remained in the public schools. Since all students in the study had applied for the scholarships and recipients were determined by lottery, the researcher had both a control group and a "treated" group to compare. After one year, the students who had received vouchers had improved their scores on national standardized math tests by 5.9 to 6.2 national percentile ranking points and their reading scores by 5.4 to 7.7 national percentile ranking points. In addition, parental satisfaction and student satisfaction were higher for those in voucher programs. The author of the study, Jay P. Greene, found that "Choice parents were also

nearly twice as likely to report being 'very satisfied' with virtually all aspects of their children's school."[629]

Two privately funded programs in North Carolina provide vouchers: the Children's Scholarship Fund–Charlotte and the Carolina Educational Opportunity Scholarship Fund. Both programs are projects of Children First America (CFA), a prominent scholarship organization that promotes school choice by assisting in the formation of privately funded voucher programs.[630]

A surge of charter school applications in 2001 resulted in an attempt by legislators to remove the limit on the number of charters allowed. Three new charter schools were approved in February 2001, bringing the total to 97; however, 33 additional applications had been submitted that year as well.[631] Four bills (House Bills 1207, 25, 26, and 29) were introduced to increase or remove the cap on charter schools, but all died in committee.[632]

In November 2001, a highly anticipated study of North Carolina charter schools was released. Researchers concluded that "wide variations in performance render any analyses that combine all charter schools together for the purpose of making comparisons largely unhelpful in estimating the 'effects' of charter schools on student achievement." The study found that charter schools, like public schools, "vary considerably among themselves," making it "difficult to speak of these schools as if they were a single entity." However, it also found that, in general, charter schools were smaller, had greater student turnover, and "served students who, for a variety of reasons, were not thriving in their regular placements." Because most charter schools were smaller than public schools, students received

626. Education Commission of the States, "Postsecondary Options: Dual/Concurrent Enrollment," July 2001.
627. NCSG 115C–238, 29.
628. Center for Education Reform, "Charter School Legislation: Profile of North Carolina's Charter School Law," 2001, at http://edreform.com/charter_schools/laws/NorthCarolina.htm.
629. Jay P. Greene, "The Effect of School Choice: An Evaluation of the Charlotte Children's Scholarship Fund Program," Manhattan Institute Civic Report No. 12, August 2000.
630. See Children First America Web Site at www.childrenfirstamerica.org.
631. Andrew Cline, "Charter School Cap Assailed as New Schools Are Approved," Carolina Journal, February 2001, p. 5.
632. See North Carolina General Assembly Web site at www.ncga.state.nc.us.

more personal attention. Also, parents were more likely to be involved in a student's education at a charter school.[633]

Gaston College Preparatory School, which was highlighted in a *New York Times* commentary, provides an example of the potential of charter schools. The commentary noted that, "In the year before they attended Gaston, only 53 percent of the first class of fifth-graders had passed the North Carolina statewide reading test. After one year at Gaston, 93 percent passed, including 82 percent of the special-education students."[634]

## Developments in 2002 and 2003

The Charlotte–Mecklenburg school district (CMS), the 23rd largest in the nation, implemented a limited districtwide school choice system for the 2002–2003 school year. Court cases delayed enactment of the school choice program until 2002. In April 2002, the Supreme Court of the United States declared CMS "unitary," which means that the district has met desegregation standards. This ruling ended a nearly 40-year conflict in the courts over the district's desegregation strategies of race-based busing and magnet schools.[635] Under a new student assignment plan adopted by the board, the district was divided into four "geographic choice zones, allowing students to attend any of the schools in their assigned zone" if space was available.[636] The plan "guarantees availability of a 'home' school assignment choice for every student."[637]

In 2003, the school choice advocacy group Assignment By Choice proposed that a program similar to that of CMS be enacted in Wake County, the state's second largest school system, which still uses "forced busing."[638]

In April 2002, $1.5 million was donated to the Children's Scholarship Fund–Charlotte by Julian Roberts, who had founded the scholarship fund in 1999 with a donation in the same amount.[639]

Several bills to raise or eliminate the cap on charter schools were introduced. H.B. 31, which would raise the cap to 110, has been passed by the House.

## Position of the Governor / Composition of the State Legislature

Governor Michael F. Easley, a Democrat, strongly opposes vouchers. Democrats control the Senate, and the House is evenly split between Democrats and Republicans.

## State Contacts

### Black Alliance for Educational Options
William Pierce, Director
NC Triangle Area
c/o Urban Ed LLC
P.O. Box 11265
Durham, NC 27703
Phone: (919) 358-3048
Web site: www.baeo.org
E-mail: wpierce@urbanedllc.com

### Children's Scholarship Fund–Charlotte
Lindalyn Kakadelis
The Great Aunt Stella Center
926 Elizabeth Avenue, Suite 403A
Charlotte, NC 28204
Phone: (704) 373-2378
Fax: (704) 373-1739
Web site: www.csfcharlotte.org

---

633. George W. Noblit and Dickson Corbett, *North Carolina Charter School Evaluation Report*, November 2001, at *www.ncpublicschools.org/accountability/evaluation/charter/evalreport.pdf*.

634. Bob Herbert, "A Chance to Learn," *The New York Times*, December 16, 2002.

635. Charlotte–Mecklenburg School System, "The History of Public Schools in Charlotte–Mecklenburg," April 3, 2003, at *www.cms.k12.nc.us/discover/history.asp*.

636. Karla Scoon Reid, "Charlotte District, Still in Limbo, Presses Ahead with Choice Plan," *Education Week*, September 5, 2001.

637. Charlotte–Mecklenburg Schools, "Board Resolution 2001," April 3, 2001, at *www.cms.k12.nc.us/studentassignment03-04/boardResolution2001.asp*. For additional information on the Charlotte–Mecklenburg school choice program, see "School Reassignment: A Parent's Complete Guide to Charlotte–Mecklenburg Schools Reassignment," *The Charlotte Observer*, at *www.print2webcorp.com/news/charlotte/reassignment/20011130/p1.asp*.

638. Dr. Karen Palasek, "Local Group Presses for School Choice in North Carolina's 2nd-Largest District," *Carolina Journal Online*, March 11, 2003, at *www.carolinajournal.com/issues/display_story.html?id=158*.

639. Foundation for the Carolinas, "Julian Robertson Makes $1.5 Million Gift to Children's Scholarship Fund," press release, April 10, 2002, at *www.fftc.org/news/press/releases/20020410_1.html*.

**John Locke Foundation**
John Hood, President
200 West Morgan Street, Suite 200
Raleigh, NC 27601
Phone: (919) 828-3876
Fax: (919) 821-5117
Web site: www.johnlocke.org
E-mail: jhood@johnlocke.org

**North Carolina Christian School Association**
Dr. Joe Haas, Executive Director
P.O. Box 231
Goldsboro, NC 27533
Phone: (919) 731-4844
Fax: (919) 731-4847
Web site: www.nccsa.org
E-mail: 1haas@nccsa.org; info@nccsa.org

**North Carolina Citizens for
a Sound Economy**
Jonathon Hill, Director
115½ West Morgan Street
Raleigh, NC 27601
Phone: (919) 807-0100
Fax: (919) 807-0400
Web site: www.cse.org/northcarolina/index.php
E-mail: nccse@cse.org

**North Carolina Department of
Public Instruction**
Office of the State Superintendent
Education Building
301 North Wilmington Street
Raleigh, NC 27601-2825

Phone: (919) 807-3300
Fax: (919) 807-3445
Web site: www.dpi.state.nc.us

**North Carolina Education Alliance**
Lindalyn Kakadelis, Director
200 West Morgan Street, Suite 200
Raleigh, NC 27601
Phone: (919) 832-9756
Fax: (919) 821-5117
Web site: www.nceducationalliance.org
E-mail: kakadelis@bellsouth.net

**North Carolinians for Home Education**
4326 Bland Road
Raleigh, NC 27609-6125
Phone: (919) 790-1100
Fax: (919) 790-1892
Web site: www.nche.com
E-mail: nche@nche.com

## State School Report Card
**Charlotte–Mecklenburg School System**
Web site: www.cms.k12.nc.us

**Greatschools.net**
Web site: www.greatschools.net/modperl/go/NC

**North Carolina Department of Public Instruction**
Web site: www.ncreportcards.org/src

# NORTH DAKOTA

## State Profile (Updated May 2003)

### School Choice Status
- Public school choice: Interdistrict/voluntary
- State constitution: Blaine amendment
- Charter school law: No
- Publicly funded private school choice: No
- Privately funded school choice: No
- Home-school law: High regulation
- Ranking on the Education Freedom Index (2001): 44th out of 50 states

### K–12 Public Schools and Students (2001–2002)
- Public school enrollment: 106,047
- Students enrolled per teacher: 12.5
- Number of schools (2000–2001): 539
- Number of districts: 231
- Current expenditures: $654,600,000
- Current per-pupil expenditure: $6,173
- Amount of revenue from the federal government: 11.6%

### K–12 Public School Teachers (2001–2002)
- Number of teachers: 8,503
- Average salary: $31,709

### K–12 Private Schools (1999–2000)
- Private school enrollment: 7,148
- Number of schools: 55
- Number of teachers: 545

### K–12 Public and Private School Student Academic Performance
- NAEP test results:

| NAEP Tests North Dakota Student Performance | State (National) 2000 Math Scale = 0–500 | | State (National) 2000 Science Scale = 0–300 | | State (National) 2000 Reading Scale = 0–500 | |
|---|---|---|---|---|---|---|
| | 4th Grade | 8th Grade | 4th Grade | 8th Grade | 4th Grade | 8th Grade |
| Average Scale Score | 231 (226) | 283 (274) | 160 (148) | 161 (149) | N/A (215) | N/A (261) |
| Advanced | 2% (3%) | 4% (5%) | 3% (3%) | 4% (4%) | N/A (6%) | N/A (2%) |
| Proficient | 23% (23%) | 27% (21%) | 35% (25%) | 36% (26%) | N/A (23%) | N/A (29%) |
| Basic | 50% (43%) | 46% (39%) | 42% (36%) | 34% (29%) | N/A (32%) | N/A (41%) |
| Below Basic | 25% (31%) | 23% (35%) | 20% (36%) | 26% (41%) | N/A (39%) | N/A (28%) |

- SAT weighted rank (2001): N/A
- ACT weighted rank (2001): 14th out of 26 states
- ALEC Academic Achievement Ranking: 16th out of 50 states and the District of Columbia

## Summary

North Dakota offers interdistict choice that enables students to attend any participating school outside their district. The state has no charter schools, and home schooling is heavily regulated.

## Background

The North Dakota Division of Independent Study (NDIS) has provided distance-learning opportunities to students for the past 67 years. The NDIS currently offers 189 courses, 75 of which are available on-line, for students in grades 4 through 12. Students submit work by mail, fax, e-mail, or on-line and may earn a state-accredited diploma through the distance-learning programs.[640] The state's dual-enrollment law allows high schools to form partnerships with colleges and universities to offer college course credit for high school students.[641]

## Developments in 2002 and 2003

In 2002, North Dakota legislators introduced House Bill 1182, which would have forced home-schooled students to meet state standards and take state tests. In January 2003, H.B. 1182 was defeated in the House by a vote of 87 to 2.[642]

In 2003, State Representative C. B. Haas (R–36) introduced H.B. 1361 to amend the state's open enrollment law. The bill would have allowed school districts to deny transfer applications if the applications would change the enrollment of the district by more than 20 percent. It also would have required districts to allow students from the same family to transfer in order to attend school in the same district. The bill was passed in the House but lost in the Senate.[643]

Governor John Hoeven signed H.B. 1086 into law in April 2003. Under this bill, parents may apply to transfer their child to a school in a neighboring district if the child has been the victim of a violent incident, if the superintendent has declared the school unsafe, or if the superintendent has determined that the school requires "program improvement for six consecutive years." The sending district would be responsible for transportation.[644]

## Position of the Governor / Composition of the State Legislature

Governor John H. Hoeven, a Republican, has no stated position on school choice. Republicans control both houses of the legislature.

## State Contacts

**North Dakota Department of Public Instruction**
600 East Boulevard Avenue, Department 201
Bismarck, ND 58505-0440
Phone: (701) 328-2260
Web site: www.dpi.state.nd.us/index.shtm

**North Dakota Family Alliance**
Christina Kindel, Executive Director
4007 State Street North, Suite 109
Bismarck, ND 58503
Phone: (701) 223-3575
Fax: (701) 223-1133
Web site: www.ndfa.org
E-mail: ndfa@riverjorden.com

**North Dakota Home School Association**
P.O. Box 7400
Bismarck, ND 58507
Phone: (701) 223-4080
Fax: (701) 223-4081
Web site: www.ndhsa.org
E-mail: ndhsa@riverjordan.com

---

640. For more information, see North Dakota Division of Independent Study Web site at *www.dis.dpi.state.nd.us/*.

641. Education Commission of the States, "Postsecondary Options: Dual/Current Enrollment," July 2001, at *www.communitycollegepolicy.org/pdf/ECSDualEnrollStateNote.pdf*.

642. See North Dakota Legislature Web site, at *www.state.nd.us/lr/assembly/*, and Home School Legal Defense Association, "Legislation Threatens Home-School Freedoms," *The Home School Court Report*, March/April 2003, at *www.hslda.org/courtreport/V19N2/V19N2ND.asp*.

643. See North Dakota Legislature Web site at *www.state.nd.us/lr/assembly/*.

644. *Ibid.*

## State School Report Card

**Greatschools.net**
Web site: www.greatschools.net/modperl/go/ND

**North Dakota Department of Public Instruction**[645]
Web site: www.dpi.state.nd.us/dpi/reports/profile/index.shtm

---

645. North Dakota provides district-level information.

# OHIO

## State Profile (Updated May 2003)

### School Choice Status
- Public school choice: Intradistrict/mandatory and interdistrict/voluntary
- State constitution: Compelled-support language
- Charter school law: Established 1997
    Strength of law: Strong
    Number of charter schools in operation (fall 2002): 131
    Number of students enrolled in charter schools (fall 2002): 28,446
- Publicly funded private school choice: Yes
- Privately funded school choice: Yes
- Home-school law: Moderate regulation
- Ranking on the Education Freedom Index (2001): 26th out of 50 states

### K–12 Public Schools and Students (2001–2002)
- Public school enrollment: 1,808,000
- Students enrolled per teacher: 15.3
- Number of schools (2000–2001): 3,827
- Number of districts: 612
- Current expenditures: $15,020,000,000
- Current per-pupil expenditure: $8,308
- Amount of revenue from the federal government: 6.0%

### K–12 Public School Teachers (2001–2002)
- Number of teachers: 118,000
- Average salary: $44,492

### K–12 Private Schools (1999–2000)
- Private school enrollment: 254,494
- Number of schools: 974
- Number of teachers: 16,165

### K–12 Public and Private School Student Academic Performance
- NAEP test results:

| NAEP Tests Ohio Student Performance | State (National) 2000 Math Scale = 0–500 | | State (National) 2000 Science Scale = 0–300 | | State (National) 2000 Reading Scale = 0–500 | |
|---|---|---|---|---|---|---|
| | 4th Grade | 8th Grade | 4th Grade | 8th Grade | 4th Grade | 8th Grade |
| Average Scale Score | 231 (226) | 283 (274) | 154 (148) | 161 (149) | N/A (215) | N/A (261) |
| Advanced | 2% (3%) | 5% (5%) | 4% (3%) | 6% (4%) | N/A (6%) | N/A (2%) |
| Proficient | 24% (23%) | 26% (21%) | 27% (25%) | 35% (26%) | N/A (23%) | N/A (29%) |
| Basic | 47% (43%) | 44% (39%) | 41% (36%) | 32% (29%) | N/A (32%) | N/A (41%) |
| Below Basic | 27% (31%) | 25% (35%) | 28% (36%) | 27% (41%) | N/A (39%) | N/A (28%) |

- SAT weighted rank (2001): N/A
- ACT weighted rank (200): 14th out of 26 states
- ALEC Academic Achievement Ranking: 16th out of 50 states and the District of Columbia

## Summary

Ohio families, particularly those in Cleveland, enjoy significant freedom in choosing a school for their children. Students may transfer to any school within a district and to schools in other participating districts. The state also has a strong charter school law. In Cleveland, in addition to being able to choose a charter school or a traditional public school, students may attend a private or parochial school with government support. High school juniors and seniors may take college courses for high school and post-secondary credit. Several private scholarship organizations provide financial assistance for poor students.

## Background

In 1989, the Ohio legislature enacted Senate Bill 140 to enable students to transfer to another school within their district as of the1993–1994 school year. The law also allows students to transfer to other schools in adjacent participating districts. Each district must establish a policy indicating whether or not it will receive transfers. Space limitations and stipulations regarding racial balance may limit transfers. Transportation is provided if students use existing bus stops. Districts may reimburse low-income parents for the transportation costs associated with interdistrict transfers.[646]

Since 1990, the state has allowed students in junior and senior high school to enroll in free college courses and receive both college and high school credit. Students in chartered private schools may also participate. Students may choose any state-approved public, private non-profit, or proprietary higher education institution that grants degrees.[647]

On June 30, 1995, then-Governor and former Cleveland Mayor George Voinovich signed a state budget bill that included a pilot voucher program for Cleveland students.[648] Starting in the 1996–1997 school year, the state provided vouchers worth up to $2,250 to 1,994 low-income students in grades K–3 to attend a public or private school of choice. (The program currently serves students in grades K–8). Although this program allows students to transfer to participating suburban schools, no suburban school has opted to participate. During the same year, 124 public school students received tutoring at state expense.[649]

On July 31, 1996, Franklin County Court of Common Pleas Judge Lisa Sadler ruled that the Cleveland voucher plan did not violate either the state constitution or the U.S. Constitution. Noting that the "nonpublic sectarian schools participating in the scholarship program are benefited only indirectly, and purely as the result of the genuinely independent and private choices of aid recipients," Judge Sadler concluded that allowing religious schools to be included in the voucher program did not violate the First Amendment.[650] Opponents of the voucher plan appealed the decision.

In May 1997, the Ohio Court of Appeals struck down the Cleveland pilot scholarship program by a vote of 3 to 0, ruling that the program violated the religious establishment clauses of the Ohio and U. S. Constitutions, as well as a provision in the state constitution requiring general laws to have statewide application. The Ohio Supreme Court granted a motion to stay on July 24, 1997, allowing the Cleveland scholarship program to continue operating while the court considered the case.[651]

After two years of failed efforts to pass a charter school bill, Governor Voinovich signed House Bill 215 on June 30, 1997.[652] The law allowed the creation of new charter "community

---

646. Informational Brief Prepared for Members of the Ohio General Assembly by the Legislative Service Commission Staff, "School Choice," Vol. 121, Issue 11, January 24, 1997, at *www.lsc.state.oh.us/membersonly/schoolchoice.pdf.*

647. *Ibid.*

648. Drew Lindsay, "Wisconsin, Ohio Back Vouchers for Religious Schools," *Education Week*, July 12, 1995.

649. See "Cleveland Scholarship and Tutoring Program" at *http://schoolchoiceinfo.org/facts/index.cfm?fl_id=2.*

650. Mark Walsh, "Ohio Court Clears Cleveland's Voucher Pilot," *Education Week*, August 7, 1996.

651. Beth Reinhard, "Ohio Supreme Court Will Allow Cleveland Voucher Program to Begin Its Second Year," *Education Week*, August 6, 1997.

schools" in Lucas County (which includes Toledo) and allowed an unlimited number of traditional public schools throughout the state to convert to charter status. The law was later amended to permit other urban districts to establish new charter schools.[653]

In 1998, Parents Advancing Choice in Education (PACE) began offering scholarships to 765 low-income students to attend a private school of choice in Dayton (250 of the students were already in private schools). Scholarships were equal to 50 percent of tuition, up to $1,200. In 2000, a study on the outcome of the program found that African–American voucher recipients in grades 2–8 scored, on average, nearly 7 percentile points higher in math than those who did not receive scholarships. The research also found greater satisfaction among parents whose children used the scholarships.[654]

In 1998, Dayton, Toledo, and Cincinnati became Children's Scholarship Fund (CSF) "partner cities." The CSF, a $100 million foundation, matches money raised by residents in its partner cities to fund private scholarships for low-income students to attend a school of choice. A lottery awards scholarships to children entering kindergarten through 8th grade for a minimum of four years. In Dayton, the CSF partnered with the city's existing private choice program, PACE.[655]

In May 1998, both houses of the legislature approved an amendment to the Cleveland voucher legislation sponsored by then-Representative Mike Wise (R–15) that required the Cleveland school district to provide transportation to students in the scholarship program.[656] This amendment significantly decreased the number of students who had to rely on taxicabs to get to their new schools of choice.[657]

In May 1999, the Ohio Supreme Court upheld the constitutionality of the Cleveland scholarship and Tutoring Program in *Simmons-Harris* v. *Goff*. Justice Paul E. Pfeifer wrote for the majority that "Whatever link between government and religion is created by the school voucher program is indirect, depending only on the genuinely independent and private choices of individual parents." The court, however, struck down the program for violating the state's requirement for "one subject" legislative bills, since the legislature had attached the Cleveland choice program language to an appropriations bill. The ruling allowed the scholarship program to continue until the end of the school year and gave the legislature the opportunity to reauthorize the scholarship plan in a one-subject bill.[658]

Soon after the law was passed, the Ohio Education Association, the American Civil Liberties Union, and People for the American Way filed suit in federal court to challenge the program on First Amendment grounds and to obtain a preliminary injunction. In August 1999, one day before the start of school, Judge Solomon Oliver of the Federal District Court for Northern Ohio granted the injunction, prompting a national outcry. Judge Oliver modified his ruling several days later to allow current voucher recipients to remain in the program but also preventing 794 new participants from entering school.[659]

A study released in September 1999 by Indiana University found that the Cleveland scholarship program was beneficial and was serving the populations for which it was intended. The program primarily served low-income, minority families headed by single mothers. The study found that families applied for the scholarships for academic and safety reasons and that 97.4 percent of voucher users and applicants who

652. "Charters in Our Midst: Charter Legislation and Contacts in the NCREL States," North Central Regional Educational Laboratory, *Policy Publications*, January 1998, at *www.ncrel.org/sdrs/pbriefs/97/97-1leg.htm*.

653. *Ibid.*

654. William G. Howell and Paul E. Peterson, "School Choice in Dayton, Ohio: An Evaluation After One Year," prepared for the Conference on Vouchers, Charters and Public Education, sponsored by the Program on Education Policy and Governance, Harvard University, March 2000.

655. See Children's Scholarship Fund Web site at *www.scholarshipfund.org*.

656. Blum Center for Parental Freedom in Education, Marquette University, *Educational Freedom Report* No. 60, June 19, 1998.

657. Jeff Archer, "Policies of Cleveland Voucher Program Faulted," *Education Week*, January 20, 1999.

658. Center for Education Reform, *Monthly Letter to Friends of The Center for Education Reform*, No. 54, June 1999. See also Institute for Justice, "Ohio School Choice Case," at *www.ij.org/cases/index.html*.

659. Institute for Justice, "Ohio School Choice Case," at *www.ij.org/cases/index.html*.

did not receive vouchers were satisfied with the program. Scholarship students showed a small but statistically significant improvement in their achievement scores in language and science after two years.[660]

A June 1999 survey published by Paul Peterson, Ph.D., revealed that more parents participating in Cleveland's voucher program were "very satisfied" with many aspects of their children's schools, including academics, safety, and discipline, than were parents of the children who remained in public schools. The research also indicated that families using vouchers were more likely to be African–American, headed by single parents, and poorer than average families that used public schools.[661]

A study released in November 1999 by the Columbus-based Buckeye Institute for Public Policy Solutions found that school choice in Cleveland provided better racial integration than did the conventional public school system. According to the study, 19 percent of Cleveland's voucher recipients were enrolled at private schools that had a racial composition approximating the average for the Cleveland area, while only 5.2 percent of the Cleveland area's public school students were in schools with comparable integration. While 61 percent of the public school students in the Cleveland area attended schools that had almost entirely white or minority enrollment, only 50 percent of voucher recipients were educated in such a homogenous environment.[662]

In November 1999, the Supreme Court of the United States granted a stay of the injunction against the Cleveland school choice program; but in December, Judge Oliver ruled that the program "has the effect of advancing religion

through government-supported religious indoctrination" and is therefore unconstitutional. The decision was appealed to the U.S. Court of Appeals for the Sixth Circuit. Meanwhile, the parties on both sides of the case agreed to allow the program's nearly 4,000 students to remain in their schools until a final decision was reached.[663]

In December 2000, by a vote of 3 to 2, the U.S. Court of Appeals for the Sixth District ruled that the Cleveland school choice program was unconstitutional, contending that government funding of private tuition promotes religious education.[664] Proponents sought a ruling from the full U.S. Court of Appeals for the Sixth Circuit. In March 2001, the U.S. Court of Appeals declined to review the lower panel's ruling. However, it did decide that the program could continue to operate while supporters sought a U.S. Supreme Court review of the decision.[665]

A new privately funded scholarship program for low-income Columbus families, Children First Columbus, was created in 2000. This program, founded by Thomas Needles and other private benefactors, is an affiliate of Children First America.[666]

A 2001 Indiana University study of the Cleveland Scholarship and Tutoring Program found that voucher recipients' test scores were higher than those of their peers in public schools. The study concluded that "Students who entered the Scholarship Program as kindergartners were achieving at significantly higher levels than other students when they entered first grade" and that, while public school students made academic gains in the first grade, students who used vouchers for three years remained ahead academically.[667]

660. Kim K. Metcalf, Ph.D., "Evaluation of the Cleveland Scholarship and Tutoring Grant Program, 1996–99," Indiana University, Indiana Center for Evaluation, September 1999.

661. Paul E. Peterson, William G. Howell, and Jay P. Greene, "An Evaluation of the Cleveland Voucher Program After Two Years," Program on Education Policy and Governance, Harvard University, June 1999.

662. Jay P. Greene, Ph.D., "Choice and Community: The Racial, Economic, and Religious Context of Parental Choice in Cleveland," Buckeye Institute for Public Policy Solutions, November 1999.

663. John Kramer, "Web Release: Parents File Cleveland School Choice Appeal, Lament Latest Public School Failures," Institute for Justice, January 12, 2000.

664. Kenneth Cooper, "Appeals Court Rejects Vouchers in Cleveland as Unconstitutional," *The Washington Post*, December 12, 2000.

665. John Kramer, "Web Release: Entire Sixth Circuit Declines to Review School Choice Case, Appeal Now Headed to U.S. Supreme Court," Institute for Justice, March 1, 2001.

666. News release, Children First Columbus, July 19, 2000.

667. Kim K. Metcalf, Ph.D., "Evaluation of the Cleveland Scholarship Program 1998–2000 Executive Summary," Indiana University, Indiana Center for Evaluation, September 2001.

In May 2001, several education groups—including the Ohio Federation of Teachers, the Cleveland Teachers Union, the Ohio School Boards Association, the Ohio League of Women Voters, and the Ohio PTA—filed a lawsuit contending that Ohio's charter school program violated the state constitution by illegally transferring funds from traditional public schools to schools that are subject to little oversight by elected school boards. The case was decided in April 2003.[668]

In 2001, several Republican lawmakers unveiled proposals to expand community school programs and voucher programs. State Senator Ron Amstutz (R–17) introduced S.B. 89, which would have increased the maximum scholarship provided under the Cleveland voucher program from $2,250 to the amount of the state's basic public school per-pupil expenditure. Another bill introduced during the 2001 session, H.B. 204, would have provided "child-centered scholarships" for students in school districts that were in a state of "academic emergency." Both bills died in committee.[669]

Representative Michael Gilb (R–Findlay) proposed H.B. 202 to allow tax credits of up to $10,000 toward the corporate franchise tax of companies that contribute to nonprofit organizations that provide scholarships to low-income students. The bill would have allowed individuals to take a credit of up to $500 for a contribution to a scholarship program or a credit of up to $100 for educational expenses. This bill also died in committee.[670]

### Developments in 2002 and 2003

In June 2002, the U.S. Supreme Court upheld the Cleveland Scholarship and Tutoring Program, ruling that the use of public money to underwrite tuition at private and religious schools does not violate the Establishment Clause of the Constitution as long as parents make the decision regarding where the voucher is used.[671] Writing for the Court, Chief Justice William Rehnquist stated, "We believe that the program challenged here is a program of true private choice, consistent with *Mueller*, *Witters*, and *Zobrest* and, thus, constitutional. As was true in those cases, the Ohio program is neutral in all respects toward religion."[672]

The program awarded scholarships to 4,456 students in kindergarten through 8th grade during the 2001–2002 school year.[673] Although the number of available vouchers was increased from 4,523 for the 2001–2002 school year to 5,523 for the 2002–2003 school year, officials say they have been forced to turn away more than 1,100 Cleveland parents who applied for vouchers because there were not enough to meet the demand.[674]

On January 7, 2003, Governor Robert Taft signed H.B. 364, which amended the charter school law, stipulating that the Ohio State Board of Education may no longer sponsor community schools and that those schools sponsored by the state board will have two years to find new sponsors. The law also gives the Ohio Department of Education greater oversight over charter sponsors; caps the number of community schools at 225 until July 1, 2005; allows private, nonprofit education organizations to authorize charter schools; and increases the number of districts where charters can be formed.[675]

H.B. 95 and a companion bill, S.B. 12, were introduced in the 2003 session to allow districts to create on-line charter schools. Governor Taft signed S.B. 12 at the end of March 2003.[676]

On April 21, 2003, Franklin County Judge Patrick McGrath dismissed the majority of the

---

668. Center for Education Reform, *Education Reform Newswire*, Vol. 5, No. 17 (April 22, 2003); "News in Brief: A State Capitals Roundup," *Education Week*, April 30, 2003.

669. See Ohio Legislative Service Commission, "124th General Assembly: Bill Analyses," at *www.lsc.state.oh.us/analyses124/index.html*.

670. *Ibid.*

671. George A. Clowes, "Parents Are Winners in Supreme Court Ruling," *School Reform News*, Vol. 6, No. 8 (August 2002).

672. *Zelman v. Simmons-Harris*, 536 U.S. 639 at 653 (2002).

673. Jacques Steinberg, "Cleveland Case Poses New Test for Vouchers," *The New York Times*, February 10, 2002.

674. Caroline Hendrie, "Applications for Cleveland Vouchers Soar After High Court Ruling," *Education Week*, September 4, 2002.

675. See Ohio Legislative Service Commission "Final Bill Analysis," at *http://lsc.state.oh.us/analyses/fnla124.nsf/All%20Bills%20and%20Resolutions/53ea*.

allegations of the lawsuit filed in May 2001 by the Ohio Federation of Teachers, the Ohio School Boards Association, the Ohio League of Women Voters, and the Ohio PTA. Although other elements of the case remain, Judge McGrath dismissed the claim that the law is unconstitutional.[677]

## Position of the Governor / Composition of the State Legislature

Governor Robert Taft, a Republican, favors all forms of parental choice in education. Republicans control both houses of the legislature.

## State Contacts

**Buckeye Institute for Public Policy Solutions**
Sam Staley, President
Joshua Hall, Director of Research and Director, Center for Education
4100 North High Street, Suite 200
Columbus, OH 43214
Phone: (614) 262-1593
Fax: (614) 262-1927
Web site: http://www.buckeyeinstitute.org
E-mail: hall@buckeyeinstitute.org

**Children First Columbus**
Tom Needles, Program Coordinator
66 East Lynn Street
Columbus, Ohio 43215
Phone: (614) 470-2442
Fax: (614) 221-9192
Web site: www.statecraftconsulting.com
E-mail: tom@statecraftconsulting.com

**Christian Home Educators of Ohio**
117 West Main Street, Suite 103
Lancaster, OH 43130
Phone: (740) 654-3331
Fax: (740) 654-3337
E-mail: CHEO.ORG@USA.NET

**Children's Scholarship Fund of Greater Cincinnati**
Lisa Claytor, Administrator
P.O. Box 361
10 North Locust Street, Suite C
Oxford, OH 45056
Phone: (513) 523-3816
Fax: (513) 523-1547
Web site: www.scholarshipfund.org
Email: csfgclc@one.net

**Northwest Ohio Scholarship Fund**
P.O. Box 985
Toledo, OH 43697
Phone: (419) 244-6711, ext. 373
Web site: www.nosf.org

**Ohio Department of Education**
25 South Front Street
Columbus, OH 43215-4183
Phone: (877) 644-6338
Web site: www.ode.state.oh.us

**Ohio Roundtable and Freedom Forum**
The School Choice Committee
David Zanotti, Chairman
Patty Hollo, Executive Director
Bert Holt, Co-Chairman
11288 Alameda Drive
Strongsville, OH 44149
Phone: (877) 696-8722
Fax: (440) 572-2128
Web site: www.schoolchoicecommittee.com
E-mail: info@schoolchoicecommittee.com

**Parents Advancing Choice in Education, Inc.**
Bonnie E. Smith, Program Manager
Angela Hayes, Program Officer
1315 North Main Street
Dayton, OH 45405
Phone: (937) 228-PACE
Fax: (937) 226-1887
Web site: www.pacedayton.org
E-mail: dariastone@pacedayton.org; angel-hayes@pacedayton.org

**Parents of Lima Advancing Choice in Education (PLACE)**
Susie Crabtree, Program Administrator
Lima Community Foundation
P.O. Box 1086
Lima, OH 45802-1086
Phone: (419) 221-5928
Fax: (419) 221-2930
E-mail: limacommunityfoundation@bright.net

## State School Report Card

**Greatschools.net**
Web site: www.greatschools.net/modperl/go/OH

**Ohio Department of Education**
Web site: www.ode.state.oh.us/reportcard

---

676. See Ohio Legislative Service Commission, "125th General Assembly, Regular Session, 2003–2004, Am. S. B. No. 12," at *www.legislature.state.oh.us/bills.cfm?ID=125_SB_12*.

677. Center for Education Reform, *Education Reform Newswire*, Vol. 5, No. 17 (April 22, 2003).

# OKLAHOMA

## State Profile (Updated May 2003)

### School Choice Status
- Public school choice: Interdistrict/mandatory
- State constitution: Blaine amendment
- Charter school law: Established 1999
  - Strength of law: Weak
  - Number of charter schools in operation (fall 2002): 10
  - Number of students enrolled in charter schools (fall 2002): 2,197
- Publicly funded private school choice: No
- Privately funded school choice: Yes
- Home-school law: No notice required
- Ranking on the Education Freedom Index (2001): 10th out of 50 states

### K–12 Public Schools and Students (2001–2002)
- Public school enrollment: 620,404
- Students enrolled per teacher: 15
- Number of schools (2000–2001): 1,811
- Number of districts: 543
- Current expenditures: $3,836,716,000
- Current per-pupil expenditure: $6,184
- Amount of revenue from the federal government: 10.7%

### K–12 Public School Teachers (2001–2002)
- Number of teachers: 41,452
- Average salary: $35,412

### K–12 Private Schools (1999–2000)
- Private school enrollment: 31,276
- Number of schools: 179
- Number of teachers: 2,727

### K–12 Public and Private School Student Academic Performance
- NAEP test results:

| NAEP Tests Oklahoma Student Performance | State (National) 2000 Math Scale = 0–500 | | State (National) 2000 Science Scale = 0–300 | | State (National) 2000 Reading Scale = 0–500 | |
|---|---|---|---|---|---|---|
| | 4th Grade | 8th Grade | 4th Grade | 8th Grade | 4th Grade | 8th Grade |
| Average Scale Score | 225 (226) | 272 (274) | 152 (148) | 149 (149) | 220 (215) | 265 (261) |
| Advanced | 1% (3%) | 2% (5%) | 2% (3%) | 2% (4%) | 5% (6%) | 1% (2%) |
| Proficient | 15% (23%) | 17% (21%) | 24% (25%) | 24% (26%) | 25% (23%) | 28% (29%) |
| Basic | 53% (43%) | 45% (39%) | 45% (36%) | 36% (29%) | 36% (32%) | 51% (41%) |
| Below Basic | 31% (31%) | 36% (35%) | 29% (36%) | 38% (41%) | 34% (39%) | 20% (28%) |

- SAT weighted rank (2001): N/A
- ACT weighted rank (2001): 18th out of 26 states
- ALEC Academic Achievement Ranking: 36th out of 50 states and the District of Columbia

## Summary

Oklahoma offers interdistrict school choice, charter schools, Enterprise Schools, and on-line schooling.[678] The Oklahoma Scholarship Fund provides private scholarships to students.

## Background

During the 1995 legislative session, Senate Joint Resolution 17 was introduced to amend the Oklahoma constitution to provide vouchers for children in elementary and secondary schools. The voucher would have been worth 50 percent to 70 percent of the state's per-pupil expenditure. The bill died in committee.[679]

In June 1999, the Oklahoma legislature enacted House Bill 1759, which allows local school boards and career-technology schools to charter public schools in districts with 5,000 or more students that are located in cities with a population of 500,000 or more (Oklahoma City and Tulsa).[680] The bill also includes the Education Open Transfer Act, which allows interdistrict public school choice. Transfers are subject to guidelines adopted by local school boards.[681]

Also in 1999, H.B. 2671 was introduced to provide parents with a non-refundable tax credit of up to $500 for tuition. The bill died in committee.[682]

The Oklahoma City School District offers Enterprise Schools, a program that enables teachers, parents, and community leaders to contract with the board of education to operate a school. Such schools have greater flexibility than traditional public schools but less than charter schools.[683]

Oklahoma is the only state whose constitution guarantees a right to home schooling. The

Home School Legal Defense Association estimates that between 20,000 and 25,000 children are homeschooled in the state.[684]

In 1999, then-Governor Frank Keating signed H.B. 1650, which established a pilot Internet schooling program, the Virtual Internet School in Oklahoma Network (VISION), to provide Web-based instruction programs in nine public school districts. The program was amended in 2000 by H.B. 2662 and was launched in 2001. In 2001, approximately 95 Oklahoma school districts offered Internet-based courses, and enrollment in these courses is expected to increase in future years.[685]

Two choice bills were introduced in 2001. H.B. 1473 would have provided a $500 tax credit to parents for tuition and fees, and H.B. 1818 would have provided an income tax credit to donors of scholarships that enable students to attend a private school. H.B. 1818 specified that, "In order to claim the credit authorized by this section, the school board for the district in which the student provided with the private-school scholarship resides must approve a measure authorizing a scholarship to fully or partially subsidize the cost of attendance by students at a public school located within such district." Both bills died in committee.[686]

## Developments in 2002 and 2003

A voucher bill for low-income preschoolers (Senate Bill 1654) was introduced during the 2002 legislative session. This bill would have used Temporary Assistance for Needy Families (TANF) funds to provide vouchers to low-income parents to send their children to private preschools.[687] The bill died in committee.[688]

---

678. Students in state-designated low-performing schools may transfer to another public school in the district.

679. See National School Boards Association Web site at *www.nsba.org/novouchers*.

680. "Oklahoma Charter School Information," at *www.uscharterschools.org/pub/sp/40*.

681. See Oklahoma Legislature Web site at *www.lsb.state.ok.us*.

682. See National School Boards Association Web site at *www.nsba.org/novouchers*.

683. See Oklahoma City Public Schools Web site, at *www.okcps.k12.ok.us/general/highlights.htm*, and Oklahoma Council of Public Affairs, "School Choice in Oklahoma, 2002," *Educational Freedom Watch*, September 2002.

684. Oklahoma Council of Public Affairs, "School Choice in Oklahoma, 2002."

685. *Ibid.* and Oklahoma Legislature Web site at *www.lsb.state.ok.us*.

686. Oklahoma Legislature Web site at *www.lsb.state.ok.us*.

Three tax credit bills—House Bills 2413, 2620, and 2676— were introduced during the 2002 legislative session. H.B. 2413 would have provided an income tax credit of up to $500 for individuals or corporations that donated money to charitable scholarship organizations to fund scholarships for families with incomes below $50,000 and credits of up to $200 for donations for public school extracurricular activities. H.B. 2620 would have provided an income tax credit of up to $1,000 to corporations for donations to charitable scholarship organizations in Tulsa. Both bills died in committee. The third bill (H.B. 2676) would have allowed the state to permit up to $2 million in tax credits for donations to scholarship organizations; organizations would have received credits for scholarships of up to $2,000 or 80 percent of the private school tuition, whichever was less. This bill also died in committee.[689]

In accordance with the federal No Child Left Behind Act of 2001, students in 30 poor-performing schools were eligible to transfer to better-performing schools. In 21 of those 30 schools, students were eligible to receive supplemental services such as tutoring.[690]

In 2003, S.B. 311 would have allowed public school officials to require home-school students to take state assessment tests. The bill also would have allowed the state board of education to create rules that would affect home-school students. The bill was defeated in the Senate on March 12, 2003, by a vote of 22 to 16.[691]

A bill to create vouchers for students with disabilities, S.B. 15, was introduced in February 2003. This bill would create the Scholarships for Students with Disabilities Program, which would begin in 2004. To qualify for these scholarships, students must have attended a public school in 2003–2004, and their selected private school must be approved to participate in the program.[692]

H.B. 1749, introduced in 2003, would create tax credits for contributions to scholarship organizations. The credits would be worth up to

$250 for an individual and $500 for couples filing jointly. The donations would have to be made to scholarship organizations that provide the majority of their tuition assistance to students who are eligible for the federal free-lunch program. No action on either bill was taken before adjournment.[693]

## Position of the Governor / Composition of the State Legislature

Governor Brad Henry, a Democrat, does not support school choice. Democrats control both houses of the legislature.

## State Contacts

**Christian Home Educators Fellowship of Oklahoma**
P.O. Box 471363
Tulsa, OK 74147-1363
Phone: (918) 583-7323
Fax: 503-218-0200
Web site: www.chefok.org
E-mail: staff@chefok.org

**Oklahoma Christian Coalition**
Kenneth Wood, Executive Director
4604 NW 60th Street
Oklahoma City, OK 73112-4605
Phone: (405) 773-9797
Fax: (405) 773-9798
Web site: www.cc.org/state/ok
E-mail: eternia@sbcglobl.net

**Oklahoma Christian Home Educators Consociation**
3801 Northwest 63rd Street
Building 3, Suite 236
Oklahoma City, OK 73116
Phone: (405) 810-0386
Fax: (405) 810-0386
Web site: www.ochec.com
E-mail: staff@ochec.com

**Oklahoma Council of Public Affairs**
Brandon Dutcher, Research Director
100 West Wilshire Boulevard, Suite C3
Oklahoma City, OK 73116

687. See National School Boards Association Web site at *www.nsba.org/novouchers*.
688. *Ibid.*
689. *Ibid.*
690. Oklahoma Council of Public Affairs, "School Choice in Oklahoma, 2002."
691. See Oklahoma Legislature Web site at *www.lsb.state.ok.us*.
692. *Ibid.*
693. *Ibid.*

Phone: (405) 843-9212
Fax: (405) 843-9436
Web site: www.ocpathink.org
E-mail: ocpa@ocpathink.org
E-mail: brandondutcher@yahoo.com

**Oklahoma Family Policy Council**
Michael L. Jestes, Executive Director
3908 North Peniel Avenue, Suite 100
Bethany, OK 73008-3458
Phone: (405) 787-7744
Fax: (405) 787-3900
Web site: www.okfamilypc.org
E-mail: info@okfamilypc.org

**Oklahoma Scholarship Fund**
Karen C. Horton, Executive Director
3030 NW Expressway, Suite 1313
Oklahoma City, OK 73112
Phone: (405) 942-5489

Fax: (405) 947-4403
E-mail: khorton@betterdays.org

**Oklahoma State Department of Education**
Wendy Pratt, Communications Director
2500 North Lincoln Boulevard
Oklahoma City, OK 73105-4599
Phone: (405) 521-3333
Fax: (405) 522-0768
Web site: www.sde.state.ok.us
E-mail: wendy_pratt@mail.sde.state.ok.us

## State School Report Card

**Greatschools.net**
Web site: www.greatschools.net/modperl/go/
OK

**Oklahoma Education Oversight Board**
Web site: www.schoolreportcard.org

# OREGON

## State Profile (Updated May 2003)

### School Choice Status
- Public school choice: Interdistrict/voluntary
- State constitution: Blaine amendment
- Charter school law: Established 1999
    Strength of law: Strong
    Number of charter schools in operation (fall 2002): 25
    Number of students enrolled (fall 2002): 2,107
- Publicly funded private school choice: No
- Privately funded school choice: Yes
- Home-school law: Moderate regulation
- Ranking on the Education Freedom Index (2001): 16th out of 50 states

### K–12 Public Schools and Students (2001–2002)
- Public school enrollment: 552,144
- Students enrolled per teacher: 17.9
- Number of schools (2000–2001): 1,263
- Number of districts: 198
- Current expenditures: $4,572,000,000
- Current per-pupil expenditure: $8,280
- Amount of revenue from the federal government: 7.1%

### K–12 Public School Teachers (2001–2002)
- Number of teachers: 30,895
- Average salary: $43,886

### K–12 Private Schools (1999–2000)
- Private school enrollment: 45,352
- Number of schools: 347
- Number of teachers: 3,473

### K–12 Public and Private School Student Academic Performance
- NAEP test results:

| NAEP Tests Oregon Student Performance | State (National) 2000 Math Scale = 0–500 | | State (National) 2000 Science Scale = 0–300 | | State (National) 2000 Reading Scale = 0–500 | |
|---|---|---|---|---|---|---|
| | 4th Grade | 8th Grade | 4th Grade | 8th Grade | 4th Grade | 8th Grade |
| Average Scale Score | 227 (226) | 281 (274) | 150 (148) | 154 (149) | 214 (215) | 266 (261) |
| Advanced | 3% (3%) | 6% (5%) | 3% (3%) | 3% (4%) | 5% (6%) | 2% (2%) |
| Proficient | 20% (23%) | 26% (21%) | 25% (25%) | 30% (26%) | 23% (23%) | 31% (29%) |
| Basic | 44% (43%) | 39% (39%) | 39% (36%) | 34% (29%) | 33% (32%) | 45% (41%) |
| Below Basic | 33% (31%) | 29% (35%) | 33% (36%) | 33% (41%) | 39% (39%) | 22% (28%) |

- SAT weighted rank (2001): 2nd out of 24 states and the District of Columbia
- ACT weighted rank (2001): N/A
- ALEC Academic Achievement Ranking: 9th out of 50 states and the District of Columbia

## Summary

Oregon has a strong charter school law, and private scholarship organizations help low-income children attend a school of choice. High school students may take college courses for high school or postsecondary credit or both.[694] Districts may contract with one another to allow students to transfer.[695] Parents and school administrators may also make arrangements to enable a student who is not meeting state academic standards to transfer to another school within or outside of the district.[696]

## Background

The debate in Oregon regarding the rights and responsibilities of parents in providing their children's education dates back nearly 80 years. In 1925, the Supreme Court of the United States struck down a 1922 Oregon law that required all children to attend public schools. Writing for the Court, Justice James C. McReynolds declared:

> [W]e think it entirely plain that the Act of 1922 unreasonably interferes with the liberty of parents and guardians to direct the upbringing and education of children under their control…. The child is not the mere creature of the state; those who nurture him and direct his destiny have the right, coupled with the high duty, to recognize and prepare him for additional obligations.[697]

In 1990, by a margin of 2 to 1, the voters rejected an initiative known as Measure 11, which would have given parents a tax credit worth up to $2,500 either to send their children to the public or private school of choice or to pay for home schooling. The initiative, introduced by a grassroots parent organization, Oregonians for School Choice, also would have mandated interdistrict public school choice.[698]

In 1997, the Oregon School Choice Task Force initiated House Joint Resolution 33, a resolution to put a school choice referendum on the ballot. Had it passed, it would have allowed voters to amend the state constitution to allow parents to use state funds to send their children to public, private, or religious schools of choice. The bill died in committee.[699]

In 1999, the House Education Committee approved House Bill 2597, which would have provided tax credits for contributions to K–12 public school foundations or private school scholarship foundations. Individuals, joint filers, and corporations would have received tax credits of up to $250, $500, and $1,000, respectively. The bill was approved by the House Education Committee on April 21 but made no further progress.[700]

Efforts to pass a charter school bill failed in 1995 and 1997, but in May 1999, then-Governor John Kitzhaber signed Senate Bill 100, Oregon's charter school law. The law allows both new charter schools and conversions from existing public schools.[701] Local boards may charter schools, and rejected charter applicants may appeal to the Oregon State Board of Education. Charters are granted for five-year periods. Charter elementary schools and middle schools receive 80 percent of the district's average per student funding, and high schools receive 95 percent.[702] In 1999, Governor Kitzhaber also

---

694. Education Commission of the States, "Postsecondary Options: Dual/Concurrent Enrollment," July 2001.

695. Oregon Revised Statute 339.125.

696. Oregon Revised Statute 329.485.

697. *Pierce* v. *Society of Sisters*, 268 U.S. 510, 534–35 (1925).

698. Joseph Bast and Robert Wittmann, "A Marketing Plan For Educational Choice," Heartland Institute *Rebuilding America's Schools Report* No. 6, May 1991.

699. Blum Center for Parental Freedom in Education, Marquette University, *Educational Freedom Report* No. 54, December 19, 1997.

700. "Parental Freedom in the States and Nation," *School Reform News*, July 1999.

701. "Oregon Charter School Information," at *www.uscharterschools.org/pub/sp/3.*

702. Center for Education Reform, "Charter School Legislation: Profile of Oregon's Charter School Law," October 2001, at *http://edreform.com/charter_schools/laws/Oregon.htm.*

signed H.B. 2550, requiring that half of the teachers in charter schools be state-certified.[703]

In 1998, Portland became one of 40 Children's Scholarship Fund (CSF) "partner cities." The CSF is a $100 million foundation that matches money raised by Portland residents to fund scholarships that enable low-income students to attend a school of choice.[704]

In May 2000, the Portland school board rejected a charter proposal from a school that desired to contract with a for-profit charter management company, arguing that the state charter law did not allow for such an arrangement.[705] In September 2000, the Oregon Attorney General overruled the Portland school board and affirmed the right of charter schools to contract with a for-profit management firm.[706]

In 2000, opponents of the charter school law obtained fewer than half of the 66,286 signatures needed to place a repeal initiative on the November ballot.[707]

In 2001, a proposal (H.J.R. 2) was introduced that would have amended the state constitution to allow the legislature to enact legislation creating tax credits or deductions for contributions to education investment accounts and for the costs of tuition and fees at public or private schools. The resolution would have required a vote by the public in the next general election.[708] Another bill (H.B. 2091) would have provided tax deductions for contributions to education investment accounts and would have made interest on such accounts tax-free. Parents would have been able to make withdrawals on their accounts for expenses associated with public K–12 education, higher education, and home schooling.[709] Both H.J.R. 2 and H.B. 2091 died in committee.

## Developments in 2002 and 2003

At the beginning of the 2003 session, House Joint Resolution 7 was introduced to provide tax credits for tuition expenses or contributions to education investment accounts. The bill has been referred to the House Committee on Rules and Public Affairs.[710]

Senate Bill 761 was also introduced in 2003 to ease restrictions on home-school students. S.B. 761, which was passed in the Senate by a vote of 20 to 9 in April and approved by the House 34 to 25 on May 29. Under this bill, parents would not have to alert state officials of their intent to homeschool, and testing requirements for home-school students would be removed.[711]

## Position of the Governor / Composition of the State Legislature

Governor Ted Kulongoski, a Democrat, does not support school choice. Republicans control the House, and the Senate is evenly split.

## State Contacts

**Cascade Policy Institute**
Steve Buckstein, President
813 SW Alder Street, Suite 450
Portland, OR 97205
Phone: (503) 242-0900
Fax: (503) 242-3822
Web site: www.CascadePolicy.org
E-mail: steve@CascadePolicy.org

**Children's Scholarship Fund–Portland**
Tamar Hare, Executive Director
813 SW Alder Street, Suite 450
Portland, OR 97205
Phone: (503) 524-2419
Fax: (503) 242-3822
Web site: www.cascadepolicy.org/csf.asp
E-mail: tamar@cascadepolicy.org

---

703. "Oregon Charter School Information," at *www.uscharterschools.org/pub/sp/3*.

704. See Children's Scholarship Fund Web site at *www.scholarshipfund.org*.

705. Betsy Hammond, "Charter School Supporters Seek State OK of For-Profit Operation," *The Oregonian*, May 24, 2000, p. B1.

706. Michael Ottwy, "Directive Allows Businesses to Run Charter Schools in State," *The Oregonian*, September 7, 2000, p. D1.

707. Center for Education Reform, *Education Reform Newswire*, Vol. 2, No. 29 (July 25, 2000).

708. Oregon Legislative Assembly, 2001 Regular Session, H.J.R. 2, H.B. 2091.

709. *Ibid.*

710. Oregon Legislative Assembly, 2003 Regular Session, H.J.R. 7.

711. Home School Legal Defense Association, "SB 761: Favorable Revisions to Homeschool Law," May 6, 2003, at *www.hslda.org/Legislation/State/or/2003/ORSB761/default.asp*.

**Oregon Christian Home Education Association Network**
17985 Falls City Road
Dallas, OR 97338
Phone: (503) 288-1285
Web site: www.oceanetwork.org
E-mail: oceanet@oceanetwork.org

**Oregon Department of Education**
255 Capitol Street, NE
Salem, OR 97310-0203
Phone: (503) 378-3569
Fax: (503) 378-5156
Web site: www.ode.state.or.us
E-mail: barbara.wolfe@state.or.us

**Oregon Education Coalition**
Rob Kremer, President
9498 SW Barbur Boulevard, Suite 302
Portland, OR 97219
Phone: (503) 244-7523

Fax: (503) 244-7523
Web site: www.oregoneducation.org
E-mail: rob@oregoneducation.org

## State School Report Card
**Greatschools.net**
Web site: www.greatschools.net/modperl/go/OR

**Oregon Department of Education**
Web site: http://reportcard.ode.state.or.us

**Portland Public Schools**
Web site: www.pps.k12.or.us/schools-c

*The Oregonian*
Web site: www.oregonlive.com/special/oregonian/education/index.ssf?/education/oregonian/schools.html

# PENNSYLVANIA

## State Profile (Updated May 2003)

### School Choice Status
- Public school choice: Interdistrict/voluntary
- State constitution: Blaine amendment and compelled-support language
- Charter school law: Established 1997
  Strength of law: Strong
  Number of charter schools in operation (fall 2002): 91
  Number of students enrolled (fall 2002): 33,656
- Publicly funded private school choice: Yes
- Privately funded school choice: Yes
- Home-school law: High regulation
- Ranking on the Education Freedom Index (2001): 22nd out of 50 states

### K–12 Public Schools and Students (2001–2002)
- Public school enrollment: 1,810,390
- Students enrolled per teacher: 15.5
- Number of schools (2000–2001): 3,183
- Number of districts: 501
- Current expenditures: $15,701,000,000
- Current per-pupil expenditure: $8,673
- Amount of revenue from the federal government: 5.1%

### K–12 Public School Teachers (2001–2002)
- Number of teachers: 116,900
- Average salary: $50,599

## K–12 Private Schools (1999–2000)
- Private school enrollment: 339,484
- Number of schools: 1,964
- Number of teachers: 24,453

### K–12 Public and Private School Student Academic Performance
- NAEP test results:

| NAEP Tests Pennsylvania Student Performance | State (National) 2000 Math Scale = 0–500 | | State (National) 2000 Science Scale = 0–300 | | State (National) 2000 Reading Scale = 0–500 | |
|---|---|---|---|---|---|---|
| | 4th Grade | 8th Grade | 4th Grade | 8th Grade | 4th Grade | 8th Grade |
| Average Scale Score | N/A (226) | N/A (274) | N/A (148) | N/A (149) | N/A (215) | N/A 261) |
| Advanced | N/A (3%) | N/A (5%) | N/A (3%) | N/A (4%) | N/A (6%) | N/A (2%) |
| Proficient | N/A (23%) | N/A (21%) | N/A (25%) | N/A (26%) | N/A (23%) | N/A (29%) |
| Basic | N/A (43%) | N/A (39%) | N/A (36%) | N/A (29%) | N/A (32%) | N/A (41%) |
| Below Basic | N/A (31%) | N/A (35%) | N/A (36%) | N/A (41%) | N/A (39%) | N/A (28%) |

- SAT weighted rank (2001): 19th out of 24 states and the District of Columbia
- ACT weighted rank (2001): N/A
- ALEC Academic Achievement Ranking: 41st out of 50 states and the District of Columbia

## Summary

Pennsylvania has a strong charter school law but offers little public school choice. The state has a strict home-school law, and legislation to ease its requirements failed in 2002. Privately funded scholarship organizations help low-income students attend schools of choice.

## Background

On June 12, 1997, Pennsylvania's charter school law, Senate Bill 123, was signed by then-Governor Tom Ridge.[712] Under this legislation, charters can be formed by teachers, parents, colleges and universities, museums, and a number of other entities. A public school can convert to a charter school with the support of 50 percent of the teachers and 50 percent of the students' parents. Charters are granted for five years.[713] Local school boards grant charters, and the state has placed no cap on the number of allowable charter schools.[714] The charter school law includes an appeals process, initiated in 1999, whereby charter applicants who have been denied by their local boards can take their cases to the state Charter School Appeal Board.[715] Students attending a charter school in their district are provided the same transportation services as other public school students. At least 75 percent of charter school teachers must be certified. Charters are funded on the basis of their district's average per-pupil expenditure during the previous school year.[716]

On May 10, 2000, Governor Ridge signed Pennsylvania's Education Empowerment Act, S.B. 652.[717] Under this act, districts with a high percentage of low-performing schools must improve test scores or undergo state takeover.[718] More than half of the students in Philadelphia and 10 other districts scored in the bottom 25th percentile on standardized tests in 1998 and 1999.[719] District leaders were required to submit proposals for school improvement to the state by the end of 2000. Leaders from Chester–Upland in Delaware County suggested that all of their public schools be converted to charter schools or managed by private firms. In 2001, management duties for the Chester–Upland school district (a district in such disarray that the state had assumed financial control in 1994) were divided between three companies: Mosaica Education, Inc., LearnNow, and Edison Schools, Inc.[720] The case of Chester–Upland is more severe than most: It is estimated that nearly 40 percent of its students drop out of school each year, and in 2000, more than two-thirds of the district's students failed standardized math and reading tests.[721]

In June 2001, State Representative Dwight Evans (D–Philadelphia) proposed the creation of a network of 16 charter schools in Philadelphia's Martin Luther King Cluster of schools.[722] Although this proposal was not enacted, Philadelphia schools would begin a turbulent process

712. Pennsylvania Department of Education, Charter School Legislation Web site, "Senate Bill No. 123 Passed June 12, 1997," at *www.pde.state.pa.us/charter_schools/cwp/view.asp?a=146&Q=46483*.

713. Pennsylvania Department of Education, Charter School Legislation Web site.

714. Center for Education Reform, "Charter School Legislation: Profile of Pennsylvania's Charter School Law," at *http://edreform.com/charter_schools/laws/Pennsylvania.htm*.

715. Pennsylvania Department of Education, Charter School Legislation Web site.

716. Center for Education Reform, "Charter School Legislation: Profile of Pennsylvania's Charter School Law."

717. Pennsylvania General Assembly, 1999–2000 Session, S.B. 652, at *www.legis.state.pa.us/WU01/LI/BI/BH/1999/0/SB0652.HTM*.

718. Susan Snyder, "A City Team Studies How to Intervene for Better Schools," *The Philadelphia Inquirer*, November 11, 2000, p. B1.

719. *Ibid.*

720. Michael A. Fletcher, "Private Firms Enlisted to Run Troubled Pa. School System," *The Washington Post*, March 23, 2001, p. A8.

721. *Ibid.*

722. Mensah M. Dean, "Evans Eyes 16 New Charter Members Looking to Convert Schools in M.L. King Cluster," *Philadelphia Daily News*, June 12, 2001, p. 9.

of converting school management to private entities later that year.[723]

On February 12, 2001, by a vote of 9 to 0, the Norristown Area School District approved the state's first K12 Internet-based charter school.[724] The Pennsylvania Virtual Charter School (PAVCS) opened in September 2002 and is operated by K12, the virtual charter school company created by former Secretary of Education William J. Bennett. In this educational program, a parent or guardian supervises a student's work, and an approved PAVCS teacher contacts each student regularly to monitor progress.[725] In December 2002, Pennsylvania Secretary of Education Charles Zogby left his post to serve as a senior manager for K12.[726]

Although more than 2,700 students were enrolled in Pennsylvania's "cyber schools" in 2001, not all virtual charters have been successful.[727] In 2001, two districts rejected E-Academy Charter School's application.[728] One of the chartering authorities, the New Hope–Solebury school board, said that by assuming that students can have a parent or responsible adult supervising them during the day, virtual charter schools were discriminating against low-income families.[729]

Voucher proposals have been unsuccessful in Pennsylvania. In 1995, Governor Ridge proposed two different voucher programs.[730] "Kids I" would have given $1,000 vouchers to families with incomes under $70,000. In complicated proceedings, the legislation died in the House. Later that year, Governor Ridge proposed "Kids II," which would have created a five-year pilot program to give vouchers worth $1,500 to students in 120 districts.[731] Kids II was also unsuccessful. In 1999, Governor Ridge again attempted to establish a pilot program, but legislation was not introduced.[732]

In 1998, Delaware County Judge Joseph F. Battle ruled against the school district's plan to give students attending schools in other districts vouchers worth up to $1,000. The district had designed the voucher proposal to ease overcrowded classrooms.[733] The $1.2 million plan would have given $250 vouchers to kindergarten students, $500 vouchers to students in grades 1 through 8, and $1,000 vouchers to high school students.[734]

Despite the failure of Pennsylvania's voucher legislation, a privately funded scholarship organization, Children's Scholarship Fund–Philadelphia, has been in operation in Philadelphia since 1998.[735] Since its founding, the organization has awarded more than 2,500 scholarships. CSF–Philadelphia functions under Children First America, a nationwide privately funded scholarship program, and matches the funds that parents pay for their children's private school tuition.

Governor Ridge was also a proponent of education-related tax credits. In 2001, legislators passed House Bill 996, Governor Ridge's plan to give corporations a tax credit for donations to scholarship organizations.[736] Under this legislation, businesses can receive a credit against their state taxes of 75 cents for every dollar they

723. Susan Snyder, "Disband School Board, Install Edison," *The Philadelphia Inquirer*, October 23, 2001, p. B10.

724. Martha Woodall, "School Board Oks Virtual Charter School," *The Philadelphia Inquirer*, February 14, 2001, p. C2.

725. Pennsylvania Virtual Charter School, "Teaching Methods," at *www.pavcs.org/program/methods.html*.

726. Ovetta Wiggins and Dale Mezzacappa, "Pa.'s Education Secretary Resigns," *The Philadelphia Inquirer*, December 18, 2002, p. B2.

727. Pennsylvania School Boards Association, Inc., "Cyber Schools Enrolling Thousands, Costing Taxpayers Millions, School Boards Group Reports," news release, October 16, 2001.

728. Oshrat Carmiel, "Application Rejected for an Online Charter," *The Philadelphia Inquirer*, February 28, 2001, p. B3.

729. *Ibid.*

730. Deirdre Shaw, "School Vouchers Are Ruled Illegal," *The Philadelphia Inquirer*, October 15, 1998, p. A1, and Friedman–Blum *Educational Freedom Report* No. 67, January 22, 1999.

731. See National School Boards Association Web site at *www.nsba.org/novouchers*.

732. *Ibid.*

733. Shaw, "School Vouchers Are Ruled Illegal."

734. *Ibid.*

735. Martha Woodall, "Program Eases Way to Private Schools," *The Philadelphia Inquirer*, August 16, 2002, p. B1.

invest.[737] The total tax credits given by the state in any year may not exceed $30 million.[738]

In 2001, the Home School Legal Defense Association (HSLDA) challenged three Pennsylvania districts for requesting "unauthorized information" and incorrectly communicating state law to home-school families.[739] The Bangor Area School District and the Perkiomen Valley School District were found to have misled parents regarding a request for student portfolios, and the Wyalusing Area School District assumed authority, not granted by state law, to "examine all textbooks and curriculum materials for home-schoolers."[740] No suit was filed, but the HSLDA responded to complaints from parents and contacted each district.

## Developments in 2002 and 2003

State officials appropriated additional funds for charter schools in the 2002–2003 budget and gave districts, which had been responsible for funding all of their charter schools, a reimbursement equal to 30 percent of their charter schools' per-pupil expenditure throughout the previous year.[741] Analysts expect districts with 100 or more charter students to benefit the most from the revised funding.

On June 29, 2002, then-Governor Mark S. Schweiker signed H.B. 4 into law, transferring chartering authority for Internet charter schools from local districts to the Pennsylvania Department of Education. The bill stipulated new administrative and supervisory details for the schools.[742]

In August 2002, Representative Samuel E. Rohrer (R–Berks County) introduced H. B. 2560 to loosen Pennsylvania's home-school law.[743] The bill would have allowed home-schooling parents simply to send a written notice to the state at least 30 days before beginning a program, easing existing regulations that require the authorization of several documents in order to home-school.[744] Representative Rohrer's bill was tabled in November.[745]

In 2002, businesses donated more than $455,000 to CSF–Philadelphia for student scholarships. This project enabled recipients to attend 205 private schools. In 2002, scholarship programs such as CSF–Philadelphia enabled 700 students to attend private schools for the first time.[746]

S.B. 384 was introduced in 2003 to allow home-school students to participate in extracurricular public school activities. The bill was referred to the Senate Committee on Education in March.[747]

736. Pennsylvania Office of the Governor, "Gov. Ridge Urges Pennsylvania Businesses to Invest in Education," news release, May 22, 2001.

737. Center for Education Reform, *Education Reform Newswire*, June 5, 2001, at *www.edreform.com/update/2001/010605.html*.

738. See National School Boards Association Web site at *www.nsba.org/novouchers*.

739. Home School Legal Defense Association, "Pennsylvania: A Barrage of School District Harassment," May 8, 2001, at *www.hslda.org/docs/news/hslda/200106182.asp*.

740. *Ibid.*

741. Benjamin Y. Lowe, "Districts Get Aid for Charter Tuitions," *The Philadelphia Inquirer*, July 15, 2002, p. B1.

742. See Pennsylvania Legislature Web site at *www.legis.state.pa.us*.

743. Ellen Sorokin, "State Eyes Reducing Home-School Filings," *The Washington Times*, August 6, 2002, p. A7.

744. *Ibid.*

745. Home School Legal Defense Association, "Pennsylvania Homeschool Legislation Effectively Dead for 2002," November 18, 2002, at *www.hslda.org/hs/state/pa/200211180.asp*.

746. Woodall, "Program Eases Way to Private Schools."

747. Home School Legal Defense Association, "Senate Bill 384: Allowing Homeschool Students to Participate in Extracurricular Activities," March 13, 2003, at *www.hslda.org/Legislation/State/pa/2003/PASB384/default.asp*.

## Position of the Governor / Composition of the State Legislature

Governor Edward G. Rendell, a Democrat, does not support school choice. Republicans control both houses of the legislature.

## State Contacts

### Allegheny Institute for Public Policy
Jake Haulk, President
Frank Gamrat, Senior Research Associate
305 Mt. Lebanon Boulevard, Suite 305
Pittsburgh, PA 15234
Phone: (412) 440-0079
Fax: (412) 440-0085
Web site: www.alleghenyinstitute.org
E-mail: Frank@alleghenyinstitute.org

### Archdiocese of Philadelphia
Guy Ciarrocchi, Esquire
Director, Office for Public Affairs
222 North 17th Street
Philadelphia, PA 19103
Phone: (215) 587-3509
Fax: (215) 587-0515
Web site: www.archdiocese-phl.org
E-mail: pubaff@adphila.org

### Catholic Homeschoolers of Pennsylvania
101 South College Street
Myerstown, PA 17067-1212
Phone: (717) 866-5425
Fax: (717) 866-9383
Web site: www.catholichomeschoolpa.org
E-mail: info@catholichomeschoolpa.org

### CEO America, Lehigh Valley
Gloria Matarelli, Administrative Assistant
33 South 7th Street, Suite 250
Allentown, PA 18101
Phone: (610) 776-8740
Fax: (610) 776-8741
Web site: www.ceoamerica.net

### Charter Schools Project
Dr. Chenzie Grignano, Director
507 Rockwell Hall, 600 Forbes Avenue
Duquesne University
Pittsburgh, PA 15282
Phone: (412) 396-4492
Fax: (412) 396-6175
Web site: www.bus.duk.edu/charter

### Children First America Delaware County
Doreen Strand, Executive Director
2512 West 2nd Street
Chester, PA 19013
Phone: (610) 497-3445
Fax: (610) 497-3451

Web site: www.childrenfirstamerica.org
E-mail: CFADelaware@aol.com

### Children's Scholarship Fund Philadelphia
Ina Lipman, Executive Director
Victoria Sambursky, Program Director
P.O. Box 22463
Philadelphia, PA 19110
Phone: (215) 670-8411
Fax: (215) 670-8413

### Children's Scholarship Fund Pittsburgh
Gael Byrnes, Executive Director
55 West Superior, Suite 3N
Chicago, IL 60610
Phone: (312) 960-0205
Fax: (312) 377-1837
Web site: www.scholarshipfund.org
E-mail: gbyrnes@csfchicago.org

### Christian Home School Association of Pennsylvania
P.O. Box 115
Mount Joy, PA 17552-0115
Phone: (717) 661-2428
Fax: (717) 653-2454
Web site: www.chapboard.org
E-mail: chap@chapboard.org

### Commonwealth Foundation for Public Policy Alternatives
Matthew Brouillette, President
225 State Street, Suite 302
Harrisburg, PA 17101
Phone: (717) 671-1901
Fax: (717) 671-1905
Web site: www.commonwealthfoundation.org
E-mail: brouillette@commonwealthfoundation.org

### Misciagna Challenge Scholarship Program
Tim Lucko, Program Coordinator
728 Ben Franklin Highway
Ebensburg, PA 15931
Phone: (814) 471-6885
Fax: (814) 472-8020
E-mail: tlucko@dioceseaj.org

### Pennsylvania Catholic Conference
Frederick Cabell, Jr., Esquire
Director, Education Department
P.O. Box 2835
223 North Street
Harrisburg, PA 17105
Phone: (717) 238-9613
Fax: (717) 238-1473
Web site: www.pacatholic.org
E-mail: fcabell@pacatholic.org

**Pennsylvania Department of Education**
Vicki L. Phillips, Secretary of Education
333 Market Street
Harrisburg, PA 17126
Phone: (717) 783-6788
Fax: (717) 787-7222
Web site: www.pde.state.pa.us

**Pennsylvania Family Institute**
Michael Geer, President
1240 North Mountain Road
Harrisburg, PA 17112
Phone: (717) 545-0600
Fax: (717) 545-8107
Web site: www.pafamily.org
E-mail: mail@pafamily.org

**Pennsylvania Leadership Council**
223 State Street
Harrisburg, PA 17101
Phone: (717) 232-5919
Fax: (717) 232-1186
E-mail: spushnik@msn.com

**Pennsylvania Virtual Charter School**
1 Montgomery Plaza, Suite 905
425 Swede Street
Norristown, PA 19401
Phone: (610) 275-8500
Fax: (610) 275-1719
Web site: www.pavcs.org
E-mail: info@pavcs.org

**REACH Alliance (Road to Educational Achievement Through Choice)**
Dennis Giorno, Executive Director
P.O. Box 1283
Harrisburg, PA 17108-1283
Phone: (717) 238-1878
Fax: (717) 703-3182
E-mail: dennis@paschoolchoice.org

**School Choice Scholarship Program–Erie**
Bea Blenner, Program Director
2171 West 38th Street
Erie, PA 16508-1925
Phone: (814) 833-3200
Fax: (814) 833-4844
Web site: www.childrenfirstamerica.org

**John P. Tramontano Jr. Education Foundation**
Bea Blenner, Program Coordinator
2171 West 38th Street
Erie, PA 16508-1925
(814) 833-3200
Fax: (814) 833-4844
E-mail: bblenner@manp.org

## State School Report Card

**GreatSchools.net**
Web site: www.greatschools.net/modperl/go/PA

**Pennsylvania Department of Education**
Web site: www.paprofiles.org

**Philadelphia Public Schools**
Web site: www.phila.k12.pa.us

# RHODE ISLAND

## State Profile (Updated May 2003)

### School Choice Status
- Public school choice: Interdistrict/voluntary
- State constitution: Compelled-support language
- Charter school law: Established 1995
- Strength of law: Weak
    Number of charter schools in operation (fall 2002): 7
    Number of students enrolled in charter schools (fall 2002): 914
    Publicly funded private school choice: No
- Privately funded school choice: No
- Home-school law: High regulation
- Ranking on the Education Freedom Index (2001): 48th out of 50 states

### K–12 Public Schools and Students (2001–2002)
- Public school enrollment: 157,599
- Students enrolled per teacher: 15.1
- Number of schools (2000–2001): 320
- Number of districts: 36
- Current expenditures: $1,610,108,000
- Current per-pupil expenditure: $10,216
- Amount of revenue from the federal government: 3.8%

### K–12 Public School Teachers (2001–2002)
- Number of teachers: 10,455
- Average salary: $49,758

### K–12 Private Schools (1999–2000)
- Private school enrollment: 24,738
- Number of schools: 127
- Number of teachers: 1,961

### K–12 Public and Private School Student Academic Performance
- NAEP test results:

| NAEP Tests Rhode Island Student Performance | State (National) 2000 Math Scale = 0–500 | | State (National) 2000 Science Scale = 0–300 | | State (National) 2000 Reading Scale = 0–500 | |
|---|---|---|---|---|---|---|
| | 4th Grade | 8th Grade | 4th Grade | 8th Grade | 4th Grade | 8th Grade |
| Average Scale Score | 225 (226) | 273 (274) | 148 (148) | 150 (149) | 218 (215) | 262 (261) |
| Advanced | 2% (3%) | 4% (5%) | 2% (3%) | 3% (4%) | 7% (6%) | 2% (2%) |
| Proficient | 21% (23%) | 20% (21%) | 25% (25%) | 26% (26%) | 25% (23%) | 28% (29%) |
| Basic | 44% (43%) | 40% (39%) | 39% (36%) | 32% (29%) | 33% (32%) | 44% (41%) |
| Below Basic | 33% (31%) | 36% (35%) | 34% (36%) | 39% (41%) | 35% (39%) | 26% (28%) |

- SAT weighted rank (2001): 15th out of 24 states and the District of Columbia
- ACT weighted rank (2001): N/A
- ALEC Academic Achievement Ranking: 34th out of 50 states and the District of Columbia

## Summary

Rhode Island offers limited public school choice. The state has a weak charter school law and no private scholarship organizations.

## Background

In 1971, the Supreme Court of the United States decided one of the earliest legal cases regarding religion and school choice—a case that had originated in Rhode Island. Before this decision, the state's practice had been to give salary bonuses to private school teachers, including those at Catholic schools, who did not teach religious courses and used public school material to teach courses also taught in public schools. The Court ended this practice in *Lemon v. Kurzman*, which set the precedent that state actions "must have a secular legislative purpose…. [I]ts principal or primary effect must be one that neither advances nor inhibits religion; [and] the statute must not foster 'an excessive government entanglement with religion.'"[748]

On June 30, 1995, then-Governor Lincoln Almond, a Republican, signed into law the Act to Establish Charter Schools. The law authorized the creation of as many as 20 charter schools, which were to serve no more than 4 percent of the students in the state. Only the Rhode Island Board of Regents would have the power to authorize a charter school, and it could do so only after a local school committee or the state Commissioner of Elementary and Secondary Education had approved the application. All teachers in a charter school were to be certified by the state and covered by the district bargaining agreement.[749]

In 1997, Senate Bill 2090 would have provided a tax credit of up to $500 for education expenses, including tuition. A similar bill, S.B.

2297, was introduced in 1999. Both bills died in committee.[750]

In 2001, an education tax credit bill was introduced. S.B. 74 would have authorized a tax credit for up to 20 percent of the first $150 of a student's educational expenses, including transportation, nonreligious textbooks, tutoring, and computer technology. Tuition was not included. The bill died in committee.

## Developments in 2002 and 2003

Two tax credit bills, House Bill 7075 and S.B. 2240, were introduced during the 2002 legislative session. These bills would have created a personal income tax credit of $200 ($250 for joint filers) for contributions to scholarship organizations. They also would have authorized corporate income tax credits of up to 75 percent for such contributions, but not to exceed $100,000. Both bills died in committee.[751]

More tax credit legislation was introduced in 2003. H.B. 5426 would create tax credits for donations to scholarship organizations. The credits could not exceed $200 for an individual and $250 per couple. The bill was referred to the House Finance Committee in February.[752] S.B. 179, a similar bill, was referred to the Senate Finance Committee in January.[753]

In April 2003, the Governor's Education Transition Team, formed at the request of Governor Don Carcieri, produced a report on suggested reforms for the state's school system. The Team's proposals included statewide open enrollment, the creation of more nontraditional schools, removing the cap on the number of possible charter schools, and creating a voucher program.[754]

---

748. *Lemon v. Kurzman*, 403 U.S. 602, at 612–613 (1971).

749. Center for Education Reform, "Charter School Legislation: Profile of Rhode Island's Charter School Law," 2001.

750. See National School Board Association Web site at *www.nsba.org/novouchers*.

751. *Ibid.*

752. See Rhode Island General Assembly Web site at *www.rilin.state.ri.us/*.

753. *Ibid.*

754. Linda Borg, "Education Panel Urges More Options for Students," *The Providence Journal*, April 23, 2003, p. B1.

## Position of the Governor / Composition of the State Legislature

Governor Don Carcieri, a Republican, supports charter schools. Democrats control both houses of the legislature.

## State Contacts

**Rhode Island Department of Elementary and Secondary Education**
Keith Oliveira, Charter Schools Division
255 Westminster Street
Providence, RI 02903
Phone: (401) 222-4600, ext. 2209
Web site: www.ridoe.net
E-mail: rid23934@ride.ri.net

**Rhode Island Guild of Home Teachers**
P.O. Box 11
Hope, RI 02831
Phone: (401) 821-7700
Web site: www.rihomeschool.com
E-mail: info@rihomeschool.com

**Rhode Islanders Sponsoring Education**
Kristin Moran, Director
80 8th Street
Providence, RI 02906
Phone: (401) 421-2010
Fax: (401) 331-2033
Web site: www.riseonline.org
E-mail: kristinhmoran@yahoo.com

## State School Report Card

**Greatschools.net**
Web site: www.greatschools.net/modperl/go/RI

**Rhode Island Department of Elementary and Secondary Education**
Web site: www.infoworks.ride.uri.edu/2002/reports

# SOUTH CAROLINA

## State Profile (Updated May 2003)

### School Choice Status
- Public school choice: Interdistrict/voluntary
- State constitution: Blaine amendment
- Charter school law: Established 1996
  - Strength of law: Weak
  - Number of charter schools in operation (fall 2002): 13
  - Number of students enrolled in charter schools (fall 2002): 1,235
- Publicly funded private school choice: No
- Privately funded school choice: Yes
- Home-school law: Moderate regulation
- Ranking on the Education Freedom Index (2001): 39th out of 50 states

### K–12 Public Schools and Students (2001–2002)
- Public school enrollment: 648,000
- Students enrolled per teacher: 14.1
- Number of schools (2000–2001): 1,067
- Number of districts: 87
- Current expenditures: $4,651,774,000
- Current per-pupil expenditure: $7,179
- Amount of revenue from the federal government: 7.8%

### K–12 Public School Teachers (2001–2002)
- Number of teachers: 46,000
- Average salary: $38,943

### K–12 Private Schools (1999–2000)
- Private school enrollment: 55,612
- Number of schools: 326
- Number of teachers: 4,912

### K–12 Public and Private School Student Academic Performance
- NAEP test results:

| NAEP Tests South Carolina Student Performance | State (National) 2000 Math Scale = 0–500 | | State (National) 2000 Science Scale = 0–300 | | State (National) 2000 Reading Scale = 0–500 | |
|---|---|---|---|---|---|---|
| | 4th Grade | 8th Grade | 4th Grade | 8th Grade | 4th Grade | 8th Grade |
| Average Scale Score | 220 (226) | 266 (274) | 141 (148) | 142 (149) | 210 (215) | 255 (261) |
| Advanced | 2% (3%) | 2% (5%) | 2% (3%) | 2% (4%) | 4% (6%) | 1% (2%) |
| Proficient | 16% (23%) | 16% (21%) | 19% (25%) | 18% (26%) | 18% (23%) | 21% (29%) |
| Basic | 42% (43%) | 37% (39%) | 35% (36%) | 30% (29%) | 33% (32%) | 43% (41%) |
| Below Basic | 40% (31%) | 45% (35%) | 44% (36%) | 50% (41%) | 45% (39%) | 35% (28%) |

- SAT weighted rank (2001): 24th out of 24 states and the District of Columbia
- ACT weighted rank (2001): N/A
- ALEC Academic Achievement: 46th out of 50 states and the District of Columbia

## Summary

South Carolina offers little public school choice and has a weak charter school law. Low-income students may apply for scholarships provided by private scholarship foundations.

## Background

On June 18, 1996, then-Governor David Beasley signed South Carolina's first charter school law, Act 447. The law was revised in 2002, but many of the original provisions were maintained. Local school boards grant charters, but an appeals provision allows the South Carolina Department of Education to overrule a local board. Charter schools can be either new schools or converted public schools. If a school results from a conversion, 10 percent of the teachers may be uncertified; if the school is a new school, 25 percent may be uncertified.[755] Although charters cannot be granted to for-profit organizations under Act 447, for-profit entities may manage a charter school.[756] In addition, the legislation mandated that a charter school evaluation must be conducted five years after the law's enactment.[757]

The original charter law also specified that "under no circumstances may a charter school enrollment differ from the racial composition of the school district by more than ten percent."[758] In May 2000, South Carolina Circuit Court Judge Jackson V. Gregory ruled the law unconstitutional because this stipulation "may require the school to use racial discrimination in its admission process."[759] The case, *Beaufort County Board of Education* v. *Lighthouse Charter School*, originated in 1997, when Beaufort County denied the Lighthouse Charter School's application (the state's first such application). Although the Beaufort district has nearly equal numbers of black and white residents, Lighthouse Charter's application was for a charter school to be located on the wealthy, predominately white Hilton Head Island.[760] Additionally, district officials expressed concern that the school would attract students who had formerly attended a private or home school, thereby increasing the number of public school students and the financial burden of the school district.[761] Before adjourning for the summer of 2000, South Carolina legislators came close to revising the law's racial-composition requirement to allow a 20 percent differential between a charter school's enrollment and that of the district's traditional public schools.[762] However, no decision was made on the issue that year.

In 1999, House 4062 was introduced to create an Open Enrollment Task Force that would "determine the feasibility" of allowing open enrollment in the state's public schools. The bill died in the House Committee on Education and Public Works, and the task force was never created.[763] H. 4070, also introduced in 1999, would have created an open enrollment program but also died in this committee.[764]

South Carolina legislators enacted Senate 727, an alternative school law, during the 1999–2000 session. Under this legislation, districts must create at least one alternative school (or be

---

755. South Carolina Legislature, 1996 Session, H. 4443, and 2002 Session, S. 12. See also Weaver B. Rogers, Ph.D., and Associates, *South Carolina Charter Schools: A Five-Year Evaluation Report*, July 1, 2002, p. 4, at *www.sde.state.sc.us/offices/ssys/alternative_education/charter_schools/CS5-yearEvaluationReport.doc*.

756. Center for Education Reform, "Charter School Legislation: Profile of South Carolina's Charter School Law," at *http://edreform.com/charter_schools/laws/SouthCarolina.htm*.

757. Rogers, *South Carolina Charter Schools*, pp. 1–2.

758. South Carolina Legislature, 1996 Session, H. 4443, and 2002 Session, S. 12.

759. Darcia Harris Bowman, "Judge Overturns South Carolina's Charter School Law," *Education Week*, May 24, 2000.

760. Lynn Schnaiberg, "Racial Makeup at Issue in S.C. Charter Debate," *Education Week*, April 30, 1997.

761. Center for Education Reform, *Education Reform Newswire*, Vol. 2, No. 26 (July 26, 2000), at *www.edreform.com/update/000706.html*, and Schnaiberg, "Racial Makeup at Issue."

762. Ken Knelly, "Charter School Plans Move Forward," *The State*, July 3, 2000, p. B1.

763. South Carolina Legislature, 1999 Session, H. 4062.

764. South Carolina Legislature, 1999 Session, H. 4070.

part of a consortium that creates an alternative school) to serve students who have been expelled or whose behavior is disruptive in the traditional school setting.[765]

In 2000, several education tax credit bills were introduced. Companion bills H. 4753 and S. 1326 would have provided tax credits of up to $500 to individuals or corporations for donations made to scholarship organizations. H. 4753 passed the House by a vote of 78 to 21 but died in the Senate Finance Committee.[766] S. 1326 also died in this committee.[767] H. 4814 would have offered phased-in tax credits to individuals or corporations for donations for scholarships. Tax credits would have started at $100 in 2000 and would have increased annually until 2004, when they would have reached $500. H. 4814 died in committee.[768]

In 2001, H. 3172 was introduced to provide tax credits similar to those of H. 4753 and S. 1326.[769] It was passed by the House but died in the Senate Finance Committee. H. 3209, also introduced in 2001, would have provided a $500 tax credit under similar conditions, but it died in the House Ways and Means Committee.[770]

## Developments in 2002 and 2003

On July 1, 2002, a five-year evaluation of South Carolina charter schools was released. The evaluation did not reach any conclusions regarding the success of charter schools or whether they should be discontinued, but it did review the original law, possible revisions to the law, and statistics from existing state charter schools. The evaluation also offered recommendations on how charters could be assisted, studied, and improved.[771]

With the state's charter law under review by the South Carolina Supreme Court because of its racial-composition guidelines, then-Governor Jim Hodges signed a new charter school law, S. 12, on July 14, 2002. The new law doubles the percentage by which the racial composition of a charter school's enrollment may differ from that of the traditional public schools in its district—increasing the level from 10 percent to 20 percent.[772] Six months later, on January 27, 2003, the State Supreme Court upheld the constitutionality of the amended law in a unanimous decision in *Beaufort County Board of Education* v. *Lighthouse Charter School*, ending the debate surrounding the charter law.[773]

The new law also established a state-level advisory committee that will review charter applications within 30 days after they are submitted and then send the application to the local school board for a decision. This committee's objective is to ensure that charter applications are judged by consistent standards. S. 12 also extends the term for charters from three years to five years.[774]

H. 3705 was introduced in February 2003 to create tax credits for donations to scholarship organizations. The scholarship organization receiving the donation must award 75 percent of its scholarships to students eligible for the federal free-lunch program. The tax credits would be worth up to $100 in the first year and increase by $100 each year for five years. This bill has been passed by the House and has been referred to a Senate committee.[775]

H. 3200 also proposes a tax credit, but this credit would be for donations to public or private schools or contributions to extracurricular activities or "character education programs" at a

765. South Carolina Legislature, 1999 Session, S. 727, and personal communication with Aveene Coleman, South Carolina Department of Education, Alternative Schools Office, Columbia, South Carolina, April 21, 2003.

766. South Carolina Legislature, 2000 Session, H. 4753.

767. South Carolina Legislature, 2000 Session, S. 1326.

768. South Carolina Legislature, 2000 Session, H. 4814.

769. See National School Boards Association Web site at *www.nsba.org/novouchers*.

770. South Carolina Legislature, 2001 Session, H. 3209.

771. Rogers, *South Carolina Charter Schools*.

772. South Carolina Legislature, 2001–2002 Session, S. 12, at *www.lpitr.state.sc.us/cgi-bin/web_bh10.exe*.

773. John Gehring, "S.C. Charter Statute Upheld by High Court," *Education Week*, March 5, 2003.

774. Personal communication with Catherine Samulski, South Carolina Department of Education, Charter Schools Office, April 21, 2003.

775. South Carolina Legislature, 2003–2004 Session, H. 3705, at *www.lpitr.state.sc.us/sess115_2003-2004/bills/3705.htm*.

public or private school. The credits for school donations would be worth up to $500 for an individual and $625 for a couple, and the credits for support of extracurricular or character education programs would be $200 for an individual and $250 for a couple filing jointly. The bill has been referred to the House Ways and Means Committee.[776]

State Representative G. Ralph Davenport, Jr. (R–37), introduced home-school legislation in March 2003. Under H. 3821, home-school parents would receive 100 percent of the district's per-pupil expenditure for their child. The bill has been referred to the House Education and Public Works Committee.[777]

## Position of the Governor / Composition of the State Legislature

Governor Mark Sanford, a Republican, supports all forms of school choice. Republicans control both the House and the Senate.

## State Contacts

**Partners Advancing Choice in Education (PACE)**
Earle W. Lingle, Ph.D.
1323 Pendleton Street
Columbia, SC 29201
Phone: (803) 254-1201
Fax: (803) 779-4953
E-mail: pacefdnsc@yahoo.com

**South Carolina Association of Independent Home Schoolers**
930 Knox Abbott Drive
Cayce, SC 29033-3320

Phone: (803) 454-0427
Fax: (803) 454-0428
Web site: www.scaihs.org
E-mail: kcarper@scaihs.org

**South Carolina Department of Education**
Rutledge Building
1429 Senate Street
Columbia, SC 29201
Phone: (803) 734-8500
Fax: (803) 734-8624
Web site: www.sde.state.sc.us
E-mail: jfoster@sde.state.sc.us

**South Carolina Home Educators Association**
P.O. Box 3231
Columbia, SC 29230-3231
Phone: (803) 772-2330
Web site: www.christianity.com/schea
E-mail: SCHEA1@aol.com

**South Carolina Policy Council**
Edward T. McMullen, Jr., President
Gerry Dickinson, Vice President for Policy
1323 Pendleton Street
Columbia, SC 29201-3708
Phone: (803) 779-5022
Fax: (803) 779-4953
Web site: www.scpolicycouncil.com
E-mail: ewl@scpolicycouncil.com

## State School Report Card

**GreatSchools.net**
Web site: http://greatschools.net/modperl/go/SC

**South Carolina Department of Education**
Web site: www.sde.state.sc.us/reports

---

776. South Carolina Legislature, 2003–2004 Session, H. 3200, at *www.lpitr.state.sc.us/sess115_2003-2004/bills/3200.htm*.

777. South Carolina Legislature, 2003–2004 Session, H. 3821, at *www.lpitr.state.sc.us/sess115_2003-2004/bills/3821.htm*.

# SOUTH DAKOTA

## State Profile (Updated May 2003)

### School Choice Status
- Public school choice: Intradistrict and interdistrict/mandatory
- State constitution: Blaine amendment and compelled-support language
- Charter school law: No
- Publicly funded private school choice: No
- Privately funded school choice: No
- Home-school law: Moderate regulation
- Ranking on the Education Freedom Index (2001): 31st out of 50 states

### K–12 Public Schools and Students (2001–2002)
- Public school enrollment: 126,560
- Students enrolled per teacher: 13.9
- Number of schools (2000–2001): 756
- Number of districts: 176
- Current expenditures: $815,244,000
- Current per-pupil expenditure: $6,442
- Amount of revenue from the federal government: 10.0%

### K–12 Public School Teachers (2001–2002)
- Number of teachers: 9,089
- Average salary: $31,295

### K–12 Private Schools (1999–2000)
- Private school enrollment: 9,364
- Number of schools: 83
- Number of teachers: 743

### K–12 Public and Private School Student Academic Performance
- NAEP test results:

| NAEP Tests South Dakota Student Performance | State (National) 2000 Math Scale = 0–500 | | State (National) 2000 Science Scale = 0–300 | | State (National) 2000 Reading Scale = 0–500 | |
|---|---|---|---|---|---|---|
| | 4th Grade | 8th Grade | 4th Grade | 8th Grade | 4th Grade | 8th Grade |
| Average Scale Score | N/A (226) | N/A (274) | N/A (148) | N/A (149) | N/A (215) | N/A (261) |
| Advanced | N/A (3%) | N/A (5%) | N/A (3%) | N/A (4%) | N/A (6%) | N/A (2%) |
| Proficient | N/A (23%) | N/A (21%) | N/A (25%) | N/A (26%) | N/A (23%) | N/A (29%) |
| Basic | N/A (43%) | N/A (39%) | N/A (36%) | N/A (29%) | N/A (32%) | N/A (41%) |
| Below Basic | N/A (31%) | N/A (35%) | N/A (36%) | N/A (41%) | N/A (39%) | N/A (28%) |

- SAT weighted rank (2001): N/A
- ACT weighted rank (2001): 9th out of 26 states
- ALEC Academic Achievement Ranking: 18th out of 50 states and the District of Columbia

## Summary

South Dakota offers statewide public school choice. High school students may take college courses at public universities for high school or postsecondary credit or both.[778]

## Background

On March 11, 1997, then-Governor William Janklow signed South Dakota's open enrollment law, House Bill 1075. Under this law, any student may attend any public school in the state. If neither the sending nor the receiving district provides transportation, it becomes the parents' responsibility.[779]

During the 2000 legislative session, two school choice bills were introduced. H.B. 1241 would have established independent, nonsectarian public "voucher schools." Students in voucher schools would have received a "nonsectarian voucher" worth $3,666 for tuition. The bill was approved in committee but was defeated on the House floor.[780]

The second bill, H.B. 1265, would have provided students with vouchers to attend accredited private schools. The vouchers would have been awarded for the amount of the private school's tuition or one-third of the state's expenditure per public school pupil, whichever was less. If test scores at participating schools failed to exceed national averages for two consecutive years, the South Dakota Department of Education and Cultural Affairs could have refused to grant vouchers for those schools. This bill likewise was approved in committee but was defeated by a House vote.[781]

### Developments in 2002 and 2003

In 2002, South Dakota lawmakers narrowly voted down a bill that would have allowed home-school students to participate in public school athletic teams. The bill, H.B. 1072, was approved by the House Education Committee by a vote of 11 to 4, but when it reached the full House, it was defeated by one vote: 34 to 33.[782]

## Position of the Governor / Composition of the State Legislature

Governor Mike Rounds, a Republican, has no stated position on school choice. Republicans control both houses of the legislature.

## State Contacts

**Citizens for Choice in Education**
Kay Glover, Founder
411 Glover Street
Sturgis, SD 57785
Phone: (605) 347-2495
Fax: (605) 347-6390

**Great Plains Public Policy Institute**
Ronald Williamson, President
P.O. Box 88138
Sioux Falls, SD 57109
Phone: (605) 334-9400
Fax: (605) 731-0043
Web site: www.greatplainsppi.org
E-mail: ron.williamson@greatplainsppi.org

**South Dakota Christian Home Educators**
P.O. Box 9571
Rapid City, SD 57709-9571
Phone: (605) 348-2001
Fax: (605) 341-2447
Web site: www.sdche.org
E-mail: gkoenig@rushmore.com

**South Dakota Department of Education and Cultural Affairs**
700 Governors Drive
Pierre, SD 57501
Phone: (605) 773-3134
Web site: http://www.state.sd.us/deca

---

778. Education Commission of the States, "Postsecondary Options: Dual/Concurrent Enrollment," July 2001.

779. See South Dakota Legislative Research Council Web site at *http://legis.state.sd.us/sessions/1997/1075.htm*.

780. See South Dakota Legislative Research Council Web site at *http://legis.state.sd.us/sessions/2000/index.cfm?FuseAction=TextSearch*.

781. *Ibid.*

782. South Dakota Legislature, 2002 Session, H. 1072, at *http://legis.state.sd.us/sessions/2002/1072.htm*; Home School Legal Defense Association, "South Dakota Rejects Interscholastic Sports for Home Schoolers," February 6, 2002, at *www.hslda.org/hs/state/SD/200202060.asp*.

## South Dakota Family Policy Council

Rob Regier, Executive Director
3130 West 57th Street, Suite 108
Sioux Falls, SD 57106
Phone: (605) 335-8100
Fax: (605) 336-1926
Web site: http://www.sdfamily.org/
E-mail: mail@sdfamily.org

## State School Report Card

**Greatschools.net**
Web site: www.greatschools.net/modperl/go/SD

**South Dakota Department of Education and Cultural Affairs**[783]
Web site: www.state.sd.us/deca/finance/Data/02digest/index.htm

---

783. South Dakota provides district-level information.

# TENNESSEE

## State Profile (Updated May 2003)

### School Choice Status
- Public school choice: Intradistrict and interdistrict/voluntary
- State constitution: Compelled-support language
- Charter school law: Established 2002
  Strength of law: Weak
  Number of charter schools in operation (fall 2002): 0
  Number of students enrolled in charter schools (fall 2002): 0
- Publicly funded private school choice: No
- Privately funded school choice: Yes
- Home-school law: Moderate regulation
- Ranking on the Education Freedom Index (2001): 40th out of 50 states

### K–12 Public Schools and Students (2001–2002)
- Public school enrollment: 938,162
- Students enrolled per teacher: 16.2
- Number of schools (2000–2001): 1,575
- Number of districts: 139
- Current expenditures: $5,131,548,000
- Current per-pupil expenditure: $5,470
- Amount of revenue from the federal government: 8.9%

### K–12 Public School Teachers (2001–2002)
- Number of teachers: 58,059
- Average salary: $38,554

### K–12 Private Schools (1999–2000)
- Private school enrollment: 93,680
- Number of schools: 533
- Number of teachers: 7,921

### K–12 Public and Private School Student Academic Performance
- NAEP test results:

| NAEP Tests Tennessee Student Performance | State (National) 2000 Math Scale = 0–500 | | State (National) 2000 Science Scale = 0–300 | | State (National) 2000 Reading Scale = 0–500 | |
|---|---|---|---|---|---|---|
| | 4th Grade | 8th Grade | 4th Grade | 8th Grade | 4th Grade | 8th Grade |
| Average Scale Score | 220 (226) | 263 (274) | 147 (148) | 146 (149) | 212 (215) | 259 (261) |
| Advanced | 1% (3%) | 2% (5%) | 3% (3%) | 2% (4%) | 5% (6%) | 1% (2%) |
| Proficient | 17% (23%) | 15% (21%) | 23% (25%) | 23% (26%) | 20% (23%) | 25% (29%) |
| Basic | 42% (43%) | 36% (39%) | 37% (36%) | 32% (29%) | 33% (32%) | 45% (41%) |
| Below Basic | 40% (31%) | 47% (35%) | 37% (36%) | 43% (41%) | 42% (39%) | 29% (28%) |

- SAT weighted rank (2001): N/A
- ACT weighted rank (2001): 24th out of 26 states
- ALEC Academic Achievement Ranking: 47th out of 50 states and the District of Columbia

## Summary

The legislature passed a weak charter school bill in 2002. Junior and senior high school students may enroll in college courses for secondary and higher education credit.[784] Privately funded scholarship programs are serving students in Chattanooga, Memphis, and Knoxville. Students in state-designated low-performing schools may transfer to other public schools in the district.

## Background

In 1998, then-Governor Don Sundquist proposed charter school legislation. House Bill 2553 would have allowed local boards to charter schools. Rejected charters could have appealed to the state.[785] The bill died in a House subcommittee.[786]

In 2000, Tennessee legislators introduced two bills to address the problem of overcrowded schools. H.B. 2706 and Senate Bill 2248 would have allowed eight districts that were categorized as "high-growth" to contract with private schools to enroll students who wanted to transfer.[787] Neither bill was successful.

In a *Chattanooga Times* and *Chattanooga Free Press* survey taken in September 2000 in Southwest Tennessee, 54 percent of respondents favored "school vouchers that allow parents to use part of the taxes they pay for public education to pay for private school tuition." Thirty-five percent opposed vouchers.[788]

The Memphis Opportunity Scholarship Trust (MOST) is a privately funded scholarship organization, formed in 1998, that serves students in the Memphis area and operates in conjunction with the nationwide Children's Scholarship Fund (CSF). MOST scholarships help low- and moderate-income families pay private school tuition. They are awarded in amounts up to $1,500 or 75 percent of the tuition fee, whichever is less, and are guaranteed for four years. In 2000, the CSF matched MOST's $3 million in scholarship awards. Since the program's first year, the number of MOST recipients has grown: 156 scholarships were awarded in 1998, 750 in 2000, and 860 in 2001. In 2001, 1,200 students were on the MOST waiting list.[789]

Chattanooga also has a privately funded voucher program, CEO Chattanooga, which provides partial scholarships for urban students (targeting students in underperforming schools) to attend private school. The program, which operates with Children First America, offers scholarships worth up to $1,700.[790] More than 200 CEO scholarships were awarded in 1998. In 1999, CEO Chattanooga joined with the Children's Scholarship Fund to provide 500 additional scholarships. Currently, more than 3,200 students are on the CEO waiting list. Studies show that students have been more successful after receiving scholarships. An April 2000 survey found that 54 percent of recipients had improved their academic performance.[791]

Knoxville also has a scholarship fund operated in conjunction with Children First America.[792] Prior to 2001, CEO Knoxville awarded 75 scholarships totaling $112,000.[793]

In 2001, Memphis parents started the first out-of-state chapter of Eta Sigma Alpha, a home-school honor society initiated in Texas to "give

784. Education Commission of the States, "Postsecondary Options: Dual/Concurrent Enrollment," July 2001.

785. Rebecca Ferrar, "Governor Allows Charter School Plan to Die for Session, Move to Study Group," *The Knoxville News–Sentinel*, April 1, 1998, p. A3.

786. National Conference of State Legislatures, "Charter Schools," June 3, 1998.

787. See National School Boards Association Web site at *www.nsba.org/novouchers*.

788. Pam Sohn, "Candidates' Education Views Differ," *Times Free Press*, September 27, 2000.

789. Jenny Havron, "Scholarship Fund Helps Students Attend Private Schools," *Memphis Business Journal*, January 22, 2001.

790. See Children First Tennessee Web site at *www.childrenfirsttn.org*.

791. Center for Education Reform, *Education Reform Newswire*, April 5, 2000, at *http://edreform.com/update/000406.html*.

792. Children First America, "Private Scholarship Initiatives," at *www.childrenfirstamerica.org*.

793. Personal communication with Tamara Ownby, Donor Services Officer, CEO Knoxville, April 24, 2003.

home-school students an advantage when applying to college." By December 2002, Eta Sigma Alpha had 20 chapters in the United States, and an application for a second chapter in Tennessee was under review.[794]

## Developments in 2002 and 2003

On July 4, 2002, then-Governor Don Sundquist signed H.B. 1131, creating Tennessee's charter school program.[795] To date, Tennessee has no charter schools.[796] Tennessee offers three types of charters: schools for students who were previously in schools that had failed to make "adequate yearly progress"; programs that are "designed to address the needs of students with special needs, as specified by the Individuals with Disabilities Education Act"; and converted public schools.[797] The Tennessee law stipulates that at least 75 percent of a converted public school's enrollment must be composed of students from a school that had not met state performance standards or students who are eligible for the free or reduced-price lunch program.[798] The local school board governs charter approval and manages charter school funding, which is 100 percent of the per-pupil expenditure from the local education agency (LEA) in which the charter is located.[799]

In 2003, S.B. 1368 and H.B. 1302, a companion bill, were introduced to provide excise tax credits for donations to tuition scholarship organizations. Taxpayers could not designate a particular student as a beneficiary of a scholarship or award more than $5 million to a single scholarship organization. The scholarship organization would be authorized to give scholarships of up to $3,500 for tuition, textbooks, and transportation to a private school, or $500 to attend a public school out of the district. The bills did not receive any action prior to adjournment.[800]

Three bills were introduced in 2003 to offer college scholarship opportunities to home-school students. H.B. 475 and S.B. 144, a companion bill, would fund the scholarships with proceeds from the state lottery. Public and private school students would be eligible for the scholarships as well and would receive the funds before entering college. Home-school students would not receive the scholarship money until after the end of their freshman year.[801] H.B. 1178 would also create scholarships from lottery proceeds; home-school students would have to outscore public and private school students on the SAT or ACT to be eligible. The legislature did not act on the bills prior to adjournment.[802]

## Position of the Governor / Composition of the State Legislature

Governor Phil Bredesen, a Democrat, has stated no position on school choice. Democrats control both houses of the legislature.

---

794. Dorren Klausnitzer, "Home-School Parents Weigh Pros, Cons of Honor Society," *The Tennesseean*, December 15, 2002.

795. Tennessee 102nd General Assembly, Archive Information regarding H.B. 1131.

796. Center for Education Reform, "Charter Schools in Tennessee," at *http://edreform.com/charter_schools/states/tennessee.htm*.

797. Tennessee Department of Education, "Summary of the Tennessee Charter Schools Act of 2002," at *www.state.tn.us/education/ci/cichartersch/index.htm*.

798. Tennessee Department of Education, "Tennessee Public Charter Schools Act of 2002," at *www.tncharters.org/tncharterschoollaw.pdf*; Tennessee Department of Education, "Summary of the Tennessee Charter Schools Act of 2002."

799. Tennessee Department of Education, "Tennessee Public Charter Schools Act of 2002."

800. See Tennessee Legislature Web site at *www.legislature.state.tn.us/*.

801. Home School Legal Defense Association, "Tennessee State Legislation," at *www.hslda.org/hs/state/TN/default.asp*; Tennessee General Assembly Web site at *www.legislature.state.tn.us*.

802. Home School Legal Defense Association, "House Bill 1178: College Scholarships for Homeschool Students," April 7, 2003, at *www.hslda.org/Legislation/State/tn/2003/TNHB1178/default.asp*.

---

## State Contacts

### Children First Tennessee Chattanooga

Gail Tyron, Administrator
102 Walnut Street
Chattanooga, TN 37403
Phone: (423) 756-0410, ext. 105
Fax: (423) 756-8250
Web site: www.childrenfirsttn.org
E-mail: gail@resourcefoundation.org

### Memphis Opportunity Scholarship Trust (MOST)

Gayle Barnwell, Executive Director
850 Ridge Lake Boulevard, Suite 330
Memphis, TN 38120
Phone: (901) 818-5290
Fax: (901) 818-5291
E-mail: gaylebarnwell@rfshotel.com

### Tennessee Department of Education

Andrew Johnson Tower, 6th Floor
710 James Robertson Parkway
Nashville, TN 37243-0375
Phone: (615) 741-2731
Web site: www.state.tn.us/education

## State School Report Card

### GreatSchools.net

Web site: www.greatschools.net/modperl/go/TN

### Tennessee Department of Education

Web site: www.k-12.state.tn.us/rptcrd02

### Tennessee Institute for Public Policy

Web site: www.tnpolicy.org/Education/Education.htm

# TEXAS

## State Profile (Updated May 2003)

### School Choice Status
- Public school choice: Intradistrict and interdistrict/voluntary
- State constitution: Blaine amendment and compelled-support language
- Charter school law: Established 1995
    Strength of law: Strong
    Number of charter schools in operation (fall 2002): 221
    Number of students enrolled in charter schools (fall 2002): 60,562
- Publicly funded private school choice: No
- Privately funded school choice: Yes
- Home-school law: No notice required
- Ranking on the Education Freedom Index (2001): 7th out of 50 states

### K–12 Public Schools and Students (2001–2002)
- Public school enrollment: 4,128,429
- Students enrolled per teacher: 14.7
- Number of schools (2000–2001): 7,519
- Number of districts: 1,215
- Current expenditures: $28,208,002,000
- Current per-pupil expenditure: $6,833
- Amount of revenue from the federal government: 9.6%

### K–12 Public School Teachers (2001–2002)
- Number of teachers: 281,427
- Average salary: $39,293

### K–12 Private Schools (1999–2000)
- Private school enrollment: 227,645
- Number of schools: 1,281
- Number of teachers: 19,777

### K–12 Public and Private School Student Academic Performance
- NAEP test results:

| NAEP Tests Texas Student Performance | State (National) 2000 Math Scale = 0–500 | | State (National) 2000 Science Scale = 0–300 | | State (National) 2000 Reading Scale = 0–500 | |
|---|---|---|---|---|---|---|
| | 4th Grade | 8th Grade | 4th Grade | 8th Grade | 4th Grade | 8th Grade |
| Average Scale Score | 223 (226) | 275 (274) | 147 (148) | 144 (149) | 217 (215) | 262 (261) |
| Advanced | 2% (3%) | 3% (5%) | 2% (3%) | 2% (4%) | 5% (6%) | 1% (2%) |
| Proficient | 25% (23%) | 21% (21%) | 22% (25%) | 21% (26%) | 24% (23%) | 27% (29%) |
| Basic | 50% (43%) | 44% (39%) | 41% (36%) | 30% (29%) | 34% (32%) | 48% (41%) |
| Below Basic | 23% (31%) | 32% (35%) | 35% (36%) | 47% (41%) | 37% (39%) | 24% (28%) |

- SAT weighted rank (2001): 21st out of 24 states and the District of Columbia
- ACT weighted rank (2001): N/A
- ALEC Academic Achievement Ranking: 37th out of 50 states and the District of Columbia

## Summary

Texas offers public school choice through the Public Education Grant (PEG), but there are significant limitations. Texas has a strong charter school law. Several state scholarship foundations offer privately funded vouchers.

## Background

In June 1993, the Texas Justice Foundation filed suit on behalf of Guadalupe and Margie Gutierrez and their children, Lupita and Vanessa, claiming that the state's monopoly on public education funding could never produce a "suitable" and "efficient" system with a "general diffusion of knowledge" as required by the state constitution. The plaintiffs asked the court to order their school district to contract with a private entity chosen by the family to educate their children. On January 30, 1995, the Texas Supreme Court ruled against the plaintiffs, holding that the state constitution does not require that education be provided by districts or a state agency and that the legislature may decide whether education should be administered by a state agency, the districts, or any other means.[803]

In 1995, then-Governor George W. Bush signed Senate Bill 1 to authorize charter schools and to set up home-rule school districts. Under this legislation, the Texas State Board of Education could authorize up to 20 open enrollment charters with institutions of higher education, nonprofit organizations, or governmental entities. School district boards may convert an existing public school to a charter school if there is sufficient support from parents and teachers.[804]

School districts may form Home-Rule Charter Districts. A Home-Rule Charter District can be initiated through a petition and a two-thirds vote of school board members. A commission must be formed to adopt a proposal. This proposal must be submitted to the Texas Secretary of State. If the Secretary of State determines that it would engender a change in district governance, the proposal must be approved by the U.S. Department of Justice or the U.S. District Court for the District of Columbia. Finally, the charter must be approved by a majority of the voters in the school district.[805] No Home-Rule Charter Districts have been established.[806]

Created in 1995, the Public Education Grant (PEG) offers students the opportunity to transfer out of schools that the state has rated as "low-performing" or in which 50 percent or more of the students have not passed the Texas Assessment of Academic Skills (TAAS) tests throughout the preceding three years. A student may apply to transfer to another school within the district or one outside of the district. The law does not require schools to accept PEG transfers.[807]

In 1996, then-District Superintendent of Schools Rod Paige initiated an innovative plan to allow students in overcrowded Houston schools the option of transferring to nonsectarian private schools. This practice, called "educational contracting," was expanded in 1998 to provide similar options for students who were struggling in failing schools. Since then, the Houston school board has voted several times to enable more students to participate in this program of limited choice.[808]

---

803. See Texas Supreme Court decision at *www.tea.state.tx.us/juris/edgewood/*.

804. See Texas Education Agency, "Texas Charter Schools Frequently Asked Questions," at *www.tea.state.tx.us/charter/faq.html*, and Center for Education Reform, "Charter School Legislation: Profile of Texas' Charter School Law," 2001, at *http://edreform.com/charter_schools/laws/Texas.htm*.

805. Anne Turnbaugh Lockwood, "Charter Districts: Much Fuss, Little Gain," American Association of School Administrators, *Issues and Insights*, November 2001.

806. See Texas Education Agency, "Texas Charter Schools Frequently Asked Questions," at *www.tea.state.tx.us/charter/faq.html*.

807. Allan E. Parker, Jr., "Public Education Grants: Your Right to Public School Choice," Texas Public Policy Foundation, August 1995.

808. Darcia Harris Bowman, "Voucher-Style Program Offers Clues to Paige's Outlook," *Education Week*, January 10, 2001.

During the 1997 legislative session, the enactment of House Bill 318 significantly improved the state's charter school bill by raising the cap on open enrollment charters to 120 and allowing for an unlimited number of charters for schools serving at-risk students.[809] An amendment by Representative Ron Wilson (D–131) would have allowed PEG participants who were rejected by a public school to attend private school at public expense. The amendment, however, was withdrawn.[810]

A poll conducted in 1998 by Scripps Howard found that 54 percent of Texans surveyed supported legislation to create a voucher program to allow students in poor-performing public schools to attend private schools.[811]

In 1999, H.B. 2118 was introduced to provide "opportunity scholarships" for students in poorly performing schools in the state's seven largest school districts. The schools' districts would have had to provide transportation, and the vouchers would have been worth the per-pupil expenditure in the district. Only 10 percent of the students in a school would have been eligible to participate. The bill died in committee.[812]

Another bill introduced in 1999, S.B. 10, would have initiated a program in the state's six most urban counties to provide vouchers for low-income students who were struggling academically. The bill was approved by the Senate Education Committee but was not taken up by the full Senate.[813]

The state's first private scholarship program, the Texas CEO Foundation, began in San Antonio in 1992 with support from USAA, the *San Antonio Express News*, David Robinson of the San Antonio Spurs, and Children First America.[814] Since 1998, CEO Horizon, a private organiza-

tion in San Antonio, has made a scholarship available to every low-income child in the predominantly Hispanic Edgewood Independent School District to attend a school of choice.

Researchers at Mathematica Policy Research, Inc., and Harvard University's Program on Education Policy and Governance released a study of San Antonio's Horizon Program in 1999. The study showed that, contrary to critics' claims, the voucher program did not "cream" the best students from the public school system and that there was no significant academic or economic difference between the students who entered the Horizon program and those who remained in the public school system.[815]

In 2001, the legislature passed H.B. 6, which capped the number of schools chartered by the state at 215. The law also placed numerous new requirements on charter schools, including standards that board members must meet and restrictions on the use of charter school funds. In addition, the law stipulates that charter schools must use a lottery system for enrollment and gives additional authority to the state Commissioner of Education. Despite these new restrictions, the law makes it easier for universities to obtain charters, placing no limit on the number of university-run charter schools.[816]

Three choice bills were introduced during the 2001 legislative session: House Bills 1240, 2666, and 2489. H.B. 1240 would have provided vouchers for poor-performing students in the six largest school districts: Dallas, Houston, Fort Worth, Austin, Northside, and El Paso. Students would have been eligible for the vouchers if they qualified to participate in the federal free and reduced-price lunch program and performed poorly on the state assessment tests or if they had been denied a transfer through the PEG program. The bill required the

809. Texas Education Agency, "Update on Approved Open-Enrollment Charter Schools and Request for Approval of Charter Amendments," November 3, 2000, at *www.tea.state.tx.us/sboe/schedule/0011/charterupdate.html*.

810. See "Texas Legislature Online," at *www.capitol.state.tx.us/*.

811. Steve Ray, "Poll: School Voucher Debate Splits State in Half," *The San Angelo Standard*, March 13, 1998.

812. See "Texas Legislature Online," at *www.capitol.state.tx.us/*.

813. *Ibid.*

814. See Children First America Web site at *www.childrenfirstamerica.org/about/backgrounder.htm*.

815. Paul E. Peterson, David Myers, and William G. Howell, "An Evaluation of the Horizon Scholarship Program in the Edgewood Independent School District, San Antonio, Texas: The First Year," Mathematica Policy Research, Inc., September 1999.

816. Texas Public Policy Foundation, "HB 6: Increased Regulation Over Charter Schools Enforcing a Double Standard," November 1, 2001, and Charter School Resource Center of Texas, "State of the State Charter School Movement," July 26, 2001, at *www.charterstexas.org/resources/state_of_the_state.php*.

state education commissioner to report an evaluation of the voucher program to the legislature by December 2004.

H.B. 2666 would have created a statewide private school voucher program in the event that the U.S. Congress passed voucher legislation. Students participating in a federal voucher program would have been able to supplement a federal voucher with local and state funding to attend a private school. The program would have been governed by federal law and regulations created by the Texas Commissioner of Education.

H.B. 2489 would have provided tax credits for corporate contributions to scholarship funds. All three bills died in committee.[817]

In 2001, Houston's Knowledge Is Power Program (KIPP) Academy, a charter school, had the highest passing rates of all middle schools in the city on state assessment tests. In math, the KIPP students scored in the 81st percentile of the nation on the Stanford–9 test.[818]

## Developments in 2002 and 2003

In 2002, researchers at the Manhattan Institute for Policy Research concluded that, in addition to helping individual students who participate in the program, the Horizon scholarship program has engendered improvements in the public school system. After controlling for differences in resources and demographic characteristics, analysts found that, from 1998 to 2001, Edgewood District students' improvement on the state's TAAS test exceeded or was equal to that of students in 85 percent of all Texas school districts. Edgewood students also fared well when compared to other Hispanic and low-income populations.[819] The program currently serves 1,713 students (approximately 12 percent of Edgewood's student population),

providing vouchers that range from $3,600 to $4,800.[820]

According to a recent examination of Texas charter schools by the National Center for Policy Analysis, 39.7 percent of students are African–American and 20.5 percent are white, while 14.4 percent of students in traditional public schools are African–American and 40.9 percent are white. The study also showed that 57.6 percent of students in charter schools are economically disadvantaged, compared to 50.4 percent in traditional public schools.[821]

Research conducted by the Texas Public Policy Foundation found that, although students who enter a charter school experience a first-year decline in test scores, students who remain in charter schools for consecutive years achieve strong academic gains. The performance of students enrolled in charter schools for two years improved at a greater rate than did the performance of students in traditional public schools.[822]

Students at Houston's KIPP charter school made gains on test scores that surpassed the achievement of students at other area schools, according to a report released in October 2002 by New American Schools. Encouraged by the results experienced by its three schools that opened last year, KIPP announced plans to open 19 new campuses across the country next year.[823]

In December 2002, State Representative Ron Wilson (D–131) pre-filed H.B. 293, a school choice bill that would provide vouchers to low-income students from six of the state's large urban districts to attend a private school. In order to participate, students must qualify for the federal free and reduced-price lunch program and must have performed poorly on the state assessment or have been denied a transfer through the PEG program. Encouraged by the

817. See National School Boards Association Web site at *www.nsba.org/novouchers*.

818. Center for Education Reform, *Spotlight on Schools*, December 2001, at *www.edreform.com*.

819. Jay P. Greene, Ph.D., and Greg Forster, Ph.D., "Rising to the Challenge: The Effect of School Choice on Public Schools in Milwaukee and San Antonio," Manhattan Institute for Policy Research, *Civic Bulletin* No. 27, October 2002.

820. Laylan Copelin, "School Vouchers Slipping as Priority of GOP," *Austin American–Statesman*, June 5, 2002, p. A1.

821. Matt Moore, "Texas Charter Schools: Do They Measure Up?" National Center for Policy Analysis, *Brief Analysis* No. 403, June 25, 2002, at *www.ncpa.org/pub/ba/ba403*.

822. Dr. Timothy Gronberg and Dr. Dennis Jansen, "Navigating Newly Chartered Waters," Texas Public Policy Foundation, April 2001, at *www.tppf.org*.

823. Jay Mathews, "Test Scores Are Up at KIPP Schools," *The Washington Post*, October 21, 2002, p. B4.

Supreme Court's decision upholding the Cleveland voucher program, Representative Wilson said, "There is no more constitutional impediment. They can't hide behind that tree anymore."[824] Representative Wilson also introduced a similar bill, H.B. 658, in 2003. Both bills were in committee upon adjournment of the regular session.[825]

Home-school advocates are supporting H.B. 1449, a bill introduced in 2003 to prohibit discrimination against home-school students regarding publicly funded scholarships for higher education. The bill was referred to the House Committee on Higher Education.[826] H.B. 944, enacted in 2003, also prohibits discrimination against home-school students in higher education. This bill will require colleges and universities to use the same admission standards for home-school students that they use for public school students.[827]

S.B. 586 is a third bill introduced in the 2003 that would affect home-school students. This bill, sponsored by Senator Gonzalo Barrientos (D–14), would require students who leave a public school to begin homeschooling to register with the Commissioner of Education.[828] The bill was referred to the Senate Eduction Committee.

Companion bills H.B. 3474 and S.B. 1822 were introduced in 2003 to create a study of the privately funded voucher program in operation in San Antonio's Edgewood Independent School District. The study would review the vouchers' effects on taxpayers, students using the vouchers, and students not using the vouchers. Neither bill received any action.[829]

H.B. 2465 would create the Education Freedom Pilot Program for districts with over 40,000 students, the majority of whom qualify for the free and reduced-priced lunch program. The House Committee on Public Education approved H.B. 2465 by a vote of 5 to 3.[830] The bill would allow some of the state funds apportioned for students who leave a public school to remain with the district. Private schools that accept voucher students would receive 90 percent of the district's per-pupil allotment.[831]

H.B. 2563 would create a tax credit for corporations that donate money to scholarship organizations. The bill specifies that organizations receiving the donations cannot award more than $3,700 annually per student. The bill did not receive a vote.[832]

In April 2003, a virtual charter school bill, H.B. 1554, was killed in the House by a vote of 75 to 66.[833] Its companion, S.B. 933, was passed in the Senate and sent to the House.[834] The bills would allow universities to contract with private companies to operate on-line schools.[835]

H.B. 2224, introduced by Representative Harold Dutton (D–Houston), would repeal some of the state's oversight provisions regarding charter schools. The bill, which passed the House on May 1, 2003, would require the Texas State Board of Education to approve any governing standards for charters proposed by the education commissioner. The bill's supporters say that too many restrictions have been placed on charter schools because of a small number of schools that have failed.[836]

---

824. Children First America, *A Voice for Choice*, December 19, 2002.

825. See Texas Legislature Online at *www.capitol.state.tx.us*.

826. Home School Legal Defense Association, "House Bill 1449: Prohibiting Discrimination of Financial Aid Grants to Homeschoolers," April 11, 2003, at *www.hslda.org/Legislation/State/tx/2003/TXHB1449/default.asp*.

827. Home School Legal Defense Association, "Texas Bill Would Require Registration of Homeschoolers," March 17, 2003, at *www.hslda.org/hs/state/tx/200303170.asp*.

828. Home School Legal Defense Association, "Texas Bill Would Require Registration of Homeschoolers."

829. *Ibid.*

830. *Ibid.*

831. Matt Frazier, "Bill Backs State Aid for Private Schooling," *Star–Telegram*, March 13, 2003.

832. See Texas Legislature Online at *www.capitol.state.tx.us*.

833. Laylan Copelin, "'Virtual Charter School' Bill Dies in House," *Austin American–Statesman*, April 24, 2003.

834. Michael King, "Small Victory, Bitter Defeats," *The Austin Chronicle*, May 2, 2003.

835. Copelin, "'Virtual Charter School' Bill Dies in House."

836. Melissa Drosjack, "House OKs Loosening of Charter Rules," *The Houston Chronicle*, May 1, 2003.

## Position of the Governor / Composition of the State Legislature

Governor Rick Perry, a Republican, supports charter schools and vouchers. Republicans control both the House and Senate.

## State Contacts

### Charter School Resource Center of Texas

Patsy O'Neill, Executive Director
40 NE Loop 410, Suite 408
San Antonio, TX 78216
Phone: (210) 348-7890
Fax: (210) 348-7899
Web site: www.charterstexas.org
E-mail: oneillp@texas.net

### CEO Austin

Jane Kilgore, Program Administrator
12407 North MoPac Expressway, Suite 100, Box 340
Austin, TX 78758
Phone: (512) 472-0153
Fax: (512) 310-1688
Web site: www.ceoaustin.org
E-mail: austinceo@aol.com

### CEO Midland

Andrea Catania, Chairman
3000 Moss
Midland, TX 79705
Phone: (915) 697-5666
Fax: (915) 683-1988
Web site: www.childrenfirstamerica.org

### CEO San Antonio/Horizon Program

Robert Aguirre, Managing Director
Teresa Treat, Program Director
8122 Datapoint Drive, Suite 316
San Antonio, TX 78229
Phone: (210) 614-0037
Fax: (210) 614-5730
Web site: www.ceofoundation.org
E-mail: tftreat@aol.com

### Children's Education Fund

Fran Sauls, Director
P.O. Box 225748
Dallas, TX 75222-5748
Phone: (972) 298-1811
Fax: (972) 572-1515
Web site: www.todayfoundation.org
E-mail: info@todayfoundation.org

### Children's Scholarship Fund Fort Worth

Patty Myers, Executive Director
Dianna Lucas, Program Director
316 Bailey Avenue, Suite 109
Fort Worth, TX 76107

Phone: (817) 332-8550
Fax: (817) 332-8825
Web site: www.scholarshipfund.org
E-mail: starcsf@lycos.com

### Christian Home Education Association of Central Texas (CHEACT)

P.O. Box 141998
Austin, TX 78714
Phone: (512) 450-0070
Web site: www.cheact.org
E-mail: info@cheact.org

### A Choice for Every Child Foundation

Martin Tyler Angell, Executive Director
9805 Walnut Street, Suite C206
Dallas, TX 75243
Phone/Fax: (972) 699-3446
Web site: www.scholarshiptaxcredit.com
E-mail: mtylerangell@earthlink.net

### Family Educators Alliance of South Texas (FEAST)

25 Burwood Lane
San Antonio, TX 78216
Phone: (210) 342-4674
Fax: (210) 541-8722
Web site: www.homeschoolfeast.com
E-mail: ruth@homeschoolfeast.com

### Fourth Partner Foundation

Fred Smith, President
601 Shelly Drive
Tyler, TX 75701
Phone: (903) 509-1771
Fax: (903) 509-1909
E-mail: fredsmith@fourthpartner.org

### Free Market Foundation

Kelly Shackelford, Executive Director
903 East 18th Street, Suite 230
Plano, TX 75074
Phone: (972) 423-8889
Fax: (972) 423-8899
Web site: www.freemarket.org
E-mail: operations@freemarket.org

### Home School Texas

P.O. Box 29307
Dallas, TX 75229
Phone: (214) 358-5723
Fax: (214) 358-2996
Web site: www.homeschooltexas.com
E-mail: info@homeschooltexas.com

### Houston CEO Foundation/Houston CSF

Herb Butrum, Executive Director
Laura Schlameus, Administrator
952 Echo Lane, Suite 350

Houston, TX 77024
Phone: (713) 722-8555
Fax: (713) 722-7442
Web site: www.hern.org/ceo

**The Justice Foundation**
Allan Parker, CEO
8122 Datapoint Drive, Suite 812
San Antonio, TX 78229
Phone: (210) 614-7157
Fax: (210) 614-6656
Web site: www.txjf.org
E-mail: aparker@txjf.org

**National Center for Policy Analysis (NCPA)**
12655 North Central Expressway, Suite 720
Dallas, TX 75243
Phone: (972) 386-6272
Fax: (972) 386-0924
Web site: www.ncpa.org
E-mail: sarnold@ncpa.org

**National Home Education Network (NHEN)**
Central Region
Laura Derrick, Director
PMB 157
5114 Balcones Woods Drive, Suite 307
Austin, TX 78759
Phone: (512) 345-4895
Fax: (512) 345-6297
Web site: www.nhen.org
E-mail: info@nhen.org

**North Texas Home Education Network (NTHEN)**
801 East Main Street, Suite G
Allen, TX 75002
Phone: (214) 495-9600
Fax: (972) 396-5053
Web site: www.nthen.org
E-mail: info@nthen.org

**Southeast Texas Home School Association (SETHSA)**
PMB 297
4950 FM 1960 West, #A7
Houston, TX 77069
Phone: (281) 370-8787
Fax: (281) 655-0963
Web site: www.sethsa.org
E-mail: sethsa@sethsa.org

**STAR Sponsorship Program**
Patty Myers, Executive Director
Dianna Lucas, Administrator
316 Bailey Avenue, Suite 109
Fort Worth, TX 76107
Phone: (817) 332-8550
Fax: (817) 332-8825
E-mail: starcsf@lycos.com

**Texas Citizens for a Sound Economy**
Peggy Venable, Director
1005 Congress Avenue, Suite 910
Austin, TX 78701
Phone: (512) 476-5905
Fax: (512) 476-5906
Web site: www.cse.org
E-mail: pvenable@cse.org

**Texas Coalition for Parental Choice in Education**
Pam Benson, President
107 Ranch Road, 620 South, Suite 34D
Austin, TX 78734
Phone: (512) 266-9012
E-mail: tcpce@aol.com

**Texas Education Agency**
Felipe Alanis, Commissioner
1701 North Congress Avenue
Austin, TX 78701-1494
Phone: (512) 463-9734
Fax: (512) 463-9838
Web site: www.tea.state.tx.us

**Texas Public Policy Foundation**
Brooke Rollins, President
Christine Patterson, Director of Research
P.O. Box 40519
San Antonio, TX 78229
Phone: (210) 614-0080
Fax: (210) 614-2649
Web site: www.tppf.org
E-mail: brollins@tppf.org or chrispat@tppf.org

## State School Report Card

### Austin Private Schools
Web site: www.austinprivateschools.com

### Greatschools.net
Web site: www.greatschools.net/modperl/go/TX

### *Houston Chronicle*
Web site: www.chron.com/content/chronicle/
special/01/schools/index.html

### Just for the Kids
Web site: www.just4kids.org/us/us_home.asp

### Texas Education Agency
Web site: www.tea.state.tx.us/perfreport/
account

# UTAH

## State Profile (Updated May 2003)

### School Choice Status
- Public school choice: Intradistrict and interdistrict/mandatory
- State constitution: Blaine amendment
- Charter school law: Established 1998
    Strength of law: Weak
    Number of charter schools in operation (fall 2002): 12
    Number of students enrolled in charter schools (fall 2002): 1,259
- Publicly funded private school choice: No
- Privately funded school choice: Yes
- Home-school law: High regulation
- Ranking on the Education Freedom Index (2001): 49th out of 50 states

### K–12 Public Schools and Students (2001–2002)
- Public school enrollment: 477,801
- Students enrolled per teacher: 21.8
- Number of schools (2000–2001): 793
- Number of districts: 40
- Current expenditures: $2,278,647,000
- Current per-pupil expenditure: $4,769
- Amount of revenue from the federal government: 7.5%

### K–12 Public School Teachers (2001–2002)
- Number of teachers: 21,900
- Average salary: $37,414

### K–12 Private Schools (1999–2000)
- Private school enrollment: 12,614
- Number of schools: 78
- Number of teachers: 1,091

### K–12 Public and Private School Student Academic Performance
- NAEP test results:

| NAEP Tests Utah Student Performance | State (National) 2000 Math Scale = 0–500 | | State (National) 2000 Science Scale = 0–300 | | State (National) 2000 Reading Scale = 0–500 | |
|---|---|---|---|---|---|---|
| | 4th Grade | 8th Grade | 4th Grade | 8th Grade | 4th Grade | 8th Grade |
| Average Scale Score | 227 (226) | 275 (274) | 155 (148) | 155 (149) | 215 (215) | 265 (261) |
| Advanced | 2% (3%) | 3% (5%) | 3% (3%) | 3% (4%) | 5% (6%) | 2% (2%) |
| Proficient | 22% (23%) | 23% (21%) | 29% (25%) | 31% (26%) | 23% (23%) | 29% (29%) |
| Basic | 46% (43%) | 42% (39%) | 43% (36%) | 34% (29%) | 34% (32%) | 46% (41%) |
| Below Basic | 30% (31%) | 32% (35%) | 25% (36%) | 32% (41%) | 38% (39%) | 23% (28%) |

- SAT weighted rank (2001): N/A
- ACT weighted rank (2001): 9th out of 26 states
- ALEC Academic Achievement Ranking: 26th out of 50 states and the District of Columbia

## Summary

Utah has public school open enrollment and charter schools. High school students may take college courses for high school or postsecondary credit or both.[837] Support for school choice has risen substantially since Utah residents voted down a tax credit proposal in 1988. Privately funded vouchers for low-income students are offered by Children First Utah, a private scholarship foundation.

## Background

On March 7, 1990, then-Governor Norman Bangerter signed a school choice bill that expanded the state's 43-year-old interdistrict school choice program. The law stipulated that the state's per-pupil contribution and half of the sending district's per-pupil allocation would follow transferring students to the new school district. Under this legislation, districts could choose not to participate, and participating districts had to establish standards for review of applications. Formerly, districts could decide whether to take a student on a case-by-case basis.[838] The law was later amended to make open enrollment mandatory.[839]

According to a 1997 survey by R. T. Nielsen, 79 percent of Utah voters supported parental choice laws that included public and private schools. The survey, conducted for the Utah Coalition for Freedom in Education, also found that 61 percent of respondents supported using tax dollars to provide scholarships to children to attend a school of choice.[840]

In 1997, the Utah Senate passed a tuition tax credit proposal, Senate Bill 61, which offered refundable state income tax credits to parents who chose to send their children to non-public

schools. The amount of the proposed credit was equal to the tuition at a private school or the per-pupil expenditure of public schools, whichever was less. The bill was defeated in the House.[841]

In 1998, the legislature approved a relatively weak charter school law. It stipulated that, to qualify for conversion to a charter school, a public school must show evidence of support from two-thirds of its parents and teachers. Charter schools receive 75 percent of public schools' per-pupil funding. The law instituted a cap of eight three-year charters and required that teachers in charter schools must be certified.[842] The Utah School Boards Association filed a lawsuit challenging the constitutionality of this charter school law on the grounds that the state constitution authorizes the Utah State Board of Education to control one uniform system. On January 19, 2001, the Utah Supreme Court upheld the law, calling the challenge "unreasonable." The court ruled that the state constitution allows the state school board to oversee charter schools, as it grants the board authority over "such other schools and programs that the Legislature may designate."[843]

Another tax credit bill was introduced in 2000. House Bill 401, the Income Tax–Private Investment in Education Act, would have provided a dollar-for-dollar tax credit to parents who transfer their children to a private school. In addition, any taxpayer (either individual or business) would have been eligible to receive a tax credit for contributions to the tuition of a child in private school, and taxpayers could have received a credit for contributions to organizations that provide private school

---

837. Education Commission of the States, "Postsecondary Options: Dual/Concurrent Enrollment," July 2001.

838. "News in Brief," *Education Week*, March 28, 1990.

839. Education Commission of the States, "School Choice: State Laws," December 2002, at *www.communitycollege-policy.org/pdf/ECSDualEnrollStateNote.pdf*.

840. Blum Center for Parental Freedom in Education, *Educational Freedom Report* No. 58, April 24, 1998.

841. See Utah State Legislature Web site at *www.le.state.ut.us/*.

842. Center for Education Reform, "Charter School Legislation: Profile of Utah's Charter School Law," 2001, at *http://edreform.com/charter_schools/laws/Utah.htm*. See also Utah State Office of Education Charter Schools Web site at *www.usoe.k12.ut.us/charterschools*.

843. Center for Education Reform, *Education Reform Newswire*, Vol. 3, No. 4 (January 23, 2001), and Associated Press, "Charter Schools Are Ruled Constitutional," *Utah Deseret News*, January 19, 2001, p. B2.

scholarships to low-income children. The bill died in the House.[844]

On March 19, 2001, Governor Michael Leavitt signed S.B. 169, the Charter School Amendments bill. The law gives school districts the authority to approve charter schools and allows schools whose charters have been rejected to appeal to the State Board of Education. The cap for state-issued charters was raised to 16 charter schools for the 2002–2003 school year.[845]

In January 2001, Children First Utah, in conjunction with Children First America, launched a $2 million, statewide, privately funded voucher program. The scholarships provide up to 50 percent of students' tuition costs each year, up to a maximum of $1,700 per child.[846]

In 2001, then-Representative John Swallow (R–Sandy) introduced H.B. 138, which would have given taxpayers a non-refundable $1,500 tax credit for tuition, textbooks, or school fees. The bill was approved in committee but received no further action.[847]

## Developments in 2002 and 2003

Three school choice bills were introduced during the 2002 legislative session. State Senator D. Chris Buttars (R–Salt Lake) introduced S.B. 69, which would have given taxpayers a credit of up to $2,116 for contributions to scholarship organizations or for the tuition costs of individual students. To be eligible to receive tuition support, either directly or through scholarship organizations, families would have had to earn less than $30,000 and students could not have been attending a private school. The bill was approved in committee but stalled in the Senate.[848]

Representative David Cox (R–56) introduced H.B. 76, which would have allowed a county commission to form new school districts out of existing districts either in response to a citizens' petition or at the request of the State Board of Education, the legislature, the governor, or the existing school district. If the bill had become law, a popular vote would have been necessary to ratify a commission's decision to create a new district. The bill was passed by the House but suffered a narrow defeat in the Senate.[849]

Governor Leavitt signed S.B. 138, the Charter School Amendments bill, on March 26, 2002. S.B. 138 allows the State Board of Education to sponsor up to six New Century High Schools (magnet charter schools focused on math, technology, and science); allows local school districts to sponsor an unlimited number of conversion schools and start-up charter schools, as long as they enroll no more than 4 percent of a district's student population; and authorizes the state superintendent to allocate grants for both start-up costs and ongoing expenses of charter schools.[850]

At the end of 2002, the Utah Employers' Education Coalition voiced support for charter schools, school choice, and tuition tax credits. The coalition presented state leaders with a proposal that $90 million be added to the budget for more school choice options.[851]

In 2003, the Utah Senate passed a tax credit bill, S.B. 34, by a vote of 20 to 8. The proposal was included in the education omnibus bill, S.B. 154. The tax credits, however, were removed from S.B. 154 before the final vote. The Utah House voted 41 to 32 to put a non-binding referendum, House Concurrent Resolution 3, on the November 2004 ballot that asks: "Should Utah's public tax dollars or potential tax dollars be used to fund private education through the use of a tuition tax credit?" The bill died in the Senate.[852]

---

844. See Utah State Legislature Web site at *www.le.state.ut.us/index.htm*.

845. *Ibid.*

846. Telephone conversation with David Salisbury, Children First Utah, January 15, 2001.

847. Jennifer Toomer-Cook, "Sponsor Yanks Private School Tax-Credit Bill," *Utah Deseret News*, February 24, 2001, p. B1.

848. See Utah State Legislature Web site at *www.le.state.ut.us/index.htm*.

849. *Ibid.*

850. See Utah State Legislature Web site at *www.le.state.ut.us/*.

851. Shinika A. Sykes, "Tuition Tax Credit an Answer to School Woes, Employers Say," *Salt Lake Tribune*, December 14, 2002, p. A1.

852. See Utah State Legislature Web site at *www.le.state.ut.us/*. See also Shinika A. Sykes, "Supporters Lobby to Save Tuition Tax Credit," *Salt Lake Tribune*, March 4, 2003.

## Position of the Governor / Composition of the State Legislature

Governor Michael Leavitt, a Republican, favors charter schools. Republicans control both houses of the legislature.

## State Contacts

### Children First Utah
Carolyn Sharette, Executive Director
455 East South Temple
Salt Lake City, UT 84111
Phone: (801) 363-0946
Fax: (801) 524-2374
Web site: www.childrenfirstutah.org
E-mail: carolyn@childrenfirstutah.org

### Education Excellence Utah
Elisa Clements, Director
4897 West Lake Park Boulevard, Suite 100
West Valley City, UT 84120
Phone: (801) 415-2813
Fax: (801) 415-2810
Web site: www.edexutah.org
E-mail: elisa@edexutah.org

### Sutherland Institute
Paul T. Mero, President
Independence Square
111 East 5600 South Street, Suite 202
Salt Lake City, UT 84107
Phone: (801) 281-2081
Fax: (801) 281-2414
Web site: www.sutherlandinstitute.org;
www.utahschools.org
E-mail: pmero@sutherlandinstitute.org

### Utah Christian Home School Association
P.O. Box 3942
Salt Lake City, UT 84110
Phone: (801) 296-7198
Web site: http://www.utch.org
E-mail: friesen_r@msn.com

### Utah State Office of Education
Larry Newton, Director of School Finance
250 East 500 South
P.O. Box 144200
Salt Lake City, UT 84114
Phone: (801) 538-7665
Fax: (801) 538-7729
Web site: www.usoe.k12.ut.us

## State School Report Card

### Greatschools.net
Web site: www.greatschools.net/modperl/go/UT

### Sutherland Institute
Web site: www.utahschools.org/us_home.php

### Utah State Office of Education
Web site: http://www.usoe.k12.ut.us

# VERMONT

VERMONT

## State Profile (Updated May 2003)

### School Choice Status
- Public school choice: Interdistrict/voluntary
- State constitution: Compelled-support language
- Charter school law: No
- Publicly funded private school choice: Yes
- Privately funded school choice: Yes
- Home-school law: High regulation
- Ranking on the Education Freedom Index (2001): 25th out of 50 states

### K–12 Public Schools and Students (2001–2002)
- Public school enrollment: 99,599
- Students enrolled per teacher: 12.1
- Number of schools (2000–2001): 353
- Number of districts: 351
- Current expenditures: $975,884,000
- Current per-pupil expenditure: $9,798
- Amount of revenue from the federal government: 6.0%

### K–12 Public School Teachers (2001–2002)
- Number of teachers: 8,250
- Average salary: $38,802

### K–12 Private Schools (1999–2000)
- Private school enrollment: 12,170
- Number of schools: 122
- Number of teachers: 1,361

### K–12 Public and Private School Student Academic Performance
- NAEP test results:

| NAEP Tests Vermont Student Performance | State (National) 2000 Math Scale = 0–500 | | State (National) 2000 Science Scale = 0–300 | | State (National) 2000 Reading Scale = 0–500 | |
|---|---|---|---|---|---|---|
| | 4th Grade | 8th Grade | 4th Grade | 8th Grade | 4th Grade | 8th Grade |
| Average Scale Score | 232 (226) | 283 (274) | 159 (148) | 161 (149) | N/A (215) | N/A (261) |
| Advanced | 4% (3%) | 6% (5%) | 4% (3%) | 4% (4%) | N/A (6%) | N/A (2%) |
| Proficient | 25% (23%) | 26% (21%) | 35% (25%) | 36% (26%) | N/A (23%) | N/A (29%) |
| Basic | 44% (43%) | 43% (39%) | 39% (36%) | 34% (29%) | N/A (32%) | N/A (41%) |
| Below Basic | 27% (31%) | 25% (35%) | 22% (36%) | 26% (41%) | N/A (39%) | N/A (28%) |

- SAT weighted rank (2001): 9th out of 24 states and the District of Columbia
- ACT weighted rank (2001): N/A
- ALEC Academic Achievement Ranking: 12th out of 50 states and the District of Columbia

## Summary

Vermont has offered a form of publicly funded private or public school choice for students in rural areas since 1869. A limited interdistrict school choice law was passed in 2000. Vermont Student Opportunity Scholarships (SOS) offers privately funded partial scholarships for students for use toward tuition in either a public school or a private school.

## Background

Under Vermont's Title 16, districts that do not have a public school provide tuition to students to attend a public or nonsectarian private school of choice. The "nonsectarian" provision of the law has been the source of much debate since 1961, when the Vermont Supreme Court ruled in *Swart* v. *South Burlington Town School District* that using state tuitioning money to send students to religious schools violated the U.S. Constitution's Establishment Clause.[853] In 1994, the Vermont Supreme Court overturned the decision in *Campbell* v. *Manchester Board of School Directors*, allowing tuitioning students to resume attendance at religious schools.[854] Five years later, the court overturned its own ruling once again in *Chittenden Town School District* v. *Vermont Department of Education*.[855] Chittenden students were using their state-funded tuition money to attend Mount St. Joseph's Academy in Rutland, and the court ruled that this violated the state constitution's "compelled support" clause.[856] On December 13, 1999, the Supreme Court of the United States declined to hear an appeal.[857]

Legislation was introduced in 1997 to permit merit pay for teachers, school choice, and the formation of charter schools. House 393 would have authorized the creation of "educational freedom districts" allowing "full parental choice" to choose charter, alternative, independent, or parochial schools.[858] Another bill, H. 364, would have created a system of vouchers that students could have used to attend nonsectarian or religious schools. Both bills died in committee.[859]

In 1999, a Vermont Public Radio–Macro poll revealed that 55 percent of survey respondents wanted parents to be able to use state funds to send their children to religious schools, while 34 percent did not.[860]

Vermont has a limited school choice law for districts with public high schools. On May 24, 2000, then-Governor Howard Dean signed Act 150.[861] Under this legislation, beginning in 2002–2003, high school students could transfer to another public school with the approval of both the sending and receiving districts. During the 2002–2003 school year, boards could limit the transfer to no more than 3 percent of a school or six students. After 2003, the limit will increase to 5 percent of a school's enrollment or 10 students.[862]

Vermont Student Opportunity Scholarships offers privately funded scholarships that are worth up to half of tuition costs or $2,000 for use toward tuition in either a public school or a private school. The average scholarship award is $1,204. SOS awarded 136 scholarships for the 1999–2000 school year.[863]

---

853. Ethan Allen Institute, "Voucher Decision Will Reverberate in Vermont," *Commentary*, July 2002, and "009: Parental Choice in Education: H.716," *Policy Brief*, March 12, 2002.

854. Act 60–What You Should Know Web site, "Full School Choice Thwarted," June 11, 1999, at *www.act60.org/chitten.htm*.

855. Institute for Justice, "Vermont School Choice," *Legal Cases*, at *www.ij.org/cases/school/VT.shtml*.

856. *Chittenden Town School District* v. *Vermont Department of Education* (97-275), 169 Vt. 310, 738 A.2d 539. See also Ethan Allen Institute, "Voucher Decision Will Reverberate in Vermont."

857. See National School Boards Association Web site at *www.nsba.org/novouchers*.

858. Vermont Legislature, 1997–1998 Session, H. 393.

859. See National School Boards Association Web site at *www.nsba.org/novouchers*.

860. Ethan Allen Institute, "009: Parental Choice in Education: H.716."

861. Vermont Legislature, 1999–2000 Session, S. 0203.

862. *Ibid.*

Legislation that would have created a pilot voucher program was introduced in 2001. H. 468 would have created a program in three counties—Orleans, Rutland, and Caledonia—where district vouchers would allow students to attend a school of choice, including religious schools. Vouchers given to students in towns that have a public school would have been capped at $2,000.[864] The bill died in committee.[865]

In 2001, charter school legislation was introduced. H. 174 would have allowed the Vermont State Board of Education to grant 15 charters. The bill would have allowed for both the creation of new schools and the conversion of public schools. The Commissioner of Education would have been given $500,000 to allot to charters for "initial start-up costs." H. 174 died in the House Education Committee.[866]

Tax-credit legislation, H. 342, was introduced in 2001. Under this legislation, individuals would have been able to receive a tax credit on 50 percent of their donation to scholarship organizations. The bill died in the House Ways and Means Committee.[867]

## Developments in 2002 and 2003

A voucher bill, S. 227, was introduced in 2002 to create vouchers worth 50 percent of public schools' per-pupil costs. Students would have been allowed to use the vouchers for tuition at a public, private, or religious school. The bill also included a provision for home-school students, granting elementary students a voucher worth $500 and high school students a voucher worth $1,000. The bill died in the Senate Education Committee.[868]

Then-State Representative Neil Randall (R–Orange) introduced H. 703, which would have eased restrictions on home-school families. Under current law, the Vermont Department of Education must respond to a parent's declaration to homeschool within 45 days. If the department does not respond or requests a hearing, home-school programs could be delayed. Representative Randall's bill would have made home-school programs operative as soon as parents filed an enrollment notice. H. 703 died in the House Education Committee.[869]

H. 716 would have allowed students to transfer to any public school if space was available. If sufficient space was not available, schools could have used a lottery to determine transfers.[870] The bill cleared the House by a vote of 72 to 67 but died in the Senate with a tie vote of 14 to 14.[871]

Under Act 150, a limited number of high school students were given the option to transfer to another public school. State officials reported 254 transfers during the 2002–2003 and 2003–2004 school years. Due to restrictions on the number of allowable transfers, a maximum of 450 students statewide could have changed schools.[872]

Several school choice bills were introduced in 2003. H. 392 would require districts that have public schools to provide vouchers worth up to $1,000 for students to attend a school of choice, including religious schools.[873] State Representative Nancy Sheltra (R–Derby) introduced H. 391 (similar to H. 468 from 2001), which would create a pilot voucher program in Orleans, Rutland, and Caledonia counties. The program would be subject to approval by the voters of a district, and vouchers would be capped at $2,000 for those districts that operate public schools.[874] H. 262 would allow school

---

863. Vermonters for Better Education, "Vermont SOS: Private Scholarship Program to Fund Public and Private Education," at *www.schoolreport.com/./vbe/articles/sos.htm.*

864. See National School Boards Association Web site at *www.nsba.org/novouchers.*

865. Vermont Legislature, 2001–2002 Session, H. 104.

866. Vermont Legislature, 2001–2002 Session, H. 174.

867. Vermont Legislature, 2001–2002 Session, H. 342.

868. Vermont Legislature, 2001–2002 Session, S. 227.

869. Home School Legal Defense Association, "House Bill 703: Home Study Enrollment," May 8, 2002, at *www.hslda.org/legislation/state/vt/2002/VTHB703/default.asp.*

870. Ethan Allen Institute, "009: Parental Choice in Education: H. 716."

871. Vermont Legislature, 2001–2002 Session, H. 716.

872. Brent Hallenbeck, "Only a Few Opt for School Choice," *Burlington Free Press,* January 18, 2003.

873. Vermont Legislature, 2003–2004 Session, H. 392.

boards to choose to reimburse parents who send their children to religious private schools. No action was taken on the bills prior to adjournment.[875]

H. 57 was introduced to create a voucher system for students with disabilities. Special-education students who are not meeting goals set in their Individualized Education Plan (IEP) would be given vouchers worth the cost of tuition at a school of choice or the state's block grant allotment, whichever is less. The bill was referred to the Education Committee.[876]

Two tax credit bills were introduced in 2003 but did not receive any action. H. 198 would allow individuals or corporations to claim a tax credit on 50 percent of a donation to a scholarship organization.[877] H. 235 would allow home-school families to claim a tax credit on expenditures for educational materials up to $500.[878]

State Representative Frank M. Mazur (R–South Burlington) introduced H. 77, which would create a charter law. Under this legislation, town, city, or district school boards and state colleges and the University of Vermont would be granted chartering authority. The charters could be granted to individuals, groups, businesses, or colleges for up to five years. The Commissioner of Education would appropriate $500,000 to use for start-up grants to charter schools. The bill was referred to the House Education Committee.[879]

S. 121 would allow parents to send their child to any public school in the state, and sending districts would pay 90 percent of state per-pupil grants. S. 121 referred to the Senate Education Committee, but received no further action in 2003.[880]

On March 23, 2003, a Chittenden resident filed suit against the state of Vermont regarding its tuitioning policy. The resident, Dr. Blane Nasveschuk, had paid to send his sons to Mount St. Joseph's Academy in Chittenden, a tuitioning town. Dr. Naveschuk has joined two other families who live in tuitioning towns but must pay out of pocket for their choice schools because the schools are religious. The Institute for Justice represents the families.[881]

## Position of the Governor / Composition of the State Legislature

Governor Jim Douglas, a Republican, supports school choice. Republicans control the House, and Democrats control the Senate.

## State Contacts

**Christian Home Educators of Vermont**
146 Sherwood Circle
Brattleboro, VT 05301
Phone: (802) 254-7697
Web site: www.sover.net/~kelrobin/chev
E-mail: rebrobin@sover.net

**Ethan Allen Institute**
John McClaughry, President
4836 Kirby Mountain Road
Concord, VT 05824
Phone: (802) 695-1448
Fax: (802) 695-1436
Web site: www.ethanallen.org
E-mail: eai@ethanallen.org

**Vermonters for Better Education**
Libby Sternberg, Executive Director
170 North Church Street
Rutland, VT 05701
Phone: (802) 773-5240
Web site: www.schoolreport.com
E-mail: lsternberg@aol.com

874. Vermont Legislature, 2003–2004 Session, H. 391.
875. Vermont Legislature, 2003–2004 Session, H. 262.
876. Vermont Legislature, 2003–2004 Session, H. 57.
877. Vermont Legislature, 2003–2004 Session, H. 198.
878. Vermont Legislature, 2003–2004 Session, H. 235.
879. Vermont Legislature, 2003–2004 Session, H. 77.
880. Vermont Legislature, 2003–2004 Session, S. 121.
881. Institute for Justice, "Fighting for Parental Liberty by Stopping Religious Discrimination," *Litigation Backgrounder*, March 20, 2003, at *www.ij.org*.

**Vermont Department of Education**
120 State Street
Montpelier, VT 05620
Phone: (802) 828-3135
Web site: www.state.vt.us/educ
E-mail: edinfo@doe.state.vt.us

**Vermont SOS Fund**
Ruth Stokes, Executive Director
2239 Oakhill Road
Williston, VT 05495
Phone: (802) 879-7460
Fax: (802) 879-2550
E-mail: vtsos@aol.com

## State School Report Card

**Greatschools.net**
Web site: www.greatschools.net/modperl/go/VT

**Independent Schools Association of Northern New England**
Web site: www.isanne.org/frame_isanne.asp?x=choose

**Vermont Department of Education**
Web site: http://maps.vcgi.org/schlrpt

# VIRGINIA

## State Profile (Updated May 2003)

### School Choice Status
- Public school choice: No
- State constitution: Blaine amendment and compelled-support language
- Charter school law: Established 1998
    Strength of law: Weak
    Number of charter schools in operation (fall 2002): 8
    Number of students enrolled in charter schools (fall 2002): 1,440
    Publicly funded private school choice: No
- Privately funded school choice: Yes
- Home-school law: Moderate regulation
- Ranking on the Education Freedom Index (2001): 42nd out of 50 states

### K–12 Public Schools and Students (2001–2002)
- Public school enrollment: 1,162,780
- Students enrolled per teacher: 13.2
- Number of schools (2000–2001): 1,841
- Number of districts: 136
- Current expenditures: $8,664,590,000
- Current per-pupil expenditure: $7,452
- Amount of revenue from the federal government: 5.7%

### K–12 Public School Teachers (2001–2002)
- Number of teachers: 87,823
- Average salary: $41,262

### K–12 Private Schools (1999–2000)
- Private school enrollment: 100,171
- Number of schools: 582
- Number of teachers: 9,389

### K–12 Public and Private School Student Academic Performance
- NAEP test results:

| NAEP Tests Virginia Student Performance | State (National) 2000 Math Scale = 0–500 | | State (National) 2000 Science Scale = 0–300 | | State (National) 2000 Reading Scale = 0–500 | |
|---|---|---|---|---|---|---|
| | 4th Grade | 8th Grade | 4th Grade | 8th Grade | 4th Grade | 8th Grade |
| Average Scale Score | 230 (226) | 277 (274) | 156 (148) | 152 (149) | 218 (215) | 266 (261) |
| Advanced | 2% (3%) | 5% (5%) | 4% (3%) | 3% (4%) | 6% (6%) | 3% (2%) |
| Proficient | 23% (23%) | 21% (21%) | 29% (25%) | 28% (26%) | 24% (23%) | 30% (29%) |
| Basic | 48% (43%) | 41% (39%) | 41% (36%) | 32% (29%) | 34% (32%) | 45% (41%) |
| Below Basic | 27% (31%) | 33% (35%) | 26% (36%) | 37% (41%) | 36% (39%) | 22% (28%) |

- SAT weighted rank (2001): 12th out of 24 states and the District of Columbia
- ACT weighted rank (2001): N/A
- ALEC Academic Achievement Ranking: 27th out of 50 states and the District of Columbia

## Summary

Virginia offers no public school choice and has a weak charter school law. Children First Virginia, a private scholarship program, provides tuition vouchers to low-income children to attend a school of choice.

## Background

When then-Governor George Allen, a Republican, took office in 1994, he showed a strong interest in education alternatives. His Commission on Champion Schools examined primary and secondary education around the state and recommended numerous statewide education reforms to promote higher academic standards and greater accountability. It also examined educational alternatives and noted that the "most discredited idea in economics is that a government monopoly is the best way to deliver services." In 1994, the commission called for a variety of choices—including charter schools, intradistrict and interdistrict choice, opportunity grants, and tuition tax credits—and suggested vouchers for parents of students whose schools lose their accreditation.[882]

In 1998, then-State Delegate Jay Katzen (R–31) introduced House Joint Resolution (H.J.) 199 to study the feasibility of granting state or local tax credits for private school tuition payments and home instruction. The bill died in committee.[883]

The state passed a weak charter school bill, House Bill 543/Senate Bill 318, in 1998. The law specifies that charter schools must adhere to most regulations applied to traditional schools regarding operations, curriculum standards, and testing and that teachers must be certified. It further stipulates that the schools must be approved by the local school board and does not offer an appeals process. Charters are limited to two charters per district or up to 10 percent of a district's total number of schools, whichever is greater.[884]

H.B. 1740 and its companion, S.B. 866, the Children's Educational Opportunity Act, were introduced in January 1999. The bill would have phased in a tax credit for individuals that make donations to organizations that give scholarships to low-income children in grades K–12. It also proposed a credit of 80 percent to 100 percent of education costs for parents of children in private, parochial, or home schools and public schools other than the child's assigned school. A taxpayer would not have been allowed to take advantage of both credits. The bills died in committee; H.B. 1740 was defeated in the Finance Committee, and S.B. 866 was never considered.[885]

The Virginia Children's Educational Opportunity Act was reintroduced in modified form in both houses of the General Assembly in 2000. H.B. 68 would have provided state tax credits of up to $2,500 for each child to defray the costs of qualifying educational expenses, including private school tuition, textbooks, and tutoring. The legislation also would have provided a tax credit of as much as $550 for each home-schooled child and a $500 tax credit for donors to a scholarship fund (or "school tuition organization") that serves low-income families. School tuition organizations would have been authorized to provide scholarships worth up to $3,100. The bill was defeated in committee on a 13 to 9 vote.[886]

In 2000, Richard and Sherry Sharp launched a new K–6 private scholarship program, Children First Virginia. The program provides low-income students in Virginia with scholarships of up to $2,000 each for tuition expenses at any school of choice. The Sharps pledged more than $4.5 million to the fund. A gift from the Children's Educational Opportunity Foundation of

---

882. *The Governor's Commission on Champion Schools: Final Report to the Governor, Commonwealth of Virginia*, January 1996, pp. 47–59.

883. See Virginia's Legislative Information System at *http://leg1.state.va.us/*.

884. Center for Education Reform, "Charter School Legislation: Profile of Virginia's Charter School Law," 2001, at *http://edreform.com/charter_schools/laws/Virginia.htm*.

885. See Virginia's Legislative Information System at *http://leg1.state.va.us/*.

886. *Ibid.*

America put the funding total at over $5 million.[887]

The 2000 General Assembly enacted H.B. 785, which required local school boards to provide public notice by December 31, 2000, of their intent to accept or not to accept applications for charter schools.[888] The Alexandria school board voted unanimously to accept applications, while the Arlington board voted 4 to 1 to refuse charter applications, saying it already offered many choices for parents.[889] In June 2001, Prince William County voted to accept charter school applications. Falls Church, Loudoun, Stafford, and Fauquier Counties also have voted to consider charter schools.[890] Throughout the state, 82 school districts voted to consider charter applications, and 50 chose not to consider them.[891]

A 2001 Virginia Commonwealth University survey found that 50 percent of respondents favored giving parents tax credits or vouchers to pay for their child's tuition at a private school of choice, while 40 percent opposed such programs. Among respondents who were 29 years old or younger, support soared to 70 percent. Only 32 percent of senior citizens supported tuition tax credits or vouchers.[892]

In 2001, Delegate Jay Katzen (R–31) introduced the Virginia Children's Educational Opportunity Act of 2001, H.B. 1961, to provide tax credits of up to $500 for contributions to scholarship organizations. In addition, the bill would have allowed parents to receive a credit of up to $2,500 per year for education expenses at private schools, provided home-schooling parents with a credit of up to $550 for expenses, and given taxpayers tax credits of up to $500 for contributions to scholarship organizations.

However, in an effort to gain majority support in the House Finance Committee, Delegate

Katzen amended the bill to delete tax credits for parents' expenditures and create a "scholarship only" tax credit program. The Finance Committee approved the scholarship-only bill on January 22, 2001, by a vote of 12 to 11. Subsequent amendments adopted by the House were hostile to the tax credit, and Katzen withdrew the measure.[893]

In 2001, then-Delegate William P. Robinson, Jr. (D–90), sponsored H.B. 2498, the Education Certificate Act, which would have created a parental choice program to provide vouchers to low-income children in grades K–12. The bill died in committee. H.J. 561, sponsored by Delegate Robert Marshall (R–13), would have established a joint subcommittee to study the issues of vouchers, tuition tax credits, and deductions and report back to the governor and the 2003 legislature. This bill also died in committee.[894]

## Developments in 2002 and 2003

The Children's Educational Opportunity Act, H.B. 1119, was introduced in 2002 to provide a tax credit of up to $500 for contributions to scholarship organizations. The organizations would have to grant scholarships to low-income students.[895] Consideration of H.B. 1119 was deferred until 2003.

During the 2002 legislative session, a resolution calling for a voucher task force, H.J. 30, was introduced. This bill would have established a joint subcommittee to study tax credits and vouchers. The bill died in committee.[896]

As a result of mandatory school choice provisions in the federal No Child Left Behind Act of 2001, students at 35 low-performing Virginia schools were eligible to transfer to better-performing public schools. The law requires districts to offer transfers and pay for transferring

887. Clare Boothe Luce Institute, "Luce Policy Institute Creates New K–6 School Choice Scholarship Program," at *www.cblpolicyinstitute.org/cfva.htm*.
888. See Virginia's Legislative Information System at *http://leg1.state.va.us/*.
889. Emily Wax, "Alexandria Votes to Consider Charter Schools," *The Washington Post*, December 21, 2000, p. B1.
890. Christina Samuels, "Board Weighs Next Step on Charter Schools," *The Washington Post*, July 1, 2001, p. T1.
891. Vaishali Honawar, "New Charters Diversify Educational Paths," *The Washington Times*, January 3, 2002, p. B1.
892. Center for Education Reform, *Education Reform Newswire*, Vol. 3, No. 22 (May 29, 2001), at *http://edreform.com/update/2001/010529.html*.
893. See Virginia's Legislative Information System at *http://leg1.state.va.us/*.
894. See National School Boards Association Web site at *www.nsba.org/novouchers*.
895. See Virginia's Legislative Information System at *http://leg1.state.va.us/*.
896. See National School Boards Association Web site at *www.nsba.org/novouchers*.

students' transportation. Low-income students were given priority to transfer.[897]

In 2002, the legislature enacted S.B. 625, which requires all school boards to review public charter school applications. Previously, boards could decide whether or not to accept proposals.[898]

Several voucher bills were introduced during the 2003 session. H.J. 545 would have created vouchers for use at private schools at any level of education, including college and graduate programs, and would have created tax credits for educational expenses. The bill was defeated in committee by a vote of 12 to 8.[899]

H.B. 2761, introduced by Delegate Kirkland Cox (R–66), would have created tax credits of up to 25 percent of donations made by corporations to scholarship organizations that serve students "at risk of educational failure," with a $2 million annual maximum of credits statewide. The bill failed to pass.[900]

House Delegate Robert G. Marshall (R–13) introduced three voucher bills, all of which were killed in separate 21 to 1 votes in the House Education Committee. H.B. 2043, the Virginia Scholarship and Tutorial Assistance Program, would have offered state-funded scholarships for public or nonsectarian private schools and tutoring grants for low-income students. H.B. 1639, which was introduced to ease overcrowded public schools, would have required that public schools with enrollments that exceed their facilities' capacity allow students to transfer. Vouchers worth between $500 and the per-pupil district expenditure would have been given to transferring students. H.B. 2042 would have created the Virginia Educational Options Program through which students in failing public schools could transfer to another school in the district. The bill further stipulated that, if all public schools in a district were underperforming by state standards, parents could receive vouchers worth up to $2,000 to be used in a nonreligious private school.[901]

## Position of the Governor / Composition of the State Legislature

Governor Mark Warner, a Democrat, does not support vouchers. Republicans control both houses of the legislature.

## State Contacts

### Children First Virginia
Judy Baucom, Program Director
9020 Stony Point Parkway, Suite 185
Richmond, VA 23235
Phone: (804) 327-9504
Fax: (804) 327-9505
E-mail: childrenfirstva@yahoo.com

### Clare Boothe Luce Policy Institute
Michelle Easton, President
Lil Tuttle, Education Director
112 Elden Street, Suite P
Herndon, VA 22170
Phone: (703) 318-0730
Fax: (703) 318-8867
Web site: www.cblpolicyinstitute.org
E-mail: tuttles@erols.com

### The Family Foundation
Wayman Bishop, Executive Director
Victoria Cobb, Director of Legislative Affairs
1 Capitol Square,
830 East Main Street, Suite 1201
Richmond, VA 23219
Phone: (804) 343-0010
Fax: (804) 343-0050
Web site: www.familyfoundation.org
E-mail: vafamily@familyfoundation.org

### Home Educators Association of Virginia
P.O. Box 6745
Richmond, VA 23230
Phone: (804) 288-1608
Fax: (804) 288-6962
Web site: www.heav.org
E-mail: office@heav.org

### Home School Legal Defense Association
Tom Washburne, Executive Director
P.O. Box 3000
Purcellville, VA 20134
Phone: (540) 338-5600
Fax: (540) 338-2733

897. Brigid Schulte, "Educators Prepare, Worry Over Effect of Transfer Law," *The Washington Post*, May 13, 2002.
898. See Virginia's Legislative Information System at *http://leg1.state.va.us/*.
899. *Ibid.*
900. *Ibid.*
901. *Ibid.*

Web site: www.hslda.org
E-mail: info@hslda.org

**Landmark Legal Foundation**
Mark Levin, President
Eric Christensen, Vice President
445-B Carlisle Drive
Herndon, VA 20170
Phone: (703) 689-2370
Fax: (703) 689-2373
Web site: www.landmarklegal.org
E-mail: info@landmarklegal.org

**Lexington Institute**
Bob Holland, Senior Fellow
Don Soifer, Executive Vice President
1600 Wilson Boulevard, Suite 900
Arlington, VA 22209
Phone: (703) 522-5828
Fax: (703) 522-5837
Web site: www.lexingtoninstitute.org
E-mail: soifer@lexingtoninstitute.org
E-mail: holland@lexingtoninstitute.org

**Rutherford Institute**
Ron Rissler, Legal Coordinator
P.O. Box 7482
Charlottesville, VA 22906-7482
Phone: (434) 978-3888
Fax: (434) 978-1789
Web site: www.rutherford.org
E-mail: staff@rutherford.org

**Thomas Jefferson Institute for Public Policy**
Michael Thompson, Chairman and President
9035 Golden Sunset Lane
Springfield, VA 22153
Phone: (703) 440-9447
Fax: (703) 455-1531
Web site: www.thomasjeffersoninst.org
E-mail: info@thomasjeffersoninst.org

**Virginia Child**
Donald Coleman, President
P.O. Box 23255
Richmond, VA 23223
Phone: (804) 304-KIDS
Web site: www.virginiachild.org

**Virginia Department of Education**
Belle S. Wheelan, Secretary of Education
P.O. Box 1475
Richmond, VA 23218
Phone: (804) 786-1151
Fax: (804) 371-0154
Web site: www.education.state.va.us
E-mail: seced@gov.state.va.us

**Virginia Institute for Public Policy**
John Taylor, President
20461 Tappahannock Place
Potomac Falls, VA 20165-4791
Phone: (703) 421-8635
Fax: (703) 421-8631
Web site: www.virginiainstitute.org
E-mail: jtaylor@virginiainstitute.org

## State School Report Card

**Chesterfield County Public Schools**
Web site: www.chesterfield.k12.va.us/Admin/
Accountability_New/home.html

**Greatschools.net**
Web site: www.greatschools.net/modperl/go/VA

**Roanoke County Schools**
Web site: www.rcs.k12.va.us

**Virginia Department of Education**
Web site: www.pen.k12.va.us/html/
reportcard.shtml

# WASHINGTON

WASHINGTON

## State Profile (Updated May 2003)

### School Choice Status
- Public school choice: Intradistrict and interdistrict/mandatory
- State constitution: Blaine amendment
- Charter school law: No
- Publicly funded private school choice: No
- Privately funded school choice: Yes
- Home-school law: High regulation
- Ranking on the Education Freedom Index (2001): 28th out of 50 states

### K–12 Public Schools and Students (2001–2002)
- Public school enrollment: 1,009,626
- Students enrolled per teacher: 19.6
- Number of schools (2000–2001): 2,141
- Number of districts: 296
- Current expenditures: $7,350,880,000
- Current per-pupil expenditure: $7,236
- Amount of revenue from the federal government: 8.6%

### K–12 Public School Teachers (2001–2002)
- Number of teachers: 51,584
- Average salary: $43,483

### K–12 Private Schools (1999–2000)
- Private school enrollment: 76,885
- Number of schools: 494
- Number of teachers: 5,697

### K–12 Public and Private School Student Academic Performance
- NAEP test results:

| NAEP Tests Washington Student Performance | State (National) 2000 Math Scale = 0–500 | | State (National) 2000 Science Scale = 0–300 | | State (National) 2000 Reading Scale = 0–500 | |
|---|---|---|---|---|---|---|
| | 4th Grade | 8th Grade | 4th Grade | 8th Grade | 4th Grade | 8th Grade |
| Average Scale Score | N/A (226) | N/A (274) | N/A (148) | N/A (149) | N/A (215) | N/A (261) |
| Advanced | N/A (3%) | N/A (5%) | N/A (3%) | N/A (4%) | 6% (6%) | 2% (2%) |
| Proficient | N/A (23%) | N/A (21%) | N/A (25%) | N/A (26%) | 23% (23%) | 30% (29%) |
| Basic | N/A (43%) | N/A (39%) | N/A (36%) | N/A (29%) | 34% (32%) | 45% (41%) |
| Below Basic | N/A (31%) | N/A (35%) | N/A (36%) | N/A (41%) | 37% (39%) | 23% (28%) |

- SAT weighted rank (2001): 1st out of 24 states and the District of Columbia
- ACT weighted rank (2001): N/A
- ALEC Academic Achievement Ranking: 2nd out of 50 states and the District of Columbia

## Summary

Washington offers postsecondary enrollment options for 11th and 12th grade students to take courses, free of charge, for high school or college credit at a community college, technical college, or select four-year university. Two private scholarship foundations, Children's Scholarship Fund Seattle–Tacoma and Children First of Whatcom County, provide vouchers to low-income children to attend a school of choice.

## Background

In 1986, the Supreme Court of the United States ruled in favor of school choice in a case involving a disabled Washington resident. In *Witters* v. *Washington Department of Services for the Blind*, the plaintiff was a blind individual who wanted to use his state assistance to attend a religious college. The Court ruled that this did not violate the First Amendment's Establishment Clause since the money did not go directly from the state to the religious institution but to an individual who determined its use.[902]

Since 1990, 11th and 12th grade students have been able to take free college courses under the state's Running Start program. Private and home-schooled students may take advantage of this option but must enroll through their local public high school, although they do not have to attend school there.[903]

During the 1997–1998 session, a charter school bill, House Bill 2019, was passed by the House but then died in the Senate.[904] Even though charter schools are public entities, the state Parent Teacher Association declared, "We're very glad this went down. We've been opposed to

use of public money for private schools, but we have to keep doing this every year."[905]

H.B. 1670 and Senate Bill 5949, introduced in 1999, would have established a pilot voucher program called the Academic Choice in Education Scholarship Program. Students in the state's five largest school districts would have received vouchers worth $3,500. To be eligible, students would have had to qualify for the federal free and reduced-price lunch program. During the 1999–2000 school year, up to 7 percent of eligible students could have participated, and the number would have risen to 15 percent the following year and subsequent years. Both bills died in committee.[906]

In 2000, supporters of charter schools introduced H.B. 2415, which would have allowed for the creation of 40 charter schools in districts with public school enrollments above 2,000. The bill died in the House Rules committee.[907]

Charter proponents collected enough signatures to place the issue on the November 2000 ballot. Initiative 729 would have authorized up to 20 charters a year for four years. The initiative enjoyed the support of Governor Gary Locke, Seattle Mayor Paul Schell, the Urban League, and 10 state newspapers.[908] Nevertheless, Initiative 729 was narrowly defeated by a margin of 52 percent to 48 percent.

Seattle became one of 40 Children's Scholarship Fund (CSF) "partner cities" in 1998. The CSF is a $100 million foundation that matches money raised by Seattle residents to fund private scholarships for low-income students to attend a school of choice.[909] Additionally, Children First Education Foundation of Whatcom County provides three-year $1,000 scholarships.[910]

---

902. *Witters* v. *Washington Department of Services for the Blind*, 474 U.S. 481 (1986), and Melanie L. Looney, "School Choice in the Courts," National Center for Policy Analysis, *Policy Backgrounder* No. 153, August 7, 2000.

903. See Office of Superintendent of Public Instruction Web site at *www.k12.wa.us/secondaryed/rstart.asp*.

904. See Washington State Legislature Web site at *www.leg.wa.gov/*.

905. Center for Education Reform, "Washington State and Charter Schools: 'When You Lie Down With Dogs, You Wake Up With Fleas,'" *News Alert*, March 5, 1998.

906. See National School Boards Association Web site at *www.nsba.org/novouchers*.

907. See Educational Excellence Coalition Web site at *www.wacharterschools.org*.

908. Center for Education Reform, *Charter Schools in Washington*, at *http://edreform.com/charter_schools/states/washington.htm*.

909. See Children's Scholarship Fund Web site at *www.scholarshipfund.org*.

Three parental choice bills were introduced in 2001. S.B. 5337 would have authorized vouchers worth up to $4,000 for students in low-performing schools to attend a private school or another public school in the same district. S.B. 5666 would have provided children with academic or behavioral difficulties with vouchers to attend private schools approved by the Washington State Board of Education. Both bills died in committee. The Senate also rejected efforts to attach a voucher amendment to another education bill during debate. The amendment would have provided a $4,000 voucher to students who attend poorly performing schools.[911]

## Developments in 2002 and 2003

In June 2002, the Washington Supreme Court, overturning a previous trial court decision, ruled that the state's Educational Opportunity Grant (EOG) Program does not violate the state constitution when college students use grants for tuition at religiously affiliated colleges. Washington's Blaine amendment prohibits public-sector funding of sectarian institutions. The state has interpreted this provision to prohibit students from using state aid to attend religious K–12 schools or colleges. The court ruled that the Blaine amendment did not apply to higher education. However, it did not consider whether the Blaine amendment itself violates the U.S. Constitution, which requires that government programs must be nondiscriminatory toward religion.[912]

On July 18, 2002, the Ninth U.S. Circuit Court of Appeals declared unconstitutional a Washington State policy that prohibits students who use state higher education scholarships to earn a degree in theology. The court declared in *Davey* v. *Locke* that "a state law may not offer a benefit to all…but exclude some on the basis of reli-

gion."[913] The case has been appealed to the Supreme Court of the United States.

In September 2002, the Institute for Justice filed a lawsuit in Washington State arguing that the state's religious establishment clause, discriminates against students at religious schools. The Washington State attorney had interpreted the clause to prohibit student teaching at religious schools. The lawsuit was filed on behalf of Carolyn Harrison, who was not allowed to finish the internship required by the University of Washington at Tacoma at the Jesuit school where she teaches. Donnell Rene Penhallurick, an education student who wished to complete her internship at a Seventh-Day Adventist school, was also represented. The Institute for Justice has launched a legal effort to ensure that state constitutions are interpreted as parallel to the U.S. Constitution—that is, that they are neutral with regard to religion.[914]

Prompted by a change in state policy, the Institute for Justice dismissed its lawsuit against Washington State for discriminating against student teachers that choose religious schools. In April 2003, the state decided to allow Carolyn Harrison to intern at her Jesuit school. The court, however, refused to grant an injunction to allow Donnell Rene Penhallurick to teach at a religious school in Moses Lake. The state now requires universities to allow students either to intern at any private school—religious or secular—or to intern at only public schools.[915]

Washington State lawmakers are holding a special session in May 2003 that may result in the enactment of a charter school law, S.B. 5012,[916] which has passed the Senate by a vote of 26 to 23.[917] Under the bill, nonprofit organizations may apply to operate charter schools, and district school boards and university boards can grant the charters. The law allows both the formation of new schools

---

910. See Children First Education Foundation of Whatcom County Web site at *www.schoolchoicenews.org/children-First.htm*.

911. See National School Boards Association Web site at *www.nsba.org/novouchers*.

912. News release, "Washington Supreme Court Sidesteps Key Issue in School Aid Case," Becket Fund for Religious Liberty, June 13, 2002.

913. *Davey* v. *Locke*, 299 F.3d 748 at 754 (9th Cir. 2002).

914. "The Next Step for School Choice: Removing State Constitutional Obstacles," Institute for Justice *Litigation Backgrounder*, at *www.ij.org/cases/index.html*.

915. Institute for Justice, "Web Release: Institute for Justice Dismisses Student Teacher Lawsuit," April 24, 2003.

916. Washington Charter Public Schools, "Good News, Bad News, on the Last Day of the Regular Session of the 2003 Legislature," April 27, 2003, at *www.wacharterschools.org/legis_special_sesion_4_28_03.html*.

917. See Washington State Legislature Web site at *www.leg.wa.gov/*.

and public school conversions.[918] Up to 70 charter schools could be created over six years.[919]

## Position of the Governor / Composition of the State Legislature

Governor Gary Locke, a Democrat, supports charter schools. Democrats control the House, and Republicans control the Senate.

## State Contacts

**Children First of Whatcom County**
Bob Warshawer, President
1225 East Sunset Drive, Suite 832
Bellingham, WA 98226
Phone: (360) 733-0925
Web site: www.schoolchoicenews.org/children-First.htm

**Children's Scholarship Fund Seattle–Tacoma**
Bob Hurlbut, Administrator
1401 East Jefferson, Suite 300
Seattle, WA 98122
Phone: (206) 726-3336
Fax: (206) 329-7415
Web site: www.childrenfirstamerica.org
E-mail: bhurlbut@msn.com

**Education Excellence Coalition**
Jim and Fawn Spady
4426 2nd Avenue, NE
Seattle, WA 98105-6191
Phone: (206) 634-0589
Fax: (206) 633-3561
Web site: www.wacharterschools.org
E-mail: JimSpady@aol.com

**Evergreen Freedom Foundation**
Bob Williams, President
P.O. Box 552
Olympia, WA 98507
Phone: (360) 956-3482
Fax: (360) 352-1874
Web site: www.effwa.org
E-mail: effwa@effwa.org

**Office of Superintendent of Public Instruction**
Old Capitol Building

P.O. Box 47200
Olympia, WA 98504
Phone: (360) 725-6000
Fax: (360) 753-6712
Web site: www.k12.wa.us
E-mail: tkelly@ospi.wednet.edu

**Washington Association of Teaching Christian Homes**
1026 224th Avenue NE
Sammamish, WA 98074
Phone: (206) 729-4804
Web site: www.watchhome.org
E-mail: info@watchhome.org

**Washington Citizens for a Sound Economy**
Russ Walker, Northwest Director, CSE
7444 Shadowwood Court, NE
Keizer, OR 97303-3937
Phone: (425) 257-9156
Web site: www.cse.org
E-mail: rwalker@cse.org

**Washington Federation of Independent Schools**
Daniel Sherman
P.O. Box 369
DuPont, WA 98327-0369
Phone: (253) 912-5808
Fax: (253) 912-5809
Web site: www.WFIS.org
E-mail: dsherman@WFIS.org

**Washington Policy Center**
Daniel Mead Smith, President
P.O. Box 3643
Seattle, WA 98124-3643
Phone: 1-888-972-9272
Fax: 1-888-943-9797
Web site: www.washingtonpolicy.org
E-mail: wpc@washingtonpolicy.org

**Washington Research Council**
Richard S. Davis, President
108 South Washington Street, Suite 406
Seattle, WA 98104
Phone: (206) 467-7088
Fax: (206) 467-6957
Web site: www.researchcouncil.org
E-mail: wrc@researchcouncil.org

---

918. *Ibid.*

919. Sarah Lorenzini, "Senate Backs Charter Schools: Legislature Saying Yes to Idea Voters Rejected," *Seattle Times*, March 14, 2003.

## State School Report Card

**Greatschool.net**
Web site: www.greatschools.net/modperl/go/
WA

**Office of Superintendent of Public Instruction**
Web site: www.k12.wa.us/EdProfile

**_Seattle Times_ School Guide**
Web site: http://texis.seattletimes.
nwsource.com/cgi-bin/texis.cgi/schoolguide/
vortex/index

# WEST VIRGINIA

## State Profile (Updated May 2003)

### School Choice Status
- Public school choice: Intradistrict and interdistrict/voluntary
- State constitution: Compelled-support language
- Charter school law: No
- Publicly funded private school choice: No
- Privately funded school choice: No
- Home-school law: High regulation
- Ranking on the Education Freedom Index (2001): 47th out of 50 states

### K–12 Public Schools and Students (2001–2002)
- Public school enrollment: 281,400
- Students enrolled per teacher: 14.1
- Number of schools (2000–2001): 794
- Number of districts: 55
- Current expenditures: $2,460,000,000
- Current per-pupil expenditure: $8,742
- Amount of revenue from the federal government: 11.5%

### K–12 Public School Teachers (2001–2002)
- Number of teachers: 19,970
- Average salary: $36,751

### K–12 Private Schools (1999–2000)
- Private school enrollment: 15,895
- Number of schools: 151
- Number of teachers: 1,486

### K–12 Public and Private School Student Academic Performance
- NAEP test results:

| NAEP Tests West Virginia Student Performance | State (National) 2000 Math Scale = 0–500 | | State (National) 2000 Science Scale = 0–300 | | State (National) 2000 Reading Scale = 0–500 | |
|---|---|---|---|---|---|---|
| | 4th Grade | 8th Grade | 4th Grade | 8th Grade | 4th Grade | 8th Grade |
| Average Scale Score | 225 (226) | 271 (274) | 150 (148) | 150 (149) | 216 (215) | 262 (261) |
| Advanced | 1% (3%) | 2% (5%) | 2% (3%) | 2% (4%) | 6% (6%) | 1% (2%) |
| Proficient | 17% (23%) | 16% (21%) | 23% (25%) | 24% (26%) | 23% (23%) | 26% (29%) |
| Basic | 50% (43%) | 44% (39%) | 44% (36%) | 35% (29%) | 33% (32%) | 47% (41%) |
| Below Basic | 32% (31%) | 38% (35%) | 31% (36%) | 39% (41%) | 38% (39%) | 26% (28%) |

- SAT weighted rank (2001): N/A
- ACT weighted rank (2001): 20th out of 26 states
- ALEC Academic Achievement Ranking: 39th out of 50 states and the District of Columbia

## Summary

West Virginia has no charter schools and offers only limited public school choice.

## Background

According to West Virginia law, students attending persistently failing schools, as determined by the state, may transfer to the nearest accredited public school, subject to the approval of the receiving school. Parents may request an interdistrict transfer and, if denied, may appeal to the State Superintendent of Schools. County boards of education are authorized to enter into agreements with one another, subject to approval by the West Virginia Board of Education, for the transfer and receipt of any and all funds determined to be fair when students elect to transfer.[920]

In 1997, House 2256 was introduced to provide a tax credit for parents who provide their children with home or private schooling. The bill died in committee. The following year, two tax credit bills were introduced. H. 2256 would have provided tax credits to parents of home-schooled or privately schooled children.[921] H. 4403 would have provided a tax credit of up to $1,000 for tuition at a private school. The legislature did not act on either bill.[922]

H. 2151 and H. 2824 were introduced in 1999 and 2000. H. 2151 would have provided a $500 tax credit per child to home-schooling parents and a $1,000 tax credit per child to parents paying private school tuition. The West Virginia Board of Education would have been prohibited from regulating the education of children whose parents received a tax credit. H. 2824 would have authorized a tax credit of 50 percent of the total amount spent on tuition, tutoring, com-

puters, uniforms, or textbooks, up to $1,000. Both bills died in committee.

Similar legislation was introduced in 2001. H. 2750 would have provided parents a $500 tax credit for home-schooling expenses and a credit of $1,000 for private schooling. H. 2269 would have provided a credit of 50 percent of the total spent on education, up to $1,000. Both bills died in committee.[923]

## Developments in 2002 and 2003

Delegate Tim Armstead (R–32) reintroduced H. 2269 to provide a 50 percent tax credit for education expenses up to $1,000. John Overington (R–55) reintroduced H. 2750 to provide a tax credit to parents for both home and private school expenses. Both bills died in committee.[924]

Senate 591, which would have established charter schools, was introduced but died in committee. The bill would have authorized county school boards to approve charters for new schools and conversions from traditional public schools. There would have been no appeals process for rejected charter applications.[925]

In 2003, Delegate John Overington (R–55) introduced H. 2507, which would have provided a tax credit of up to $500 for home schooling and $1,000 for private schooling. The bill died in committee.[926]

## Position of the Governor / Composition of the State Legislature

Governor Bob Wise, a Democrat, opposes vouchers. Democrats control both houses of the legislature.

---

920. See West Virginia Code, Chapter 18, at *http://129.71.164.29/wvcode_chap/wvcode_chapfrm.htm*.

921. See West Virginia Legislature Web site at *http://129.71.164.29/Bill_Status/bstat_intro.html*.

922. See National School Boards Association Web site at *www.nsba.org/novouchers*.

923. See West Virginia Legislature Web site at *http://129.71.164.29/Bill_Status/bstat_intro.html*.

924. *Ibid.*

925. *Ibid.*

926. *Ibid.*

## State Contacts

**Christian Home Educators of West Virginia**
P.O. Box 8770
Charleston, WV 25303
Phone: (304) 776-4664
Web site: www.chewv.org
E-mail: executivedirector@chewv.org

**West Virginia Department of Education**
1900 Kanawha Boulevard East
Charleston, WV 25305
Phone: (304) 558-1598

Fax: (304) 558-1613
Web site: wvde.state.wv.us

## State School Report Card

**Greatschools.net**
Web site: www.greatschools.net/modperl/go/
WV

**West Virginia Department of Education**
Web site: http://wvde.state.wv.us/data/
report_cards

# WISCONSIN

## State Profile (Updated May 2003)

### School Choice Status
- Public school choice: Interdistrict mandatory
- State constitution: Blaine amendment and compelled-support language
- Charter school law: Established 1993
  Strength of law: Strong
  Number of charter schools in operation (fall 2002): 130
  Number of students enrolled in charter schools (fall 2002): 26,797
- Publicly funded school choice: Yes
- Privately funded private school choice: Yes
- Home-school law: Low regulation
- Ranking on the Education Freedom Index (2001): 6th out of 50 states

### K–12 Public Schools and Students (2001–2002)
- Public school enrollment: 878,809
- Students enrolled per teacher: 14.7
- Number of schools (2000–2001): 2,180
- Number of districts: 426
- Current expenditures: $7,605,190,000
- Current per-pupil expenditure: $8,654
- Amount of revenue from the federal government: 4.8%

### K–12 Public School Teachers (2001–2002)
- Number of teachers: 59,783
- Average salary: $43,114

### K–12 Private Schools (1999–2000)
- Private school enrollment: 139,455
- Number of schools: 991
- Number of teachers: 10,025

### K–12 Public and Private School Student Academic Performance
- NAEP test results:

| NAEP Tests Wisconsin Student Performance | State (National) 2000 Math Scale = 0–500 | | State (National) 2000 Science Scale = 0–300 | | State (National) 2000 Reading Scale = 0–500 | |
|---|---|---|---|---|---|---|
| | 4th Grade | 8th Grade | 4th Grade | 8th Grade | 4th Grade | 8th Grade |
| Average Scale Score | N/A (226) | N/A (274) | N/A (148) | N/A (149) | 224 (215) | 266 (261) |
| Advanced | N/A (3%) | N/A (5%) | N/A (3%) | N/A (4%) | 6% (6%) | 2% (2%) |
| Proficient | N/A (23%) | N/A (21%) | N/A (25%) | N/A (26%) | 28% (23%) | 31% (29%) |
| Basic | N/A (43%) | N/A (39%) | N/A (36%) | N/A (29%) | 38% (32%) | 46% (41%) |
| Below Basic | N/A (31%) | N/A (35%) | N/A (36%) | N/A (41%) | 28% (39%) | 21% (28%) |

- SAT weighted rank (2001): N/A
- ACT weighted rank (2001): 1st of out 26 states
- ALEC Academic Achievement Ranking: 1st out of 50 states and the District of Columbia

## Summary

Wisconsin offers families numerous choices in the education of their children. The state has a strong charter school law, and students may transfer to other schools within their district (intradistrict) with the district's approval and to schools in other districts (interdistrict) with the permission of the receiving district. In Milwaukee, low-income children may attend private schools at public expense. Additionally, students in private and home schools may take up to two classes a semester at a public high school in their district. Juniors and seniors in public high schools who meet certain conditions may take classes for high school and college credit at a University of Wisconsin (UW) campus, a Wisconsin technical college, a tribally controlled college, or a participating state private nonprofit university.

## Background

In 1975, the legislature enacted Assembly Bill 1040. This legislation initiated a program of public school choice, known as the Chapter 220, with a goal of promoting greater integration in Milwaukee metropolitan schools. Faced with a declining white population in city schools and a federal desegregation order, the legislature sought to achieve racial balance through this state-funded program of voluntary school choice. The city of Milwaukee and its 12 suburban districts developed a plan to draw minority students into predominately white schools. The program provided intradistrict choice within the city as well as the opportunity to transfer to schools outside of the city.[927]

In 1990, then-Governor Tommy Thompson, a Republican, signed legislation spearheaded by State Representative Annette "Polly" Williams (D–Milwaukee) to give low-income Milwaukee parents the opportunity to send their children to a non-sectarian school of choice.[928] In 1995, the legislature expanded the program to include religious schools. The Milwaukee plan offers this alternative to families whose incomes are at or below 175 percent of the federal poverty level. The vouchers are limited to 15 percent of a district's public school enrollment. Participating schools must meet health and safety standards as well as certain academic and attendance benchmarks.[929] In 2002–2003, 11,621 students with scholarships of up to $5,783 each attended 102 private or religious schools of choice.[930]

In 1998, the Wisconsin Supreme Court upheld the program in *Jackson* v. *Benson*, ending a grueling round of constitutional challenges.[931] Since that time, participation in the Milwaukee Parental Choice Program (MPCP) has grown every year by nearly 1,000 students.[932]

Since 1992, junior and senior high school students have been able to take postsecondary courses at a UW institution, a Wisconsin technical college, one of the state's participating private nonprofit institutions of higher education, or a tribally controlled college. Approved courses are free to the student, and students receive credit toward high school graduation and college credit for the courses.[933]

Governor Thompson signed Wisconsin's charter school law in 1993. Currently, an unlimited number of charter schools can be approved by a variety of institutions, including school boards

---

927. Public Policy Forum, "Interdistrict Chapter 220: Changing Goals and Perspectives," February 2000, at *www.publicpolicyforum.org/josh/interdistrict220.pdf*.

928. Lynn Olson, "Choice Plan's Architect Relishes Her Role As State Legislature's 'Lone Independent'," *Education Week*, September 12, 1990.

929. 2001 Wisconsin Statutes 119.23 at *http://folio.legis.state.wi.us/cgi-bin/om_isapi.dll?clientID=317421&infobase=stats.nfo&j1=119.23&jump=119.23&softpage=Browse_Frame_Pg*.

930. Wisconsin Department of Public Instruction, "MPCP Facts and Figures for 2002–2003," at *www.dpi.state.wi.us/dpi/dfm/sms/doc/mpc02fnf.doc*.

931. *Jackson* v. *Benson*, 578 NW 2nd 602 (Wis. 1998).

932. Sarah Carr, "School Voucher Program Continues to Grow," *The Milwaukee Journal–Sentinel*, October 10, 2002.

933. See Wisconsin Department of Public Instruction, "Wisconsin's Youth Options Program," at *www.dpi.state.wi.us/dpi/dlsis/let/youthop1.html*.

outside of Milwaukee, the Milwaukee City Council, the technical college district board of Milwaukee, and the chancellors of both UW–Milwaukee and UW–Parkside.[934]

Between 1991 and 1995, political science professor John Witte from the University of Wisconsin, Madison, submitted annual reports on the state's school choice program. While these reports did not indicate a significant difference in the academic progress of voucher students compared with peers who did not use vouchers, research completed in 1996 by Harvard University and Houston's Center for Public Policy reanalyzed Witte's data and found different results.[935] This analysis reported "attendance at a choice school for three or more years enhances academic performance, as measured by standardized math and reading test scores." Voucher students' reading scores averaged 3 to 5 percentile points higher than those of counterparts in public schools, and math scores averaged 5 to 12 percentile points higher.[936] In a surprising turn of events, Witte published a book in 2000 supporting school choice, *The Market Approach to Education: An Analysis of America's First Voucher Program*, in which he wrote that "Choice can be a useful tool to aid families and educators."[937]

In 1997, the legislature enacted Wisconsin Act 27 authorizing interdistrict public school choice that would start in 1998. Through the Open Enrollment program, a student may attend schools outside of his or her district if both the sending and receiving districts approve the student's application. Districts may reject applica-

tions if space is not available, if the transfer would interfere with a Chapter 220 plan, if the district cannot accommodate a student's special needs, or if the student has previously been expelled. Districts may also limit the number of students who can leave to 8 percent of the district's enrollment. Transportation is provided for Chapter 220 students and low-income students.[938]

A 1997 amendment to the charter school law (signed into law as Act 238) broadened Wisconsin's law so that any individual, group, or "corporate body" could submit a charter application.[939] The state does not have an appeals process, and each charter school must negotiate its funding with its district. Although the law stipulates that teachers in charter schools must be certified, it provides those who have a college degree with an option of earning an alternative charter school certification.[940]

Since 1998, home-schooled and privately schooled high school students have been allowed to enroll in up to two courses per semester in a public high school in the districts in which they live. Course enrollment is subject to space limitations, and the district may provide transportation.[941]

On August 24, 2000, former Superintendent of Milwaukee Public Schools Howard Fuller launched the Black Alliance for Educational Options (BAEO) to promote school choice and to help black parents evaluate school choice options for their children.[942] By 2002, the BAEO was active in 33 cities in 25 states.[943]

934. See uscharterschools.org, "Wisconsin Charter School Information," at *www.uscharterschools.org/pub/sp/9*.

935. Jay P. Greene, Paul E. Peterson, Jiangtao Du, Leesa Boeger, and Curtis L. Frazier, *The Effectiveness of School Choice in Milwaukee: A Secondary Analysis of Data from the Program's Evaluation*, August 14, 1996, at *www.ksg.harvard.edu/pepg/op/evaluate.htm*.

936. *Ibid.*

937. Joe Williams, "Ex-Milwaukee Evaluator Endorses School Choice," *The Milwaukee Journal–Sentinel*, January 9, 2000, p. 1.

938. See Wisconsin Department of Public Instruction Web site at *www.dpi.state.wi.us/dpi/dfm/sms/psctoc.html*, and Julie Mead, Ph.D., "Publicly Funded School Choice Options in Milwaukee: An Examination of the Legal Issues," Public Policy Forum *Research Brief*, July 21, 2000.

939. North Central Regional Educational Laboratory, "Charter School Activities: Wisconsin," at *www.ncrel.org/sdrs/timely/wiact.htm*.

940. Center for Education Reform, "Charter School Legislation: Profile of Wisconsin's Charter School Law," at *http://edreform.com/charter_schools/laws/Wisconsin.htm*.

941. See Wisconsin Department of Public Instruction Web site at *www.dpi.state.wi.us/dpi/dfm/sms/bascinf.html*.

942. Black Alliance for Educational Options, "About BAEO: History and Purpose," at *www.baeo.org/about/history.htm*.

943. Black Alliance for Educational Options, "Supreme Court Voucher Ruling Affirms School Choice," press release, June 27, 2002.

Two reports released in 2001 provided evidence that Milwaukee's choice system was beneficial for schools with both high and low populations of choice students. Research by Harvard professor Caroline Hoxby showed that students improved faster in schools where a large number of students qualified to receive vouchers than at schools where fewer students did, suggesting that competition presented by vouchers inspired schools to improve their efforts.[944] In addition, the Hoover Institution reported that from 1991 to 2001, students in Milwaukee showed more improvement on local, state, and national assessments than students in the rest of the state.[945]

## Developments in 2002 and 2003

In September 2002, the parents of 586 Milwaukee students requested transfers to higher-performing schools in accordance with the federal No Child Left Behind Act. More than 45,000 parents had received letters detailing their child's option to transfer. Because of space constraints, a lottery determines which transfer requests are approved.[946]

In October 2002, the U.S. Department of Education awarded the BAEO $600,000 in funding to promote parental awareness of school choice options throughout the nation. The BAEO is using the funds for pilot programs in Philadelphia, Dallas, Detroit, and Milwaukee that assist low-income parents whose children attend low-performing schools to make informed decisions regarding their placement.[947]

A report produced by the Public Policy Forum in January 2003 shows that one-third of MPCP students are now attending nonreligious schools and that total enrollment for the program increased by 7 percent in 2002–2003. The report also shows that 59 percent of schools that have gained students since 2001–2002 have made structural renovations in their facilities.[948]

Three voucher bills were introduced in 2003. Representative Scott Jensen (R–98) introduced A.B. 260, which would expand the MPCP to include all private schools in Milwaukee County.[949] MPCP eligibility requirements would be loosened under A.B. 259, which would allow students to remain in the program even if their family's income exceeds program limits after the student is enrolled in the program. A.B. 259 would also remove the limit on the number of students per district allowed to enroll in the MPCP.[950] The bills are in committee.

## Position of the Governor / Composition of the State Legislature

Governor Jim Doyle, a Democrat, does not support vouchers or charter schools. Republicans control both houses of the legislature.

## State Contacts

**American Education Reform Council (AERC)**
Susan Mitchell, President
Abigail Winger, Research Associate
2025 North Summit Avenue, Suite 103
Milwaukee, WI 53202
Phone: (414) 319-9160
Fax: (414) 765-0220
Web site: www.SchoolChoiceInfo.org
E-mail: mitchell@parentchoice.org
E-mail: winger@parentchoice.org

**Black Alliance for Educational Options**
Milwaukee Chapter
Deborah McGriff, Chair
3290 North 44th Street
Milwaukee, WI 53216
Phone: (414) 444-6086
Fax: (414) 449-2507
Web site: www.baeo.org
E-mail: dmmcgriff@aol.com
E-mail: kaleenc@aol.com

---

944. Associated Press, "City's Public School Gains Linked to Vouchers," *St. Paul Pioneer Press*, April 25, 2001, p. B3.

945. Hanna Skandera and Richard Sousa, "School Choice: The Evidence Comes In," *Hoover Digest*, Spring Issue 2001, No. 2, at *www-hoover.stanford.edu/publications/digest/012/skandera.html*.

946. Sarah Carr, "586 Seek Transfers Out of MPS Schools on 'Improve' List," *The Milwaukee Journal–Sentinel*, September 25, 2002, p. A1.

947. Chris Brennan, "Fed$ Aid Parents on School Options," *Philadelphia Daily News*, October 16, 2002, p. 10.

948. Public Policy Forum, "Beyond an Experiment: 13 Years of Growth in School Choice Program," *Research Brief*, Vol. 91, No. 1 (January 24, 2003).

949. Wisconsin Legislature, A.B. 260, at *www.legis.state.wi.us/2003/data/AB260hst.html*.

950. Wisconsin Legislature, A.B. 259, at *www.legis.state.wi.us/2003/data/AB259hst.html*.

**Institute for the Transformation of Learning**
Dr. Howard Fuller, Director
Marquette University
750 North 18th Street
Milwaukee, WI 53233
Phone: (414) 288-5774
Web site: www.itl.mu.edu

**Parents for School Choice**
Zakiya Courtney, Executive Director
2541 North 46th Street
Milwaukee, WI 53210
Phone: (414) 288-3054
Fax: (414) 288-6199

**Partners Advancing Values
in Education (PAVE)**
Daniel McKinley, Executive Director
1841 North Martin Luther King Drive
Milwaukee, WI 53212
Phone: (414) 263-2970
Fax: (414) 263-2975
Web site: www.pave.org
E-mail: mckinleyd@pave.org

**Wisconsin Christian Home Educators
Association**
2307 Carmel Avenue
Racine, WI 53405
Phone: (262) 637-5127
Fax: (262) 638-8127
Web site: www.wisconsinchea.com
E-mail: jang@wisconsinchea.com

**Wisconsin Department of Public Instruction**
Milwaukee Parental Choice Program
Tricia Collins
125 South Webster Street
Box 7841
Madison, WI 53707-7841
Phone: (608) 266-2853
Fax: (608) 266-2840
Web site: www.dpi.state.wi.us/dpi/dfm/sms/
choice.html
E-mail: tricia.collins@dpi.state.wi.us

**Wisconsin Policy Research Institute**
James Miller, President
P.O. Box 487
Thiensville, WI 53092
Phone: (414) 241-0514
Fax: (414) 241-0774
Web site: www.wpri.org
E-mail: wpri@execpc.com

## State School Report Card

**Greatschools.net**
Web site: www.greatschools.net/modperl/go/WI

**Madison Metropolitan School District**
Web site: www.madison.k12.wi.us/schools.htm

**Wisconsin Department of Public Instruction**
Web site: www.dpi.state.wi.us/dpi/spr/
index.html

# WYOMING

## State Profile (Updated May 2003)

### School Choice Status
- Public school choice: Interdistrict/voluntary
- State constitution: Blaine amendment
- Charter school law: Established 1995
    Strength of law: Weak
    Number of charter schools in operation
    (fall 2002): 1
    Number of students enrolled in charter schools (fall 2002): 110
- Publicly funded private school choice: No
- Privately funded school choice: No
- Home-school law: Low regulation
- Ranking on the Education Freedom Index (2001): 30th out of 50 states

### K–12 Public Schools and Students (2001–2002)
- Public school enrollment: 87,768
- Students enrolled per teacher: 13
- Number of schools (2000–2001): 387
- Number of districts: 48
- Current expenditures: $720,000,000
- Current per-pupil expenditure: $8,203
- Amount of revenue from the federal government: 8.2%

### K–12 Public School Teachers (2001–2002)
- Number of teachers: 6,730
- Average salary: $37,841

### K–12 Private Schools (1999–2000)
- Private school enrollment: 2,221
- Number of schools: 41
- Number of teachers: 241

### K–12 Public and Private School Student Academic Performance
- NAEP test results:

| NAEP Tests Wyoming Student Performance | State (National) 2000 Math Scale = 0–500 | | State (National) 2000 Science Scale = 0–300 | | State (National) 2000 Reading Scale = 0–500 | |
|---|---|---|---|---|---|---|
| | 4th Grade | 8th Grade | 4th Grade | 8th Grade | 4th Grade | 8th Grade |
| Average Scale Score | 229 (226) | 277 (274) | 158 (148) | 158 (149) | 219 (215) | 262 (261) |
| Advanced | 2% (3%) | 4% (5%) | 3% (3%) | 3% (4%) | 6% (6%) | 2% (2%) |
| Proficient | 23% (23%) | 21% (21%) | 30% (25%) | 33% (26%) | 24% (23%) | 27% (29%) |
| Basic | 48% (43%) | 45% (39%) | 47% (36%) | 35% (29%) | 35% (32%) | 47% (41%) |
| Below Basic | 27% (31%) | 30% (35%) | 20% (36%) | 29% (41%) | 35% (39%) | 24% (28%) |

- SAT weighted rank (2001): N/A
- ACT weighted rank (2001): 6th out of 26 states
- ALEC Academic Achievement Ranking: 15th out of 50 states and the District of Columbia

## Summary

Many school districts in Wyoming offer open enrollment, through which students may enroll in a different district with the approval of the sending and receiving districts. Some districts offer magnet schools or allow high school students to enroll in college courses for concurrent credit and/or advanced placement. The state has a weak charter school law.

## Background

In 1995, Wyoming adopted a charter school law that, although it set no limit on the number of charters that could be granted, gave local schools the sole authority to grant charters. Charter schools receive only limited legal autonomy and must apply for waivers from state and district regulations and policies.[951]

In the 2000 session, State Senator Mike Massie (D–9th District) introduced the School Choice–Charter School Assistance bill, which would have provided funds for school districts operating choice and charter programs. The bill was not enacted.[952]

In 2001, a pilot voucher program that would have provided 100 students with a $3,500 voucher was introduced as an amendment to the state supplemental budget. The legislation required a comparison of the test scores of 200 students: 100 who received a voucher and 100 who would serve as a public school control group. Legislators would have decided whether to continue the program beyond the pilot on the basis of this comparison. The amendment failed to pass.[953]

Two attempts to open a charter school were made in 2000. In the first attempt, the applicants were turned down; in the second, the peti-

tions for the school were withdrawn. Although these attempts were not successful, they brought legislators' attention to the weakness of the state's charter school statute and prompted them to change the law.[954]

In 2001, the legislature amended Wyoming's charter school statute to make it easier to open charter schools. The amended law allows charter school applicants to appeal to the Wyoming State Board of Education if a local school district denies their application; it also guarantees charter schools 95 percent of the state's per-pupil funding for public schools.[955]

## Developments in 2002 and 2003

In the fall of 2002, Wyoming's first charter school, the Snowy Range Academy, opened as a Core Knowledge School. Initially serving students in grades K–6, the school plans eventually to include grades 7 and 8 as well.

Legislation similar to the proposed 2001 amendment to establish a pilot voucher program was passed by the Senate but was defeated in the House.[956]

In 2003, Senator Kathryn Sessions (D) introduced Senate File 110 to require home-schooled students to take state assessments. If the student failed to score at the proficient level, the parent would have to present a "remediation plan." The bill died in committee.[957]

## Position of the Governor / Composition of the State Legislature

Governor Dave Freudenthal, a Democrat, has stated no position on school choice. Republicans control both houses of the legislature.

951. Center for Education Reform, "Charter School Legislation: Profile of Wyoming's Charter School Law," at *www.edreform.com/charter_schools/laws/Wyoming.htm.*

952. See *http://legisweb.state.wy.us/20sessin/sfiles/SF0072.htm.*

953. See National School Boards Association Web site at *www.nsba.org/novouchers.*

954. Phone conversation with Nancy Hamilton, Wyoming Citizens for Educational Choice, April 17, 2001.

955. Center for Education Reform, "State by State Summary of Laws Passed (May 2000–April 2001)," at *http://edreform.com/charter_schools/laws/summary.htm#wyoming.*

956. See National School Boards Association Web site at *www.nsba.org/novouchers.*

957. See Wyoming State Legislature Web site at *http://legisweb.state.wy.us/.*

## State Contacts

### Homeschoolers of Wyoming
Cindy Munger
P.O. Box 3151
Jackson, WY 83001
Phone: (307) 883-0618
Fax: (307) 883-0618
Web site: http://www.homeschoolersofwy.org
E-mail: contact@homeschoolersofwy.org

### Wyoming Department of Education
Dianne Frazer,
Charter School Program Consultant
2300 Capitol Avenue
Hathaway Building, 2nd Floor
Cheyenne, WY 82002

Phone: (307) 777-3544
Fax: (307) 777-6234
Web site: www.k12.wy.us
E-mail: dfraze@educ.state.wy.us

## State School Report Card

### Greatschools.net
Web site: www.greatschools.net/modperl/go/WY

### Wyoming Department of Education
Web site: www.k12.wy.us/pls/stats/esc.show_menu

# A SCHOOL CHOICE GLOSSARY

**Charter school:** A public school sponsored by a local school board, university, state board of education, or other state governing body and operated by groups of parents, teachers, other individuals, or private organizations. Charter schools are granted more autonomy than district-run public schools and are held accountable for student performance. Charter school laws vary by state.

**Child-centered funding:** An education financing plan that allows a specific dollar amount, representing both operations and capital funding costs, to follow each student to the school chosen by his or her parents.

**Controlled choice:** A program that provides parental choice while promoting racial integration. Generally, parents are allowed to choose a school within a specified zone. Racial quotas regulate student admittance.

**Dual enrollment:** Programs that allow students to enroll in courses at institutions of higher education for secondary and/or postsecondary credit. Depending on state and local policy, the student, the state, or the district pays for the courses.

**Education savings accounts:** Accounts that are largely free from taxation and for used toward K–16 educational expenses.

**Interdistrict choice:** Parental freedom to send students to public schools outside the district of residence. In some states, the policy is voluntary, and districts may or may not participate. In others, interdistrict choice is mandatory, and all districts must allow transfers.

**Intradistrict choice:** Parental freedom to choose from schools within the district of residence. In some states, districts set transfer policies. In others, intradistrict choice is mandatory.

**Magnet schools:** Public schools offering programs to students with particular interests (such as the arts or technology). Often used as a voluntary method to achieve racial balance.

**Open enrollment:** Policy that allows parents to choose from any school in their state. With voluntary open enrollment, the district is not required to offer a choice. With mandatory open enrollment, the district must allow parents this option.

**Private voucher programs:** Scholarship programs that are supported by individuals or corporations. The scholarships are awarded by lottery to applicants for use at private schools. Also known as privately funded school choice.

**Publicly funded private school choice:** Choice programs that include publicly funded scholarships to be applied toward tuition fees at a private or religious school.

**Public school choice:** Systems that allow parents to choose from among different public schools.

**Scholarships:** Certificates of a designated dollar value that are applied toward tuition and/or fees at a public or private school. Also called vouchers, tuition scholarships, or opportunity scholarships.

**Tax credits and/or deductions:** Tax policies that (1) empower parents to claim a credit or deduction against their taxes for approved educational expenses, including private school tuition, books, tutors, or transportation or (2) enable individuals or corporations to receive a tax credit for contributions to tuition scholarship organizations.

**Tuitioning programs:** Programs under which school districts or towns without public schools pay for the cost of sending students to private or public schools in another district or state. Maine and Vermont are the only states that have tuitioning laws.

**Vouchers:** Certificates with a designated dollar value that may be applied toward tuition or fees at a public or private educational institution of choice. Vouchers are similar to the federal government's Pell Grant program, under which a student receives a designated dollar amount in the form of a scholarship to apply toward tuition at a public, private, or religious college or university of choice.

# APPENDIX

## Select List of National Organizations that Promote School Choice

**American Education Reform Council**
2025 North Summit Avenue, Suite 103
Milwaukee, WI 53202
Phone: (414) 319-9160
Fax: (414) 765-0220
Web site: www.schoolchoiceinfo.org

**American Enterprise Institute**
1150 17th Street, NW
Washington, DC 20036
Phone: (202) 862-5800
Fax: (202) 862-7177
Web site: www.aei.org

**American Legislative Exchange Council (ALEC)**
1129 20th Street, NW, Suite 500
Washington, DC 20036
Phone: (202) 466-3800
Fax: (202) 466-3801
Web site: www.alec.org

**Association of American Educators**
25201 Paseo de Alicia, Suite 104
Laguna Hills, CA 92653
Phone: (949) 595-7979
Fax: (949) 595-7970
Web site: www.aaeteachers.org

**Black Alliance for Educational Options (BAEO)**
501 C Street, NE, Suite 3
Washington, DC 20002
Phone: (202) 544-9870
Fax: (202) 544-7680
Web site: www.baeo.org/home/index.php

**Cato Institute**
1000 Massachusetts Avenue, NW
Washington, DC 20001
Phone: (202) 842-0200
Fax: (202) 842-3490
Web site: www.cato.org

**Center for Education Reform**
1001 Connecticut Avenue, NW, Suite 204
Washington, DC 20036
Phone: (202) 822-9000
Fax: (202) 822-5077
Web site: www.edreform.com

**Children First America**
Austin, TX 78755
Phone: (512) 345-1083
Fax: (512) 345-1280
Web site: www.childrenfirstamerica.org

**Children's Scholarship Fund (CSF)**
8 West 38th Street, 9th Floor
New York, NY 10018
Phone: (212) 515-7100
Fax: (212) 515-7111
Web site: www.scholarshipfund.org

**Citizens for Educational Freedom**
9333 Clayton Road
St. Louis, MO 63124
Phone: (314) 997-6361
Fax: (314) 997-6321
Web site: www.educational-freedom.org

**Education Leaders Council**
1225 19th Street, NW, Suite 400
Washington, DC 20036
Phone: (202) 261-2600
Fax: (202) 261-2638
Web site: www.educationleaders.org

**Education Policy Institute**
4401-A Connecticut Avenue, NW, PMB 294
Washington, DC 20008-2322
Phone: (202) 244-7535
Fax: (202) 244-7584
Web site: www.educationpolicy.org

**Empower America**
1801 K Street, NW, Suite 410
Washington, DC 20006
Phone: (202) 452-8200
Fax: (202) 833-0388
Web site: www.empoweramerica.org

**Family Research Council**
801 G Street, NW
Washington, DC 20001
Phone: (202) 393-2100
Fax: (202) 393-2134
Web site: www.frc.org

For updates go to: *heritage.org*

259

**Thomas B. Fordham Foundation**
1627 K Street, NW, Suite 600
Washington, DC 20006
Phone: (202) 223-5452
Fax: (202) 223-9226
Web site: www.edexcellence.net

**Milton & Rose D. Friedman Foundation**
One American Square, Suite 1750
P.O. Box 82078
Indianapolis, IN 46282
Phone: (317) 681-0745
Fax: (317) 681-0945
Web site: www.friedmanfoundation.org

**Heartland Institute**
19 South LaSalle, Suite 903
Chicago, IL 60603
Phone: (312) 377-4000
Web site: www.heartland.org

**The Heritage Foundation**
214 Massachusetts Avenue, NE
Washington, DC 20002-4999
Phone: (202) 546-4400
Fax: (202) 546-8328
Web site: www.heritage.org/schools

**The Hoover Institution**
Stanford University
Stanford, CA 94305
Phone: (650) 723-1754
Fax: (650) 723-1687
Web site: www.hoover.org

**Institute for Justice**
1717 Pennsylvania Avenue, NW, Suite 200
Washington, DC 20006
Phone: (202) 955-1300

Fax: (202) 955-1329
Web site: www.ij.org

**Institute for the Transformation of Learning**
750 North 18th Street
Milwaukee, WI 53233
Phone: (414) 288-5775
Fax: (414) 288-6199
Web site: www.itlmuonline.org

**Lexington Institute**
1600 Wilson Boulevard, Suite 900
Arlington, VA 22209
Phone: (703) 522-5828
Fax: (703) 522-5837
Web site: www.lexingtoninstitute.org

**Manhattan Institute for Policy Research**
52 Vanderbilt Avenue
New York, NY 10017
Phone: (212) 599-7000
Fax: (212) 599-3494
Web site: www.manhattan-institute.org

**Program on Education Policy
and Governance**
John F. Kennedy School of Government
Harvard University
79 JFK Street, T308
Cambridge, MA 02138
Phone: (617) 495-7976
Fax: (617) 496-4428
Web site: www.ksg.harvard.edu/pepg